AF707192

LEGALISM

Legalism

Property and Ownership

Edited by

GEORGY KANTOR, TOM LAMBERT,
AND HANNAH SKODA

OXFORD
UNIVERSITY PRESS

OXFORD
UNIVERSITY PRESS

Great Clarendon Street, Oxford, OX2 6DP,
United Kingdom

Oxford University Press is a department of the University of Oxford. It furthers the University's objective of excellence in research, scholarship, and education by publishing worldwide. Oxford is a registered trade mark of Oxford University Press in the UK and in certain other countries

© The several contributors 2017

The moral rights of the authors have been asserted

First Edition published in 2017

All rights reserved. No part of this publication may be reproduced, stored in a retrieval system, or transmitted, in any form or by any means, without the prior permission in writing of Oxford University Press, or as expressly permitted by law, by licence or under terms agreed with the appropriate reprographics rights organization. Enquiries concerning reproduction outside the scope of the above should be sent to the Rights Department, Oxford University Press, at the address above

You must not circulate this work in any other form and you must impose this same condition on any acquirer

Crown copyright material is reproduced under Class Licence Number C01P0000148 with the permission of OPSI and the Queen's Printer for Scotland

Published in the United States of America by Oxford University Press
198 Madison Avenue, New York, NY 10016, United States of America

British Library Cataloguing in Publication Data
Data available

Library of Congress Control Number: 2017947317

ISBN 978–0–19–881341–5

Links to third party websites are provided by Oxford in good faith and for information only. Oxford disclaims any responsibility for the materials contained in any third party website referenced in this work.

Preface and Acknowledgements

This is the fourth volume in a series. *Legalism: Anthropology and History* appeared in 2012, *Legalism: Community and Justice* in 2014, and *Legalism: Rules and Categories* in 2015. The book is in many ways the product of wonderfully stimulating weekly discussions and papers at the Oxford Legalism seminar, now in its ninth year. We would like to begin by thanking those funding bodies which have made possible the series, as well as the more intensive workshops which have punctuated its existence. The St John's College Research Centre has been outstandingly generous over a number of years, allowing for the rich continuity which has proved intellectually so fruitful. We would also like to thank the Oxford Centre for Socio-Legal Studies for crucial support, the Oxford History Faculty, and the Craven Fund.

These regular discussions owe so much to the commitment of the participants in the seminars and the project as a whole. We would like to thank all who have attended and given papers over the years, in particular Lisa Eberle, Paul Hyams, and Martin Ingram. In January 2016, a workshop on the specific theme of 'property and ownership' was organized, which could not have functioned without the scholarly input of the contributors to this volume as well as the intellectual generosity of those who agreed to act as respondents, including Morgan Clarke, Simon Douglas, Joshua Getzler, Tom Johnson, Luke Rostill, and Ting Xu. The clarity of this volume has been helped by the editorial assistance of Anna Boeles-Rowland.

Finally, we would like to thank three people who provided the impetus behind the project in the first place, and whose intellectual generosity and clarity of thought have been truly inspiring. Fernanda Pirie's intellectual acuity, and her constancy of interest and support, lie at the heart of this. Judith Scheele has been a crucial presence at the seminar, providing meticulous organizational support, but more than this, generous-spirited, nuanced, and articulate insights. And Paul Dresch has been an inspiration to us all. The breadth of his reading, depth of his conceptual grasp, and willingness to share his expertise provide a pinnacle to which we can only aspire.

G. K., T. L., and H. S.
March 2017

Contents

List of Figures

List of Contributors

T. M. Charles-Edwards is an Emeritus Fellow, formerly Professor of Celtic Studies at Jesus College, Oxford. He has published extensively across early Irish and Welsh history and literature. Many of his publications have focused on early legalism, including *Lawyers and Laymen* (edited with Morfydd Owen and D. B. Walters, 1986), *The Welsh Laws* (1989), *The Welsh King and His Court* (edited with Morfydd Owen and Paul Russell, 2000), and *Tair Colofn Cyfraith: The Three Columns of Law in Medieval Wales: Homicide, Theft and Fire* (edited with Paul Russell, 2005). Most recently, he has published *Wales and the Britons 350–1064* (2013).

Jatin Dua is an assistant professor in anthropology at the University of Michigan, Ann Arbor. He works on legal and economic anthropology, particularly on maritime piracy in the Western Indian Ocean, and on broader histories of governance, law, and economy along the East African coast.

Matthew S. Erie is an associate professor of modern Chinese studies at the University of Oxford. He is a comparativist lawyer and anthropologist whose research examines illiberal law, specifically, questions of development, freedom, and 'rule of law'. His research has been published in such journals as *American Ethnologist, Islamic Law & Society*, and *Law & Social Inquiry.* His first book *China and Islam: The Prophet, the Party, and Law* (2016) is an ethnographic study of the contemporary practice of *sharīʿah* by Chinese Muslims.

Georgy Kantor is a fellow and tutor in ancient history at St John's College, Oxford. He works on Roman legal and institutional history, particularly on the eastern provinces of the Roman Empire, and on Greek and Latin inscriptions of the Roman period. He is also an associate editor of the *Supplementum Epigraphicum Graecum.*

Tom Lambert is the Osborn Fellow in Early Medieval History and Culture at Sidney Sussex College, Cambridge. His publications include *Law and Order in Anglo-Saxon England* (2017), and he co-edited (with David Rollason), *Peace and Protection in the Middle Ages* (2009). His other publications range across early English history, engaging with such themes as hospitality, ecclesiastical sanctuary, theft, and homicide.

Walter Rech is a postdoctoral researcher at the Erik Castrén Institute of International Law and Human Rights, University of Helsinki. His main research interests are in political philosophy and the theory and history of international law and international relations. Among Walter's recent publications is the volume *International Law and Empire: Historical Explorations* (2017), which he co-edited with Martti Koskenniemi and Manuel Jiménez Fonseca.

Judith Scheele is a social anthropologist and a post-doctoral research fellow at All Souls College, Oxford. Her publications include *Village Matters: Knowledge, Politics and Community in Kabylia* (2009) and *Smugglers and Saints of the Sahara: Regional Connectivity in the Twentieth Century* (2012). She has co-edited, with Fernanda Pirie, *Legalism: Community and Justice* (2014), and, with Paul Dresch, *Legalism: Rules and Categories* (2015).

Hannah Skoda is an associate professor of history at the University of Oxford and a Fellow of St John's College. She is author of *Medieval Violence: Physical Brutality in Northern France, c.1270–c.1330* (2012), and co-editor (with Patrick Lantschner and Robert Shaw) of *Contact and Exchange in Later Medieval Europe* (2012) and (with Paul Dresch) of *Legalism: Anthropology and History* (2012). She has published on diverse themes of later medieval social and cultural history, from experiences of disability, to misbehaving students, and is currently working on expressions of nostalgia in the fourteenth century.

William Wheeler completed his PhD in the Anthropology Department, Goldsmiths College, University of London. His research concerns the relationship between environmental and political-economic change in the Aral Sea region of Kazakhstan.

Introduction

Property and Ownership: An Overview

GEORGY KANTOR, TOM LAMBERT, AND HANNAH SKODA

Anthropologists like to see property as 'relationships between people with respect to things' (Ackerman 1977: 26).[1] But how far does such a phrase get us? Property is a famously slippery idea, such that '[e]veryone knows what it is, but no one can define it' (Bell and Parchomovsky 2005: 533); it is one of those words which we all assume we understand, but can rarely pin down.[2] In this volume, we attempt a further distinction between property and ownership. Property we see as a field of study which encompasses a wide range of property rights, property relationships, and property regimes. Of course, even in scholarly texts, these terms are often used as synonyms, but we suspect that the tendency to frame property questions always in terms of ownership is an artefact of approaches based largely on Roman law (see Hann

[1] e.g. Busse (2012: 124), a recent survey of the field. Property can be defined as 'the rights that people hold over things which guarantee them a future income stream. They "own" only incorporeal rights, not the thing itself. Property relations are consequently better seen as social relations between people' (Hann 1998: 4–5); 'Property ... is not a thing, but a network of social relations that governs the conduct of people with respect to the use and disposition of things' (Hoebel 1966: 424); 'The study of property rules in general, and of land tenure in particular, is the study of relations between people' (Davis 1973: 157, both quoted in Hann 1998: 5); 'Property in the most general sense concerns the ways in which the relations between society's members with respect to valuables are given form and significance' (von Benda-Beckmann, von Benda Beckmann, and Wiber 2006: 14–15). For an excellent state-of-the-art article on the anthropology of property, see Hann (2007).

[2] Another problem lies in translation—to state the obvious, languages have varying terms for 'property', each carrying subtly different sets of connotations (Hann 2007: 289–90). The problem is not just one of geographical variety, but also of historical change—see e.g. Seipp's discussion of the changing meanings of property in medieval England (1994: particularly 70), and Hyams's discussion of the language of property in Old English (Hyams 2016). This linguistic variation really matters, and can become highly politically charged: e.g. Maddock (1983).

Introduction—Property and Ownership: An Overview. Georgy Kantor, Tom Lambert, and Hannah Skoda. © Georgy Kantor, Tom Lambert, and Hannah Skoda, 2017. Published 2017 by Oxford University Press.

2007: 289).[3] A whole host of distinctions could be brought into play: the classic Romanist division of ownership and possession (explicated in slightly different terms by Kant [1797] 1996: 37), for example, or the categorization by economists of property into open access, common property, state property, and private property (von Benda-Beckmann, von Benda-Beckmann, and Wiber 2006: 8). But our own approach is simple. Fundamentally, ownership concerns humans' propensity to claim and control elements of the world around them, particularly at a distance.[4] If we treat ownership as the simple fact of being able to describe something as 'mine' or 'yours', and distinguish property as the discursive field which allows the articulation of attendant rights, relationships, and obligations, analytical comparisons across time and space become more fruitful.[5]

A significant proportion of children's literature addresses ideas of property and ownership in one way or another.[6] One reason for this is the seemingly universal tendency of small children to say 'mine' in petulant tones. Many of these books therefore try to encourage sharing, or respect for the property of others, and they contain endless moralizing aphorisms on the subject. But there is a second reason: fictional accounts of ownership engage small children because it is such a hard concept to convey, and to make sense of.

In Oliver Jeffers's *This Moose Belongs to Me* (2012), a young boy named Wilfred not only befriends a moose, but claims him as his own, going so far as to name him Marcel. He makes up a series of complex rules to ensure that his moose behaves, and can be controlled by him. Needless to say, the moose 'obeys' in only the most arbitrary fashion. But the true shock for Wilfred comes when he discovers that he is not the only person claiming ownership, and indeed that he is not the only person to have given a name to the animal. By the end of the story, Wilfred is forced to acknowledge that he can never fully own the moose, who, he realizes, will obey his rules only 'when

[3] For origins of the western notion of property as a legal right in the Roman tradition, see Garnsey (2007: 177–203).

[4] We owe this phrase to discussion with Paul Dresch, who suggested Kant as a source to think with. It is reminiscent of Parry and Bloch's definition of money which 'permits possession at a distance' (1989: 5). For the centrality of simple 'mine' and 'thine', see Dresch (2012b: 162; 2015: 73).

[5] While contributions to this volume approach the problems of property from historical and anthropological, rather than legal theoretical perspectives, there are correspondences here, for example with Dagan's (2011 and 2014) notion of 'structural pluralism' and with Waldron's (1990) influential idea of 'contestant uses' of property.

[6] e.g. *That Rabbit Belongs to Emily Brown* (Cowell 2006); *All Mine* (Hicks 2015); *The Tale of Peter Rabbit* (Potter 1902); *Charlie and the Chocolate Factory* (Dahl 1964); *The Velveteen Rabbit* (Williams 1922); *Mister Magnolia* (Blake 1980); *This Is Not My Hat* (Klassen 2012); *This Moose Belongs to Me* (Jeffers 2012); *The Highway Rat* (Donaldson 2011).

it suited him'. The complexity of the child's thinking is set, with delightful nonchalance, beside the absolute indifference of the moose.

The story reminds us of the seemingly universal tendency to claim ownership.[7] But it also indicates that ownership can be textured and contested. The boy in the story assumes that the moose belongs to him in absolute terms, and his certainty echoes the famous claim of Blackstone that property is 'that sole and despotic dominion which one man claims and exercises over the external things of the world, in total exclusion of the right of any other individual in the universe' ([1766] 2016: 1). When this claim is invalidated by the appearance of other putative owners,[8] property becomes the anthropologically inflected 'relationships *between people* with respect to things', as discussed e.g. by Ackerman 1977). Blackstonian certainty gives way to the more relational view of property introduced into legal theory by Hohfeld in the early twentieth century (Hohfeld 1913 and 1917). The complex web of relations between human beings so often centres around ideas of property and ownership that the subject cannot be left to purely legal scholarship: it deserves the same sort of attention from historians and anthropologists as has been given to a topic like kinship.[9]

Wilfred, in fact, gets over his shock at discovering that other people are laying claims to 'his' moose. His primary concern remains the moose itself. Anthropological interest in relations between people, with the things owned as mere objects through which those relationships are mediated, risks missing the point here. The fundamental attachment of an owner to an object can become obscured. Of course, part of the role of legal articulations of property is to regulate that attachment with regard to potential interference by other people (many writers on law might suggest that this is property's essence), but nevertheless, the heart of the matter lies with the object itself.

[7] Dresch raised at the workshop the puzzle of children everywhere learning 'mine'. Given deixis or indexicality, this is hardly something that works by ostensive definition like 'spoon' or 'plate', yet children usually claim things are 'mine' by the age of 2, or 2 and a half. At the same time, it is important to acknowledge that ownership is not always articulated in legalistic terms. Among the Panara in Amazonia there is little sense of legalism: '[t]here is no term for property other than "things" (*soti*), but things normally have an owner, so one speaks for instance of "Karapo's pot" (*Karapo yo kukyati*)' (Ewart 2015: 214 n. 5). Also, *soti* can refer to what in a sense, though not a lawyer's sense, are 'incorporeal things', such as traditions or cultural practices.

[8] As Birks points out, 'absolute' property in the literal sense is in the end an impossibility (Birks 1985: 1–2).

[9] Apart from children's books, the natural home of property analysis is in legal theory. However, given the importance and relevance of the topic, it is surprising that Hann's 1998 call for a renewal of the anthropological tradition of conceptualizing property has not stimulated a burgeoning field: there are of course some significant exceptions (e.g. Verdery and Humphrey 2004; Widlock and Tadesse 2004).

One response to the child's conundrum—what can it possibly mean to say that one owns a moose, and how can this be achieved?—might be to turn to legal theories of a 'bundle of rights'. The metaphor was first used by Maine (1861), articulated in detail by Hohfeld (1913 and 1917), and famously elaborated by Honoré (1961).[10] Fundamentally, the 'bundle of rights' paradigm is an acknowledgement of the fact that, as Wilfred discovers, any single-sentence definition of property is impossible. As expounded by Honoré, property involves rights of possession; profitability; transferability; legal protection; product of labour; alienability; use and enjoyment; exclusion; and destruction (1961: 107–47). From a legal perspective, the list may be helpful analytically, and it discourages over-simple views.

Conceptually, though, as recent legal theorists have pointed out (e.g. Smith 2012), this kind of approach leaves much to be desired. The first and most obvious problem regards the rights which make up the bundle. Much work has focused on unpicking the bundle and showing the malleability of its elements. The point is made nicely in the story of the moose, as Wilfred struggles to understand whether rights to exclusion are intrinsic to ownership and whether he can still believe he owns the moose even if he cannot entirely control it. If the moose does not do what he tells it to, does it still belong to him?[11] Compromise is unavoidable, and the bundle of rights paradigm as it stands does not easily allow for this conceptual flexibility.

Second, and more conceptually, the 'bundle of rights' paradigm is so focused on legally enshrined rights that other dimensions of property may be obscured. Most obviously, the relationship between property and personhood is one which philosophers and legal theorists have explored in convincing terms,[12] although, as Judith Scheele (Chapter 1, this volume) points out, their preoccupation with the individual often belies their own cultural assumptions, while others have criticized the exaggeratedly normative and consensual nature of the model (Schnably 1993: 347–467). In many cases, we hope for legal protection for the things we think we own not just because of an abstract concept of right, but because we are emotionally attached to these things. In many cultures, owning a house is seen as a fundamental step towards fully realized selfhood.[13] In many families, ownership of family heirlooms, or of tokens such as wedding rings, matters because these things

[10] A useful history (and defence) of the approach is found in Baron (2014).

[11] In law, much has turned on whether a species is wild by its nature (*ferae naturae*); the example of Roman bees is famous, see Frier (1982–3 and 1994).

[12] See e.g. Hegel [1821] 1967: para. 41a; Green [1895] 1941; Radin 1982.

[13] An odd position, one might think—but one which a western generation of 'millennials' currently tends to feel acutely, as house prices have risen beyond the grasp of many in a society where real estate is a major form of investment. In other societies, the house may have quite other values but be just as central (see Carsten and Hugh-Jones 1995).

are seen as markers of identity: they are often intrinsic to both our personhood and our sense of kin.

Third, the 'bundle of rights', in its focus on formalist legal analysis, fails to account for the ways in which societies justify property in the first place: in other words, the paradigm offers little in the way of conceptualizing property as an idea.[14] And thinking about the origins of property need not be the sole preserve of philosophers. It is bound up with our notions of the ways in which ownership can be regulated and made meaningful. In the delightful simplicity of the story about the moose, the child seems to evoke a number of different ways of thinking about the justification for, and meaningfulness of, property. But when he first came across the moose he 'knew, just knew' that it was meant to be his (Jeffers 2012: 4). We often feel an instinctive claim to something we define as ours. There is also in the story a hint of Lockean theory of appropriation ([1689] 1988: ch. 5; on the medieval antecedents of this idea, see Swanson 1997): Wilfred believes he finds the moose first, 'trains it', and therefore it must be his. Social systems seem full of such assumptions regarding property, assumptions which gain their social and indeed legal purchase primarily because they seem so obvious, and seem to align so straightforwardly with natural inclination (even if this is most often wishful thinking). The story takes further what it means to own something, by integrating a Radin-like theory of personhood as selfhood becomes intertwined with ownership.[15] Wilfred identifies with the moose, treats him as a kind of friend, and crucially, names him.

Most strikingly, and most comically, the child attempts to assert ownership by imposing a series of rules on the animal.[16] The story's final compromise in this respect suggests that this ability to control lies at the heart of

[14] Thomas Grey comments that 'The substitution of a bundle-of-rights for a thing-ownership conception of property has the ultimate consequence that property ceases to be an important category in legal and political theory' (cited in Bell and Parchomovsky 2005: 546). From another viewpoint, one might say almost the opposite, that it places the idea of property beyond discussion by shifting the emphasis to 'types' of property-relation.

[15] Radin suggests that 'to achieve proper self-development—to be a person—an individual needs some control over resources in the external environment' (1982: 957); the argument is used to distinguish two levels of property, the personal and the fungible. For an attempt to distinguish between ownership as a 'concept' of 'a correlation between individual names and particular objects, such that the decision of the named individual about what should be done with an object is taken as socially conclusive', as opposed to particular 'conceptions' of that concept in different legal systems—compare Waldron (1990: 47–53, quotation from p. 52).

[16] The animal's indifference to this recalls Latour's notion of the 'unruliness of things' (e.g. Latour 2010). We may invent rules and complex categories, but the matter they concern will often not be so easily objectified and contained. This was explored in a contribution to this seminar by Tom Johnson (forthcoming 2017), which considered the impact of coastal erosion on property rights in late medieval England; see also Johnson 2015 and the discussion of the legal status of the alluvial lands at the mouth of the Maeander in Roman Asia Minor in Thonemann (2011: 306–14).

defining degrees of ownership. The crux seems to be the ability to control something at a distance, both in itself (the more intransigent problem with the moose) and, which matters to analysts, as regards others.

> That is *rightfully mine* (meum iuris) with which I am so connected that another's use of it without my consent would wrong me. The subjective condition of any possible use is *possession.*
>
> But something external to me would be mine only if I may assume that I could be wronged by another's use of a thing even *though I am not in possession of it* (Kant 1797 [1996]: 37).

What Kant means is simply that I need not have my hand on it or have it in my grasp. As he moves to specific cases, his language becomes easier:

> can anyone have a thing of his own on land no part of which belongs to someone? Yes, as in Mongolia where, since all land belongs to the people, the use of it belongs to each individual, so that anyone can leave his pack lying on it or recover possession of his horse if it runs away, since it his (Kant [1797] 1996: 53).

This idea of ownership as control at a distance affords a reasonable purchase on comparison. It allows us to examine the ways in which control is exercised, made meaningful, contested, and protected. It allows us to examine the interaction of legal modes of articulating these elements, with practical, ethical, economic, and religious discourses.

At this point in the discussion, the notion of legalism is required in order for any meaningful sense of property and ownership to emerge. Legalism evokes generalizing concepts as a way of understanding reality, which provide meaning and purchase for the idea of control. As was said at the start of the present series of volumes, legalism is 'an appeal to rules that are distinct from practice, the explicit use of generalising concepts, and a disposition to address in such terms the conduct of human life' (Dresch 2012a: 1).[17] The simple use of such concepts is enough to conjure the spectre of property, though not full-blown property law, from mere attachment to things.

Arguing that law lies at the heart of property is of course an age-old trope. Bentham's assertion that law and property naturally go together—that one cannot exist without the other (Bentham [1802] 1931)—resonates with a far older Christian narrative of expulsion from Eden, followed by the eruption of violence over property and laws to protect property made necessary by mankind's sinfulness (Coleman 1988: 615–22).[18] Montesquieu's perspective

[17] For further discussion of legalism as a concept, see also Pirie (2015).

[18] This is, of course, a central topic in the historical philosophy of property. One might think of Hobbes's and Hume's arguments that property is effectively created by the state (Hobbes [1647] 1983; Hume [1739] 1978) or Kant's proposal that property must be sanctioned in a way which benefits all, thus necessitating the rule of law (Kant [1797] 1996). The most obvious exponent of natural rights, complete with a narrative of the development of perverted desires

on this transition is a subtle one, arguing that the advent of property was bound up with the development of agriculture, money, and civil society and required civil law, which at an early stage were 'moeurs' rather than 'lois' (Montesquieu [1748] 1989: book XVIII, ch. 13). Modern legal theorists are equally keen to demonstrate that law of some kind lies at the heart of any definition of property, often by arguing, from a utilitarian perspective, that law protects labour value (e.g. Bell and Parchomovsky 2005).[19] Certainly, legal traditions have often had property at their heart.

In Roman law, a key distinction is made between ownership and possession. For historians of the common law in England, tracing the emergence of this distinction has lain at the heart of attempts to discern the extent of Roman influence on the emergence of the common law (Palmer 1985 expanding upon the position of Milsom 1981 as against Pollock and Maitland 1898; the debate is revivified and nuanced by Tate 2006).[20] What these forensic analyses reveal most convincingly is the contingency of distinctions upon which we now tend to rely when discussing property in any context. Notably, David Seipp's writing on the common law of England has demonstrated that between 1290 and 1490, the word 'property' was not used to refer to land (1994: 29–91).[21]

A simple conclusion to draw is that property does not always mean the same thing—or at least the articulations of property and ownership can be configured in very different ways, and draw upon different distinctions. As Wilfred discovers with his moose, there are degrees of property, competing definitions, and all kinds of complexities involved in trying to assess what objects or creatures can, so to speak, be 'propertized'. People themselves can be rendered as property in some circumstances, although the conceptual problems this throws up tend to be complex, as well as ethically abhorrent to most of us at present. Different societies have come up with various solutions to the question of which animals might be meaningfully 'propertized'. Can water be rendered as property? More recently, legislators and

and the need for property law is Rousseau ([1755] 1994: part II). A useful starting point is Waldron (2004) in the *Stanford Encyclopedia of Philosophy*.

[19] 'Most scholars today base their understandings of property on a model where property is justified by utilitarianism, defined by positive law rather than upon natural rights theory' (Bell and Parchomovsky 2005: 542).

[20] For a detailed and clear comparison between Roman and common law in this respect, see Buckland and McNair (1965: 62–88). They emphasize the absence of any sharp distinction in common law and state strikingly that 'in English law, at any rate in the law of moveables, there is hardly such a thing as ownership' (quote from p. 76).

[21] Seipp has some tantalizing thoughts to explain this shift, one of which suggests the transfer of terminology from goods to land, by upwardly mobile merchants becoming powerful landowners in the late medieval context (1994: 88).

academics have been grappling with the challenges of intellectual property and the commoditization of body parts (Strathern 1996: 17).[22]

Ultimately, legalism provides a way of classifying and categorizing that makes possible, and debatable, the process of control at a distance. To return to Wilfred and his moose, legalism and generalizing concepts of ownership can make sense of his relationship with others with respect to the moose, but also crucially they are bound up with his own relationship with the animal and the extent of his control over it. The comedy of the story lies in the moose's sheer indifference to the whole narrative.

The chapters in this volume take as their starting point the definitions and concepts evoked above, and together, draw out a series of tensions and interwoven ways of thinking about property. The Benda-Beckmanns and Wiber argue that property is constituted through multiple layers, both discursive and prescriptive (von Benda-Beckmann, von Benda-Beckmann, and Wiber 2006). It is a process and a relationship which is shaped not only by law, but by economics, by moral philosophy and religious ethics, by political prerogatives, by kinship ties, and by the dictates of natural law. Set beside their notion of legal pluralism, with multiple nodes and processes of various forms of law and legal authority operating together and in conflict, this provides a vision in which law is just one of many ways of articulating property.[23] Replace law with legalism, however, and a subtly different picture emerges.[24] If legalism is broadly an appeal to rules and generalizing categories (Dresch 2012a: 1), then we are no longer constrained to identify the ways in which discrete systems of law might interact formally and counteract each other and other discrete normalizing frameworks.[25] It is not just one among many ways of thinking about property. Rather, legalism permeates the thicker tapestry which makes up property relations and distinguishes them from simple attachment or felt identity.

Property discussions and relationships are shot through with ideas of morality, natural law, religious ethics, economics, political prerogatives, and

[22] Siegrist suggests that intellectual property has been an important category since the seventeenth century (2003, cited in Hann 2007: 288). Medievalists would argue that nuanced discussions about whether knowledge could be bought and sold date at least to the fourteenth century (Post, Giocarinis, and Kay 1955).

[23] In this sense, laws of property, as legal theorists point out, have four main purposes: (1) to identify *what* things law protects; (2) in relation to whom; (3) 'with what rights'; and (4) 'by what enforcement mechanism' (Bell and Parchomovsky 2005: 575–6).

[24] Not least, this approach permits us to avoid such misleading distinctions as '[w]hile lawyers discuss who owns what, philosophers ask why anyone can legitimately claim to own anything' (Gray 1991: 292).

[25] This also provides a rather different frame of analysis to that proposed by Hann who suggests a base and superstructure model: 'precisely the fascination and challenge of property, which necessarily involved both economy (base) and the jural–ideological domain of superstructure' (Hann 2007: 290).

that perennial favourite of anthropologists, kinship networks. But, in turn, legalism suffuses all these threads. The status of ownership which legalism apparently bestows is often sustained through moral, religious, or political logics. One might describe legalism as lying at the interface of the various discursive frameworks, but one should also be attentive to the ways in which it structures and makes meaningful these other discourses. Legalism carries a certain formalism: it shapes and categorizes where property relations can seem otherwise disconcertingly chaotic. It also brings a kind of moral authority: much legalism is reinforced by ideas of justice, however nebulous, and exerts a powerful rhetorical pull. And it serves an ordering function: it is a way in which societies are able to make sense of competing claims to define and hold property. Indeed, it is precisely because property is so hard to pin down, defined and driven by so many different and competing forces, that legalism's authoritative, formalizing and ordering role may be so pervasive. This is not to say that legalism resolves tensions. It is, though, a powerful way to articulate and negotiate them.

INTERTWINED LOGICS OF PROPERTY: NATURAL LAW, RELIGION, POLITICS

The basic logic of property can seem to be rooted in the apparent universalism of human needs and with the associated moral pressures that may be understood as natural law. But where does natural law stop and morality begin? In the western tradition, they are concepts which have traditionally been allied very closely, and which provoked considerable debate in the later Middle Ages, for example (Coleman 1988: 618).[26] Although philosophers have been keen to demonstrate the origins of property in natural law—from Grotius to Locke (respectively [1625] 2005: book 2; [1689] 1988: ch. 5)—many societies reject the causation this implies. Indeed, this rejection lies at the heart of anthropological enquiry. For western medieval theologians, natural law did not necessarily institute property, but nor did it produce pressing reasons to undermine property, as defined by civil law (see Tierney 1997). Indeed, the question of property served often to highlight the relationship between different forms of law: if civil law protected the accumulation of wealth, canon law did not explicitly forbid this, and natural law was not contravened even if it did not encourage accumulation.

[26] Coleman points out that Gratian, the 'father of canon law', meant two different things by natural law: on the one hand, it designated a kind of primitive, even prelapsarian state of being; on the other hand, it meant the ways in which people normally behaved, 'a sort of moral economy' (1988: 618).

This problem is brought into particular focus by the institution of slavery. In many ways, the greatest challenge for theorists and jurists has always been to define *what* is property, rather than how it then operates: rendering people as property touches the heart of this problem, and it seems no coincidence that classical discussions often substantiate their points by referring to slaves. Ulpian, as incorporated in the Digest of Justinian, famously claimed that the origins of slavery could not be found in natural law, and that this was why the law of nations was necessary to justify, define, and encode it (*Digest* 1.1.4; 1.5.4; 50.17.32).[27] Hannah Skoda (Chapter 9, this volume) shows how such juxtapositions underpinned much of the logic surrounding slavery in fifteenth-century Dubrovnik. If owning slaves was left unexplained and unjustified by natural law, statutes, and contracts were needed to prescribe, regulate, and categorize. Yet, as Skoda shows, this positive legalism did not resolve the tensions inherent in slavery, but, if anything, served to articulate the natural law difficulties implicit in the practice.

On the other hand, in the modern West, we tend to assume that land is the archetypal form of property:[28] again, 'natural' rights to land are often held in uneasy tension with positive law. The conceptual work of defining land as property by natural right, as in Locke's theory of first occupation (Locke [1689] 1988: ch. 5), may not contribute much to the early history of property rights, but the philosophical and ethical problems with which this is freighted might be said to lie at the heart of much subsequent history.[29] What those natural rights and laws might be can throw up very antagonistic problems, perhaps because land seems peculiarly charged emotionally. Land is clearly a category apart from other forms of things owned (Linklater 2013: 375). Perhaps it is the spatial dimension—one can occupy land, live on it or in it, experience it—as opposed to the mere tangibility of other resources which sets land apart; also, as Seipp (1994) points out, it is largely

[27] See Honoré (2012: 9), for further examples from other Roman jurists of the classical period included in the Digest. The view can be traced back to the fifth-century BC Greek sophist Alcidamas of Elis, mentioned by Aristotle, *Rhetoric* 1.13.2.1373b18.

[28] Though see Seipp (1994) whose work on medieval English common law problematizes this. In ancient Greek legal traditions land ownership was considerably more restricted than the ownership of moveables, particularly in the notorious and complex case of Sparta, for which see MacDowell (1986: 89–110); while it is true that in early Roman law 'the overwhelming stress in the property provisions is on farming' (Watson 1975: 165), there are considerable difficulties with the chronology and content of Roman land ownership (see Kantor, Chapter 2, this volume).

[29] For recent discussions, see Garnsey (2007: 136–54); Alexander and Peñalver (2012: 35–56). Contrast the Marxist critique, assuming communal property in land as the earliest form of historical development, often no less ahistorically (see e.g. Sayers 2011: 110–12), or Aristotle's assertion that 'the state is by nature clearly prior to the family and to the individual' (*Politics* 1.2.1253a18–19, transl. B. Jowett and W. D. Ross). For premodern theories of the origins of property, see Garnsey (2007: 107–35).

permanent. Again and again, land ownership, although outwardly drily legal, proves emotionally fraught and politically subversive. Matthew Erie (Chapter 4, this volume) demonstrates how, in twentieth- and twenty-first-century China, land ownership tends to be bound up with a sense of selfhood. The moral and apparently natural underpinnings of this emotional attachment are articulated legalistically through generalizing categories which enable litigation and resistance, but obviously conflict with top-down state law attempting to redefine who owns what (even while attempting to resist it, often on its own terms). Erie draws attention to a different kind of legalism rooted in a sense of 'what is right', to the extent that emotional attachment can produce a kind of 'afterlife' of property sustained by parties unwilling to accept the quashing of their claims.

Some of Erie's informants are Chinese Muslims (Hui). They reject attempts to commoditize land which they deem to be sacred: religious prerogatives provide another way of thinking about property. These claims of sacrality seem rooted as much in family and historical ties as they are in Islamic thought: but they are inflected in religious terms, as, for them, the meaningfulness of the property depends upon religious categories. And of course, within Islamic thought, the legalistic and the religio-ethical cannot be easily disentangled. Likewise, the legalistic dimension of religious ethics is prominent in a western canon law context. Canon law is effectively an attempt to work Christian ethics into a systematic and enforceable legal framework (Brundage 1995). These kinds of religious categories overlap with moral and emotional categories, but often establish themselves in opposition to state legalism and its trenchant demands. These various ways of articulating property do not, then, just pit religion against law, but are themselves shot through with legalistic reasoning. In fifteenth-century Dubrovnik, Skoda shows the legalism of Christian canon law and that of the civil law of slavery to have been in uneasy tension. Notably, in Dubrovnik slaves were required to be 'present and consenting' at the signing of the contract of their sale. The presence of this clause remains mysterious (it is almost unique in late medieval slaving societies, and has no precedent in Roman law), but one reason may be that canon law forbade the enslaving of fellow Christians: if a slave converted to Christianity, his or her status remained unchanged, but if the conversion took place before the moment of enslavement, the enslavement was illegitimate, in both canon and civil law. The 'present and consenting' clause may have been a way to morally obfuscate a practice which Christians remained uneasy about, as well as a way to protect against future litigation by slaves drawing upon canon law.

A different kind of interweaving characterizes the Islamic underpinnings of property discourse in the Abéché customary court in Eastern Chad, as described by Judith Scheele. Legal definitions of property are relatively straightforward, and drawn from *sharīʿah* law.[30] But how property relations are managed in practice is far more unstable, shifts over time, and is dependent upon a web of social networks and prerogatives.[31] More processual legalisms are then nested within a clearer dogmatic religious legal framework: this is not a point about pluralism, or indeed about contradictory frameworks, but rather the interweaving of different ways of thinking about property.

The work of the Islamic scholar Sayyid Qutb, as analysed by Walter Rech (Chapter 6, this volume), situates itself explicitly within an Islamic framework. Qutb's ideas of social justice, underpinned by discussions about the redistribution of property, treat the relations between legalism and religion rather differently. On the one hand, he describes the need to limit private ownership within a framework of religious obligation and the public good. Qutb manages to combine the social teachings of the Qur'an with a call for a centralized and interventionist state. All this relies on the existence of a quite sophisticated form of legalism, and appeal to generalizing categories (although he seems to avoid any explicit detail as to how any of this might actually function in practice). But the discussion is also shot through with what one might term 'anti-legalism'. As Qutb presents it, the expertise and pedantry of advanced legalism, particularly as practised by the *ulamā'*, powered inegalitarian forms of property and lost sight of religious ethics and the common good. This religious framework, then, provoked an oscillation between legalism and anti-legalism.

If religion shapes property discourse partly through its own legalism, so too does politics. Palmer, writing on the early common law of England, goes so far as to state that 'The complex interplay between present-oriented politics or juridical decisions, and bureaucratic rigor generated a legal system' (1985: 2); while such a statement sits uneasily with many of the cases studied here, the intertwining of legalism with political prerogatives certainly generates both norms and tensions. Indeed, political pressures can shape the definition of property itself. For example, in Roman law the concept of *dominium* becomes inextricably linked with Italian soil and Roman citizenship, leading to convoluted redefinitions of 'non-Roman ownership' (Kantor, Chapter 2, this volume).[32] In the Aral Sea region in Kazakhstan, William

[30] For introductions to Islamic law, see Coulson (1964); Schacht (1964); Islam (1999); Hallaq (2009).

[31] Put differently, it is impossible to analyse practice solely by reference to learned law, but everyone in practice knows there is such law. An interesting comparative case is discussed in Scheele (2012).

[32] *Dominium* raises useful questions, not least for medievalists, in that it may often be as well translated 'ownership' or 'lordship'. Classicists have a different agenda, addressing more specific questions that arise from a different place and period.

Wheeler (Chapter 8, this volume) shows how political prerogatives are also interwoven through the economics and legalism of fishing quotas. In previous nomadic economies, fish were not deemed property objects (in contrast to livestock); over the colonial, Soviet, and post-Soviet periods, they have been 'propertized' in ways to engage the ideologies of successive regimes. The interweaving of various ways of thinking about fish points to a situation far more complex than any image of local resistance against a dominant state. Likewise, Jatin Dua (Chapter 7, this volume) rejects, for Somalia, the common scholarly vision of a failed state, unable to regulate and impose the rule of law. He stresses instead the centrality of capture as a generalizing principle underpinning Somalian pastoralism, fishing, and, in due course, piracy. In a sense, he describes a series of legalisms nested within one another, from international institutions, to state-level governance, to the logic of pastoralism transplanted into the sea, to local social networks, and coastguard initiatives. In both Somalia and Kazakhstan, as elsewhere in different forms, we find 'rent-seeking' which assumes control at distance through generalizing claims to property.

In many cases, then, politics is more complex than the study of a centralized state and/or its failure. In the early Celtic societies described by Thomas Charles-Edwards (Chapter 3, this volume), the politics of clientship does not just shape property relations, but is made meaningful through property. Politics makes sense through property, and vice versa, and is enabled to do so by the categories of legalism. Charles-Edwards draws a contrast between the elaboration, in Wales, of an explicit set of concepts to deal with property; and, in Ireland, the focus rather on distinctions implied by complex legal rituals.

In Erie's China, by contrast, the informants present their cases as direct conflicts between individuals or communities, and the state. This must be driven not only by the emotional attachment of the owners themselves to their land, but by the high-handedness and changeability of state law. Of course, the justifiability of expropriation of property has lain at the heart of property discourse for many centuries.[33] Counterintuitively perhaps, it seems to be the very instability of state legalism which is the problem. The

[33] Montesquieu was deeply concerned by the implications of expropriation, and commented that 'c'est un paralogisme de dire que le bien particulier doit céder au bien public ... parce que le bien public est toujours que chacun conserve invariablement la propriété que lui donnent les lois civiles' (Montesquieu [1748] 1989: book XXVI, ch. 15). His position appears to have influenced the Declaration of the Rights of Man and the Citizen, Art. 17, on the centrality of property to civic rights (for a useful reference tool, and a discussion of these citations, see Bart 2013). One might also turn, for example, to St German's sixteenth-century discussion of the political contingency of property rights ([1532] 1874), pace Fortescue's insistence on the inviolable natural origins of property ([*c*.1460] 1869, 82, 149–50). These are cited, together with an informative discussion, in Seipp (1994: 78–9).

informants argue for a conception of property which is not subject to the vagaries of politics, but detached from it. To some extent, what is at stake here, is a contestation about the extent of the links between politics and law. It raises, then, a fundamental set of questions about the extent to which legality might be rooted in natural law and morals, as opposed to time-bound economics and politics. Property lies at the heart of this conflict.

EMBEDDEDNESS

Property discourse, then, is articulated through a range of frameworks—of natural law, of religion, and of politics—often competing and held in uneasy tension. Of course, property necessarily centres on concepts of value (whether straightforwardly financial, or more broadly cultural). In this sense, economic and socio-economic frameworks provide another set of prerogatives, often articulated legalistically. It is impossible to disentangle property from the wider social, political, and economic contexts in which it is found: it is, as Polanyi would have it, 'embedded' ([1944] 2001; 1957). Many contributions to this volume accordingly situate legalistic property regimes within the wider context of socio-economic relations. The relationship is a reciprocal one: external measures of success (or otherwise) of the property regimes are analysed, as well as the role of property regimes in shaping the economic dimension of particular societies. From Erie's account of the tensions between cultural, political, and economic motivations in claiming real estate rights in China, to the complex commoditization of fish in Wheeler and Dua's chapters, property regimes cannot be disentangled from socio-economic and political pressures.

The relationship between property regimes and wider economic pressures in particular has provoked fraught and politically influential debate, which has been long dominated by two interlocked (but not necessarily compatible) hypotheses and reactions to them. Hardin's (1968) influential, but commonly misconstrued, hypothesis of the 'tragedy of the commons' suggests that individuals cannot be trusted not to pursue selfish interests at the expense of resource management and the common good: law is needed to ensure that property regimes are economically beneficial rather than catastrophically wasteful. On the other hand, the approach of the new institutional economics interprets property law as a way towards driving down transaction costs and thereby establishing a more economically efficient community. The two views can often be combined through an optimistic reading of the effects of a particular 'western' interpretation of private property, the roots of which are often sought in Graeco-Roman antiquity, notably in the work of the 'Stanford school'. So, for instance, an influential interpretation of the rise of classical Greece by Josiah Ober accords crucial importance both to low transaction costs produced by the rule of law and to 'rule egalitarianism' protecting and clarifying the rules of property (2015: 101–22).[34]

The connection is not an inevitable one, however. Hardin's argument for the need for coercion in situations of resource scarcity is fundamentally rooted in a pessimistic view of human nature.[35] But many scholars have a more optimistic view of the efficiency of private property regimes: for example, the work of Demsetz (1967) or its more limited and plausible version advanced by Ellickson (1993), commonly accepted at least implicitly in the new institutional economics, suggest that coercion is unnecessary, at least within close-knit groups.[36] Moreover, the new institutional economics view that property regimes drive down transaction costs need not necessarily lead to the acceptance of a modern liberal interpretation of property as an ultimate goal; this would clearly be misleading in the cases studied here which show a far more complex interweaving of motivations. If we were to accept that all societies tend to arrive at maximally efficient property regimes for themselves, as Demsetz and Ellickson argue, measuring them against each other would be a meaningless exercise.

Neither argument satisfactorily accounts for the cases studied in this volume. Anthropologists (see particularly Dua, Scheele, and Wheeler) are able to demonstrate that Hardin's resolutely individualistic conception of motivation simply does not match the collective approaches adopted in many areas. Nor, as Wheeler for instance shows, do communities tend to adopt anything as straightforward as the 'grab it while you can' approach implied by Hardin. As for the reduction of transaction costs, while the cases studied here certainly suggest the importance of economic imperatives, the commoditization made possible through legalism's provision of apparently stable categories is itself a source of critical tensions.

The 'economistic' interpretation of property regimes has provoked a number of challenges, both from theoretical and from historical perspectives. These challenges tend to focus on precisely the point drawn out by

[34] For interpretation of Roman law on these terms, see Jakab (2015) and Kehoe (2015); wider perspectives on ancient law are in Frier and Kehoe (2007); Kehoe, Ratzan, and Yiftach (2015); an interesting attempt to connect ancient philosophical thinking about wealth and property with the new institutional economics in Swain (2013: 145–256). Contrast Zurbach (2013), grounding the emergence of landed property in concerns for community cohesion.

[35] A quite different perspective is proposed by Sen who argues conversely that intransigent attitudes to property rights can be responsible for the misuse and unjustifiable running down of resources: '"absurdism" does not belong to the attaching of intrinsic value to property rights, but to regarding these rights as simply acceptable, regardless of their consequences [i.e. potential famine]' (1988: 63).

[36] The contradiction is stressed by Ellickson (1993: 1320).

the cases here: that economics is just one frame of reference amidst a more complex social texture. Rebuttal comes from more pluralistic approaches to the ultimate efficiency of legal regimes, such as Aristotelian 'human flourishing' (Alexander and Peñalver 2012: 80–101). It also takes the form of variants on Polanyi's 'embeddedness' thesis, which always seemed to gain more traction with historians and anthropologists than with legal theorists.[37] According to one influential view, at least in so far as property in land was concerned, 'social and familial solidarities' prevailed over economic up until the Industrial Revolution (Le Goff 2012: 123–6); historians of medieval Europe have used the 'bundle of rights' metaphor to emphasize social controls over property and assert that 'absolute property exists nowhere except in the minds and polemics of those who are anxious to defend their rights either against governments or against those who claim conflicting rights' (Reynolds 1994: 53). The analysis of post-socialist transition (Heller 1998; Hann 2014) challenged the efficiency claims of the liberal 'bundle' of ownership rights on their own terms. Economic frameworks are central to property regimes, but make little sense if treated in isolation.

Legalism, seen as 'an appeal to rules that are distinct from practice, the explicit use of generalizing concepts, and a disposition to address in such terms the conduct of human life' (Dresch 2012a: 1), but not limiting itself to 'legal systems' in the legal theorists' sense, offers a perspective on these debates, while resonating with the 'embeddedness' thesis. Thus, in their distinct ways, property in livestock in Abéché in Eastern Chad (Scheele, Chapter 1, this volume) or in early medieval Ireland and Wales (Charles-Edwards, Chapter 3, this volume) or, to tread on a ground more familiar to legal theory, in land in Roman provinces (Kantor, Chapter 2, this volume) can be shown to be a community concern at least as important as a 'personal right'. In the words of Scheele (Chapter 1, this volume), 'while in western legal systems, legal philosophers agonize about the individual "state of mind" that defines property transactions, these questions are here a matter of public opinion'. In some cases, as with ownership of jurisdictional rights in Anglo-Saxon England or even of radio spectrum bandwidths in modern law (Lambert, Chapter 5, this volume), this 'matter of public opinion' generates a category of property *ex nihilo*.[38]

The concerns explored here are often neither theoretical nor exclusively economic: rather, boundaries of the community, maintenance of family and kinship ties or individual honour could be at stake. Early Irish law on pledges seems to accord special significance to horses and to festival

[37] See now Hann (1998; 2007); von Benda-Beckmann, von Benda-Beckmann, and Wiber (2006).

[38] See for a similar argument Pirie (2015: 56).

garments (Charles-Edwards), for instance, while among the Aral Sea fishermen and their European markets, the cultural value of particular kinds of fish appears to determine attitudes to them as suitable for market transactions (Wheeler). This does not, however, imply lack of sophistication: as, for instance, Charles-Edwards convincingly demonstrates, within its own terms medieval Irish property law was complex and clear, and attitudes to it included 'an appreciation of what might be called cleverness or sharp practice'.

Kinship ties are often central to property, including to conceptions of its value.[39] From Kazakhstan to Somalia, medieval Wales to twentieth-century Chad, property rules form part of social webs founded upon kinship ties. As described by Scheele, in Eastern Chad, property relations lie at the heart of social definitions and transactions, kinship, and marriage. If property is, to some extent, about economic value, that only becomes meaningful in a wider social context. The relationship is reciprocal: property relations are also conditioned and upheld through these same social ties. Property tends to depend upon the use of guarantors and witnesses. It is not that kinship trumps legalism, but that it provides a set of categories which function legalistically to underpin property processes. The emotional dimension seems particularly raw in the case of China, as described by Erie, where kinship is shown to generate its own forms of legalism. His informants challenge and contest state legalism and its implications for their own property holdings, often precisely because they reject the economic prerogatives driving that state legalism. Subjecting land in particular to a set of economic categorizations seems to be to deny the connection of that land with the moral identities of its tenants. And a more wholesale rejection of theories of value is of course possible. Qutb's writings discussed by Rech in this volume amount, essentially, to a rejection of the modern western economic underpinnings of property. His balance of legalist and anti-legalist thought provides an alternative basis and route for property. And despite the ascendency of modern neoliberalism, it is not unusual to find economic frameworks of property contested by other logics. Indeed, one of the reasons to undertake a comparative study of property is precisely in order to challenge assumptions that economic theory provides its ultimate logic.

[39] A parallel between law and kinship was suggested in the first volume of this series (Dresch 2012a: 37), where reference was made to Shryock and Smail (2011); see also Dresch (2015: 68–9). As soon as one has a category such as 'cross cousin' one has the possibility of what physics once called 'action at a distance'. Anthropologists' worries about whether they should speak of 'kinship' or 'relatedness' (Carsten 2000) turn on many of the same analytic problems that confront historians of property.

INSTABILITY AND INTANGIBILITY

The embeddedness of property regimes in social and economic interactions (even if that involves a rejection of those pressures) leads to the problem of 'the practical instability of a category that is central to all social relations', as Scheele (Chapter 1, this volume) observes in regard of the treatment of property relations in Abéché courts. Socio-economic and political contexts fluctuate: so too, then, does property. The problem of property's 'instability' emerges across most contributions to this volume: the complex interaction of the *sharīʿah* and local rules in Chad (Scheele); Roman and Greek law in Roman provinces with their different and community-determined 'bundles of rights' (Kantor); the understanding of property rights generated by fishing within local communities, in government regulation and in market transactions, explored in different settings by Dua and by Wheeler; the conflict between positive law, western influences and Islamic ideology of Sayyid Qutb, discussed by Rech; or the tension between state property regimes and community-accepted forms of legalism in contemporary China, studied by Erie. The failure to negotiate such tensions in contemporary Somalia leads to transition from catching fish to capturing fishing vessels and then to other forms of maritime piracy (Dua, this volume), but an argument may be made that the presence of interpretative tensions is inherent to the way property gets conceptualized as a rule-bound category. Existing as it does at the cross-section of different social (and indeed economic) concerns with their competing discourses, it becomes a category in need of constant redefinition.[40] For inhabitants of medieval Dubrovnik, grappling with religious, moral, economic, and diplomatic dimensions of slave ownership, 'law was a useful way of negotiating these dilemmas. The idea of property was fragile and problematic, but capacious' (Skoda, Chapter 9, this volume).

If property discourse allows one to 'pursue claims to control at a distance',[41] its role is also to define something *as* property in the first place. And it is where those things are hard to grasp, where the distance is not just

[40] As Paul Dresch has pointed out, the point is not simply that particular types of property shift over time, as they plainly do, but that the most general category may also shift. One can imagine a particular place seeing periods when property was much talked of and other periods when the talk was all of custom, relatedness, propinquity, or royal power.

[41] This is not to say formal law derives in any simple way from practice. In legal discussion, the very concept of property may not be salient. Birks writes that the Roman lawyers' 'habit of mind' was to attend to the thing owned: 'Once the thing ... had been defined—something more difficult where the thing was abstract—there was in a sense nothing more to say' (Birks 1985: 3). 'The differentiation of ownership from other superiorities ... [e.g. patriarchal domination] takes us back to the *classification of things*. If the thing in view is extra-patrimonial [in the Roman case], the relationship is not ownership' (ibid.: 26). In the Roman case, there is no discussion of, say, the origins of ownership as there is in Grotius.

spatial but conceptual, that legalism and its appeal to categories are particularly powerful. So, while economic prerogatives might underlie many notions of property, they most often need to be articulated in legalistic terms. The argument proposed by Lambert to explain the growth of private jurisdictional rights in the Middle Ages, makes just such a point. Whereas these jurisdictional rights are most often explained in a political narrative of post-Conquest England, Lambert suggests that it was competition for newly valuable legal revenues which ultimately led to the clearer articulation of jurisdictional rights and their establishment as property. In turn, this allows us to tease apart exactly what aristocratic landed property consisted of; beyond the land itself this was something rather hard to grasp, and the formalism of law helped to make sense of it.

By a similar logic, commodification depends on the formalism offered by legal categories. Transactions are well-nigh impossible without classification of the particular types of property or commodity being transferred. It is the very instability and intangibility of the objects which legalism addresses, and which must therefore underpin any economic approach. Adam Smith posited a contrast between hunter-gatherer societies, where property was a marginal concern, and agricultural settled societies, where exchange and money were central ([1776] 2014: particularly book 1).[42] The contrast is, of course, somewhat misleading, but it is striking that so many commodities are, so to speak, hunted, so that there must be a moment before they *become* property. That process—of becoming property—is worth studying in its own right. Two of the nine papers in this volume are about property in fish (Dua and Wheeler, Chapters 7 and 8, this volume). In many ways, fish are archetypal commodities, and yet they cannot even be quantified until they are caught. Dua describes a legalism, in the broadest sense, of capture in the Gulf of Aden. Intangible commodities like fish, and in turn, ships, can only become property (of fishermen or of pirates) once caught. The economic framework of value within which they are defined hinges on a legalism of capture.

For the Aral Sea, Wheeler describes a situation of competing and failed legalisms. Two economic orders, the one trying to maximize output, the other trying to conserve resources, are articulated through various legal orders, rules, and categories. He describes the post-socialist desire both to protect fish stocks and to institute a successful new political regime operating through a system of quotas. Fish are rendered as property before they

[42] For this observation, we would again like to thank Paul Dresch, who drew attention at the workshop to how little Adam Smith resembles the character promoted by the Adam Smith Institute. Quite apart from Smith's views on early society and his moral distrust of rent, the layout of *The Wealth of Nations* suggests a manual of statecraft, not a eulogy to individualism.

are even caught, a form of virtual categorization which should satisfy economic prerogatives. But 'virtual fish' are not really there. No one knows how many fish will actually be caught on each trip; numbers caught are determined as much by local rules, financial constraints, and webs of social relations as they are by complex quota systems whose management depends upon local kinship networks. The presence of NGOs proposing further ways to categorize and to conserve insist upon another overlapping legalistic framework. The instability of the resource—in terms of its potential scarcity, its unpredictability, and its embeddedness in political, economic, and cultural habits—mobilizes legalistic ways of thinking. It is precisely because fish are such an uncertain commodity that the formal categories of legalism are necessary and meaningful.

MATERIALITY AND TEMPORALITY

Instability is tied, then, not just to socio-economic 'embeddedness', but also to the simple fact of materiality. This raises another tension—between the apparent timelessness and abstract intangibility of legalistic property discourses and the strikingly contingent notions of materiality and temporality that emerge when specific forms of property are examined in depth.

Legalism, as Dresch notes, suggests 'an order of affairs that outlasts the moment' (2012a: 15), and in this volume we repeatedly see appeals to legalism which are simultaneously future-oriented and reliant upon precedent and the authority of history—claims of ownership that, whether maintained to buttress or to reconfigure present realities, draw their legitimacy from assertions of unbroken formal continuity. At the Abéché customary court in 1937, the assertion with witnesses that a she-camel had been 'born between his hands' allowed a claimant to take ownership of her, his title theoretically secure for the future. The real-world shift here was significant—a valuable camel changed hands—but it was effected on the basis of a legal narrative in which property rights remained reassuringly stable: the man's ownership of the camel was no novelty, she had always belonged to him (Scheele, Chapter 1, this volume). Likewise, Erie (Chapter 4, this volume) describes Hua Xinmin's struggle to assert ownership of her 'ancestral house' (*zuzhai*), appropriated by the government in 1958. Here it seems that the claim of enduring rightful ownership is almost an end in itself; Hua's prospects of persuading the state to adopt the idiosyncratic interpretation of the development of Chinese property law on which her claim is founded are very slim, but she presses on, seemingly driven by the impossibility of accepting a future in which her family's link to this property is accepted as having been less than permanent. And as the anxious insistence that slaves sold in medieval Dubrovnik were 'present and consenting' reminds us, a buyer's future security of ownership depends not only on the validity of the present transaction but on the validity of the vendor's title in the first place, both of which—however contradictory the implications—were emphasized by such clauses (Skoda, Chapter 9, this volume).

The timeless order apparently offered by legalism can be alluring precisely because it promises to cut through much messier realities, in which the identities of individual camels are matters for dispute, states assert the authority to reshape property law for political ends, and slaves (or at least those who were Christians at the time of their enslavement) might plausibly sue those who held them. Law, as Scheele puts it, 'provides at least an illusion of permanence' (see Chapter 1, this volume), and such illusions can be valuable both for those seeking to reinforce present classifications and distributions of things and for those seeking to reconfigure them. Often, this sense of permanence is embodied in the production of documents. As soon as property in land becomes historically meaningful, we tend to find inscriptions, documents, and boxes of archives often treasured long after they were written.[43] Erie shows Chinese litigants brandishing documentary claims, as if the piece of paper itself might counter the fluctuations of government policy.

Owned things, however, come in many different forms, often with temporal frameworks of their own. Land provides a particularly striking example. In several of the case studies examined here it is seen as the ultimate form of permanent property. Charles-Edwards explains the medieval Welsh legal concept of *priodolder* ('proprietorship'), the most secure form of land ownership which was attained only after it had been passed down by inheritance to the fourth generation; until that point conflicts over rightful occupation were supposed to be resolved in favour of the party which could demonstrate the longest chain of inheritance, making the acquisition of land through gift or purchase a difficult enterprise of dubious legitimacy (see Chapter 3, this volume). Similarly, in early medieval Ireland, individuals were understood to have the right to a share of the land that belonged permanently to their kindreds, the wider family's inalienable link to the land signalled by burials on its boundaries (see Chapter 3). The idea that one cannot legitimately

[43] On the early importance of documents in this respect, see e.g. Meyer (2004) or Clanchy (1993). A fruitful area of study is that of medieval forgery. The relative frequency of forgery in the Middle Ages attests to the perceived importance of having a documentary claim whose status would counter the vagaries of time. An interesting example is held in the Archives of St John's College, Oxford (Muniment V.A.1): the document purports to attest to a gift by one Robert d'Oilly in the 1140s, but actually dates from the late twelfth or early thirteenth centuries. Most often, such forgeries did not attempt to sustain false claims, but rather to give a sense of permanence and authority to claims which were known to exist.

alienate land inherited from one's ancestors, especially land marked by their burials, comes through just as strongly in Erie's case studies from early twenty first-century China, though of course such notions are here in tension with the state's formal landed property regime. The Roman association between full ownership (*dominium*) and the right to render land *religiosum* by burying family members within it perhaps reflects a similar constellation of ideas (Kantor, Chapter 2, this volume). Effectively immobile and indestructible in many (though certainly not all) contexts, land's material properties make it an appropriate medium for long-term symbolic value; it can be constitutive of apparently timeless personhood to the point where people choose to immolate themselves rather than accept their severance from it (Erie, Chapter 4, this volume).[44] Elsewhere this would make little sense. As Wheeler notes, land is not a particularly significant form of property for fishermen operating on the Small Aral Sea in Kazakhstan: there is abundant unowned land on which livestock graze freely, and which can easily be acquired for the construction of new houses for a small registration fee. In Eastern Chad, likewise, the Abeché customary court adjudicated on all manner of property disputes but those involving land are conspicuously absent in its records (at least until the 2000s, when they rapidly become the majority of cases—Scheele, Chapter 1, this volume).

Property in fish has very different associations. They appear in our case studies as nature's bounty, to be enjoyed in the moment rather than stored for the future. As the Kazakh proverbs have it, 'the fisherman's wealth lasts until his sleeve dries' and 'the sower dreams for the year, the fisherman dreams for the day' (Wheeler, Chapter 7, this volume). Fish are the archetypal form of transient wealth, a form of property ill-suited to the constitution of selves, their material and temporal inadequacy especially salient in traditionally pastoralist societies. Cows and camels, as is well known to anthropologists but perhaps still rather less apparent to others, can very readily function as constitutive property: the long-term capital accumulated by a family and the form of wealth suitable for symbolically significant transactions relating to marriage or compensation for harm (e.g. Evans-Pritchard 1940: ch. 1; Hutchinson 1992). In Somalia, as Dua is informed by a wealthy camel trader, 'a person who owns a camel is a man, someone who owns a goat is half a man, and a fisherman is no man at all' (Chapter 7, this volume), and indeed the successful fishermen we learn about on both the

[44] As William James has observed in *The Principles of Psychology*, '[w]e feel about certain things that are ours very much as we feel and act about ourselves. Our fame, our children, the work of our hands, may be as dear to us as our bodies are, and arouse the same feelings and the same acts of reprisal if attacked' (1890, i.291). What these things are varies hugely by place and period.

Somali coast and the Small Aral Sea also keep livestock on their pastoral hinterlands, accumulating the capital necessary for exchange on a prestigious, person-constituting, and more lasting level. In recent years, refrigeration technology and the development of transport infrastructure have facilitated the transformation of fish into a commodity, a source of cash and thus a viable means of accumulating wealth in the long term. Notions of abundance remain deeply embedded in fishermen's assumptions, however, such that neither future-oriented environmentalist discourses predicated on scarcity nor the formal legalism of quotas and 'virtual fish' can gain traction. The tensions between presentism and long-term thinking, between the authority of the past and future-oriented goals, work very differently across different property regimes.

COMMODITIES AND PERSONHOOD

One reason why the future-oriented dimension of legalism is ridden with tensions is because it classifies and commodifies where individuality and heterogeneity is often not so easily suppressed. Commodification is often driven by marketization, and it attempts to resist the consideration of things as specific or individual. Property regimes must always then engage with the uneasy tension between useful and reassuring categories, and accommodation of individuality. This point was famously fundamental to Karl Marx's view of capitalist private property as a vehicle of 'alienation' and commodification of human beings in his early manuscripts of 1844: for him, in contemporary property frameworks 'the dominion of material property bulks so large that it aims to destroy everything which is not capable of being possessed by everyone as private property. It wants to eliminate talent, etc. by *force*. Immediate physical possession seems to it the unique goal of life and existence' (Marx 1963: 153).[45] While Marx never fully elaborated his view of the dialectic supersession of capitalist property (as opposed to the denial of property by 'crude communism', which for him would have presented a different form of alienation), this humanistic critique influenced anthropological thinking about property beyond the confines of Marxism, notably in the work of Polanyi and his school.[46]

[45] For Marx's early writings on property ('The relationship of private property', 'Private property and labour', 'Private property and communism'), see e.g. Marx (1963: 137–67). For a recent sympathetic analysis, Sayers (2011: 101–32). Note also his suggestion in the *Grundrisse* (Marx 1973: 252) that in the capitalist system landed property 'cannot exist without capital as its presupposition'.

[46] For Polanyi's intellectual debt to Marx, see e.g. Isaac (2012: 20–1).

Fish are relatively easily commodified because, as Wheeler puts it, they 'resist individuation: they are fungible and impersonal; the span of a fisherman's engagement with them is brief, hence a certain immediatism in practices surrounding them' (Chapter 7, this volume). Their individual identities matter to no one so they can simply be classified by weight and species, and sold. Schemes of classification and measurement apply to livestock and plots of land as well, of course, but their individuality—as a camel born between one's hands, or as the house of one's grandfather—can remain crucially important. Skoda's discussion of medieval Dubrovnik shows that there, at least, efforts to reduce slaves to categorized commodities had to struggle constantly against the fact of their individuality and humanity, with legalistic discourses serving as one means of negotiating and obfuscating the tension.

The point could perhaps be further generalized. If the identification of property can constitute personhood, legalism can provide a conceptual language for managing the personal trauma associated with its loss, with or without the owner's consent. Here property shades interestingly into personal injury. Late ninth-century West Saxon freemen would not, one imagines, consent to exchanging their right arms for 80 shillings, willingly treating their own bodies as commodities, yet their laws provide an authoritative scheme of classification and valuation that might enable them to accept a sum of that order as appropriate compensation for its loss (Attenborough 1922: 90–1). 'Yusuf', a Hui farmer whose house and farmland had been seized by the Chinese government, could perhaps be seen as engaging with law in a similar way, in simultaneously maintaining that his land was sacred to the Hui community, therefore inalienable and invaluable, and determinedly insisting that it be classified as urban land and compensated at the rate of RMB 700,000/*mu* rather than the RMB 81,550/*mu* he had been offered (Erie, Chapter 4, this volume). As Erie notes, 'a sceptic may interpret such behaviour as acceptance of the commodification of sacred property, signalling an attempt to maximize individual material benefit' (Chapter 4, this volume), and the motives of those who accepted compensation could be impugned on the same logic in medieval societies—in Icelandic sagas men are accused of 'carrying their kin in their purse' (Miller 2006: 26). However, this criticism was levelled at individual greed, often intended as a spur to violence, not at compensation in principle. It was uncontroversial that people or families who suffered irreversible personal harm to which they would never have consented, could legitimately accept financial compensation, and angry dismissal of compensation offers that undervalued their loss would have been well understood (Byock 1982). Legalism provides a framework and language in which things that are understood as inseparable from persons, and thus invaluable because in no sense fungible, can be classified and valued, thereby—however problematically, temporarily, or even deniably—obfuscating the contradictions inherent in such acts of violation and helping to manage the tensions they created.[47]

On the other end of the spectrum, perhaps particularly where the things in question pose few obstacles to their conceptualization as fungible commodities, the salient forms of property tend towards the immaterial—the ownership of rights relating to things rather than things themselves—and shade into notions not of personhood but sovereignty. This is very much the case in Sayyid Qutb's thought, where property is considered on an abstract, albeit also self-consciously anti-legalistic, theoretical level (Rech, Chapter 6, this volume), but we see it also in practical examples. For Lambert (Chapter 5, this volume), it is the monetization of legal revenues consequent upon late tenth-century marketization and urbanization that underpins the appearance of jurisdictional rights in Anglo-Saxon England: the resulting competition to receive fines first leads to a more complex system of classification for legal privilege, and ultimately drives sheriffs and lords not just to assert the right to take specific fines but to claim exclusive rights to perform associated legal functions—rights that would have been incomprehensible a century earlier. In Somalia, similarly, we find, first, international demand for ambergris leading to the emergence of salvage rights along carefully demarcated stretches of shoreline, followed by the globalization of the fishing industry prompting the emergence of a state licensing regime. It was this system which, with the collapse of the Siyad Barre regime, became a focus of competition, with various groups asserting the right to sell licences and protection to foreign trawlers (Dua). Again, the focus of competition would have made little sense in earlier decades, the form of property at issue being not the right to fish itself, but the right to issue licences defining who has the right to fish. Rights in this register can be a form of property in themselves, or at least—as in the medieval English case—be integral to bundles of rights that constitute particular forms of property, but their symbolic significance is as much about authority as ownership. If this is property that constitutes persons, they are constituted as lords, rulers—men of power and authority.

[47] Not all goods or possessions are alienable. If Radin (1987) highlighted the complexities of modern western law, Weiner (1992) placed inalienable possession at the centre of individual and group identity in Melanesia. Elsewhere one thinks of jewellery, weapons, animals that simply cannot be separated from what clumsily we call their 'owner'. On the conceptual and ethnographic problems of straightforward separation of subject and object, see Strathern (1996).

CONCLUSION

Property, then, may take a whole host of forms, corporeal and incorporeal. Despite its claims to permanence, it may be fleeting in the rights conferred. And the twigs which make up the bundle may vary wildly across time and place. But despite the dizzying array of forms and implications of property, it really matters. Indeed, property lies at the heart of the vast majority of social relations, and even of how we conceive of ourselves in a social context. Very few humans have ever been able to conceive of themselves without referring in some way to what they own: even the ultimate abnegators, the medieval mendicants, self-defined in terms of what they *did not* own (and, of course, were unable to resist the siren call of ownership for very long) (e.g. Lambert 1998).

These same medieval mendicants provoked and led the elaborate, convoluted but passionate debates of the fourteenth century about the nature and origins of property, and the relationship between ownership and use. The irresistibility for the friars of material possessions (even if those might be the rather more justifiable books and basic accommodation) meant that labyrinths of tangled arguments about how one might possess and use without transgressing against more direct prohibitions on ownership were constructed (Coleman 1988: 133; Mäkinen 2001; Brunner 2014).[48] The matter culminated with the famous declaration of John XXII that Christ and his apostles had never known absolute poverty, and that outright ownership was unproblematic: 'Is it heretical to assert that Christ and the apostles had none of the things that come into use in human life either in regard to ownership or of dominion over them?' (Leff 1967: 247–9; Jones 1999; Garnsey 2007: 84–106).

The example is a nice one of both the fraught and the entangled nature of discussions about property. These discussions lie at the heart of political debate, social relations, cultural advances, and religious ethics. Indeed, disentwining the various strands of these conversations, and trying to isolate the various pressure points is well-nigh impossible. What is clear, however, is that legalism lies at the heart of talk about property. Legalism, in its appeal to generalizing concepts and categories, its ability to convey meaning, its moral force, permits the expression of complex wranglings about what make property and ownership meaningful, justifiable, and sustainable.

[48] The implications are extremely far-reaching and this particular debate shaped further discussion in the Middle Ages and the Renaissance about conceptions of property, the origins of law, the nature and extent of papal power, and economic practices like usury. The justification of the latter depended on how one conceptualized ownership and use: when lending money, did one hand over ownership or just use? (Brundage 1989).

In this respect, this volume is intended as a call to anthropologists, historians, and legal theorists to think comparatively about the forms of property they encounter in their own research. It is a call to think about the conceptual basis of the 'ruliness' which underpins so much 'property talk'. In the nineteenth century, many eminent legal historians provided meticulous accounts of the development of phenomena such as the English common law (e.g. Pollock and Maitland 1898). In what is perhaps a reaction against the potentially myopic dimension of such an approach, twentieth-century historians have tended, in a spirit of seeking the mentalities of a given epoch, to skirt around and elide the legal minutiae of the developments they discuss. What legalism offers is a way to examine the conceptual role rules play in a society, a role somewhat taken for granted by older legal theorists and obscured by the interests of more recent scholars. Property lies at the heart of what we all think we are working on, and the various articulations of property rely on the logic and grammar of rules.

1

Cows and the *sharīʿah* in the Abéché Customary Court (Eastern Chad)

JUDITH SCHEELE

> Crops and dwellings can be destroyed, but cattle can be confiscated and taken home. This quality . . . has given pastoral people a bias in favour of the arts of war rather than the arts of peace . . .; a condition that has shaped their character, economy, and political structure (Evans-Pritchard 1940: 50).

Abéché, the main town and largest market in eastern Chad, used to be the capital of the Waddaï sultanate. It still houses the sultan's court, which, through reference to the *sharīʿah* and partial incorporation into the Chadian state, has largely become autonomous from his influence. Accessible court records go back to the beginning of the twentieth century. Like other examples discussed in the legalism series, their emphasis is on attempts to arbitrate, categorize, apportion, and define rather than to impose or govern in any practical way. Legalism in this sense includes 'an appeal to rules that are distinct from practice, the explicit use of generalizing concepts, and a disposition to address in such terms the conduct of human life' (Dresch 2012a: 1). The cases the Abéché court records describe, moreover, allow us to approach the theme of this particular volume from an oblique angle: as is the case with much of the ethnography of north-east Africa, property, and in particular property in livestock, is at the heart of all social relations these court records describe and define. Family relations, for instance, depend on the transfer of goods. Marriage is about continuing transfers of property, and children go where the cows are. Yet property itself is often unclear: not because of any apparent uncertainties about the law, but because it is difficult to fix and identify people and things. In fact, this can only be done through reliance on guarantors and witnesses.

Cows and the Sharīʿah *in the Abéché Customary Court (Eastern Chad).* Judith Scheele. © Judith Scheele, 2017. Published 2017 by Oxford University Press.

Property thus emerges as an inherently relational and unstable category; and while in western legal systems, legal philosophers agonize about the individual 'state of mind' that defines property transactions, these questions are here a matter of public opinion. In the historical and legal literature, such a reliance on guarantors is often described as a temporary remedy to patch up the absence or practical shortcomings of 'central authority'; in Abéché, however, it coexists and has long coexisted with several states, 'traditional' or otherwise. Justice, similarly, is inherently transactional: everything—from lost braids to civil war—can be dealt with through compensation, and state officials tend to act as parties to these transactions rather than as representatives of an overarching authority. Indeed, the transactional aspect of the cases described, and the limited role played by the state, seem to make them more rather than less congenial to the *sharīʿah*, which as a body of scholarship, is arguably marked by a long-standing suspicion of political authority (Hallaq 2003–4: 251) and an assumption of socially situated personhood (Hallaq 2009: 2). Suretyship, then, and the preponderance of property as a precondition for moral personhood and a key metaphor for social interaction that it implies, might in fact hide a different approach to the notion of 'authority' itself, giving us insights into the peculiar functioning of the Chadian state (and similar political formations elsewhere). Here as elsewhere, then, legalism 'directs us towards classification more than towards power' (Dresch 2012a: 1).

ABÉCHÉ, WADDAÏ, THE SULTAN

The city of Abéché was built in 1851, to act as the new capital of the Waddaï sultanate, which had been founded in the seventeenth century in the Maba mountains to the north-west of the city.[1] Historians interpret the sultanate's move to Abéché as symptomatic of a larger development through which Waddaï changed from a Maba kingdom to a cosmopolitan and multilingual empire in which much room was made for trade and traders (Cordell 1977: 24). Abéché was in fact situated at a crossroads, where a newly opened trans-Saharan trade route via Kufra met a long-standing west–east corridor from Lake Chad to Darfur and Egypt, and slave supply routes from the south. Trans-regional trade of this kind overlaid and relied on regional connections that are familiar from the desert edge elsewhere, and that thrived (and still thrive) on the exchange of agricultural against pastoral

[1] On the Waddaï sultanate, see Tubiana (1960); Moukhtar (1982); Khayar (1994).

produce, including livestock and salt mined in the southern Saharan oases.[2] From the mid-nineteenth century onwards, the Waddaï sultan did everything he could to attract Hausa and Kanuri pilgrims from the west, Sanūsī merchants from the north, and *jallāba* traders from Egypt and the Sudan (Nachtigal 1889: 54, 63; Cordell 1977: 24); and French colonial sources dating from before the conquest describe Waddaï as a 'country of pastoralists and traffickers'.[3] Administrative, judicial, and economic institutions were developed to accommodate this diversity (Khayar 1994: 83, see also Nachtigal 1889: 234). Abéché, then, was from the outset a cosmopolitan market town, relying on interregional trade and its surrounding pastoral economies. In the words of one colonial observer, writing in the 1950s:

> Abéché is first of all a very large and very important market ... It is inhabited by a population who are rich, active, well informed, reasonable, difficult to handle, and to whom are added the cousins, little brothers, employees of the soldiers stationed there, the families of African civil servants, and finally, the many labourers and servants, prostitutes and vagrants who are drawn to the market every day.[4]

Abéché firmly and consciously belonged to the Islamic world. The ruling dynasty of the Waddaï sultanate derived much of its legitimacy from its privileged connections with Islam (Khayar 1994: 79), not only claiming 'Abbāsī descent, but also sending the brighter of their princes to be educated in Egypt (Jomard 1851: vii). In the 1830s, the Tunisian traveller al-Tūnisī, whose father had spent many years as a minister at the court of Waddaï, noted that the most lucrative imports to Waddaï were gold coins, writing paper, and books of Islamic jurisprudence (El-Tounsy 1851: 340–1); he also (probably with some exaggeration) stated that he knew of no country where Islam was as thoroughly adhered to as in Waddaï. Thirty years later, the German traveller Gustav Nachtigal, again probably with some exaggeration, claimed that there was a qur'ānic school in every village, and that 'compulsory school attendance' was on a par with that of Prussia (Nachtigal 1889: 248). He also noted that the sultan himself mostly spoke Arabic (Nachtigal 1889: 59). As Khayar (1994: 116) concludes, 'the Waddaï nobility needed Islamic knowledge in order to continue to exist'. This Islamic legacy carried on into colonial times, when Abéché was a (moderate) centre of reformist thought

[2] On patterns of regional trade along the southern edge of the Sahara, see Baier and Lovejoy (1975); on the particular case of northern Chad, see Arditi (1993, 1995); and Marty, Eberschweiler, and Dangbet (2009); and Archives Nationales d'outre-mer (ANOM) Afrique IV Dossier 36 ter Ouadaï—Darfour. 'Rapport Mangin', 1907.

[3] ANOM AEF 2D20, Capitaine Robillot, 'Projet de mission dans le Ouaddaï', 1898.

[4] Archives Nationales du Tchad (ANT), box W 140, 'Étude sur la monarchie ouaddaïenne', n.d. (1950s).

(Gardinier 1989), and when a majority of Chadian students in Cairo were from Waddaï (Moukhtar 1982).

Central to the Islamic reputation of pre-colonial Waddaï was judgement by the sultan's *sharīʿah* court:

> Habitually, the sultan holds an audience twice a week. He receives all complaints and reclamations from everybody, whoever he might be ... Court sessions take place in the centre of the square ... where the judges sit down, facing the sultan's palace. They arrive at the court in the morning, and only stay away during the hottest time of the day and when it rains ... Their daily sessions in the main square, their juridical function, their obligation to write minutes of the matters brought before their tribunal, to turn these into a transcript that is then submitted to the sultan: all of this amounts to a kind of deliberative and consultative council, a sort of legal court (El-Tounsy 1851: 365–6, 370, see also Nachtigal 1889: 239).

Court records were shown to the sultan, who also had the power to declare the death penalty; the supreme legal authority, however, resided with the *fuqahā'* (El-Tounsy 1851: 363; Nachtigal 1889: 240).[5] The court followed the prescriptions of Islamic law: 'In Waddaï, the sanctions imposed by religious law are applied exactly as prescribed in the Qur'ān', writes al-Tūnisī (1851: 327), and favourably compared its legal practice to that current in Egypt and in his own home country (El-Tounsy 1851: 255, 327). Al-Tūnisī was probably an overly lenient judge—more versed in female intrigue and the delights of millet beer than in the fine details of the *sharīʿah*—the sultan's and his court's actual power was no doubt limited on the ground (see Nachtigal 1889: 64), and many of the details al-Tūnisī gives would have appeared strange to people accustomed to Islamic courts elsewhere. Nonetheless, local and royal aspirations to Islamic justice, and their rhetorical power, cannot be doubted.

The French conquered Abéché in 1909. Waddaï had seemed to them the most formidable enemy in the territory that was to become the colony of Chad, partly because it was seen as strategically important (marking the boundary with British and Italian dominions) yet closely connected to the Arab world, and hence understood to be hostile to the French 'civilizing mission'; partly because it was the best organized and most populous political entity in the region; partly because the French committed even more fatal military blunders here than elsewhere (Debos 2008). Repression of any real or assumed resistance was thus bloody; and by the end of the conquest,

[5] This makes Waddaï judicial practice similar to that practised in neighbouring and better-documented sultanates: on Darfur, which was probably the most direct influence on Waddaï, see O'Fahey (1977); on Sokoto, see Tabiu (1989).

French military sources estimated that half of the population of Waddaï had died or fled (Djian [1915–16] 1996: 55, see also Largeau [1913] 2001: 277).[6] This hostility expressed itself in the ambiguous relationship the French colonial administration maintained with the sultan and his religious and judicial institutions: first imposing their own candidate to the post, then abolishing the sultanate altogether, then, in 1935, re-establishing it as part of their administrative apparatus.[7] The sultan's court thereby became the first trial court in the region, and was, theoretically at least, subsumed within the colonial legal system.[8] As such, it became a bone of contention during the last decade of colonial rule: like other 'colonial chiefs', the sultan and his jurisdiction were contested by the nationalist movement, while the colonial administrators' tone, in speaking of the sultan's court, became increasingly derogatory.[9] The popularity of the court, however, does not seem to have suffered from this, as it remained 'besieged' by claimants.[10]

This ambiguity continued into independence. In 1960, as most of Chad officially became independent from French rule, the Waddaï sultanate was once more abolished.[11] It was re-established ten years later, as part of the Chadian state:

> Title II: Sultans. Article 4: the Sultan is appointed in a Cabinet Meeting, following proposition by the Minister of the Interior. The Sultan controls and directs the perception of taxes and is answerable to the Prefect, the Sub-Prefect and the relevant heads of administrative posts. He is in charge, under the surveillance of the administrative authorities, of order, security, and public hygiene.[12]

[6] The French conquest of Waddaï coincided with a Sahel-wide drought in the 1910s, making its impact even more lethal.

[7] Chad was conquered at a time when imperial enthusiasm in France was past its peak, for no obvious reason apart from strategic concerns, and at times despite orders to the contrary. There was agreement in France that any further colony would have to pay for itself (Gervais 1982); this made the conquest more rather than less bloody, but it impeded from the start the establishment of a functioning colonial state. Distinctions between direct and indirect rule—the 'French' and the 'British' system—are thus inapplicable here (as there are in Cameroon: Geschiere 1993), as officers, underpaid and overburdened, dithered between both, or gave up on the idea of ruling anybody beyond their own staff altogether.

[8] 'Étude sur la monarchie ouaddaïenne'. See also Kelinguen (1957).

[9] See e.g. ANT W 44, 'Bulletin mensuel de renseignements', Ouaddaï, July 1958: 'The customary court is more or less all that is left of Ali Silek's remit . . . as he has no control whatsoever over the Arabs and the urban population. He has thus fallen back on the law and cares very much about this prerogative.' See also ANT W 44 'Bulletins mensuels de renseignements', Ouaddaï, December 1958 and January 1959. For the nationalist struggle, see Le Cornec (1963).

[10] 'Étude sur la monarchie ouaddaïenne'.

[11] As Mann (2015: 68) notes, the struggle over the status of 'traditional chiefs', although today often forgotten, was in fact key to the negotiations leading up to independence throughout French colonial Africa.

[12] République du Tchad, Ministre de l'Intérieur, 'Décret n° 102/PR.INT', 18/05/1970.

Despite his rather narrow prerogative, the sultan's scope of action is in practice both broader and less well defined, as his influence waxes and wanes with circumstances, as does his relationship to the state (which, in the Chadian context of repeated civil war and rebellion, is a moving target).[13] Neither can be understood according to mechanical models of replacement or co-optation: the enthronement of the current Waddaï sultan, Mohamed Ourada Ibrahim, in April 2005 drew an impressively large crowd (Favre 2007: 362), although the sultan's actual influence—in the midst of rebellion and civil war—was perhaps at its lowest point at that time. The *sharīʿah* court, meanwhile, was abolished in 1967 and re-established in 1970; its jurisdiction, for civil matters, was again confirmed in 1998,[14] in a context where 'traditional' authorities throughout Chad were increasingly incorporated into the state structure (Marchal 2006: 149; Debos 2013: 53; Brachet and Scheele 2015: 739).[15]

THE COURT AND ITS RECORDS

Today, the court is run exclusively by *fuqahā'* who rule according to the *sharīʿah* and their conscience, with little (official) reference made to the sultan. Court sessions still take place, every day of the week, in the 'audience building' that was built by the French in 1942, just opposite the sultan's palace. The palace is by now largely abandoned, the sultan and his family having moved to a more comfortable residence elsewhere. The court of justice contrasts sharply with this air of abandonment and decline, as it is beleaguered, from the early hours of the morning, by claimants and their friends and family. The court sits in a large rectangular room, with two entrances: one for claimants, guarded by members of the sultan's armed guard (who, ever since the French colonial period, are on state payroll, but none of whom are in the first throes of youth), the other for the *fuqahā'*,

[13] Rebellion against the central Chadian government broke out in eastern Chad in 1965, five years after independence. 'Peace' is seen to have returned with the routing of the Libyan army (who by then occupied the northern third of the country) in 1987; but it has been fragile, and interspersed with armed rebellion, in particular in the north and east of the country.

[14] République du Tchad, 'Ordonnance du 21/03/1967'; République du Tchad, 'Ordonnance n° 7 du 7/05/1970'; and République du Tchad, 'Loi n° 004/PR/98, article 81'. See also Néné Tassi (2000: 4).

[15] As Lund (2006: 686) notes with regard to sub-Saharan African states more generally, 'it is difficult to ascribe exercised authority to the "state" as a coherent institution; rather, public authority becomes the amalgamated result of the exercise of power by a variety of local institutions and the imposition of external institutions, conjugated with the *idea* of a state ... For this reason, it is often unrewarding to attempt an analytical distinction between state and civil society.' On the 'return of the kings' elsewhere in sub-Saharan Africa, see Perrot and Aymar (2003).

court scribes, the curious anthropologist, and whoever else can manage to gain access this way. Apart from the presence of the guards, nothing visibly sets apart the court proceedings from everyday life: claimants do not dress in any particular way, for instance, nor are women obliged to veil on entering the court (as is the case in contemporary *sharīʿah* courts in the Middle East), although most women in Abéché are veiled anyway. The *fuqahāʾ* sit on a low wooden platform that is divided from the claimants by a low wooden barrier painted bright blue; they sit directly on the floor, with piles of well-thumbed Arabic volumes of Islamic jurisprudence in front of them. They are clad in white robes with a white turban, bearded, and of an age that locally qualifies as venerable. Other learned men or otherwise important figures step onto the platform for a while, sit there, talk, have a cup of tea, and disappear again; yet others stand behind the platform and listen in, or even voice their opinion. The general atmosphere is thus one of informality, with no room for secrecy or privacy, however intimate the matters at hand. The court scribe has a desk next to the claimants' entrance; he is the only person who sits on a chair.

Court sessions are animated and noisy, with everybody speaking at once, and frequent appeals for quiet and respect. Conversation is in Chadian Arabic, interspersed with local languages (by the claimants) and the odd qur'ānic citation in classical Arabic (by the *fuqahāʾ*).[16] Both parties are present at the same time, and both bring as many possible and impossible witnesses, guarantors, and family members as they can, to the point where the *fuqahāʾ* periodically ask the guards to clear the room. Women are as much or even more in evidence than men, and the tone rises quickly. The only adornment in the room, a list of fixed fines painted directly on the wall (in Arabic), gives an idea of the prevalent tone of argument:

> Defamation of a person: its penalty (*ḥukmihi*), 10,000 *riyāl*.[17]
> Defamation of a tribe: its penalty, 120,000 *riyāl*.
> Unusual vilification: its penalty, 6,000 *riyāl*.
> Usual vilification: its penalty, 5,000 *riyāl*.
> Outrage of good manners: its penalty, 4,000 *riyāl*.
> The curse: its penalty, 10,000 *riyāl*.

Disputes can go on for days and weeks, as people are sent away and asked to return with additional witnesses. Eventually, however, they are concluded with the payment of compensation, which is settled immediately; the two

[16] On the development, peculiarities, and current use of Chadian Arabic, see Jullien de Pommerol (1994).

[17] The term *riyāl* is still widely used in Chadian Arabic, and today refers to the sum of 5 francs CFA. 1,000 F CFA are worth £1; the average monthly income in Chad is less than 45,000 F CFA (or 9,000 *riyāl*).

parties can then obtain an official written judgement from the scribe on a narrow slip of paper, and most do so. People explained to me that they prefer attending the *sharīʿah* court because it was 'cheaper than the others' (i.e., the official judicial system which since independence has its own trial court, to which the *sharīʿah* court might refer any of its claimants);[18] the court is clearly still associated, as it was in colonial times, with the rural and urban poor, and market-folk.[19] Others, however, insisted simply that they preferred 'God's justice' to that of the (notoriously corrupt) Chadian state.

Besides handing out written 'judgements' to individual claimants, stamped with the sultan's seal, the court scribe holds the official court registers. These registers are kept in the court's archives, a dusty room at the back that contains a collection of broken furniture, old typewriters, banners, books, and other items of no immediate use. I was shown and allowed to photograph court records from 1937 through to 2012, although the sultan's brother—who granted access to the archives—was adamant that records went back to pre-colonial times, as is also confirmed by al-Tūnisī's observations quoted above. Almost all judgements were written in Arabic, with a few years recorded in French or in both languages. This, people agreed, was not a matter of policy but of convenience, and depended on the linguistic skill of the scribe that the court employed at the time. Although the style and appearance of judgements vary over time, change is neither linear nor consistent in any way. Events that appear significant in the historical record—such as, most strikingly, the abolition of the sultanate and its court—are invisible in the court records. Nor do the various periods of civil war and armed rebellion that frequently removed (and still remove) Waddaï from the immediate grasp of the Chadian state appear in the records, which carry on regardless. With regard to a certain 'normalization' of warfare and violence in Chad (Debos 2011: 412), this continuity is clearly partly an optical illusion which tells us much about the nature of law as conceived locally: law, or rather, the *sharīʿah*, is not just another expression of 'power'; and compared to the vagaries of politics and armed struggle, it provides at least an illusion of permanence. This is a striking contrast with Erie's observations in China (Chapter 2, this volume), where frequent reference to anachronistic legal regulations underlines the permanence of moral claims as opposed to the fragility of political arrangements: in Abéché, law is conceived to be beyond and outside 'politics', and indeed encompasses it; it 'stands apart from the

[18] Officially, none of these courts require the payment of a fee, although in practice they all do (see Arditi 2000), and this one perhaps less than others.

[19] 'With regards to legal matters, Mohamed Ourada operated a very busy court, as the poor man from the bush had soon understood that *sayyidnā* ['our lord'] was ready to listen to and justly arbitrate his disputes' ('Étude sur la monarchie ouaddaïenne').

flux of events and personalities, suggesting an order of affairs that outlasts the moment' (Dresch 2012a: 15). It is impossible, then, to use these archives to write a political history of the Waddaï sultanate, or to chart a 'decline of traditional authorities' in favour of an overbearing state: no narrative either of 'legal progress', of secularization or of the growing influence of Islamic models—of the kind proposed by Layish (2006) for southern Libya, for instance—is plausible at first sight.

There is one notable exception to this impression of permanence: matters concerning property in land are conspicuously absent in the court records until the 2000s, when they rather suddenly start to constitute the majority of cases. This change is part of a larger development, observed in much of sub-Saharan Africa, from the periodic allocation of use-rights towards private property in land.[20] In Abéché as in similar contexts (e.g. Berry 2013), such changes of status in most cases do not indicate an actual transfer of land, but a transformation in the notion of property, or rather, in the terms and references within which access rights are expressed and legitimized:

N° 005/2008
5/11/2008

> To inform whoever sees this document that the *amīr* of the faithful the sultan Muhammad Ourada the exalted indeed gave to the man Adam al-Nūr from the tribe Awlād Rashīd and its assembly a piece of residential land measuring 100 x 100 m [here follows an exact description]. And the present is passed in the presence of the shaykh 'Aūd [and two others].

N° 008/2009
16/3/2009.

> So that whoever sees this document knows there came forward Muhammad Yābis and the man 'Abd al-Rahīm in Dar Tama. Every one of them owned a piece of arable land in the *wādi* Kakarā to the west of the sultan's estate. Indeed Muhammad Yābis [says] the land was his and 'Abd al-Rahīm bought a part of it in the year 1984. Muhammad has three *mukhammas* and 'Abd al-Rahīm has one *mukhammas*: between them they have it all.

Although these entries touch directly on questions of 'governance' and the influence of 'traditional authorities' that will be addressed below, this chapter will focus on earlier transactions, as individual ownership of (rather than use-rights in) land has long been controversial in many of the major legal traditions, including the *sharīʿah*, and was in cases such as Waddaï simply

[20] See e.g. Leroy (1987), Bertrand (1990), Berry (2013), and the special issue of *Africa*, 80/1 (2010).

irrelevant until very recently.[21] These earlier transactions are almost exclusively in moveables: jewellery, money, and, most importantly, livestock. As such, they pose their own set of problems.

PROPERTY AND FAMILY RELATIONS

Moveable property is key to the court records, both as an object of dispute—cases that are in one way or another connected with the transfer of property make up for the majority of entries—and as the principal ways in which disputes can be mitigated, most commonly through restitution or compensation payment. Beyond this, and in keeping with east African ethnography, property seems to be key for the representation, legitimization, and maintenance of social relations. 'The foundations of the study of the customary law of property' in sub-Saharan Africa, writes Chanock (1991: 68), 'must be the shifting and uncertain structure of the law of marriage, succession, and family property generally'. Here, we can make the reverse claim: the fragility of property rights over time allows us insights into the complexity and adaptability of social relations, and into the ways in which this complexity is maintained over time, while creating an illusion of stability. This is so because the notion of property as implied in the court records is inherently contradictory: in keeping with Islamic law, it is conceived of as an individual and freely alienable right; in fact, however, it is necessarily socially affirmed, and almost always hides more complex arrangements on the ground. Family members do not hesitate to bring internal disputes to court; and if we include struggles over bridewealth and maintenance payments, the vast majority of cases concern property disputes between kin or affines, perhaps with a bias towards those—women, widows, 'strangers'—who otherwise might find it more difficult to have their voices heard.[22] At the same time, disputes remain motivated by a strong sense of practicalities, and although property rights are kept rhetorically distinct from possession throughout, judgements are frequently followed by a compromise that means that all parties get something at the end. There can be no doubt that property locally is seen to serve the

[21] In pre-colonial Waddaï, as Nachtigal (1889: 245) notes, land grants were seen as leases, and land was distributed periodically by minor officials on the ground. For a similar system in neighbouring Darfur, see O'Fahey (1997). In Waddaï, similar practices seem to have continued until very recently, when, with the influx of foreign investment and international humanitarian involvement in Darfur, land value started to rise steeply.

[22] This is a general feature of *sharī'ah* courts throughout the Muslim world. As Peirce (1998: 317) notes, 'one of the principal functions of the court is to open up a forum for the voices of the community. It gives a public status to voices that otherwise might not be heard.'

purpose of making rather than breaking social relations conceived to be legitimate.[23]

Hence, in November 1937, Khadījah bint ʻAbd Allāh from the village of Am Djadou took her half-brother to court, claiming that he had 'made disappear' two cows that she had entrusted to him. Her brother acquiesced, and was condemned to restore two similar cows to his sister. The latter then decided to give one of these back to him, 'as a present'.[24] Similarly, when, in 1938, three daughters accused their mother of having 'concealed' twenty-eight cattle from their father's estate, the court first obliged the latter to provide exact accounts of what happened to these cattle. As the *fuqahā'* asked the mother to swear on the Qur'ān to the truth of the information provided, however, 'the three daughters stop her, throwing themselves at her feet and apologize profusely' for this breach of filial duty.[25] Husbands and wives kept exact accounts of what belonged to whom, and of mutual debts, although it often remained impossible to enforce these. Several years ago, stated Hawa b. Fatashi in 1938, she lent fifteen cattle to her husband Adūm who had to pay compensation for the theft of four camels. She was never repaid, and now, after an unrelated quarrel, was suing for divorce. Although the court legally upheld her right to her fifteen heads of cattle, she seemed happy to obtain four cows and a remission of the reimbursement of her dower (which would fall due as she initiated the divorce).[26] Hence, the tension between the notion of individual rights and actual entanglements on the ground partakes fully in the fluid character of Waddaï social and economic life, where family units themselves were fragile and easily contested.

Not surprisingly, then, the perhaps largest number of cases is concerned with matters of bridewealth: payments that take place outside families, but in view of constituting families in the future. According to Islamic law, marriage requires agreement by both parties, a marriage contract, the *fātiḥa*, and the payment of a dower (*ṣadāq*). Reading through the documents, one cannot help feeling that it was the latter that was locally understood to be central to the process:

> 28/5/1956. Jamiya bint Muhammad against Ḥassān Sharikū.
>
> The plaintiff: my cousin Ḥassān Sharikū who had asked me to marry him found me one day in the bush and took my virginity. Then he took me to his house

[23] This is more widely the case in courts throughout the Islamic world: 'The Muslim court was embedded in a social fabric that demanded a moral logic of social equity rather than a logic of winner-takes-all resolutions. Restoring parties to the social roles they enjoyed before appearing in court required social and moral compromise, where each party was allowed to claim at least a partial gain' (Hallaq 2009: 166).

[24] 8/11/37, Khadījah bint ʻAbd Allāh against ʻAbd Allāh b. Adā.

[25] 7/11/38, Sūgūjah bint Adūm, Faran bint Adūm and Manzallu bint Adūm against their mother Kaliah b. Bahū.

[26] 21/3/38. Hawa b. Fatashi against her husband Adūm b. ʻAbd Allāh.

> and kept me like his wife although there was no marriage contract between us. Because I am an orphan he hit me every time I grumbled and he kept me like this for a whole year. He hasn't paid my dower (*ṣadāq*). He recently violently hit me again when I insisted he pay my dower. This is why I came to this court so that justice will be done.
>
> The defendant: it is exact that I asked my cousin Jamiya who is an orphan on her father's side to marry me and I even advanced a sum of 2,500 F and a cow to her mother as a first instalment of her *ṣadāq*. But before the marriage was contracted I managed to deflower my fiancée and I took her to my house, she has been with me for a year. She behaved very well until these last days when, encouraged by her mother, she started to behave badly and this is why I hit her. If I didn't give anything to her mother apart from the cow and the 2,500 F it's because I am poor.

The witnesses were then called to testify, two on each side. They said that they had urged Ḥassān to give a little more. The marriage was declared invalid because the *sharīʿah* demands a contract, a dower, and two witnesses. The two were separated, but Jamiya was able to keep the cow and the money as damages for her lost virginity. Throughout the case, little was made of the rape and subsequent cohabitation; all attention focused on the dower.

The dower was only part of the story, however. It seems that for a marriage to be truly valid and to be recognized as such, property transfers had to be ongoing. If they ceased, it was relatively easy for women to garner local support to dissolve the marriage, within or without the court. Hence, in 1944, Rūmān bint Abūnā was divorced from her husband ʿAbd al-Raḥmān who left three years earlier to look for work in Bangui in what is today the Central African Republic, saying that she 'cannot stay in a house without food or clothes'; her one witness was her husband's uncle, who clearly supported her case.[27] In 1954, Hawa bint Billa was divorced by the court from her husband who, two years prior, went to Sudan. Hawa was tired of waiting, 'since I am a girl and I am wasting my life for nothing at all', but the court seemed more impressed by the lack of maintenance.[28] Conversely, husbands tended to have recourse to the *sharīʿah* court to get their wives back:

> The plaintiff: at the beginning of the year 1955, I went to Sudan to work. When I left, I gave my wife everything that is necessary: two lactating cows, one and a half camel load of millet, nine litres of butter, two pieces of cloth and a donkey at her disposal. I came back after only six months and I was surprised to learn that my wife had got herself divorced by the tribunal and then got married to

[27] 12/07/1944, Rūmān bint Abūnā against ʿAbd al-Raḥmān b. Muḥammad.
[28] 12/07/1954, Hawa bint Billa against her husband Bukhārī b. Adūm.

> another man. I have done what I could to take her back but to no avail. I do not agree with the divorce and want it to be reversed.[29]

The wife had succeeded in obtaining a divorce because she had claimed that her husband had been away for three years. Her witnesses now recanted, and the divorce was annulled. She stayed married to the first husband, and had to reimburse the dower to the second. Similarly, in 1956, a husband appealed against his wife's divorce and subsequent remarriage, granted to her by the court after he had been on pilgrimage for two years, leaving her nothing but a camel load of millet and 900 F.[30] Given the husband's venerable age—70 years—his wife might have been rather keen to make the best of a bad situation.

If court-initiated divorce proceedings based on the absence of maintenance payments were easily phrased in terms of the Islamic legal obligation to provide maintenance (*nafaqah*) (as the *fuqahā'* state in a similar case, 'according to Muslim custom, when a boy goes to Sudan and does not leave anything the Khalīl divorces the girl'),[31] local social pressure clearly seems to have been on the wife's side, and associated marriage with the continuous supply of food and clothes, even beyond the *sharīʿah*'s provision.[32] No assumption seemed to be made, in any case, that the wife's family would automatically step in to provide for her. Following a similar logic, children were attributed to those who could provide maintenance. After the death of her daughter, Gamaramissa had taken care of her 7-month-old grandson, until his father claimed him back before the court. There was nothing unusual about this in Islamic legal terms, but the reasons given for the decision were predominantly material: 'as Gamaramissa is blind and has nothing to eat, Muslim custom and the Khalīl give the child to his father to feed him'.[33] And when, in 1956, Barkaī b. Abākar paid for the naming ceremony of his absent friend's sister's child, he was promptly accused of adultery: material provision equated to an assumption of parenthood.

> I have just heard that the man named Barkaī has organized a naming ceremony for the bastard child borne by the woman named Marū, wife of Sumāʿin ʿAbd al-Karīm who is currently absent. I hence consider Barkaī as if it was he who gave the child to Sumāʿin's wife during his absence.

[29] 21/5/1956, names illegible.

[30] 10/05/1956, al-Hājj ʿUthmān against Khazzāl b. Jibrīn.

[31] 12/7/1954, Hawa bint Billa against Bukhārī b. Adūm. The 'Khalīl' is a standard work of Malīkī jurisprudence used throughout north and west Africa.

[32] In other Islamic contexts, it is much more difficult for an abandoned wife to obtain a divorce: see e.g. Haykel (2002: 209) on Yemen.

[33] 9/07/1954, ʿAbbās b. Ibrahīm against Gamaramissa bint Muḥammad.

This accusation was refuted, based on an overwhelming number of character witnesses; and Barkaī promptly and successfully sued the plaintiff for defamation.[34]

This connection between property transfers and the establishment and maintenance of social ties is an old anthropological hat, especially with regard to the predominantly pastoral societies of southern and north-east Africa (Kuper 1982; but see also Charles-Edwards, Chapter 3, this volume). According to Evans-Pritchard's classic account:

> Kinship among the Nuer is largely defined by reference to bridewealth ... Bridewealth rights ... are the most rigidly formulated of all the privileges of kinship. A man may neglect, elude, or defy the more fluid customary duties to kin without severing the bonds of kinship or even without seriously weakening them, but refusal to give a man the bridewealth cattle to which he is entitled is a total breach of kinship (1951: 49 and 153).

Descent follows bridewealth payments, leading to such anthropological classics as 'ghost-marriage' and marriage between two women, who beget children in the cattle-giver's name. Cattle hence emerge as 'the medium of transformation ... between a material economy of things and a moral economy of persons' (Comaroff and Comaroff 1990: 196):

> Because cattle and people were in some sense 'one', individuals were able to transcend some of the profoundest of human frailties, and thereby achieve a greater sense of mastery over their world: death became surmountable, infertility reversible, and illness something that could be actively defined and cured (Hutchinson 1992: 296).

As a result, 'man's fundamental need for a woman as mother of his children was transformed via cattle into a broadened and deepened dependency on other men' (Hutchinson 1992: 297), in particular as most bridewealth payments remained unpaid debts (Glickman 1971).

Abéché, of course, is not and never has been anything like Nuerland. It is and long has been deeply Islamicized, with a mobile and floating population. Wealth was inherently fragile, and property rights largely defined in individual terms. Although property transfers and presumably also debts seem to have been as crucial to the constitution of social ties here as they were among the Nuer, these were difficult to enforce, leading to a chronic instability not only of ownership rights, but also, it seems, of family and other social connections. Here as in similar socio-economic contexts, this should not be read in terms of a social 'breakdown', however, but rather as a structural given, in an environment marked by periodic crises, population movements,

[34] 11/5/1956, Yūsuf b. Ḥalū against Barkaī b. Abākar.

the dominance of regional and trans-regional trade, pastoral and agricultural mobility, political instability, and regional interdependence and hence vulnerability. The role of the *sharīʿah* court here is thus not so much one, as an older literature would have it, of accommodation of 'proper' Islamic law to messy realities or even 'custom'; or, conversely, of the pernicious imposition of Islamic law on a formerly coherent communal order. Rather, as Hallaq observes with regard to Islam courts more generally, 'the *qāḍī* mediated a dialectic between, on the one hand, the social and moral imperatives—of which he was an integral part—and, on the other hand, the demands of legal doctrine which in turn recognized the supremacy of the unwritten codes of morality and morally grounded social relations' (2009: 169). In this case, inherently fluid social realities came to be described and formalized through individualizing legal norms, resulting in a conceptual overlap that might help explain the court's ongoing popularity, whatever the political context.

THEFT, SALE, AND GUARANTORS

This fluidity becomes even more apparent when we look at property in non-family contexts. In the Abéché court records, most non-family transactions can be categorized as either theft or sale, or as compensation payments. Although we tend to think of theft and sale as fundamentally different types of transaction, they are in fact structurally similar: both only necessitate short-term social interactions and generally do not lead to the establishment of lasting social ties; and both ideally characterize interactions among strangers (although they might in fact be more effective among known people). Hence, when, in 1937, Muqaddam b. Mūna claimed that he was robbed of the proceeds of sixteen heads of cattle that he had taken to market in Abéché, it turns out that he was probably just taking advantage of the anonymity granted by the Abéché market to keep the money—or the cattle—to himself. The cattle, in any case, seem to have disappeared with no trace even before reaching the market.[35]

Theft and sale moreover easily shade into each other, as the same transaction might be experienced—or at least described—as either by the two parties concerned.[36] Take the following example:

> Abéché Wadāy, the 10/12/1952 AC, the 22 Rabīʿ al-Awwal 1383.
>
> The matter of Abūr Qayt . . . wronged by the man Wunīs . . . . He stole ten sheep from me. And the *sharīʿah* asked Wunīs where did you get the ten sheep from?

[35] 18/10/37, Muqaddam b. Mūna against Mordo b. 'Uthmān, Mūsā b. Mayna and Bilāl b. Mūsā.

[36] For similar problems of definition in highly legalized contexts, see Melissaris (2007).

> And he said Abūr Qayt gave them to me in order to buy tea and sugar and there was one witness present, ʻAbd al-ʻAzīz . . . . And the *sharīʻah* acquits him in the presence of the *qāḍī* al-Mahdī al-Sanūsī and the imam Badr and the *faqīh* Nūr Shīn and the trustworthy Naʻam and Muḥammad al-ʻAīn.

We will never know whether Abūr Qayt was just trying it on, or whether he was cheated; the potential for ambiguity, in any case, is real. Theft and sale were also necessarily related on a practical level, as theft—and especially livestock theft—inevitably led to the sale of the animals thus acquired, since they would otherwise be tracked down by their original owner. This necessary link between cattle theft and the possibility of anonymously selling stolen animals is attested throughout the literature on east African cattle raiding (see e.g. Anderson 1986: 408 on Kenya, and Fleisher 2000: 746 on Tanzania). It reminds us that none of the problems with property in the Abéché court are in any sense due to 'premodern' eccentricities, but are rather at the heart of market relations and large-scale pastoral economies oriented towards international export—as Waddaï has long been.

Hannah Skoda (Chapter 9, this volume) illustrates how the excess of individual moral personhood inherent in slaves made fifteenth-century commercial transactions in them even in contemporary terms morally dubious, or even impossible: 'The categorization of a person as a thing is an act of violence which is likely to be contested' (p. 237). And it has been argued that the law of property is largely about identifying and delineating, if not creating, things as things (Smith 2012: 1703, 1725). Cattle are differently paradoxical in this regard. They are archetypical capital: both in Ancient Greek and Arabic, the word for capital is derived from that for livestock, an etymology that has survived into our world through the idea that capital, given time, naturally increases. Moreover, within Islamic law and comparable transactional systems, cattle are the currency that expresses crucial values such as that of the *diyah* (blood money). Yet cattle are also highly individualized: as Pouillon (1988: 179) notes, pastoralists rarely count their livestock, to ward off the evil eye, but also because they know their beasts individually, and by their position in the herd. In the Abéché court records, although animals are categorized—according to sex, age, reproductive capacity—so that their monetary value can be determined, it is the fact that they can be individually known that makes them ownable in any practical way, as this is how they can be identified should they go astray. Hence, when Banat b. ʻAbd al-Karīm recognized his donkey on a trip to the city in the hands of Ibrahīm b. Muḥammad, two witnesses from his native village came to swear to the donkey's identity, and the animal was returned to Banat.[37] Similarly, in 1937,

[37] 24/10/1937, Banat b. ʻAbd al-Karīm against Ibrahīm b. Muḥammad.

'Aliya b. Ḥamza successfully claimed ownership of a she-camel after he could prove, summoning two witnesses, that she had been 'born between his hands'.[38] Such individual ties did not wane with time: in 1973, Dalik b. Tāhir from Oum Chalouba claimed to have recognized a camel that he had lost six years ago in a village near Am-Dam in central Chad—but to no avail, as the defendant could provide witnesses for the sale by which he had acquired the beast.[39]

Ultimately, then, even an animal's individual identity relies on social consensus; and ownership was most commonly proven by following the chain of transactions it was subject to:

> 3/11/37. Jibrīn b. Aḥmad against Muḥammad b. Sibīn [both resident in Abéché].
>
> He found his donkey held by the other and said he was the owner. The other says that he bought it from Mu'allim b. Abū Ḥāma (Hausa quarter). This one says that he bought it from Kūlū [from a village in Oum Hadjer]. As [Muḥammad] cannot indicate the last seller, Jibrīn remains the owner of his donkey after he presents [two witnesses] who swear on the Qur'ān.

In a context where livestock sales fed into regional trading connections and crossed international boundaries, this was not always easy, however, and practical compromise often replaced questions of ownership:

> 10/07/1975. The matter of Ḥassān b. Abākar Brindī ... against Sāliḥ b. Salam.
>
> I was the victim of the loss of a camel. As I was looking for it, I found it in the hands of Sāliḥ b. Salam. I asked him to give it back to me.
>
> Sāliḥ: I bought this camel in al-Janayna in Sudan.
>
> The court asks Sāliḥ to present his seller within reasonable time. During this time, the camel is to be looked after by the representative Idrīs Ab Sāliḥ. Two years have passed and Sāliḥ has not come back. The camel has died. His brother Mālik b. Salam came and paid [the value of] the camel to Ḥassān in the presence of his representative.

Property thus fully emerges as a social category, a relationship between people with regard to things; and it inherently depends on other people. Hence, where in the West, lawyers agonize about the 'state of mind' ('the development of proprietary subjectivity') as defining 'appropriation' (Melissaris 2007: 592), here, legitimate appropriation is a majority decision.[40]

[38] 6/10/1937, Ḥusayn b. Qūtān against 'Aliya b. Ḥamza.

[39] 6/01/1973, Dalik b. Tāhir against Mawda b. Karda.

[40] 'There is nothing in the sensibly observable world alone that can tip the scales and can determine whether the handling of a thing is an instance of appropriation or not ... The rights of the owner are not tangible or observable in nature. They refer to a mental link between

Concretely, this means that property cannot be stable over time, or even just spatially neutral. The *sharīʿah* court and the documents it produces attempt to fix these social relations for a time; but as the court inherently depends on living witnesses, its declarations remain limited in time and place.[41] The cattle market in Abéché—the town's most important economic asset even today—hence could only work with the help of guarantors who took it upon themselves to bridge the gap between ideal transactions and the much messier realities on the ground. They did this by engaging their reputation and their own property:

> 25/11/37. Sassāl acted as a guarantor for the sale of an ox bought by ʿAbd al-Raḥmān. When he arrived at Oum Hadjer, ʿAwda took the animal saying it was his. The court asks Sassāl to give the animal to ʿAwda or to present the seller. Having looked for the seller, Sassāl can't find him, and he pays 185F, the value of the ox, to ʿAbd al-Raḥmān.

> 9/5/1956. Mūsā Sanūsī, agriculturalist, wronged by Ḥassan b. Abū Bakr, chief of the Zaghawa.
>
> A few months ago a Zaghawa Arab whose guarantor was Ḥassan b. Abū Bakr sold me an ox. This ox has now been recognized by another Arab who says he is his owner. He showed me a proof and I gave him the ox. As the Zaghawa who sold him to me is unknown in the area, his guarantor has to pay.

Ḥassan b. Abū Bakr asked the court for time to find the culprit. As he failed to do so, he himself had to reimburse the plaintiff.

Today, transactions on the Abéché cattle market still rely on guarantors. Cattle sales thus involve at least four people: the seller, his guarantor (*ḍāmin*, plural *ḍumanāʾ*), who is often an appointed resident from the seller's home area or linguistic group, the buyer, and in many cases also the buyer's guarantor (*dallāl*). Currently, seventy-five people are officially recognized as guarantors on the Abéché cattle market. Added to this is the 'guarantor of the market' (*ḍāmin al-sūq*), who is nominally the sultan and in practice one of his officials; and in most cases an intermediary (*rakāj*), who establishes first contacts between the buyer and seller. If sales, like thefts, are thus stereotypically characterized by the absence of prior social ties—as this is what makes a commodity a commodity, according to the anthropological canon—in Abéché, this clearly poses a problem. It is not just theft that is at issue here:

the owner and the thing. Therefore, they are not exhausted in their exercise' (Melissaris 2007: 585).

[41] 'Proof', as Baber Johansen (1990: 17) notes, 'is a power (*wilāyah*) exerted by the witness and the judges and through which they reconstitute and redefine the reality of appearances (*ẓāhir*), according to set procedures'.

> 4/01/1973. Jadīd b. Ādum … against Baḥr al-Dīn b. Mūsā, trader.
>
> Plaintiff: I sold my camel to Baḥr al-Dīn for 41,000 F. He gave me 19,500 F. Hence I am asking for the remaining 21,500 F.
>
> Defendant: Yes, I bought the camel for 41,000 F. Having bought it, it fell down. I think the owner poisoned it.

In order to avoid such problems, some semblance of binding social relations has to be created ad hoc.[42] This is done at some cost to all parties: the seller and buyer who have to pay small sums for their guarantors' services, and the guarantors who might find themselves obliged to pay for defaulting buyers, or to reimburse the price of animals that turn out to be stolen. The *ḍumanā*'s prime motivation in any case, so everybody agrees, is one of social reputation rather than wealth: if one is asked to be a *ḍāmin*, it is difficult to refuse, as one is 'helping one's poor countrymen'.[43] Intermediaries, on the other hand, and even *dallālīn*, are seen as rapacious, and the moral condemnation that often adheres to market folk—especially in areas that have long relied on market transactions for their daily survival (see e.g. Dresch 1998: 127)—sticks to them like cow dung.[44]

Looking for analyses of suretyship in the wider legal literature, one is more often than not confronted with narratives of legal evolution:

> What distinguishes archaic from developed law … is the widespread reliance of the former on suretyship to fence in obligations of all kinds, substantive and procedural, in a society which did not command adequate impersonal means to hold men to their obligations (Walters 1986: 97–8).

Contemporary Abéché would thus present us with a paradox: an overwhelming reliance on guarantors in a system where there are not only one, but two 'central authorities' (the sultan and the Chadian state), and where moreover one of these authorities, as *ḍāmin al-sūq*, is itself treated like an overarching 'guarantor' (and where, today at least, boundaries between 'traditional' guarantors and state functionaries are notoriously fluid: Debos 2013). The question might thus be less one of the presence or absence of central authority but rather, and more fundamentally, of the perception of political authority itself. Hence, Stewart, in his analysis of surety in Bedouin customary law, warns us that functionalist comparisons between guarantors and the

[42] Dresch (1998: 120) makes a similar observation with regard to the need for contracts and witnesses in Islamic law.

[43] As Stewart (2003: 183) notes in his analysis of Bedouin customary law: 'a man who cannot give a guaranty cannot be a leader', but leaders do not automatically act as guarantors. See also Dresch (2006: 264).

[44] The *dallāl* (broker, 'the one who points out') is a common figure on cattle markets in East and North-East Africa: see for instance Samatar, Salisbury, and Bascom (1988) and Little (1992) on Somalia; and Mahmood (2008: 563) on Kenya.

state as the 'locus of formal authority to ensure either performance of the contract or damages for failure to perform' need to be carried out 'with caution': guarantors act as 'buffers' or mediators rather than law enforcers; their use is a matter of the division (rather than the imposition) of duty and liability (Stewart 2003: 223, 222, 229, 276). Similarly, Dresch (2006: 269) concludes that 'the prominence of surety implies not certainty of outcome so much as clarity of definition ... guaranty pins down answerability'.

APPORTIONING RESPONSIBILITY

Matters of definition, identification, and answerability are indeed at the heart of the Abéché court records. If it is difficult to identify camels, donkeys, and cows, people are no easier matter. Over the decades, court documents make an increased use of fingerprints, and claimants tend to be identified by their place of residence; yet the most common and probably also the most efficient way of identifying people is through other people. Abūr Qayt, whose lost sheep were discussed above, is thus fully identified as

> Abūr Qayt son of Muḥammad and his mother is Amḥayda, his group is Zaghawa and his Qashimbayt ['tribal section'] Fatḥ and he was born in 1910, his *shaykh* is al-Saghīr Sa'īd and his *kabīr* is Yusūf Ḥawzim [from] Am Dam.

His witness is

> 'Abd al-'Azīz son of al-Tāhir his mother is Zahra his group 'Arabā and Zayd, he is born in 1910. His *shaykh* is the *'aqīd* 'Aīssa son of Khābur and his *kabīr* is Muḥammad Ibrahīm.

While the title of *shaykh* and *kabīr* refer both to pre-colonial administrative traditions and their recuperation by the French colonial state, reference to the state cannot exhaust them: rather, their mention apportions responsibility to the people named. This reference to others evaluates the claimants' worth and reliability, but it also indicates how to get hold of them, or of somebody who is responsible for them and who is weighty enough to be visible beyond doubt—who cannot just be 'made to disappear'.[45]

If, then, Radin (1982: 952) is correct that 'almost any theory of private property rights can be referred to some notion of personhood', and if the reliance on guarantors indicates a vision of the person as inherently

[45] Legal systems everywhere have to confront this problem of identity; and in Islamic law more generally, identity is ultimately established through repute, or *shuhra* (Haykel 2002: 195, 214).

relational, questions about the influence of 'central authority' might simply be neither here nor there.

> Much Western (and now global) argument proceeds on individualist lines as if persons pre-existed society. Only contract would link them morally, or otherwise a state align them. Most other traditions, by contrast—Arab tribalism is an obvious case—have recognized people as collected of their nature and seen groups, whether transient or permanent, as deriving their value from relations in a broader world (Dresch 2006: 287).

The Waddaï system of governance, both in its pre-colonial and contemporary guise, is perhaps best understood as a complex layering of suretyship, rather than as a 'central political authority'. As such, it is rather congenial to Islamic law, which has no public prosecutors; which leaves what we would consider as 'penal law' largely to the discretion of the ruler (Peters 2005); which arbitrates as much as it adjudicates; and, most importantly, which assumes to be dealing not with subjects, but with socially situated persons (Hallaq 2009: 162, 159). Although Waddaï thus appears at first as a marginal example, it might raise issues that are at the heart of the Islamic tradition, in a way more established or 'efficient' states do not. Meanwhile, the fact that an investigation of local notions and practices of property leads to a reflection of the nature of political authority should not surprise us: not only can one be expressed in terms of the other (and often is, see e.g. Chanock 1991: 66; Berry 2013: 37), but as a central distinction between mine and thine, or, more frequently, ours and yours, basic notions of property forcibly pose questions of sovereignty and the apportioning of responsibility which are at the heart not only of notions of 'political authority' but also of moral personhood. Classic distinctions between wealth-in-people and wealth-in-things might thus in fact be malleable (see also Berry 2013: 52).

These issues are raised most clearly in the last type of non-family interaction: compensation payments. In the court records, everything seems to have a price: braids, earlobes, a wasted youth, ravaged virginity, a quarter of a horse's miscarriage, insulted honour.

> 4/10/1937, Maryam bint Gindi against Birra b. Abūnā and Labada b. Muḥammad.
>
> The plaintiff declares that:
>
> 1. Birra b. Abūnā had promised to marry her. He had given her six pieces of cloth with 36 francs. In the meantime, he fell in love with the girl, deflowered her and got her pregnant. He did not keep his word and abandoned her.
> 2. Labada got engaged to her and promised to marry her. Some time after that he got her pregnant. Seeing the state she was in, he abandoned her.

> The tribunal condemns Birra and Labada to pay two and one cows respectively to the plaintiff, within thirty days.
>
> 17/02/1973, 'A'īsha bint Ḥalū against Zarqa bint 'Uthmān, Ajabo bint 'Uthmān and Mitara bint Fadif.
>
> These three women ambushed me, beat me and tore out my hair, of which 22 [strands of hair] were attached and 17 hanging down ... [After five witnesses were presented], the tribunal condemns the accused to the payment of 1,400 F.

As the Nuer would have put it: 'no error exceeds the cow' (Hutchinson 1992: 296). This 'transactional' approach to justice is also reflected in the vocabulary employed throughout the records: what I have so far translated as 'judgements' is rendered in Arabic as *sulḥ* (conciliation) or *qadiyah* (matter); the root *ḥ-k-m*, whence is derived the more usual Arabic term for judgment (*ḥukm*, see the quotation above), tends to be reserved for state activities (as in *ḥakīm*, the governor, a term that is, paradoxically perhaps, especially prominent in the 1970s when the civil war was in full swing).

Even civil war, if and when it appears in the records, is dealt with in terms of compensation payments:

> 24/5/1975. Annahal b. Khāli, Zaghawa, wronged by Dagash b. Daybū.
>
> Summary: Dagash has taken advantage of the situation and killed my son Dambū. I ask for the *diyah*.
>
> Defendant: no, no, I did not kill his son. Because the people from our village did, because Dambū is a rebel known to wear the uniform of the outlaws. He introduced eight outlaws into our section and they tortured five men from the section [names]. They took everything [these men] owned: three pastures of cows.

Witnesses were called and confirmed this. The parties were reconciled, and no *diyah* was owed, not because war erased the personal nature of killings and thereby suspended ordinary social interactions, but because some kind of balance seemed to have been achieved anyway. In neighbouring Borkou, the local administrative archives are replete with similar demands for compensation payments for people killed during the war. Hence, in 1980 the Frolinat (Front pour la libération nationale du Tchad) paid the *diyah*—a garden and 312.000 F cash—for a woman killed following 'physical pressure'; in 1986, a former fighter sued a former military commander who is 'now serving in the presidential guard' for compensation for his camel, slaughtered ten years earlier during the war.[46] Although such claims to compensation for material damage (and at a push, a woman's death might count among these)

[46] Archives de la Préfecture de Faya (APF), CCFAN, 'Jugement', 24/7/1980; and 'Le préfet du B.E.T. à N'Djamena au Commandant en chef des FANT', 12/8/1986.

might look at first sight more familiar, the personal nature of these claims is striking.

As a result, there seems to be little room for state enforcement, either by the sultanate or by the modern Chadian state; nor are reparations ever made in the name of the 'common good', which, within Islamic law also, remains limited. What emerges rather is a transactional view of the world, in which law, morality, and centralized power are not coterminous: the state does not grant legal status and hence does not encompass all possible legal and social action, but the underlying assumption is of 'a set of minor, often personal, sovereignties that in a pressing sense precede the law' (Dresch 2012b: 152). This is only possible if moral space is divided (Dresch 2012b: 163); a division that is congenial to concepts of property as fundamentally a problem of 'delineation' (Smith 2012: 1705) or, as in the documents cited above, identification. The inherent dependency of notions of legitimate property on the current social consensus thus takes on a particular relevance: compensation payments can only function as a mode of political interaction if the cows are yours to give. In the same way, the instability of property that has been pointed out throughout can be read in a new light, not as a shortcoming of an 'imperfect' legal system, but rather as a crucial component of its inherent flexibility: as Dresch (1989: 107) notes, 'where there is no fixed level of moral reference, no bounded community that can judge its members in all circumstances, there is little chance of definitive problems and definitive answers'.

This, however, should not lead us to reason in terms of 'parallel justice' established to avoid state interference:

> Unable, for various human and material reasons, to organise itself fully everywhere in the country, the [Chadian] state exercises its judicial power in a certain measure through traditional authorities (Néné Tassi 2000: 13).

Rather, the question is one of encompassment. It is never fully resolved. On the one hand, the *sharīʿah* court through its association with the sultan is in a sense part of the Chadian national state (although this participation does not exhaust its relevance or legitimacy), and the Chadian state has frequently attempted to regulate compensation payments. Lists of 'proper' amounts for *diyah* payments are periodically issued as part of state law, much to the chagrin of the French-educated Chadian elites (Alifa 2000: 29–31).[47] On the other, the state and its representatives routinely pay the *diyah* themselves, thus acting as parties within the system, rather than

[47] For an example of one of these official decrees, see République du Tchad, Ministère de l'Intérieur et de l'Administration du Territoire, 'Dispositions relatives au règlement de la diya', 26/06/1986.

as representatives of an overarching legitimizing instance. Hence, when, in 2003, quarrels between nomadic pastoralists and farmers to the south-west of Waddaï resulted in more than 100 deaths, two sultans, several members of parliament, and one minister intervened; and the Chadian national government paid the *diyah* for all those killed to both groups (Favre 2007: 358–9). The difference between 'traditional' states such as the Waddaï and the contemporary Chadian nation state is thus one of degree rather than kind (see also Favre 2008: 168). Both draw on modes of interaction that are engrained in wider social practice, but that are only badly apprehended in terms of a 'central authority', or even just a legitimate monopoly of violence. Rather, violence itself, and its traditional remedy, compensation payments, 'ha[ve] become a defining mode of political sociability' for all political actors in Chad (Debos 2011: 414). If elsewhere, then, the 'modern state' is generally held responsible for the creation of private property and the 'self-regulating market' (Hann 2007: 288), here, notions of property as backed up through guarantors pre-exist and encompass central authority, and indeed allow it to act—albeit in a rather specific and limited way.

CONCLUSION

The most obvious way to frame a presentation of the records produced by the *sharīʿah* court in Abéché would be to set up a tension between 'proper' Islamic law and 'customary practice', and then to focus either on cases where this tension is particularly apparent, or on those that clearly go against the grain of common interpretations of the *sharīʿah*. This would contribute to a broader discourse of marginality, of what is easily called 'sub-Saharan Islam' with regard to the Islamic heartland, and of 'colonially tainted' practices when compared to 'pristine' ones (which are themselves illusory of course). Such an approach (although it easily feeds into internal Islamic rhetoric, the colonial literature, contemporary news coverage, and both contemporary Middle Eastern and academic prejudice) would do justice neither to the complexity of the *sharīʿah* nor to that of 'custom'. As O'Fahey (1977: 111) writes of neighbouring Darfur, 'the Fur and the Islamic, the indigenous and the external were seemingly present together from the beginning, sometimes competing, sometimes complementing each other'. In the same way, analyses based on a narrative of legal evolution, from non-state or 'fragile' state contexts to one where a central authority would do away with uncertainties of all kinds, whether of identity or ownership, would mask the specificity of the role played both by the Waddaï sultanate and the Chadian state. Starting with specific problems—in this case, those posed by property—results in a more fruitful approach, one that not only approaches the legal language used in its own terms, but that also allows us to ask questions about local visions of social relations, personhood, and liability, and about the nature of political authority, past and present.

In the Abéché court records, property is everywhere: it is at the heart of the constitution and maintenance of families, marriage, and divorce, and, as a necessary prerequisite to compensation payments, also of what we would think of as 'criminal law'. It mediates state intervention, the effects of civil war, and interactions with officials of all kinds. Yet property, especially in a context where it refers primarily to moveable goods, is in itself unstable, as attempts to enforce it face endless problems of definition, identification, and localization. This apparent paradox—the practical instability of a category that is central to all social relations—points perhaps not so much to legal shortcomings as to productive tensions that animate social interactions. Abéché is a cosmopolitan market town deriving its wealth from the large-scale pastoral or mixed economies that surround it; people rely on trans-regional trade for their livelihood, but also divorce easily and worry about the possible disappearance of even their closest family members and patrimony. Property thus emerges both as an individual right and as a temporary social agreement on legitimate possession, which is not granted to all equally; it is made possible through a momentary fixing of relations and identification of people of things, which in turn can only be achieved through multiple social relations. Conversely, a reputation of wealth bears with it social responsibility as it is almost impossible to refuse to act as a guarantor when asked to do so; and wealth might thus easily disappear down the traces of absconding clients, so that the moral apportioning of responsibility can remain intact. This emphasis on personal suretyship and, more broadly, on transactional justice takes us away from the centrality of (or perhaps rather encompassment by) the state, but it might, in its own way, be peculiarly congenial to reference to the *sharīʿah*, a 'jurists' law' that assumes legal personhood to derive from social relations, and, ultimately, each individual believer's moral responsibility before God. In transactional systems, as Dresch (2006: 280) notes with regard to Yemen, 'men of full legal status are commonly treated as minor sovereignties'. Despite the contrasting nature of Yemen and Chad, something similar seems to be at play here—and notions of property, fluctuating and uncertain as they might be, are at the heart of it.

2

Property in Land in Roman Provinces

GEORGY KANTOR

It is a commonplace that classical Roman law of property holds a special place in the history of western legalistic thinking about property, and one which extends beyond its role as a fount and origin of continental legal systems.[1] Key Roman legal notions—most notably the revolutionary distinction between ownership (*dominium*) and possession (*possessio*)—even if not precisely synonymous with the modern law of property (particularly in the countries outside the civilian tradition) have proved central to juristic thinking about property and to our toolkit of legal–historical analysis. An important consequence of that is that Roman property law, as it developed by the time of sixth-century Justinianic codifications, appears transparent for a modern jurist, who can seemingly enter into dialogue with Gaius or Ulpian in a way which is plainly not possible with, for example, an ancient Greek lawgiver, an Anglo-Saxon king, or village authorities in the Algerian Touat.

These intellectual developments, however, often tend to be viewed in disconnect from the concerns of historians of Roman agrarian regimes. The work of Roman historians, in so far as it engages with juristic notions, is still mostly concentrated on the late Republican agrarian redistributions and (for the imperial period) on the work of land measurers (*agrimensores*) and the legal position of tenants on the imperial estates (note in particular Kehoe 2007 and Chouquer 2010). When dealing with the concept of ownership, this

Ancient authors are quoted according to standard divisions of their works into books and chapters, and inscriptions and papyri by their numbers in standard collections. For abbreviations of the papyrological editions, see <http://scriptorium.lib.duke.edu/papyrus/texts/clist.html>. Writings of Roman land surveyors are quoted by page and line of the edition of Campbell 2000. I am very grateful to my fellow editors and to the participants of the Oxford colloquium, particularly to Lisa Eberle, for their comments on an earlier version of this chapter.

[1] Garnsey (2007: 177–203). For a still useful comparison with common law notions of property, see Buckland and McNair (1965: 60–126).

Property in Land in Roman Provinces. Georgy Kantor. © Georgy Kantor, 2017. Published 2017 by Oxford University Press.

scholarship often tends to deal with the economic impact of the rules rather than with their conceptual development.[2] At the same time, the work of specialists in Roman law often considers notions of mature Roman property law outside the historical context of Roman civic community and Roman imperialism to which they originally belonged: these scholars only seek to contextualize law when studying its early, pre-juristic development. Moreover, treatments of Roman law of property and ownership in legal scholarship, with the partial exception of the work on the law of Egyptian papyri, tend to be limited to the city of Rome and Italy and leave the provincial situation out of consideration.[3]

The concept of *dominium*, as the Justinianic codifiers of the sixth-century AD inherited it, emerged only in the later Roman republic and was not defined in any comprehensive way until the work of medieval glossators centuries later.[4] Acceptance that 'ownership (*dominium*) in Roman law is difficult to define' (Johnston 1999: 53) and the rejection of over-elaborate nineteenth-century pandectist constructions of Roman legal notions, while salutary in themselves, have led to something of an overreaction against the use of juristic notions of property.[5] Typically, Chouquer (2010: 142) puts considerable weight on the fact that the term *dominium* only appears in the Augustan age in the work of the historian Livy in our surviving sources. In fact, however, a remarkably close terminology appears already in the epigraphically

[2] Note, however, Crook (1976) (on the economic impact of Roman rules of property sale) and the monumental work of Dubouloz (2011) on all aspects of urban property in Rome and Italy from the Augustan age to the late antiquity; Frier (1980) focuses more narrowly on urban leases in Ostia and Rome in a penetrating way. For the scholarly approach concentrating on 'Roman law as action, not Roman law as abstraction', still prevalent among ancient historians (as opposed to Roman law scholars), see Humfress (2007: 122). For the most recent overview of Roman law of property from the economic standpoint, see Epstein (2016).

[3] Provincial landholding outside Egypt is still predominantly viewed from the socio-economic point of view (an important but isolated exception has been Luzzato et al. 1974). For a treatment of Egyptian evidence in the context of Roman property law, see Jördens (2016), with references to earlier literature. On the practicalities of landholding in the Greek East under Rome and Roman citizen landowners in the territories of Greek cities, see the contributions to Lerouxel and Pont (2016).

[4] On the late—sometimes modern—origin of some (now standard) terminology of Roman property law see the famous and highly entertaining discussion in Daube (1969: 13–24). For two different views on the Roman concept of ownership before the late second-century BC, Kaser (1964) and Watson (1968: 91–6). For convenient introductions to the contribution of the glossators, see Garnsey (2007: 195–203); Capogrossi Colognesi (1998: 252–64); for the role of the seventeenth-century theorists, Waelkens (2015: 277–322). For the concept of *dominium utile*, which will be important for us below, see Feenstra (1971) and Rüfner (2010).

[5] For an engaging introduction to the German 'pandectist' school of Roman law, see Feenstra (1992: 416–19). For Jhering's famous criticism of the 'jurisprudence of concepts' (*Begriffsjurisprudenz*) and an important attempt to re-evaluate the role of rules in classical Roman law, see Humfress (2015). For a rejection of the pandectist notions of ownership as an 'absolute and unlimited' right as not grounded in Roman law, see Feenstra (1968), Birks (1985), and Jakab (2015).

preserved agrarian law of 111 BC, and Antistius Labeo, the most eminent jurist of the Augustan age, uses the term *dominium* in a context which seems to indicate that it was well established by his time (*Digest* 18.1.80.3).[6]

This chapter examines the concept of ownership in Roman provincial contexts (i.e. in the Roman Empire outside Italy) during the High Empire (*c.*30 BC–AD 284), alongside its connection to Roman notions of citizenship, community, and imperial rule. In doing so, it will address the material long familiar to ancient historians from a somewhat different angle, exploring in particular the implications of 'legal pluralism' for the ideas of ownership.[7]

'A CONVEYANCER'S FANTASY'?

Gaius, a second-century AD provincial jurist, in his *Institutes*, arguably the most influential student handbook of Roman law ever written, and which later formed the basis of Justinian's *Institutes*, begins his treatment of the law of property by discussing the division of things (*res*) into classes. After noting (*Institutes* II.1) that they can be 'either in our private ownership (*in nostro patrimonio*) or regarded as outside private ownership', he proceeds to discuss what is for him the fundamental distinction, namely that between things subject to 'divine law' (*divini iuris*) or 'human law' (*humani iuris*), and elaborates further on subclasses of things governed by divine law: *res sacrae* (consecrated by a public act to gods in heaven), *res religiosae* ('dedicated to the gods below', primarily burial places), and *res sanctae* (city walls and sacred boundaries).[8] This leads him to a following observation on the different status of consecration in provinces:

> A thing is made *religiosum* by the act of a private person, when we bury a corpse in our own land, provided that the dead person's funeral is our affair. In the

[6] Crawford (1996, no. 2, l. 27): '[that land or piece of land] is to be private to its owners (*[do]mneis priuatus esto*)'. The arguments of Sacchi (2006) against this reading have been convincingly refuted by Crawford (2010) and do not deserve further consideration. On the development of the term *dominus*, see Capogrossi Colognesi (1969: 414–51), and more briefly Capogrossi Colognesi (2016). A crucial passage is Varro, *On Agriculture* 2.10.4, on six modes of becoming a 'lawful owner' (*dominus legitimus*), on which see Watson (1968: 69). For the emergence of systematic juristic thought in the same period, see Frier (1985), with an important critique in Birks (1987). For an attempt to put its emergence as a central legal concept in the context of late Republican political thought, see Straumann (2016: 139–45 and 168–90), who does not, however, address legal developments as such and seems to date some of them much earlier than the current consensus. For the (slow) development of distinction between *dominium* and other categories of property rights, see Feenstra (1989). For 'bonitary ownership' and the ideas of *duplex dominium*, see below.

[7] For recent re-evaluations of Roman 'legal pluralism' of the imperial period and its implications, see Ando (2011: 19–36), Kantor (2012), Humfress (2013), and Alonso (2013).

[8] For these categories of *res* going back to the late Republican law, see Watson (1968: 1–15); a recent study by Rives (2012) takes the passage of Gaius discussed here as its starting point

> provinces, however, the general opinion (*placet plerisque*) is that land does not become *religiosum*, because the ownership of provincial land belongs to the Roman people or to the emperor (*dominium in solo provinciali populi Romani est vel Caesaris*), and individuals have only possession and enjoyment of it (*possessionem tantum vel usumfructum*). Still, even if it be not *religiosum*, it is considered as such. Again, though a thing consecrated in the provinces other than under the authority of the Roman people is not strictly *sacrum*, it is nevertheless considered as such.[9]

His statement is further explained and qualified by two observations further on in Book II of the *Institutes*. First, Gaius connects the different status of provincial land with the concepts of more archaic Roman law, *mancipatio* (a ritual form of sale reserved for land, slaves, beasts of burden, and some agricultural implements, known collectively as the *res mancipi*, and available only to Roman citizens) and *nexum* (which for Gaius seems to be synonymous with *mancipatio*).[10] Second, he seems to connect this with the taxable

but has more to say about earlier developments. The understudied notion of *patrimonium*, as pointed out to me by Lisa Eberle, allows us to look at Roman notions of property from a different angle: focusing on the person of the owner and his or her social role, rather than on the thing and the relationship of the person to it.

[9] Gaius, *Institutes* II.6–7a, trans. F. de Zulueta, slightly updated. On the state of the text (not necessarily as secure at this point as we would wish), Grelle (1990: 170–2). The passage is paraphrased in Greek in the work of the sixth-century jurist Theophilus, *Paraphrase of the Institutes of Justinian* 2.1.40; see Grelle (1966) on that passage. On its significance for the survival of the notion of provincial sovereignty of the 'Roman people' (*populus Romanus*), see Millar (2002: 319). For the rule that two persons cannot have the same rights of ownership or possession in the same thing, see Ulpian in *Digest* 13.6.5.15. On making a plot of land *religiosum* through burial and possible legal disputes connected with that, see also the imperial constitutions assembled in the *Code of Justinian* 3.44, and Ulpian in *Digest* 11.7.2.7, who stresses that where the usufruct (enjoyment) of the land belongs to someone different from the owner, neither the owner nor the holder of the usufruct can make it *religiosum*, a rule relevant to the situation envisaged by Gaius.

[10] 'Things are further divided into *mancipi* and *nec mancipi*. *Mancipi* are lands and houses on Italic soil; likewise slaves and animals that are commonly broken to draught or burden, such as oxen, horses, mules and asses; likewise, rustic praedial servitudes, whereas urban praedial servitudes are *nec mancipi*. *Nec mancipi* are also stipendiary and tributary lands' (Gaius, *Institutes* II.14a); 'we must further note that the saying of the old lawyers, that there is *nexum* of Italic, but not of provincial land, means that Italic land is *mancipi* and provincial *nec mancipi*. For in ancient speech the act had a different name, and what for them was *nexum* is for us *mancipatio*' (Gaius, *Institutes* II.27). For *nexum* in this sense, see Varro, *On the Latin Language* VII.105 (ancient dispute about the exact meaning of the term) and Watson (1975: 111–24); for possible wider meanings that may render Gaius's equation not entirely accurate, see Eberle (2016: 57–8), with further references. On the much-debated concept of *mancipium* and the criteria uniting *res mancipi*, see e.g. de Visscher (1966); Watson (1968: 16–20); Capogrossi Colognesi (1969: 288–348); Capogrossi Colognesi (1986: 199–217); Diosdi (1970: 62–84); Watson (1971: 58–72); Dozhdev (1996: 50–70); Giachi and Marotta (2014: 65–73). For the *res mancipi* as more valuable things 'within an economy that was still essentially agrarian', see Capogrossi Colognesi (2016: 524). For a survey of earlier historiography, starting with the glossators, see Capogrossi Colognesi (1969: 18–146).

status of provincial land (direct taxation in Italy itself was abolished since 167 BC) classified by him as 'tributary or stipendiary' according to the type of direct taxation introduced in particular provinces.[11]

These passages of Gaius have attracted a rather considerable bibliography and a brief historiographical excursus is required at this point. The great German historian of ancient Rome, Theodor Mommsen, assumed on the basis of Gaius's phrase in *Institutes* 2.7 that provincial land, apart from territories of the privileged 'free' or 'treaty' communities (*civitates liberae/foederatae*) became 'public land of the Roman people' (*ager publicus populi Romani*), a key element in his influential conception of a radical dichotomy between 'free' and 'subject' communities.[12] Rules governing property were for him only one part of the wider package of what he termed the 'tolerated autonomy' of provincial communities, which extended to the status of local law and jurisdiction, taxation regimes and rights of citizenship, only given precarious recognition by Roman authority. Mommsen himself ascribed the origins of this concept of provincial land to the activities of Gaius Gracchus (tribune of the people in 123–122 BC) and his introduction of Roman taxation in Asia Minor, but other scholars who followed his general scheme traced it back to an even earlier period of Roman history.[13]

Mommsen's theory continues to underpin much modern scholarship of the legal aspects of Roman provincial government and the organization of provincial judicial systems, but it has been largely abandoned in more recent scholarship as regards fiscal aspects of Roman rule. This revised historiography of provincial fiscality challenges Mommsen's characterization of provincial land: not all of it became *ager publicus*, local ownership and control by local communities remained possible. W. M. Ramsay and M. Rostovtzeff (in his early work prior to the First World War on Roman colonate) already advanced a more limited conception of the *ager publicus* in the 1890s and 1900s, suggesting a direct line of succession from the Hellenistic 'royal land' (*gē* or *chora basilikē*) to the *ager publicus* of the Roman Republican period and

[11] 'The same applies to provincial lands, some of which we call stipendiary and others tributary. Stipendiary are lands in the provinces that are considered as belonging to the Roman people (*propriae populi Romani*), tributary those in the provinces that are held to belong to the emperor' (Gaius, *Institutes* II.21). For the later abolition of the distinction between stipendiary and tributary land and Italian land by Justinian, see *IJ* 2.1.40. It is significant that even at that late date the distinction was worth including in an elementary law textbook. For the fullest overview of Roman provincial land taxes, see Neesen (1980: 19–98); for the eastern provinces, see also Migeotte (2014: 410–22).

[12] Mommsen (1887: 687; 728–31), followed e.g. by Buckland (1963: 190), who viewed provincial land ownership as 'permanent holdings at a fixed rent'. Mommsen's distinction was central to the groundbreaking—and still not fully replaced—study of provincial legal situation by Ludwig Mitteis (1891: 85–94). On the legal status of *ager publicus* in Italy (for which evidence is far more abundant), see Roselaar (2010: 86–145).

[13] e.g. Klingmüller (1910).

then to the imperial estates, and thus excluding the territory of subject communities.[14] While this is a model which might be valid for some parts of the Roman world (notably the lands of the Attalid kings of Pergamum in the modern Gallipoli peninsula), subsequent research has shown that the extent of imperial estates elsewhere was often even more limited, and any direct continuity with the Republican *ager publicus* or Hellenistic royal domains is hard to trace.[15] Furthermore, it is clear that imperial estates could be expanded through purchase, including acquisition of land and houses on the open market: imperial ownership of fiscal land in this respect appears to be closer in status to private ownership than to the status of the Republican *ager publicus* (Dalla Rosa 2014). That should lead us to the conclusion that imperial landholding in the provinces existed in a world in which local land ownership and indeed local legal regimes governing it were not necessarily rendered obsolete by Roman conquest or reduced to precarious conventions of tenancy.

It is in fact notable that the two distinctions which do not seem to be addressed at all by Gaius (or Roman land measurers, on whose evidence more below) are precisely that between the civic land (*gē politikē*) and royal land (*gē basilikē*), crucial for the Hellenistic period,[16] and that between imperial estates and the rest of provincial land. In so far as Gaius is concerned, ownership of the whole is vested, in some sense, in the Roman people or the emperor, which seems to elide these important distinctions and give no special status to the imperial properties. This seeming lack of connection with administrative practice has led Tenney Frank and A. H. M. Jones (from whose influential article on this subject the quotation used as a title of this section is taken) to conclude that Gaius's theory of provincial property is to be dismissed as an intellectually sterile way of explaining why the standard

[14] Ramsay (1890: 172ff.; 1895–7, vol. 1, 280–95; 1906, 305–14). Rostovtzeff defined the royal land as 'alles, was nicht zu den Stadt- oder Tempelterritorien gehört' (Rostowzew 1910: 247), which obviously does not cover the territory of the subject cities.

[15] The most recent treatment of the status of imperial estates is Maiuro (2012); for a checklist (badly in need of updating), see D. J. Crawford (1976: 57–70). On the lack of continuity in Asia Minor, see Broughton (1934); Levick (1967: 215–26); Mitchell (1980, esp. at p. 1079: 'no imperial holdings on the central plateau can be securely dated before the reign of Hadrian'). Rostovtzeff's view of imperial estates in Egypt has been comprehensively criticized by Monson (2012). Imperial estates within civic territory are attested at Ephesus (*Inschriften von Ephesos* I 42); Lenski (2016: 173) is wrong to assume they could have come into the emperor's hands only by confiscation.

[16] The most comprehensive study (limited to Asia Minor) is Mileta (2008). For a briefer introduction with broader geographical scope, see Bresson (2016: 110–17), with further references, stressing in particular the cases where land was granted by the kings with the right to incorporate it in the *polis* territory. For an example of such a grant, see the exemplary discussion of the considerable land grant to a certain Aristodicides of Assus by Antiochus I, incorporated by the royal permission in the territory of the city of Ilion, in Bencivenni (2004).

ways of transferring ownership of land in Italy, the transactions of *mancipatio* and *in iure cessio*, could not be used in provinces. Jones turns instead to a different Roman notion, well known from Livy's account of Roman imperial conquest: the return of 'their laws and their fields' to a subject community after its surrender to Rome. Provincial land, with the exception of what was retained as *ager Romanus* or imperial estates (in neither of which private ownership seems to have been possible) was to be interpreted, according to Jones, rather as 'the land of non-Roman communities', at any rate before the extension of Roman citizenship to the whole of the free provincial population in AD 212, and thus the territory where the *dominium ex iure Quiritium*, 'ownership according to the law of the Romans', could not exist.[17]

Independently of Jones and in a subtly different way, the great German Romanist Max Kaser argued that documentary evidence shows a range of transactions in provincial land which imply a status not radically different from that of Roman *dominium*; he suggested that legal rights in provincial land should be recognized as 'a right of property, to which only the name of property was denied'.[18] He further developed his ideas in his vastly influential handbook of Roman private law, suggesting that Gaius's denial of the full name of *dominium* to provincial ownership was a consequence of the Greek understanding of property as 'a kind of qualified possession'.[19]

However, this cannot be quite right. Notably, a funerary inscription for a Roman citizen Minucius Pollio and his family from the city of Smyrna in Asia Minor show them 'to have the full property rights (*panktesia*) for burial niches'.[20] Clearly, a fuller form of the right of ownership in Greek law

[17] Frank (1927); Jones (1941) (quotation from p. 148); see Kniep (1912: 117) (seemingly not used by Jones): 'nichts anderes als eine unfruchtbare theoretische Wortplänkelei'. See further Bleicken (1974) and Grelle (1990). For incorporation of former royal land within a Roman province, compare *Supplementum epigraphicum Graecum* XXXIX 1180 (ed. and trans. Cottier et al. 2008), ll. 26/27: 'The person importing by land [is to] declare [and register], in those places [in which] there is [a customs station on the boundaries of the land] formerly of the monarchy (*basileias*) or of free cities or of peoples or of communities'. For the *dominium ex iure Quiritium*, see nn. 22 and 23.

[18] Kaser (1942, quotation from p. 80, my translation).

[19] Kaser (1971–5, i.403). For the idea of Greek ownership as a qualified right, see Kränzlein (1963), directly acknowledged by Kaser as an influence. For more recent reactions to Kränzlein's thesis, Jakab (2014: 330–1) provides a useful survey; note in particular the discussion between Thür (2008) and Harris (2008). For a stark contrast between the Athenian terminology (always used in the sense of better claim to a thing than that of someone else) and the classical Roman *dominium* (which did not admit of grades in the thought of Roman jurists), Harrison (1968: 201–3, note also pp. 228–30 for the lack of a distinction similar to that between the *res mancipi* and *nec mancipi*); for the view of ownership as a relative right only in archaic Roman law, see Kaser (1964). On the Hellenistic evidence for the so-called *panktesia* or *panktetike kyrieia* ('full ownership') and its possible meaning, see Velissaropoulos-Karakostas (2011: ii.63–7). On the 'liberal' and individualistic character of classical Roman law of ownership, Schulz (1951: 334–7) is a controversial classic, building on the 'pandectist' tradition in some respects.

[20] G. Petzl, *Inschriften von Smyrna* I 193, l. 6 (Roman imperial period).

was seen as worth acquiring by at least some Roman citizens resident in the provinces: why then was it denied the name of *dominium* by Gaius, who wrote a commentary on the provincial edict and generally should have been familiar with provincial legal practice? Even more difficulty is presented by Western provinces, where local legal traditions were for the most part effectively subsumed by the local adoption of Roman law. A particularly important case is Spain, where after the grant of the 'Latin rights' (effectively, Roman citizenship restricted to its private law aspects) by the emperor Vespasian (probably in AD 73) local courts were to apply the rules from the *album* of the provincial governor, a list of 'writs' accepted by the governor's court (irrigation rules, as often, are attested as an exception to this rule).[21]

A further problem is presented by the seeming distinction between the status of the provincial land and the so-called 'bonitary ownership' in Roman law, which might have been considered a natural category for it. As the more flexible rules of the praetor's edict developed in parallel to the archaic statutory *ius civile*, Roman jurists developed the concept of holding 'among one's things' (*in bonis*) for the cases where ownership of *res mancipi* was transferred via informal *traditio*, rather than using the ritual of *mancipatio*.[22] For the period until the *dominium ex iure Quiritium*, full 'ownership according to Roman law', was transferred by the length of uninterrupted possession (*usucapio*), the holder *in bonis* was given absolute protection, including from the *dominus* (by means of the so-called *exceptio rei venditae et traditae*), and was already to all intents and purposes the owner of the thing.[23] While the

[21] Galsterer (1987). For irrigation rules, see Buzzacchi (2013) (Roman Spain); a recently found 'water law' from Laodicea (reported in the *Hurriyet Daily News*, 21 August 2015) provides a glimpse of a similar approach in the eastern provinces. Compare Scheele (2012) for local irrigation rules in a colonial context in a different historical period.

[22] For a clear introductory account in English, Buckland (1963: 191–5). More recent approaches are well surveyed in Guarino (2001: 684–8), and in more detail, in Vacca (2015: 1–31). On the absolute character of protection of 'bonitary' rights, above all, see Ankum (1985). For the later abolition of the *dominium ex iure Quiritium*, see *Codex of Justinian* 7.25.1; Guarino (2001: 690–1) connects this with the extension of *tributum* (land tax) to Italian land under the emperor Aurelian two decades earlier. One may compare the medieval distinction between *dominium directum* (which, according to the thirteenth-century jurist Jacques de Revigny, existed only in Italy—see Waelkens 2015: 295) and *dominium utile*, which in many ways resembles the distinction in Gaius, but uses a different terminology (see n. 4). For the argument that this distinction was rooted in the academic culture of Roman law and had little in common with social practice, see above all Reynolds (1994: 53–74); for the discovery of the Verona palimpsest of Gaius coinciding with its disappearance and as a result having limited impact on the understanding of Roman ownership, see Feenstra (1968: 57).

[23] For an introduction on the *usucapio* (which allowed to acquire full ownership rights in Italian land acquired by *traditio* after two years, and in other *res mancipi* after a year) and its later cousin *longi temporis praescriptio*, initially introduced for provincial lands, where *usucapio*, like *mancipatio*, was not available, see Buckland (1963: 241–52), or Brégi (2009: 166–74); detailed discussion e.g. in Vacca (2015: 79–282). Jakab (2015: 120–4) addresses it from the viewpoint of the New Institutional Economics.

term *bonitarium dominium* for this mode of property holding only emerged in post-Justinianic commentators, Gaius himself (*Inst.* 1.54; 2.40) could already view the difference between a *dominus ex iure Quiritium* and a holder *in bonis* as a case of 'double ownership' (*duplex dominium*).[24] While the rights of the bonitary holder received an absolute protection in private law, they were limited in some aspects of public law and personal status, for instance, conveying Roman citizenship to one's freed slaves or exercising guardianship over one's underage freedmen.[25]

This was not, however, the way Gaius nor other Roman jurists treated provincial land. Indeed, interestingly, Gaius contrasts his notion of *duplex dominium* with how ownership is understood outside Roman law, and so by implication among provincials: 'among non-citizens (*peregrini*) there is only one ownership: a man either is owner or is not considered owner' (*Inst.* 2.40). They chose instead the analogy of *possessio* and of usufruct (two notions rather problematically connected in Roman law).[26] The terminology employed by Gaius in the passages quoted above emerges as early as the Roman statute about the city of Termessus Maior in Asia Minor of 68 BC, in which the citizens of Termessus were given, as part of their autonomous status, the right 'to hold, possess, use and enjoy' their fields and buildings (*Roman Statutes* 19, col. I, l. 35). The terms *dominium* and *dominus* are first applied to tributary land as late as AD 291 (*Fragmenta Vaticana* 315 and 316). While that in itself should not be overestimated, as the texts applying the term *dominus* to the owner *in bonis* are rare and perhaps non-technical, it is surely telling that Gaius does not envisage the provincial situation as one of 'double ownership'.[27]

[24] Feenstra (1968) is fundamental on the *duplex dominium*. For post-Justinianic terminology, Kaser (1971–5, i.403 n. 21). I am using the term 'absolute' here simply as a shorthand for 'fullest possible and undifferentiated' ('distinct, singular, and exclusive', in the words of Birks 1985: 31), without arguing for a return to the untenable 'absolute ownership' view in the sense of the right of ownership unrestricted by any public authority (see n. 5).

[25] Buckland (1908: 549); on guardianship, see Sirks (1983: 248–50).

[26] See Bozza (1942, esp. 68–75), and for later legal developments, Bozza (1943), still useful. For an overview, see Guarino (2001: 688–91), with further references to recent publications. For usufructuary having *possessio*, see Cicero, *In Defence of Caecina* 94, dismissed by Watson (1968: 85) as not 'good law'. Baldus (2016: 548) terms *possessio vel ususfructus* 'a specifically provincial form of control'. It would perhaps be better to speak of an explanatory device applied by Gaius to the provincial situation. The contrast between provincial ownership and bonitary ownership has been emphasized by Grosso (1974: 68); see further Vacca (2015: 283–302). This terminology seems to have penetrated into the provincial legal usage: *Digest* 34.1.4 pr records a confusion between *usus fructus* and *plenum dominium* on the island of Chios in the third century AD.

[27] For the terminology used for 'bonitary ownership', see e.g. Buckland (1963: 190–1, n. 11). The use of the terminology of *possessio* for ownership of provincial land may be the explanation for the use of *possessio* as 'the general term suitable to express ownership' in late antique 'vulgar law': Levy (1951: 19–91, quote from p. 62) is a classic; see also Kaser (1971–5, ii.247–8). See n. 35 for the *formula* (writ) used for reclaiming provincial land.

'DIVERSITY OF THE PROVINCES'

The views of Jones and Kaser still largely dominate the field in standard treatments of both Roman law and Roman provincial administration.[28] However, while they undoubtedly single out salient features of provincial legal situation passed over in Mommsen's treatment of Gaius's passage, there are considerable problems with airy dismissal of Gaius's interpretation as just an idiosyncratic pedagogical device of a provincial law lecturer. To begin with, Gaius's view was hardly idiosyncratic. In fact, the fullest statement of the different legal status of provincial land comes in a practical treatise on land surveying, ascribed to a certain Agennius Urbicus. This treatise has often been dismissed by legal historians, since it is not very legally perceptive and appears to elide the differences between ownership and possession.

> The first category of landholding (*condicio possidendi*) occurs in Italy, of a kind where no land is liable to tribute, but belongs to a colony, or a *municipium*, or some *castellum*, or *conciliabulum*, or private estate.
>
> But if we consider the provinces, they contain lands of colonial status, which are exempt from taxes; they have in addition colonial lands which do pay taxes; moreover the provinces also contain lands belonging to *municipia* or to non-Roman communities, also in general lands subject to tax, which are not subject to *nexum*, and cannot be acquired by anyone else by *usucapio*. They are, however, possessed by private individuals but on different legal terms. These lands are also sold, but there cannot be *mancipatio* governed by *lex* in their case. For those individuals are permitted to take possession of the land as for the purpose of reaping the harvest and on condition of payment of the land tax. Nevertheless, they lay claim to boundaries among themselves, just as if they were the boundaries of private lands. For it is proper for them to be obliged to have a demarcated boundary, so that each person knows that it is right for him to cultivate, and the legal possessor (*qui iure possidet*) knows that he possesses. They engage with one another in the kinds of dispute that occur in lands not subject to tax and privately owned. Nevertheless, we shall see whether anyone can use an *interdictum*, that is appeal to an *interdictum*, concerning possession of this type.
>
> Many different cases occur, which relate to the normal legal process, because of the diversity of the provinces. For instance, in Italy no small dispute is provoked over keeping out rain water, whereas in Africa a dispute on the same matter takes a quite different direction: because it is a very dry region, a person

[28] One recent exception I am aware of is Du Plessis (2015: 189–90), who asserts that 'all "provincial land" belonged to the state (senatorial and imperial provinces) and thus could not be privately owned in the sense that *dominium* could be acquired over it'; there is a similar view in Brégi (2009: 106–7), who straightforwardly paraphrases Gaius.

> has no greater reason for complaint than if someone prevents rain water from flowing onto his property.[29]

While Jones was no doubt right that different modes of acquiring ownership in land are crucial here, he underestimated the significance of these differences. It is in fact a key question why *mancipatio* or *in iure cessio* or *usucapio* (acquisition of ownership by uncontested possession) were not valid outside the borders of Italy, even in the case of transactions between Roman citizens. The question seems to have had a practical significance for Roman policymakers: it not only concerned the land surveyors but also, from the age of Augustus onwards, led to grants to some provincial communities of the so-called 'Italian rights' (*ius Italicum*), which meant treating their land as if it was in Italy from the legal point of view. Significantly, in one early case, that of the city of Antipolis in the province of Narbonese Gaul (modern Antibes), the decision to acknowledge its 'Italian rights' proceeded from a legal dispute with a neighbouring city, showing the practical relevance of the status.[30]

There is also a clear connection with tax regimes, recognized already by Cicero in the late Republic. Attacking a Roman citizen witness in the extortion trial of a former governor of the province of Asia (western Asia Minor) in 59 BC, Cicero addresses the legal consequences of his decision to settle in the city of Apollonis:

> I ask these questions: are those estates capable of being returned in the census, do they admit of Roman civil law (*habeant ius civile*), are they capable of being mancipated or not (*sint necne sint mancipi*), can they be entered as a surety at the treasury or with the censor? Finally, in what tribe did you register those estates? You rendered yourself liable, had some crisis occurred, to have those same estates assessed for tribute at both Apollonis and Rome.[31]

[29] Agennius Urbicus, *On Land Disputes* p. 20.1–20, trans. B. Campbell. Compare Hyginus, *Categories of Land* p. 82.1–2 on the status of provincial taxable lands (*agri vectigales*). The final paragraph of Agennius Urbicus's passage is of interest for the rare explicit statement on difference between legal regimes in different provinces.

[30] 'Antipolis is classed among the Italiote cities, having been so adjudged in a suit against the Massiliotes and thereby freed from their orders' (Strabo, *Geography* 4.1.9.184C, trans. H. L. Jones). For fuller treatment and a checklist, see von Premerstein (1919, col. 1249 on Antipolis); Sherwin-White (1973: 275–7; 316–22); Malavolta (1985); Campbell (2000: 334–6, addressing Jones's theory). For other early testimonies for the *ius Italicum*, note Pliny, *Natural History* 3.25; 3.139. For the possibility that the career of Gaius took place in three cities with the *ius Italicum* (Dyrrachium, Alexandria Troas, Berytus) discussed by him in *Digest* 50.15.7, see Honoré (1962: 85–96, perhaps imaginative). For a possible unique attestation of the *ius Italicum* as a personal status, see *Inschriften von Didyma* 331, l. 5, with Triantaphyllopoulos (1974).

[31] Cicero, *In Defence of Flaccus* 80, trans. C. Macdonald, with minor modifications. See Grelle (1990: 183, n. 53), and above all Eberle (2014: 135–47), and Eberle (2016: 54–60), who stresses the important political implications of the different status of provincial holdings and provides a detailed discussion of the passage.

Beyond the already manifest concern with *mancipatio* recurrent in later texts discussed above, what is notable in Cicero's argument is the concern with tax liability and also with the ability of a citizen to enter property in the Roman *census*, which would determine his property class and thus (in the Republican and even Augustan age) his political rights and civic liabilities.[32]

Crucially, while it is true that rules about *mancipatio* go back to the period before the classical terminology of ownership and possession was quite settled, the inability to use Italian modes of acquisition of property outside Italy was intertwined with the emergence of a clear-cut distinction between Italy and provinces. The development of a territorial conception of empire was underpinned by differences in property laws, and property was thus central to how Romans conceptualized imperial space. On the practical level, this was accompanied by the development of the provincial census in parallel to the census of Roman citizens to determine poll and land tax liabilities, and the increasing role of Roman land measurers as agents of provincial administration.[33] The symbolic distinction between Italy and provinces was downplayed in the imperial period in some respects (for instance, when the emperor Claudius changed the qualification for extending the *pomerium*, the sacred boundary of the city of Rome, from extending the boundaries of Italy to 'extending the boundaries of the Roman people' anywhere), but this does not seem to have affected the distinctions in the sphere of ownership.[34]

And despite the importance of legal analogy as a procedural tool for the Roman understanding of the law (on show in the passages of Gaius with which we started our discussion), differences in the status of Italian and provincial consecration could still matter in the High Empire.[35] Pliny the Younger, governor of the province of Pontus-Bithynia (on the southern

[32] On the centrality of *census* to the definition of a Roman citizen in the Republican period, see Nicolet (1976: 71–121).

[33] On the development of the territorial concept of empire, see Richardson (2008) is fundamental, but excludes documentary sources and thus dates some important developments several decades too late. On provincial census as an instrument of Roman domination, see Nicolet (1991: 123–47). On direct taxation of property in the Greek world, see Migeotte (2014: 230–44) rejecting the old orthodoxy on non-emergency direct taxation as a sign of loss of sovereignty, which undermines the idea that land subject to taxation could not be viewed as private within Greek law itself. On provincial cadastres and the role of land surveyors, to which I return below, see Nicolet (1991: 149–69).

[34] On the right to extend the *pomerium*, see most recently Carlà (2015: 607–16). The Claudian change presumably implied that provincial territories were now viewed as being as much 'Roman' as the territory of Italy itself.

[35] On the use of legal analogy, Ando (2015: 35–40) is a groundbreaking discussion; see also Ando (2011: 115–31), for evidence on the use of fiction in Roman law. Note that the *formula* for recovery of provincial land might have referred to the right *habere possidere frui* ('to have, use and enjoy'), rather than to ownership: Lenel (1927: 188–9); Mantovani (1999: 44–5); Guarino (2001: 689). For a more sceptical take on our ability to reconstruct the *formula*, see Buckland (1963: 190, n. 5).

shore of the Black Sea) in AD 109–111, in one of his letters to the emperor Trajan expresses a concern about the project to redevelop the main square in the city of Nicomedia which required moving the temple of the Great Mother, and asks Trajan for an official pronouncement in his capacity as a supreme pontiff. Trajan's reply belongs within the same framework as the discussions in Gaius and in Agennius Urbicus, but notably fails to apply analogy:

> You need have no religious scruple, my dear Pliny, about moving the temple of the Mother of the Gods to a more convenient place if a change of site seems desirable; nor need you worry if you can find no conditions laid down for consecration, as the soil of an alien country is not capable of being consecrated according to our laws.[36]

This official exchange makes it clear that the distinction between Roman and provincial soil indeed mattered in Roman litigation in so far as the owner's rights of consecration were concerned. Nor is the matter simply limited to the precedence of Nicomedian law: the decision rests with the Roman governor and he is in fact concerned about the application of Roman law. It is Roman and not local rules that prevent him from doing so (admittedly, this was convenient for him, as he wanted the project to go ahead). The rules formulated by Gaius are prescriptive rather than just descriptive.[37]

Clifford Ando in his important new work on key ideological notions underlying Roman social framework, looks in the right direction when he attempts to take Gaius's evidence more seriously:

> In the present context I draw your attention to three things only: the elevation of soil over territory to a status of legal primary; the importance of soil as recipient of ritual action; and the simultaneous sustaining and upending of a legal principle inherent in the use of fiction: the absolute distinction between Roman and alien soil is nominally honoured, even as the substitive *pro* potentially assimilates the whole of the latter to the status of the former in practice.[38]

The specifics of his vision may be disputed, however. The distinction between soil and territory is not the one which either Gaius or land surveyors really use, and while the 'importance of soil as recipient of ritual action' is undoubtedly there, what may be more striking is the binding of the possibility of valid consecration to the possibility of the (Roman) right of

[36] Pliny, *Letters* 10.50, trans. W. Williams (Pliny's request to Trajan in *Letters* 10.49). Importantly, Trajan took a different line when a building project in the city of Prusa involved reuse of an imperial cult shrine (Pliny, *Letters* 10.70–71).

[37] On the typology of legal rules, see Dresch and Scheele (2015).

[38] Ando (2015: 21–2); see also Ando (2011: 26).

ownership. The idea of ownership is here made central to how Roman rule over provinces is defined.

'TO USE THEIR LAWS AND THEIR FIELDS'

Central to A. H. M. Jones's argument for the provincial inapplicability of Roman law of property is the notion of the restoration by the Roman authorities of their 'own laws and territory' to newly subjected cities: a classic early example would be the actions of the Roman general Lucius Aemilius Regillus at Phocaea in Asia Minor (Livy 37.32.14). For some scholars, such grants entirely abolished the legal consequences of surrender to the Romans (*deditio*).[39] It is at any rate clear that the restricted personal status of the *dediticii* (one category of free provincial population seemingly excluded from the universal grant of citizenship in AD 212), however it originated, did not apply to citizens of provincial non-Roman communities, and thus would not have been a permanent legal consequence of a *deditio*. Certainly, if taken literally, such grants would imply the abrogation of any Roman right to intervene in local property relations and legal regimes. Indeed, in the case of more privileged communities (which even Mommsen would have excluded from the sphere of application of Gaius's dictum) it is explicitly confirmed that local rules took precedence. For instance, in what was probably a dispute concerning ownership, an Augustan proconsul confirmed to the islanders of Chios that, in accordance with a senatorial decree of 80 BC, 'the Romans among them should obey Chian laws'.[40]

However, the reality on the ground (at least outside the most privileged communities like Chios) could be very different even in the very early years of Roman rule when the Roman attitude to the rights of communities was on the whole less cavalier. An exciting new document from the immediate aftermath of the final Roman victory over the Macedonian kingdom in 167 BC is a case in point.[41] Fragments of a marble stele contained a list of properties in the territory of the city of Gonnoi in Thessaly (northern Greece) confiscated from their earlier owners, followed by two letters of the Roman proconsul Lucius Aemilius Paullus to the Gonnoi authorities on behalf of a certain Demophilos from the neighbouring city of Doliche. It was presumably Demophilos himself who had the texts engraved, as the stele has been found

[39] Heuss (1933: 94–108) is the best statement of this still influential view.

[40] R. K. Sherk, *Roman Documents in the Greek East* 70, ll. 17/18. On possible connection with property disputes, see Marshall (1969) (dated in other respects).

[41] Edition and commentary in Bouchon (2014). I am grateful to Supratik Baralay for first calling this inscription to my attention.

in his home city. Demophilos had some land and a house in the territory of Gonnoi granted to him in accordance with the decision of Paullus himself and of the 'ten commissioners', conventionally assigned by the Senate to a victorious general to help in the task of organizing the conquered lands. The civic authorities understandably procrastinated when confronted with the task of confiscating land from their own citizens for the benefit of an outsider: they attempted to deny that Demophilos had the proper authority from the proconsul and his commission, and then further delayed implementing the order after Paullus's first letter. His second, much angrier, missive, threatening the archons with 'greater punishment' and accusing them of dishonesty and conspiracy, seems to have done the trick.

Aemilius Paullus's high-handed action is revealing on two different levels. First, there is an apparent contradiction between it and the rhetoric of 'restoring their fields and their laws'—as a Roman magistrate, he was deciding upon questions of land ownership in a community beyond the moment when the community's corporate existence was restored. Even though this case arose from the personal decisions of Paullus and the senatorial commissioners at the constitutive moment, this can hardly be construed as a restoration of their 'own laws'. Second, in their disregard of the connection between *polis* citizenship and the right to own land in the city's territory, done not even on behalf of a Roman citizen but of another Thessalian, the actions of Paullus appear to foreshadow the later sense that *dominium* in the provinces somehow rested with the Roman state.[42] Again, a qualification is needed, as Thessaly had a federal organization, perhaps implying the recognition of the rights of ownership in the land of member-cities; however, the agency clearly lies with the Roman authorities and there is no attempt to treat Demophilos as a local at Gonnoi.[43]

There is a way to square this circle of ostensible desire to respect local property law and Roman intervention. As E. J. Bickerman has argued, Roman grants of liberty and autonomy, at least unless confirmed by a formal treaty, were regarded as conditional on Roman goodwill, in continuation of a Hellenistic royal practice.[44] The evidence for this goes all the way back to the Roman revocation of the Rhodian jurisdiction over Caria and

[42] The treatment of the place of property regimes as a constitutive element of Greek civic communities in the period of Roman expansion and of the acquisition of property rights by the Roman diaspora in the Greek East by Eberle (2014) is fundamental; for some case studies, see Lerouxel and Pont (2016).

[43] On Thessalian federalism in that period, see Hatzopoulos (2015: 84–5), and Bouchon and Helly (2015, esp. p. 243 on lack of federal involvement in local lawsuits).

[44] Bikerman (1939) is his most influential contribution to this problem; subsequent historiography magisterially surveyed by Ma (2002: 150–73). On continuity into the Roman period (on the example of Asia Minor), see Kantor (2014).

Lycia, granted in 188 BC, carried out in response to local objections in two stages in 177 (Polybius 25.4.5; Livy 41.6.12) and 167 BC (Polybius 30.5.12). This was emulated in the early imperial period in a number of revocations of the free status in punishment for the infringement of conditions: for instance, Cyzicus in 20 BC (Cassius Dio 54.7.6) and AD 25 (Tacitus, *Annals* 4.36.2), Thessaly under Augustus (Plutarch, *Moralia* 815D), Lycia in AD 43 (Cassius Dio 60.17.3), Rhodes in AD 44 (Cassius Dio 60.24.4). Implications for the ideas of territory and ownership are obvious: recognition of a right in an area under Roman imperial authority, while it could be absolute in practical terms, was not absolute in theory. While this returns in a sense to Mommsen's *Prekaritätstheorie*, we need not assume a complete free-for-all for Roman authorities, as he tended to do in the *Römisches Staatsrecht*. A hierarchy of authority would not, in Roman thinking, diminish or contradict the binding force of an authority within its own level: 'unlike normative force, authority comes in grades, because it is not an absolute, dogmatic category, but a crossroad between the social, the political and the legal' (Alonso 2013: 403).[45]

Concomitantly (although this was clearly not a typical situation), it seems possible that at least in some provincial contexts rights of public or religious entities over what was at the same time seen as private property could be recognized by Roman provincial authorities. An example is the levy of '2 drachms out of 20' (*didrachmia*) levelled on landed property transactions by the priests of the crocodile god Souchos at Tebtunis and Crocodilopolis in Roman Egypt, in parallel to the provincial tax on property transfers, the *enkyklion*.[46] In a certain sense, the land remained in the temple domain, while at the same time it was viewed as privately owned and arguably was also treated as the 'royal land' after the reforms of the prefect of Egypt Publius Petronius (24–22 BC).[47] Whatever changes in the legal regime of Egyptian land were introduced in the process of provincialization, the rights of the temple continued through that change, despite being difficult to categorize in Roman law. This does not, however, fully conform to A. H. M. Jones's model of local rules taking precedence—the reforms of Petronius

[45] On hierarchy of authority as opposed to 'rules of recognition' as the basis of Roman idea of legalism, see Kantor (2012).

[46] Recent comprehensive study in Winkler (2015). It does not resolve the issues addressed here if we reclassify the 'temple tax' as 'a rent paid to the temple' (quote from p. 256). For the concept of ownership in Ptolemaic law, see Jakab (2014), who stresses that 'ownership over land was never absolute, unlimited and exclusive' (quote from p. 334) and distinguishes it sharply from other forms of ownership in that period.

[47] On the changes in the status of 'sacred land' following the Roman annexation, see *P.Tebt.* II 302, with Monson (2012: 131–41); Winkler (2015: 253–8).

were clearly 'Roman' (even though they did not introduce the same law as used in Rome and Italy).[48]

It is interesting that, for instance, Josephine Blei in her study of early medieval property structures in the former Roman province of Raetia attempts to link them with the limited Roman understanding of provincial ownership (seemingly unaware of the dismissal of Gaius's evidence in much of recent scholarship).[49] The attempt to strip Roman law of its medieval feudal baggage, to which the work of Savigny and his school was dedicated, may, in fact, have gone too far in so far as the situation in Roman provinces is concerned.[50]

MEASURING THE LAND

Another problem arises from the attitude of Gaius and land measurers towards ownership rights in provincial land as opposed to Italian (including in the latter case cities with the *ius Italicum*): the continued use of local land measures. Land measurement was brought to the level of a systematic discipline by the Romans. Roman centuriation, often still visible from aerial photography in the twentieth century, remains one of the key signs of Roman colonization and often provided the initial setting for asserting ownership rights in Roman law.[51] A recent treatment of Roman land measurement from that angle even argues that '[o]riginally, private ownership in its full sense (with a full bundle of rights in the hands of individuals) existed only on surveyed and assigned land according to Roman law'.[52] While this is perhaps too strongly worded, the exclusion of provincial land from the Republican and early imperial census of Roman citizens, and the parallel introduction of

[48] 'Provincial', rather than 'imperial', law in the definition of Crone (1987: 1–17). On the problem of 'the Romanity of Roman Egypt', Rathbone (2013) surveys several decades of scholarly controversy.

[49] See Blei (2013), esp. 65–78 on the concept of *dominium populi Romani vel Caesaris* in the Roman period. See also n. 27 on the use of the term *possessio* in the so-called 'vulgar Roman law'. I am grateful to Conrad Leyser for asking me whether Roman provincial land ownership was feudal.

[50] On Savigny and his rejection of the feudal distinction between *dominium directum* and *dominium utile* (for which see nn. 4 and 23), see e.g. Stein (1999: 119–20).

[51] For introduction to the writings of the land surveyors, see Dilke (1971) and Campbell (2000: pp. xxvii–xliv). For the broader context in the late Republic and the early Empire, see Moatti (1993), and for extension of these practices into provinces, see n. 33. The fullest epigraphic documentation, providing a wealth of information on Roman landholding, survives from the Roman colony of Arausio (Orange): Piganiol (1962).

[52] Jakab (2015: 115–17, quotation from p. 117), using the 'bundle of rights' understanding of property legitimized in Roman legal scholarship by Honoré (1961) (see Introduction to this volume for a fuller discussion). For the role of land measurers in confiscations of provincial land from local owners at the establishment of Roman colonies, see Gagliardi (2015).

Roman taxation census in provinces, discussed above, is certainly relevant in this context.

It is significant, then, that in so far as provincial land outside the territory of Roman colonies is concerned, writers on land measurement show detailed interest in local systems of measures, arguably reflecting in yet another way the distinct status of provincial soil. A characteristic quote comes once again from 'Agennius Urbicus':

> Moreover, I shall not omit to mention something I discovered in the province of Cyrene. Here there are Roman lands, that is, lands that King Ptolemy bequeathed to the Roman People. They are *plinthides*, that is, square blocks of land like *centuriae*, enclosed by *limites* of 6,000 feet; each block of land has 1,250 *iugera*. There are stones inscribed with the name of the divine Vespasian with the following clause, 'land occupied by private individuals: he restored it to the Roman people'. Moreover, their measurement of one foot, which is called the Ptolemaic foot, is equivalent to one Roman foot plus 1/24.[53]

This interest in the use of pre-Roman land measures, even (in the case of Cyrene) in the public land of the Roman people in provinces rather than the territory of local communities is further attested in documentary evidence and can be shown to have affected landholding patterns. It was part of a wider Roman interest in maintaining local legal regimes, while also assuming authority over them and in effect reinventing them:

> Copy of the letter of Caesar written to Quietus. If it is not clear how large are the portions called *kleroi*, into which the land dedicated to Juppiter of Aezani was divided by the kings, it is best, as you also believe, that a mean should be observed, corresponding neither to the largest nor to the smallest *kleroi* in neighbouring cities. And if, when Mettius Modestus decreed that a levy should be paid for them, it is established which were the cleruchic lands, it is fair that the levy should be paid from this time.[54]

[53] Agennius Urbicus, *Categories of Land*, p. 88.33–90.4. Compare the anonymous treatise *On Land Boundaries*, p. 270.28–31: 'The Gauls call *candetum* an area of 100 feet in urban areas, like *centetum*; in rural areas they give the name *iustum candetum* to 150 square feet'; Isidorus of Seville, *Etymologiae* 15.15.4–6 (ed. W. M. Lindsay) for local names of land measures in the province of Baetica (southern Spain). On the use of standard Roman measures in tax assessment, Oxé (1923) conveniently assembles the illustrative material from the land measurers. For Roman *iugera* used as a check on the *versus* (local measure of area) in Dalmatia, see Hyginus, *Categories of Land* p. 88.23–90.12, with Cuomo (2007: 216), who makes important observations on the 'Romanization' of official metrology. On the local civic registration of landed property in the Greek East under Rome, see Le Teuff (2016), and for Egypt, Jördens (2016: 563–4), with further references.

[54] Hadrian's letter to the proconsul Avidius Quietus, AD 125/6, trans. B. Levick and S. Mitchell, *Monumenta Asiae Minoris antiqua* IX, pp. xxviii–xxix. The fullest treatments (arguing for a different translation at this point) are Laffi (1967) and Nörr (2012).

The desire of the emperor Hadrian, from whose chancery this inscribed letter emanates, to maintain the decisions of the Attalid kings (by that point more than 250 years in the past and using an obsolete legal category of 'cleruchic lands', lands given by Hellenistic kings to military settlers on condition of service) on the lands of the temple of Zeus at Aezani is obvious in this document, as is the impact this antiquarian exploration would have had on the rights of local landholders and landowners. At the same time, the agency and authority are assumed by the imperial power, not by the city of Aezani, and in the absence of any solution authorized by its antiquity the common sense of the governor—even if based on approximation of the local practice—is to prevail, not the 'own laws' of Aezani.

Importantly, Hadrian was not attempting to apply any of the highly developed Roman systems of land division to the land of Aezani. Yet, a century later, in the aftermath of the enfranchisement of the provincial population under the emperor Caracalla, an attempt to do exactly that is made on imperial authority elsewhere in the same province:

> Good fortune! Imperator Caesar Marcus Aurelius Antoninus [titles follow] ordered the land on the entire territory of Pessinous to be measured according to the sacred ?measuring rod? (*grame*), under the supervision of Caesius Felicissimus, leading centurion, in the consulships of Catius Sabinus (for the second time) and Cornelius Anullinus [AD 216].[55]

Was this the first step towards the disappearance of the legal distinction between Italian and provincial soil achieved by the time of Justinian?[56] If so, however, the effort could hardly have been systematic at that date and its impact was very gradual even after the introduction of the standard land-taxation unit, the *iugum*, by the tetrarchic emperors (Diocletian and his co-rulers) in the late third century. As Peter Thonemann has recently shown in his meticulous study of the tetrarchic age land registers from Asia Minor, with the exception of a single senatorial estate of 75.16 *iuga* (= 2,038 acres) at Magnesia, local patterns of landholding were still prevalent in the lower Meander valley in *c.* AD 310, with most estates still fragmented into small parcels corresponding to traditional units of measurement (Thonemann 2007).

[55] First edition by Devreker (1971) [whence *L'Année épigraphique* (1975) no. 808; J. Strubbe, *The Inscriptions of Pessinous* I 166, trans. Levick 2000, no. 65]; cf. J. and L. Robert, *Bulletin épigraphique* (1972) no. 482 for a different interpretation.

[56] See n. 11. For the striking expression 'to a province of Roman soil (*in Romani soli provinciam*)' in the fifth-century *Life of St Severinus* 31.6, see Ando (2011: 26–7).

CONCLUSIONS

Several important points stand out from our discussion. First, the right of ownership, despite many significant similarities, had different content on provincial and Italian soil, not limited to the difference between Roman law and local legal systems. The refusal of Roman systematizers to apply to it the label of *dominium* was not frivolous.[57]

Second, the distinctions between Italian and provincial concepts of ownership were in key respects caused by the imposition of Roman imperial authority: the concept of 'full ownership' (*panktesia*) was developing in the Greek East before the arrival of Rome, while in Roman Spain rules similar to those used in Italy were applied as if local, so the absence of full *dominium* there cannot be explained by the absence of the notion in a local legalistic framework. The inaccessibility of certain forms of transactions outside Italy was imposed by Roman authorities for their own ideological reasons, but it did not necessarily reflect differences in local practice.

Third, rules governing ownership emerge as one of the central planks in defining the political, fiscal, and religious status of territory, and are arguably connected to different attitudes to land measurement in Italian and provincial soil. This context for the development of the concept of *dominium* suggests an important dichotomy. On the one hand, it could be viewed as the most absolute property right, Blackstone's 'sole and despotic dominion'. On the other, it was seen as a socially contingent right, dependent on civic status, on the status of the territory, on available legal remedies and on taxation regimes, and coexistent with different property regimes, which could admit of different grades in the right of ownership.

In comparative perspective, it is important to notice significant similarities with later legal systems which would emerge not from the study of classical or Justinianic law as presented in the great codifications, but from other sources. As direct continuity remains mostly implausible this should lead us to questions regarding the social 'embeddedness' of ownership and its connection to the self-definition of political society.

[57] For the view that the modern notion of ownership in continental legal systems is related more closely to the provincial property regimes than to the Italian *dominium*, see Waelkens (2015: 298).

3

Property and Possession in Medieval Celtic Societies

T. M. CHARLES-EDWARDS

My main sources are legal and come from pre-Viking Ireland and post-Norman Wales, that is to say, the Irish sources belong to the seventh and eighth centuries, the Welsh ones to the twelfth and thirteenth. They are manuals not legislation, addressed to readers who are learning the law and hope to be judges. Their purpose is shown by such remarks as 'If you would be a judge, you must know X' (Kelly 1988; Charles-Edwards 1989). In spite of the difference of date there are points of contact between Irish and Welsh law which go beyond the nature of the sources, but, on the whole, the Irish material offers the more entertaining insights into the topic of property and possession. The phrase, 'Celtic societies', might make one think of the Iron-Age Celtic-speaking peoples. My Celts, however, are later and have ceased to be aware that they spoke closely related languages.

Maitland, in a passage that caught my attention when I was an undergraduate, wrote in his *Domesday Book and Beyond* (1897: 9):

> Too often we allow ourselves to suppose that, could we get back to the beginning, we should find that all was intelligible and should then be able to watch the process whereby simple ideas were smothered under subtleties and technicalities. But it is not so. Simplicity is the outcome of technical subtlety; it is the goal not the starting-point. As we go backwards the familiar outlines become blurred; the ideas become fluid, and instead of the simple we find the indefinite.

No doubt there is some truth in all this, but when Maitland summed up the difficulty by writing, 'The grown man will find it easier to think the thoughts of the school-boy than to think the thoughts of the baby', I rise in revolt. Neither early Irish law nor medieval Welsh law could be described as 'the thoughts of the baby'. On the contrary, the Irish lawyers in particular were,

Property and Possession in Medieval Celtic Societies. T. M. Charles-Edwards. © T. M. Charles-Edwards, 2017. Published 2017 by Oxford University Press.

on occasion, notably subtle and ingenious, as I hope to demonstrate in this very matter of property and possession.

IRISH CLIENTSHIP

Since property relations are firmly in the cross-over zone between law, the economy, and society, it is important to acknowledge that the economies of pre-Viking Ireland and post-Norman Wales were very different. True, both were overwhelmingly rural; in both the mix of arable and livestock was crucial; and in both the normal exploitation of the land was by households in which a married couple cooperated but with distinct spheres of responsibility. So far, they resembled most of Europe. But the role of livestock in the economy and in social relations was very different. The free Irish (there were not just slaves but also the 'half-free') were divided between the nobles and the ordinary, non-noble free. The nobles were noble because they had clients who owed them food-renders; and these clients, who were themselves the ordinary non-noble freemen, owed food-renders because, although they had enough land by inheritance, they did not have enough livestock to practise the normal mixed farming. The other side of this coin is that the nobles were noble because they had made grants to ordinary freemen of livestock thereby obliging the grantees to deliver fixed annual food-renders: they were noble because they were the lords of men who did not, by themselves, have enough cattle, pigs, and sheep (but principally cattle). As the lawyers described society, most of the free population were either noble or free commoners, either lords or clients, and that meant that free society fell into two complementary classes: they were either those who were entitled to receive or those who were obliged to deliver food-renders. There were a few in between: some were rising in status because they had started to grant livestock to clients, but in order to become noble in status a particular line of descent had to have made such grants for three generations; one was noble by grants of livestock by oneself, one's father, and one's grandfather. One further point is crucial: the livestock granted to the client remained the property of the lord during his lifetime. But if he died before his client, the livestock became the property of the client. On the other hand, if the client died before his lord, the client's heirs had to step into his shoes and continue to deliver the food-renders. During the lifetime of the lord, therefore, the client had possession of the livestock and their offspring and had the right to employ them in his farming, but he had, for example, no right to alienate them to a third party. The distinction between property and possession was thus intrinsic to early Irish social relationships. The original grant was a contract by which the lord performed his side of the bargain straight away, but the client performed his side over the lifetime of the lord. Since, as I have just said, the great bulk of the free population of Ireland was composed of clients, the difference between property and possession was intrinsic, not just to some small segment of the population, but to the economy of the entire island.[1]

This much is the broad outline of what the legal sources tell us, but underlying what they say are some assumptions, critical but unstated. The implication of the delay in acquiring full nobility—namely that one only became a noble when three generations had been lords, so that nobility was inherited lordship—is that, by and large, the sons of lords were themselves lords (Thurneysen 1923–5: 245). Yet the initial impulse behind the whole system of lordship and clientship was the client's need for livestock; but if the livestock became the property of the client at the lord's death, why would the client then, or his son after his death, need to seek a lord in order to have enough livestock? I think that one has to assume that the annual food-renders and the client's own consumption gradually diminished his livestock. This is consistent with something else revealed by the sources, namely that a client might well seek a second or even a third lord, not instead of, but rather in addition to, the first. It is also consistent with another aspect of clientship: he was obliged to offer annual hospitality to his lord together with a company of limited size. This hospitality was regularly in the winter between the beginning of the year and the beginning of Lent; and it was in the winter up to Lent that meat-consumption appears to have been highest, whereas dairy products formed a large element of the diet in the summer.

WELSH PRIODOLDER

Clientship of this kind was not characteristic of medieval Wales. Livestock seems to have been inherited along with land and thus passed from generation to generation by partible inheritance. In Wales as in Ireland, however, a sharp distinction remained between inherited land and acquired land and between land and movables. Where Wales has something interesting and distinctive to add is the concept of *priodolder. Priod* is a borrowing from Latin *priuātus*, but in a range of senses that developed within Welsh. A husband is a *gŵr priod*, as it were a 'private man', a wife a *gwraig briod*, and their marriage is *priodas*. The notion seems to be one of exclusion: another partner is excluded by the marriage. The connotations are similar with property

[1] The crucial text is edited and translated by Thurneysen (1923–5); discussions may be found in Gerriets (1983), Kelly (1988: 29–33), and Charles-Edwards (1993: 337–63).

in land, only here the concept is tied into notions of inheritance and kinship. Someone who has inherited land from his father, his grandfather, and his great-grandfather is a *priodor*, and by this is meant that he cannot be deprived of the land by someone else using any legal means: his ownership is now secure in law. Before the fourth generation of heirs, however, it was conceivable that someone else might come with a superior claim. *Priodolder* excludes this possibility.

One way in which *priodolder* works is illustrated by an early thirteenth-century lawbook from north Wales, *Llyfr Iorwerth*, 'The Book of Iorwerth' (translated in Jenkins 1986). In this translation *priodor* is rendered by 'proprietor'; the 'maintainers' are neighbours of the land in dispute who have a privileged status as witnesses in cases over land. The 'second man' is the person who, following his father before him, has been in occupation of the land (the 'sitting' in the passage), and similarly the 'third man' is in the third generation of occupants; the 'second man' is also called 'the patrimonial' (Jenkins 1986: 91–2):

> If it happens that a non-proprietor has maintainers for his being in occupation of land and earth as second man or as third, and that a proprietor claims against him and has maintainers for his proprietorship, the non-proprietor will move away before him. If it happens that he claims by reason of being second man or third and that a proprietor is sitting against him, the proprietor will not move before him from the land. A proprietor displaces a third man. A third man displaces a patrimonial—a son whom the father leaves after him on the land. A patrimonial displaces an incomer: this is the incomer—a man who comes of himself to land, and of whose kin no-one has been on the land before him. And so their status proceeds according to their priority of occupation.

Here then possession is graded according to the number of generations until, at the fourth generation, it becomes proprietorship, property secure from legal claim by someone else. No such neat grading of possession by generations is found in the Irish texts; the closest analogy is the grading of lordship over clients according to whether the lord is in the first generation to possess lordship, or the second, or the third.

Land, or rather some land, could pass from one owner to another other than by inheritance in both Ireland and Wales. There seems to have been a small land-market even in pre-Viking Ireland. This was probably mainly within the Church: there is evidence, for example, of major churches exchanging lands so as to consolidate their estates. But Irish laymen were able to grant even land to a church, provided that it was acquired rather than inherited. Even with acquired land, however, a layman was required to leave a proportion to his kindred. In general, any grant of inherited land required the consent of his kinsmen. In Wales, it was clearly possible to grant land to a church: there is good charter evidence for such grants from the ninth century at the latest, but the legal conditions are not set out as fully as they are in Irish law.

THE RIGHTS THAT CONSTITUTED PROPERTY

Especially for the Irish legal texts, but also for the Welsh, the notion of property needs to be taken apart and the different rights that constitute property distinguished: property in one society will be a particular combination of such rights, property in another society a different combination. The early Irish freeman was entitled to cultivate his own inherited land; even his kinsmen were only involved by agreement through cooperative farming arrangements or as a backup if he was an absentee. We shall meet, at the end of this chapter, one exception to this right in the case of the watermill and the mill-race, but, almost always, he had the right that others, even close kinsmen, should not exploit his land except with his agreement. However, he also had a duty to his neighbours (who were often his kinsmen) to maintain his land so that, for example, his fences were solid enough to prevent livestock trespassing. As for changes of ownership, he had the right that others should not transfer his property to anyone else, but he himself could not alienate inherited land without the permission of all his close kinsmen and could not even alienate all his acquired land (Charles-Edwards 1993: 67–9).

CLAIMING LAND

Respect for property in land is exemplified by the procedure used to claim it as one's inheritance (Kelly 1988: 186–9; Charles-Edwards 1993: 259–73). The context is that the seventh and eighth centuries were the high point of a particular dispersed settlement-type, the so-called 'rath' (from OIr. *ráith*) or 'ring-fort'; 'ring-fort' is something of a misnomer, since it was not normally a fort at all but a farmstead, normally at some distance from other farmsteads, enclosed by a roughly circular rampart and ditch: over 45,000 such farmsteads have been located (Stout 1997). There was a sharp distinction in law between the area within the enclosure and land outside, but also a distinction between land close to the enclosure, probably more intensively cultivated, and land further away. At this period, also, burial in a church cemetery had not yet become the norm for the laity; instead the legal text on claiming land assumes that, within any kindred, some individuals at least were buried on the boundary. The boundary in question appears to be the boundary of the portions of land belonging to members of a kindred; this may also be the boundary of the individual kinsman's land, but that will not always be the case. Confirmation comes from Irish canon law of the early eighth century, in which the cemetery is described as the *sepulcrum paternum*, distinguished sharply from a church cemetery, and the practice is given scriptural justification by citing the example of Joseph commanding his body to be brought back from Egypt and buried *ad sepulcrum patrum suorum* (Wasserschleben 1885: 56–7). Furthermore, claims might be by someone who had been denied a share of a kindred's lands and the claim was then against the kindred rather than against any particular kinsman.[2]

The procedure used for claiming land as inheritance began with the claimant entering the land with one witness leading two horses yoked together; he and his pair of horses entered over a grave on the boundary, but they were only permitted to penetrate halfway into the holding that they were claiming. If the occupant or occupants failed to submit to judgment, the claimant entered ten days later with four horses and two witnesses; this time the horses were unyoked and free to graze. Again, if the defendants fail to go to judgment, the claimant entered a third time after a further ten days but now with eight horses and three witnesses. On this third occasion, he might stable the horses; the implication is that he had entered the enclosed farmstead across the ditch and rampart. Whereas on the previous occasions he withdrew and waited for some days to see if the defendant agreed to submit the case to judgment, this third time any agreement to go to judgment had to be immediate. If agreement was not forthcoming, the claimant entered the house and kindled a fire on the hearth. He now had the right to occupy the farmstead and to cultivate the land and to exclude the defendant. The previous occupant had forfeited his rights in house and land by refusing to respond to the claim, that is, by not agreeing to submit the case to judgment. The procedure thus distinguished between land and farmstead; it exhibited the basis of the claim by allowing the claimant to enter up to three times over the members of the kindred buried on the boundary, and it brought repeated and increasing pressure on the defendant to go to judgment (Binchy 1978: i. 210).

Useful corroborative evidence comes from narrative texts, first from a short account of a dispute, legendary but apparently intended to illustrate the law of 'Taking Possession', and second from a saga partially based on historical personages. The first text tells the story of someone called Nin or Ninne (Binchy 1978: iii. 907 and v. 1859). Ninne rode with two kinsmen across the frontier into Ulster. The purpose of the journey was to visit Ninne's

[2] A passage from the tract called *Din Techtugud* 'On Taking Possession', Binchy (1978: i. 207. 22–209. 23), ed. and trans. D. A. Binchy *apud* Watkins (1963: 227–8).

kinsmen in Ulster. After crossing the frontier, they unyoked their horses on land that had previously belonged to their kindred, although they were unaware of this circumstance and the act of unyoking is specifically said not to have been for the purpose of claiming a share in that land. The man who had the land told them to remove their horses, to which Ninne's companions replied by saying that it would not profit them to unyoke horses there since they were not seeking a share. To this the man in occupation replied, 'That's not so easy, it belonged to you previously.' At this point Ninne and his companions, now informed that they had a hereditary right, did not remove their horses, which were then driven off by force by the occupant. They took the case to the king, who judged that the occupant was liable to a fine for unlawful removal, and they gained possession in that way by the act of entering the land.

This story contains three lessons. It confirms that it was common for the procedure of 'entry' to be used to claim a share in land rather than outright ownership of the whole. Admittedly the procedure appears to be directed at a single occupant, but he, for his part, is likely to claim that he holds his land by right of inheritance within a kindred, the kindred whose earlier members lie dead in the graves over which the claimant has made his entry. This claimant is thus claiming a share in the inheritance, and his claim, if successful, is likely to force a redistribution of land within the kindred. Second, the story also implies that the ritual of entering and unyoking horses was legally effective whatever the intentions of those who entered. Third, it focuses on one stage in the legal process, namely the second entry when the horses were unyoked. This is portrayed as the crucial claim, suggesting perhaps that the first entry, when the horses were not unyoked, acted as a warning or notice and was not the effective action in law. In Ninne's case it was not possible to go on to a third entry, since the occupant had cut short the whole process by forcibly expelling the horses. The same focus on the second entry and on the act of unyoking appears in a saga set in seventh-century Leinster. The king, Rónán, is uttering a lament for Máel Fothartaig, the son whose death he has been induced by a false accusation to order. One verse goes as follows (Greene 1955: 10):

> My son, Máel Fothertaig,
> For whom the wide wood was a home;
> Without keeping watch on all sides,
> No king or prince would unyoke on his land.

Again, unyoking appears to be the decisive act. One reason why it was at the second entry, with the accompanying unyoking of the horses, that the procedure becomes effective may be that it was then that ritual began to mimic ownership. Entry without unyoking, even though it took place across the burial place of the kindred on the border of its land, merely announced a claim of kinship with those buried there. Also, he only went half way in: the main scene of activity remained the boundary. But once the person making the entry unyoked his horses and allowed them to graze anywhere in the land, he was beginning to do the things characteristic of an owner. On the third entry, this mimicking went further: the claimant now stabled his horses within the enclosure and entered the house. There he performed the act that was the culmination of the ritual: he kindled a fire on the hearth. The different stages of the full legal process of claiming land by hereditary right distinguish the boundary from the core of the holding and the land outside the 'rath' from the farmstead itself. In a rising crescendo the claimant acts out more and more of the role of an owner further and further into the land.

The mimicking of ownership in the later stages of the procedure is also evident in the version used by women. Whereas in her first entry across a grave a woman comes with two ewes, rather than the horses used by a man, in the third entry she arrives with the implements for baking bread, a kneading-trough, and a sieve. According to a story explaining how Machae (probably a goddess) came to give her name to Emain Machae (near Armagh), she took an ordinary commoner as her husband by coming to his house, kindling a fire, fetching a kneading-trough, and a sieve, and making food (Hull 1968: 28). She was, that is, following the procedure by which a woman took possession of house and land.

PLEDGES

As was noted earlier, Irish law made a sharp division between land and movables, and it is in connection with movables that some of the more ingenious distinctions between property and possession occur. We may take first the law of pledges, that is, things of value given to guarantee discharge of a debt (Bemmer 2013 and 2016). One should note here that in discussions of Irish law it has been normal to use 'surety' of the personal guarantor but pledge of the thing, rather than 'pledge' for the person who acts as surety and 'gage' for the thing, as in medieval English law.

The standard form of pledge-giving is straightforward; the ingenuities come when we turn to non-standard forms. By 'the standard form' I mean the situation when X owes some object or service to Y and hands over to Y a valuable item to guarantee that the debt will be discharged by some agreed time. Already this is mildly interesting, since Y now possesses the pledge but does not own it and, conversely, X owns it but does not possess it. Nor is that the end of the matter, since if X fails to discharge the debt, the pledge will, either immediately or after an interval, pass into the ownership of Y when it has already been in his possession since it was given as a pledge. Pledge-giving, that is, makes play with the difference between ownership and possession.

The first deviation from the standard was the subject of an entire legal tract (translated in Bemmer 2016): this was when X owned the thing given by Y as a pledge to Z. X owned the pledge, but, if Y was not already in possession of it, X handed it over to Y, so that it was Y who then handed it over to Z as a pledge. Y was likely to owe X some fee for this service of providing the pledge, and Y might even give a pledge to X to guarantee, first, that he would not make X's pledge forfeit by failing to discharge the debt and, second, that the fee would be paid. One pledge might thus beget a second pledge. In this scenario X, the owner of the pledge used to guarantee Y's payment of his debt to Z, might well be Y's lord. We shall see later why this possibility is a very serious one.

In a second deviation from the standard, Y specified a pledge to guarantee a debt, but, instead of handing the pledge over to Z, he retained it in his own possession. He might still forfeit his pledge as in the standard case by failing to discharge the debt, but, in the meantime, although the pledge is his and remains in his possession, he is not entitled to alienate it. He cannot give it or exchange it with a third party, nor could he pledge it to someone else, either on his own behalf or on behalf of another. So, his property has changed in nature: a power that he would normally have because he owned this valuable he no longer has. It is in his possession but he must be able and may be obliged to hand it over into Z's possession and Z may become the owner. Earlier, in the simplest form of pledging, we already saw the play with the distinction between possession and ownership; but now we have, in addition, the play extending to the kinds of use of things that would normally accompany ownership, such as the right to alienate.

A likely reason why this form of pledging merited an entire tract to itself is that the ordinary freeman, as we have seen, farmed his land (mainly inherited) with livestock granted to him by a lord; and although the livestock so granted continued in the possession of the client, they belonged to the lord for the latter's lifetime. Some especially well-off freemen had the kind of valuables regarded as relatively immune from decay—gold, silver, or yew[3]—that were preferred as pledges, but most probably did not; their movable assets were largely livestock (Binchy 1941: 9, l. 222). Hence it would make excellent sense for the lord to agree that his client might pledge an animal or animals, animals that the client possessed but his lord owned; and

[3] Early Irish tableware was normally of wood and, compared with other wood, yew was long-lasting: Kelly (1997: 383).

it made equally good sense for the recipient of the pledge, for he now had an assurance that the debtor would be subject to effective pressure from his lord to pay the debt and so redeem the pledge.

A third deviation from the standard form of pledge-giving occurred when someone gave a pledge in advance of any debt being incurred. Two contexts seem to have been important for advance pledging. First, a kindred had a head, sometimes called a 'noble of constraint': when a member of the kindred misbehaved in relation to king or Church, they, that is king or Church, were entitled to bring pressure to bear on the 'noble of constraint'. To make sure that they had pressure to bring, this head of the kindred gave a pledge to king and to 'the synod' in advance of any misbehaviour by one of his kin (Binchy 1941: 11–12, § 20). Another context was the formation of a group of neighbouring farmers. Each member of the group gave an advance pledge to guarantee that he would pay a fine if his livestock were to trespass or if some other infringement of neighbourhood law were to occur.

A further complication arises from the nature of what is given as a pledge. Again, there is a standard but also deviations. The standard is something precious, but not a living thing. Gold, silver, bronze, and yew were mentioned as suitable materials. Iron was not desirable, for it rusts. Animals were not desirable, for they needed to be grazed and were liable to die. If the pledgee is not entitled to make use of them while they are in his possession until they become forfeit, they are a pure liability; but if he does use them and they are injured or killed while in use, then he may become liable to the pledgor and moreover, if they died, he no longer had his pledge. Yet, in spite of the drawbacks, animals clearly were given as pledges, and this is not wholly surprising, since cattle, in particular, were a standard exchangeable asset.

There are some entertaining complications in this area of the law. The Irish then, as now, were keen on racing horses, although it seems to have been more by chariot-racing than by riding. Now, if a racehorse belonging to X was given by Y, with X's permission, as a pledge and the pledge was not redeemed in time for the great race-meeting of the year, on Lugnasad, that is on 1 August and the following days, the penalties owed by Y included X's honour-price, for X was dishonoured by being deprived of the very special use of the horse that he owned. Here, too, X was very probably of high status and may well have been Y's lord. Similarly, people wore their best clothes on festival and other special days and the law of pledging thus distinguished between everyday working clothes and festival clothes. If the latter were pledged and were not redeemed by the next feast day after the agreed date for redemption, again honour-price was due. It looks as though such garments or horses may have been particularly desired as pledges by the pledgee, since with them there was serious pressure on the pledgor to discharge the debt by the agreed time.

DISTRAINT

Similar issues over ownership, possession, and the right to use arose in another area of the law, namely distraint (Binchy 1973a: 22–71). This was, and remained throughout the medieval period, a standard way of enforcing payment of debt. In the sixteenth century, it produced a serious clash of legal cultures between the native Irish and Tudor administrators. The latter regarded distraint as illegal and, indeed, as theft; and hence native Irishmen who used this procedure according to their own law were liable to be condemned as thieves and executed. As described in the pre-Viking laws, however, there was a wide gulf between distraint and violent or covert seizure of someone else's property. It went roughly as follows: first, the creditor gave notice that he proposed to distrain unless the debt owed to him was discharged; then he waited for a fixed period, defined in accordance with the nature of the debt; then he distrained, accompanied by his legal agent, and took the animals to a pound, which might be his own enclosed pasture adjacent to his home or some other suitable place; then he waited again, and at the end of this second period of waiting, the animals started to become forfeit, not all at once but gradually—the value of two cows and one heifer on the first day and then one cow and a heifer on each subsequent day. One should note one further point: admittedly, distraint was a means to induce a debtor to discharge his debt, but what the debtor could do, and so recover possession of his livestock, was to give a pledge that he would, before the end of some future defined period, discharge the debt.

In both cases of enforcement of debt, whether by distraint or by pledge, the distinction between ownership and possession was vital. Possession changed hands at one point, ownership at another. One form of distraint offered particular difficulty, and here we need to add a third concept, that of the right to use (a right that was also crucial, as we have seen, in one form of pledge-giving). The context is of distraint against 'people of art' as they were called, that is persons whose main asset was a skill. This included smiths, wrights, poets, and scholars. A smith, for example, lived by his skill rather than by his cattle. The assumption is not that he does not have cattle: he would have been a very unsuccessful smith if he were not paid in livestock or in silver with which he could buy livestock, but his animals were not his principal point of vulnerability as they were with the ordinary farmers. Early Irish law, faced with this problem, resorted to ritual in order to deprive him of the use of hammer and anvil, namely the tools that were essential to his skill. But the claimant did not remove the hammer and anvil: he tied a withe round the anvil as a sign that the smith was not to use his tools until he had satisfied the claim. This form of ritual was probably widely understood, since it appears in the longest of all early Irish sagas, *Táin Bó Cúailnge*, 'The Cattle-Raid of Cooley' (O'Rahilly 1976: 8, ll. 225–6, trans. p. 131). In this case, therefore, the smith still owns the hammer and anvil and they also remain in his possession, but he is not entitled to use them. The point about the use of the withe is not so much that it has some mysterious power to afflict the smith who carries on regardless using his tools. What seems to be the case is that violation of this recognized form of prohibition raised the stakes: the smith who used the anvil in spite of the prohibition would then be liable to pay double the original debt. It would shift back to the normal distraint of livestock but at a higher rate (Binchy 1973b).

MILLS AND MILL-RACES

Another aspect of early Irish property law was the creation of what in other traditions would be called servitudes. The same period that saw the high point in the use of the rath as a form of settlement also saw a wider use of watermills. A legal tract, probably of the seventh century and thus from the period when very many watermills were being built, discusses the issue created when the owner of the mill proposes to dig a mill-race to bring the water from a stream or river to his mill and the mill-race has to cross someone else's land (Binchy 1955). It is clear from the tract that this is only one context in which the law must be settled: another, less problematic, is when a group of neighbours, probably kinsmen, decide to construct a watermill on their land. We may take first, however, the situation in which one person or one institution, such as a church, is the sole owner of the mill, but does not own all the land which the mill-race must cross. In this context, the owner of the land to be crossed cannot refuse to allow the mill-race to be dug, but he does receive a single payment or he can choose instead to have a day at unstated intervals in which he can grind his corn at the mill for free. When the owner of the land, his heir, and his heir's heir have accepted the particular route of the mill-race, the owner of the mill acquires an absolute title to the mill-race. The owner of the land cannot demand that it be moved. Many mills, however, as we have seen, seem to have been built by a group, usually of kinsmen, cooperating together. Here the possibility is envisaged that the mill-race starts in one person's land, crosses one or more holdings to reach the mill-pond, which is on another person's holding, and finally reaches the mill which is on yet another person's land. All those involved may well be kinsmen; and, in this situation, the group establishes a rota by which each has the right to mill his grain on a day or days. The underlying situation is one in which each member of the group has his own holding of land; the mill itself is on just one holding; but all those whose land has been used for any part of this asset, whether the mill-race or the pond or the mill itself, has the right to use it. A slightly later tract, of the early eighth century, assumes that the normal non-noble freeman will have a share in a mill rather than owning one outright. The corresponding assumption is likely to be that the sole owner of a mill was, if not an institution, then a noble. The tract, therefore, caters for both scenarios: the group of commoners collaborating together to build the mill and dig the mill-race and mill-pond and the noble who can build a mill with his own resources but must bring the mill-race across his neighbours' land.

By now I hope it will be clear that early Irish law, and the same will go for medieval Welsh law, was not baby talk, not some primitive confusion, as one might have supposed from the passage I quoted from Maitland at the start. What is true, however, is that it was not a philosophical or jurisprudential law with an elaborate hierarchy of technical concepts all with their place in a logical system. Possession was just physical possession: there was no special legal sense of the term. Where there was systematic thinking it tended to be under the surface, often by analogies between one part of the law and another (Charles-Edwards 1999: 23–4). Outside the legal texts there is good evidence for a wide acquaintance with the points of law I have discussed. There is also an appreciation of what might be called cleverness or sharp practice. An excellent example is in an early life of St Brigit (probably of the seventh century). Brigit was the child of a free father by his slave woman; the father, Dubthach, was married at the time and his wife brought pressure to bear on him to sell Brigit's mother. So, he did, but he avoided selling the child he had just begotten and so reclaimed Brigit when she had been born. He had been forced to sell one slave but had acquired another, Brigit (Connolly 1989: 15, ch. 4).

4

The Afterlife of Property

Affect, Time, Value

MATTHEW S. ERIE

> [Chinese law] acknowledges the indissoluble link that binds everything to its original owner. Even today an individual who has sold an item of his property, even a movable good, preserves his whole life through, *vis-à-vis* the buyer, a kind of right 'to weep for his property' (Mauss [1950] 1990: 63).
>
> [A traveller from the future] envies the people who live in their own time, who can act at will, oblivious of the future, ignorant of the effects of their actions. But he cannot act. He is an inert gas, a ghost, a sheet without soul. He has lost his personhood. He is an exile of time (Lightman 2004: 25).

BETWEEN PERSONS AND THINGS

In this chapter, I pursue the idea that property rights are constitutive of the self (Radin 1987, 1993)[1] and bring this line of thought into dialogue with anthropological understandings of the relationships between persons and things. My thinking is particularly animated by the possibility of an anthropology of value (Verdery 2003; Lambek 2008; Hann and Hart 2011; Otto and Willerslev 2013) that focuses on the ways in which social actors esteem certain things or actions as important and decide, as David Graeber stated,

I want to thank Georgy Kantor, Tom Lambert, and Hannah Skoda for their helpful comments in improving this chapter.

[1] In so doing, Radin departed from previous theories of property, including the 'bundle of sticks' metaphor and the view that property is a means to attain certain values such as freedom, social welfare, or democracy (Purdy 2010; Alexander 2011, 2013, 2016; Dagan 2011).

The Afterlife of Property: Affect, Time, Value. Matthew S. Erie. © Matthew S. Erie, 2017. Published 2017 by Oxford University Press.

'what it is that makes life worth living' (2001: 88). Assuming, first, that the state is usually the guarantor of the values of property, and, second, that specific forms of property may be constitutive of personhood, my central query is what happens in a situation in which state legalism (not just positive law but its categories and prerogatives) no longer recognizes those forms of property which constitute persons? In other words, if property has a 'life' providing the material and ideological means for self-flourishing, can it then also have an 'afterlife'?

'Afterlife' suggests temporal disconnects between emotion and law (that otherwise protects property) and thus gives rise to a kind of affective displacement or haunting. I argue that this question has implications for the study of legalism in the sense of (aspirational) forms of justice that may not be reducible to 'law' but which nonetheless elucidate foundational aspects of social ordering. I use ethnographic evidence for an afterlife of property in China where it has been particularly susceptible to regime change. Whereas scholars have described property rights in postsocialist China as 'fuzzy' (Verdery 1998, 1999; Sturgeon and Sikor 2004; Erie 2007) or, following Hayek, as 'spontaneous order' (Ho 2013; Qiao and Upham 2015), the temporal dimensions of those surviving and reviving property forms in contemporary China open new analytical windows onto understanding the role of property in transitional economies from a user-end perspective.

One consequence of property regime transformation has been to abandon certain forms of property rather than others. Those with affective ties to now obsolete forms may continue to ground their property values not only in state law or market exchange, but in notions of home, local history, and myth that produce legalisms distinct from that of the state. These referents for property values may transcend the state or market through affect,[2] but are nevertheless circumscribed jurally and economically by the modern state and global capitalism.

Therein lies the rub. Owners continue to make property claims through and against legal systems that give them no such standing. I examine this irony through a number of cases that span different property regimes in time. An afterlife of property is not necessarily dependent on the religious nature of property and, in fact, secular forms can also have a life-after-expropriation. Hence while I focus on religious minorities, specifically, Chinese Muslims (Hui) across the urban–rural spectrum in north-west China, I begin with a case of a Han Chinese woman in the centre of Beijing. The cases show actors conceptualizing property as immanent in selves beyond

[2] By 'affect', I mean not just emotion but those faculties, senses, and reflections that viscerally influence human judgments and are not reducible to reason and rationality which are often viewed as the basis of law.

the individual as 'legal person', that is, in reference to family, lineage, and community. As a result of these multiple discourses on property, actors may argue their property's value lies beyond the market; and, yet, because of the nature of socialist law, some owners do assign monetary value to their property for purposes of compensation. These tensions operate across the cases with various effects.

DREAMING OF PRIVATE PROPERTY

In China's cities, young people view acquisition of real estate as a sine qua non for the financial security needed to start a family. As a result of real estate fever, investment in the sector has been a cornerstone of China's economic growth for more than thirty years, and has fuelled one of the greatest urbanization drives in world history.[3] Under the current property regime, residents cannot own real estate; they effectively lease residential property for a seventy-year period.[4] It was only in 2007 with the Property Law that citizens obtained de facto personal property rights through automatic renewal of residential land.[5] While working for an international law firm in Beijing in the mid 2000s, I conducted fieldwork on the impacts of quasi-privatization on Beijing residents, specifically, the process called *chaiqian* (demolition and relocation). During my fieldwork, I interviewed people's court judges who heard administrative actions against the local government by residents who argued their property was taken illegally.[6] Several times, I heard of homeowners who, encountering only frustration in their attempts to mobilize the legal system to protect their rights, set themselves on fire. Self-immolation was a last resort to immortalize their tie to their property: just as their property was being razed, so too would they destroy

[3] To give a few metrics, China's urban population increased by more than 500 million people from 1978 to 2012 with plans to move an additional 250 million rural residents into cities over the next decade; real estate investment grew from a mere 4 per cent of GDP in 1997 to 15 per cent in 2014; and residential investment comprises 15 per cent of total urban employment (Johnson 2013; Wallace 2014; World Bank and Development Research Center of the State Council of the People's Republic of China 2014: 5; Chivakul et al. 2015: 3).

[4] See, e.g., Art. 12 of the Interim Regulations of the PRC Concerning the Assignment and Transfer of the Right to the Use of State-Owned Land in the Urban Areas (*Zhongghua renmin gongheguo chengzhen guoyou tudi shiyongquan churang he zhuanrang zanxing tiaoli*), issued by the State Council on 19 May 1990.

[5] See Art. 149 of the PRC Property Law (*Renmin gongheguo wuquanfa*), adopted by the National People's Congress on 16 March 2007 and effective 1 October 2007.

[6] An illegal taking is defined as one that violates the relevant law, either substantively (e.g. violating the requirement of 'public interest') or procedurally (e.g. inadequate due process). For discussions of illegal takings and suggested reforms, especially regarding the so-called 'second generation of demolition' (*chai erdai*) see Cheng (2015) and Chen (2010).

their bodies.[7] Such extraordinary sacrifices for property first exposed me to the vital links between life and home.

In one case I encountered in 2006, a woman named Hua Xinmin[8] sought the restitution of her family's courtyard home in the *hutong* (narrow alleys) of Beijing by lodging a series of lawsuits against governmental authorities, petitioning the government, and mobilizing new media. Her central argument was that China had a form of private property rights that had survived the land reforms beginning in the 1950s. Specifically, Hua conceptualized the early Communist era as having a dual housing structure: free social housing and private houses. Ownership of the latter was based on title deed (*diqi*) that was converted to 'real estate ownership certificates' (*fangdichan suoyouzheng*), of which her family possessed one. They inhabited one portion of their courtyard and rented out another. After 1958, during a period of social and land reforms, her house was taken over by the local government as a *jingzufang* (administered rented house). According to Hua, a regulation stated that a person could retain ownership even if one part of the house was appropriated by the government for renting out and administered by the land bureau. However, during the Cultural Revolution (1966–76), Red Guards took the ownership certificates. The reform era saw the return of some properties to families in such places as Fujian, Guangdong, and Yunnan: Hua claimed Beijing, by contrast, did not have such a return policy, although other Beijing residents I spoke to said local governments did return properties in limited cases.

According to Hua, in 2001, under the Regulations on Administration of Urban Housing Demolition and Relocation, a developer could commence the process of expropriation by obtaining consent from a tenant even if he or she was not the holder of the ownership certificate.[9] After this transfer, the property could then be confiscated by the government without consulting the actual owner, who held the certificate. This arrangement invited, in Hua's eyes, a 'battle of forms', the rental contract versus the 'ownership certificate'. Based on my research, in almost all cases, the

[7] For a comparative reference point, see the special issue in *Cultural Anthropology* (McGranahan and Litzinger 2012) on the self-immolation of Tibetan monks who destroy their bodies not because of the destruction not of property but of religious traditions. Also, it should be recalled that it was the self-immolation of Ben Ali in Tunis that led to protests that culminated in the 'Jasmine Revolution' in Tunisia.

[8] I include Hua's actual name as it is of public record (part of which she has created), but use pseudonyms for my other interlocutors.

[9] Hua points to the problematic language of the regulation: for example, the person being relocated is defined as the 'owner' (*suoyouren*) of the housing, instead of the person in possession of the certificate. See Regulations on Administration of Urban Housing Demolition and Relocation (*Chengshi fangwu chaiqian guanli tiaoli*), promulgated by the State Council on 13 June 2001 and implemented 1 November 2001, Art. 4.

government recognized the former over the latter and the property was expropriated.

The foregoing provides a brief synopsis of the process of *chaiqian*.[10] However, while the 'legal' processes of the expropriation of privately owned buildings that Hua described were familiar to other Beijing residents, the conditions surrounding her property's history were quite exceptional. Hua was born in Beijing in 1954 to a Chinese father who was a city planner and a French mother who was a journalist. She was raised in France, and it was only in the 1990s that she returned to find that the courtyard built by her grandfather in the 1920s had been destroyed. Her grandfather Hua Nangui had been a well-known architect who had also studied abroad in France, unusually for his generation, and who married the Polish-born novelist Stephanie Rosen.[11] This was no common family. As a result of her upbringing, Hua had a strong 'legal consciousness' (Merry 1990; Gallagher 2006) in the mould of state legalism, yet her international background helped her create critical distance from it. Alone among the dozens of people I talked to about property disputes in advance of the demolition and reconstruction of Beijing for the 2008 Summer Olympics, Hua belonged to the transnational elite. Urban labourers (e.g. factory workers, construction workers, or taxi drivers), who may also have cultivated a critical view of state legalism, did not have Hua's material and linguistic resources to combat it. Nonetheless, in conducting subsequent fieldwork outside Beijing, I realized Hua's experience did resonate with others' for it revolved around a certain conception of time outside official chronologies, one that mapped the legalisms of family onto property ownership.

Hua's interpretation of the relevant land law was built on a wilful anachronism. People's Republic of China (PRC) urban land law has undergone a series of reforms—only some of which Hua accepts. Before the Communists established power in 1949, some wealthy families indeed owned private property, but after 1949 the Party-State[12] gradually nationalized such property. This transformation applied only to private property that was used for commercial purposes, in this case, the portion of Hua's family's estate that was rented. The main form of socialist transformation in the 1950s was 'state trusteeship' whereby the Party-State managed privately

[10] For fuller treatments, see Pils (2005: 245–55) and Erie (2012: 40–1).

[11] Rosen subsequently adopted the Chinese name Hua Luochen and lived with her husband in Beijing after the fall of the Qing in 1911. Her novel *Love and Duty* (1924) was translated into Chinese and became a bestseller in China.

[12] In this chapter, I use 'Party-State' to refer to the agglomeration of the organs of the Chinese Communist Party (CCP) with the functions of the state as administration apparatus. I refer to 'state' in its more generic sense, including the historical succession of states in China and those beyond China.

owned real property and theoretically paid 20 to 40 per cent of the rent it received to former private owners for a period of time (although usually, these payments were not forthcoming). Upon expiration of a fifteen-year period, the Party-State assumed full ownership over the formerly privately owned property (Randolph and Lou 2000: 9–10).

Under this arrangement, Hua's family retained ownership of the portion of the property that they occupied until the Cultural Revolution in the 1960s and 1970s, when it was unlawfully taken not through operation of law but through pure force. Most of these properties have not been returned and the Party-State has yet to deal with the full consequences of the Cultural Revolution, a temporal state of exception to the development of China's legal system.[13] Nonetheless, even if Hua could make the Party-State confront its illegal behaviour during the Cultural Revolution, the 1982 Constitution declared that the state is the owner of 'all urban land': the Constitution effectively, then, ended private ownership of real estate, including that of Hua's family, while permitting the possibility of de facto ownership through extended usufruct rights. Ironically her claim is now stymied as much by the economic pressures underpinning state legalism as by socialist prerogatives.

In talking to Hua, I was struck by her ardour that bordered on a kind of zeal. She showed me her family's 1951 ownership certificate, and identified her father as holder of the ownership right, calling it her *zuzhai* ('grandfather's residence' or 'ancestral house'). She told me, 'There are rights on paper and then there is the reality ... But there is no contradiction between private property and socialism'. She became extremely agitated talking about the history of her family's property, her passion mixing with her reasoning. But what was most remarkable about her was her obstinate sense of time. She held onto the 1951 certificate, which she had brought to courts and petition centres and posted online, shaking it, refusing to acknowledge that the land bureau or people's courts no longer recognized it. Hua's assertions suggest that whereas the state may endorse a monolithic view of property, property holders may contest or reinterpret state legalism based on arguments that both continue to draw upon that law and, at the same time, are grounded in property's links to family and other moral authorities.

In his seminal essay, Marcel Mauss ([1950] 1990) proposes that in non-market economies, a gift incorporates the spirit or soul (he uses the Maori

[13] The official response to the Cultural Revolution is found in the Resolution on Certain Questions in the History of Our Party since the Founding of the PRC (*Guanyu jianguo yilai dang de ruogan lishi wenti de jueyi*, hereinafter, Resolution), adopted by the Sixth Plenary Session of the Eleventh Central Committee of the Communist Party of China on 27 June 1981. The Resolution identifies Mao Zedong as the instigator of the Cultural Revolution and names the Party as the main victim.

term, *hau*) of the giver. Graeber (2001: 211) furthers Mauss's analysis to argue that such 'constitutive property'—which sounds similar to Radin's 'personhood' minus the assumptions of classical liberalism—is exemplified most clearly in inheritance. Yet, for Hua, she cannot pass down her grandfather's property to her beneficiaries. It has been taken from her; all that she has, as her grandfather's inheritance, are legal documents that she is told are void. As a consequence of the state's rejection of her claims, the legacies of her architect grandfather and city planner father have come to define her life and work as a '*hutong* defender': writing petitions, planning lawsuits, contacting journalists and scholars, and blogging about her experiences, many reflections on which are inflected with nostalgia for a period before the market reforms or even before the Communists' assumption of power (e.g. Hua 2011, 2014). Formal law was thus only one means of obtaining the compensation she sought. For Hua and others, the state does not have the monopoly on interpreting law; rather, popular justice, often rooted in ancestral ownership of property, has its own morality, independent of economic discourses.

Hua's attachment to her place of birth is not unique. For instance, Wilhelmina Dery, one of the petitioners in the infamous US eminent domain case *Kelo* v. *City of New London*, was born in the house in question in 1918 and lived there her whole life.[14] Property law scholar Frank Upham wrote of Dery's home, 'Its loss, at 87 years of age in Wilhelmina's case, could kill her, certainly spiritually and conceivably literally' (2014: 46). Indeed, she died in 2006, only a year after the Supreme Court made its decision in favour of the city, after years of litigation and unprecedented media attention. On the one hand, holdout petitioners like Dery or Hua appear out of touch with the times by refusing arguments based on profit-maximizing law and economics, especially as defined by development, whether for an economically depressed New England town or a postsocialist Chinese megalopolis. Yet, on the other hand, and this is precisely the point, their valuation of their property outside of the 'time–space compression' of market capitalism (Harvey 1990), but also state regulation thereof, suggests alternatives to the value of (inequitable) efficiency, as the litmus of property rights allocation (see also Dagan 2011). Rather than market logic or state law, values toward property can be rooted in notions of morality and justice that, from a subjective standpoint, may trump the values of the current regime, even as they may resort to that regime's institutions of dispute resolution to obtain compensation.

[14] See *Kelo* v. *City of New London* 545 US 469, 475 (2005) (cited in Upham 2014: 46 fn. 23).

C-TRANSFORMS

The archaeologist Michael Schiffer wrote in his *Formation Processes of the Archaeological Record* (1987) that an archaeological site is the result of a number of processes, some natural and others caused by human (i.e. 'cultural') activity. These processes, which he terms 'N-transforms' and 'C-transforms', respectively, can potentially move any given artefact within or between strata, so that where it is excavated does not correspond to its provenance. If, as the Party-State would have it, the modern history of Chinese property reform is conceptualized as a series of strata (e.g. privatization, communization, decollectivization, marketization, and partial (re)privatization)[15] (see Pils 2009), then it would seem that a legal interpretation, in this case, one of ownership, would 'belong' to the stratum within which it originated. Yet, as in Hua's case, property claims may refuse to stay buried. Due to the actions of would-be property owners like Hua, affective ties to property from time 'period one' (privatization) may shift to time 'period five' (marketization) resulting in incongruities between popular conceptions of property and state law. The point is that whereas state chronologies of property are often taken for granted, they interact with other chronologies, such as those of diasporic families, which also engage with property. The result is that property holders may not completely reject the state's legalism but nonetheless contest its interpretation and meaning.

One of the reasons for temporal discontinuities is property holders' interpreting property through religious and ethical frameworks. This was the case when I conducted fieldwork on popular practices of *sharīʿah*, a legal–ethical order unrecognized by state law but which nonetheless has its own legalistic categories, among Chinese Muslim minorities (Hui) in north-western China in 2009 to 2015. There I learned of a variety of property arrangements tied to lineage, place, religion, and political and military authority that were sometimes at odds with the property values of the Communists.[16] These cases further demonstrate how the loss of property can become an obsession, defining a life.[17]

[15] These periods correspond roughly to the first few years of the PRC when the CCP confiscated land from landlords and distributed holdings among landless peasants under the Agrarian Reform Law in 1950 ('privatization'); the introduction of communes under the First Five Year Plan in 1953 ('collectivization'); the disbanding of collective farms and introduction of the household responsibility system in 1978 ('decollectivization'); and the creation of a market based on partial private property rights with the 2007 Property Law ('marketization').

[16] There is a growing literature on plural property rights in greater China (Qiao 2013, 2015; Clarke 2014; Gillespie and Fu 2014; Xu 2014).

[17] For a study, inspired by Agamben's writings on 'bare life', of how different understandings of memory can sustain and destroy a life in China, see Zhang (2013).

> My father was a general in the Guomindang (GMD) army and fought against the Japanese in the Sino-Japanese War. His family owned property ... for several generations. During the Cultural Revolution, beginning in 1968, my family's property was taken ... Today, it is divided into several smaller lots, one of which is occupied by governmental cadres.

The elderly Hui man told me his account, as we rubbed our hands to warm them over his black stove on a winter's day in 2010.

I first met Mr Ma while interviewing the owners of what were locally known as 'information stalls' (*xinxibu*), single-proprietorship real estate brokerages that lined the streets of a predominantly Hui city in south-western Gansu, to understand how localized practices of Islamic justice interacted with emerging real estate markets in smaller cities. Ma sought to regain property, namely, a large courtyard, which his family once owned, but which had subsequently been forcibly requisitioned by the Party-State, extinguishing his claim. As we sat before his stove, he moved the boiling water atop it aside, took up a brightly coloured piece of chalk that he used for the small blackboard outside his stall to announce housing prices, and began to write out on the stovetop key elements of his story. He continued

> I have been petitioning for over ten years. I have tried the municipal government, the prefectural government, and the prefectural CCP Committee. The prefectural government told me that the municipal government must deal with the matter. When I went to visit the municipal Party secretary, he simply said that he had signed off on that matter. The national constitution is very good, but the land laws are hindered by local corruption; we cannot obtain our usufruct rights. The problem is local corruption; the local government is too corrupt. The government and the developers collude together.

As he wrote '*guanshang goujie*' (government–commercial corruption), he ran out of space on the perimeter of the stovetop, and wrote the final character within the burning circle, upon which the pot usually rests. The chalk fizzled on the hot surface and remained there even after he erased the chalk writing with a discoloured rag.

Ma pulled out from one corner of his small stall a box containing a loose pile of dog-eared documents. The ones on top proved that his father was a general for the GMD. He told me that the former GMD were part of a group whose property was specifically identified for return after the Cultural Revolution. He held up as legal source of this assertion an internal Party memorandum in which the following text was underlined: 'Real estate that was seized during the Cultural Revolution, must be returned' (*'Wenge' zhong bei jizhan de fangchan bixu tuihuan*).[18] There were additional documents from

[18] See the Notice on the Summary of Minutes of the Expanded Meeting of the Central Committee's Implementing Policies Small Group (*'Zhongyang luoshi zhengce xiaozu kuoda huiyi*

his petitions that included his drawings of the property, its location, size, and a list of current buildings occupying the property including a CCP building. Three portions of his former property had been sold for a total of 1.7 million renminbi (RMB), of which he had received nothing. He and others began petitioning in 2000: before that any attempts to bring attention to their case had resulted in their detention.[19] In 2009, he was again detained by the police for four hours during which they tried to force him to sign documents to the effect that he was satisfied with the status quo, which he refused to do.

For Ma, his valuation of his family's property was tied to his relationship with his late father. Like Hua, Ma conceived of the loss of his property as a threat to his family, including his forebears. His perception was one rooted in time. Anthropological studies suggest that memories are reproduced through ritual, practice, protest—and, I would add, legalisms—and can in fact contest and subvert official histories (Jing 1996; Mueggler 2001). When Ma told me of the Cultural Revolution as the time when his father was labelled a 'counterrevolutionary' (*fangeming*) and was subject to 'criticism sessions' (*pidouhui*), forcing the family of five to live off the street for more than a year, he was recounting a memory, a subjective experience that was visceral and scarring.

Such memories, however, also underpin an understanding of the relationship between time and property law. Whereas in the pre-Communist era, his family's property received nominal protection by the extant legal system,[20] the arrival of the Communists and the establishment of a socialist order (that included but was not limited to law), militated explicitly against the interests of GMD landowners, their ideological foes. The Chinese state has appropriated history, and thus is able to define the legitimacy of property rights (e.g. lease terms, bank loans, vested interests, recordings and registrations, mortgages, and any other term of years in property contracts) in temporal terms according to the chronology of state property reforms. Kinship, family, and faith, however, can produce their own temporalities, of which property can be a material, affective, and pious manifestation. Thinking through property outside the PRC's property law reform shows how actors work against the grain of political amnesia (Fang 1990; Chan 2011; Lim 2014), as supplemented by the market (Graeber 2001: 79).

jiyao' de tongzhi) transmitted by the General Office of the Central Committee of the CCP on 23 August 1984.

[19] Petitioning is a form of complaint, parallel to the formal judicial system, that long predates the Communists. It is predicated on the notion that higher-level officials can prevent local injustices.

[20] Gansu in the 1920s and 1930s was subject to a number of overlapping jurisdictions in what is known as the 'warlord period'. Hui military generals, most of whom were aligned with the GMD established their own patchwork court system. I address the question of this system's provision of protected property rights, including those under Islamic law, in Erie (forthcoming 2018).

Ma, like Hua, points then to a different relationship between time and law, and the orders that underpin it. Like Hua, Ma used a variety of means to obtain redress, only one of which was administrative litigation—an option that encountered early roadblocks. Rather, petitioning, an extralegal method[21] (and one Hua used, as well), became his grindstone. Nonetheless, this method was also circumscribed by state authority, and unlike Hua, Ma did not have the transnational connections to mobilize media (print or Internet-based). Crucially, whereas Hua emphasized the illegality of current official interpretations of prior state wrongs, Ma called attention to contemporary corruption in the local real estate industry, echoes of prior Cultural Revolution-era wrongs. Hua gave more credence to state law's ability to correct injustices, whereas for Ma, formal law is a tool of corrupt officials. Neither, however, challenged the legitimacy of the Party-State itself, and thus despite their protests, their claims were bounded by categories determined by the Party-State.

The state's claims to history are not uncontested. Instead, the state's arbitrary use of violence or corrupt legal practices opens up challenges to its monopoly on legal interpretation. For descendants of homeowners, the state's particular temporality of law with its own mutability excludes their own subjective understandings: illegal seizures during the Cultural Revolution or ongoing corruption are not passively accepted. For these protestors, a vision of law embedded in public morality transcends the vicissitudes of a Party-led legal regime (see Zhu and Wang 2008). It is ironic then that Ma and several others petitioning the government for illegal takings (there were 130 such families in 2010 in total, of which only a small fraction were 'second-generation GMD' as Ma identified himself), participated in the residential real estate market as brokers. Every transaction entails the potential for a forgetting of the history of ownership (Zhao and Bell 2005), that is, market exchange may erase the bases for property ownership according to alternative legalisms.

INVALUABLE PROPERTY

PRC legal experts have observed that in property disputes, one of the most contentious issues in China's development is compensation: failure to agree on the amount of compensation is often claimed to be the reason for homeowners' resistance to redevelopment schemes that would

[21] Petitioning (*xinfang*) is a system of dispute resolution parallel to or outside of the courts that predates the establishment of the modern state and consists of bringing a complaint to an office specific for such purposes, usually at a higher administrative level (Minzner 2006; Fang 2009).

result in the destruction of their homes (Schwarzwalder et al. 2003; Ping 2007). While this is incontrovertible, to conclude that compensation is the crux of property conflicts is to fail to recognize that many evictees and owners question the very notion that their properties can be assigned a market value. Furthermore, they often question the invocation of 'public interest' to legitimize expropriation by the state (Erie 2007: 943). These putative owners engage with law through compensation, but challenge its hegemony through questioning the appropriateness of that compensation.

One of the key insights of neo-Maussian anthropology is that property can have value outside the market pricing system. Mauss looked to economic systems (e.g. Polynesian gift exchanges, north-west American Indian potlatches, Trobriand *kula* rings, and even Chinese 'face' in gifting) that were not yet integrated into global capitalism to explain how and why they compel obligations even without the familiar mechanisms of enforcement often associated with modern law. One of the reasons, Mauss surmised, was that gifted property, because it contained some aspect of the spirit of the giver, obligated the recipient until the gift was returned via a counter-gift. The value, then, of the gift was not determined by an objectifying market price, but rather though a subjective impression that was shared and reciprocated, often cyclically, forming social ties.

The 'substantivists' of the 1960s added to anthropological models of exchange to examine human volition as a basis for other economic activities (e.g. reciprocity, redistribution, ports of trade) and not necessarily reducible to interest maximization (Polanyi [1944] 2001; 1957). In his attempt to find an accommodation between Marxist and Maussian thought, Graeber (2001) argued that value need not be commensurate with market forces and that alternatives persist in varying degrees of relation with global capitalism. If valuation lies at the heart of legal ownership, its level is contested and rests in those producers, traders, donors, consumers, inheritors, and trustees who compare forms of value, even if some of their options are limited for reasons beyond their control.

In conducting fieldwork on the revival of Islam in north-west China, I was struck by those property disputes where owners either refused the government's compensation or the possibility that their property could be compensated through monetary value at all. By way of background, Ma's city is one of many in north-west China where 'urban renewal' projects are encountering the increased presence of Islam in public life (Gladney [1991] 1996, 1999; Erie and Carlson 2014; Famularo 2015). Existing state law and policy restricts the financing and construction of 'religious' buildings. Commercial developers have also encroached upon those properties where Hui have existing constructions, either for religious activities or residential purposes.

In a city in Gansu, one Hui group waged an eleven-year battle with the municipal government and real estate developers over the preservation of their property. This group was singular for both their particular doctrinal interpretation of Islam and their success as a commercially oriented Muslim group; for that reason, they had been historically ostracized by other Hui groups, and, at certain points in history, had been the object of the Party-State's attacks, as well.[22] The property in question consisted of a four-floor building on approximately two *mu* (⅓ acre) of land, consisting of a large kitchen and living space for eight families on the lower floors, and an office and prayer space on the upper floors. When I first visited the building in 2009, its front view was obscured by an immense billboard sign selling Chinese liquor in front of a major intersection. The building itself was made of concrete slabs that were sparsely decorated; the inside was poorly lit, but clean.

The Hui trace the history of the property to 1904 when members of their group travelled from their base in the Tibetan grasslands to the city to settle a lawsuit with a rival order.[23] During the course of the dispute, a community formed that grew as converts joined. They eventually built a mosque on the site, which was also a market for timber cultivated by the Hui in the foothills of the Himalayas. In 1958, during an anti-rightist campaign, experienced among Hui in Gansu as an anti-religious movement, the Hui buildings were destroyed and they were forced out. In the Cultural Revolution, their members were forced to wear 'counter-revolutionary' hats and were put in jail where many died. They returned in 1989 and subsequently acquired formal legal status when they registered the building as a 'religious activity area' (*zongjiao huodong changsuo*) two years later, at the religious bureau of the relevant city district. Registration conferred usufruct rights in the land.[24]

In February 2002, a governmental official notified the Hui group that their property would be expropriated to build a new city centre. Specifically, the notification announced the government would 'reclaim' (*huishou*) the group's usufruct rights. The group quickly mobilized. They sought administrative reconsideration at the provincial law bureau,[25] and petitioned the

[22] For more on the history of sectarianism in China, see Gladney (1987, [1991] 1996, 1999). On the history of the litigiousness of Hui, see Lipman (1999, 2005).

[23] The second group claimed that the Hui were heterodox and should be declared illegal. The dispute was settled not by the imperial court but by a Hui imam named Zhang Jingde who led a large community composed of some eleven mosques. Zhang ruled that the Hui group in question should be allowed to continue to practise their faith.

[24] They have been a number of documents to prove this, including from the mayor's office, the municipal housing management bureau, and the municipal food service company, dated 1988 and 1989. The property, however, was not deemed to be 'residential' even though some Hui families lived there and thus does not fall under the protection of Art. 149 of the 2007 Property Law.

[25] Expropriation is considered an administrative action under relevant PRC law. See Regulations for Expropriation of and Compensation for Houses on State-Owned Land (*Guoyu*

department of urban planning and land bureau, as well as the provincial government, and even the national government in Beijing. They reached out to the bureau of religious affairs, the United Front Work Department, and other organs of the CCP. They even wrote letters to the central leadership, then-president Hu Jintao and premier Wen Jiabao. At the same time, news spread among the group and several thousand members congregated at the spot in protest, calling the site of the building 'sublimely sacred' (*chonggao shensheng*) and 'religiously pure land' (*zongjiao jingdi*). In one statement issued to the government, the followers said of the site: 'even if what was waiting for us inside was our own grave, we would not hesitate to go in, lie down, and be buried' (*jishi nali you yi zuo fenmu zai dengdaizhe women, women ye yao haobu youyu di tang jinqu, ren tu yanmai*), such was their attachment to the land.

Privately, like Ma, the Hui complained to me of collusion between city officials and private developers: the municipal government had illegally sold their ownership rights to the developer who sought to evict them in contravention of relevant state law. In accordance with Chinese law, they negotiated directly only with the government and not with the developers. In 2003, the city mayor was sacked for receiving kickbacks for commercial real estate deals, a fact which the Hui pointed out in their letters. Still, the local officials maintained that the Hui would have to move. For their part, the Hui would not budge and neither would they accept compensation from the local land bureau.

After several years of negotiations, in 2009, the Hui won the right to maintain ownership over part of their property, although they had to conform to the city plan. The developer procured rights over five parcels of the land in question whereas the Hui retained two.[26] As part of the city centre plan, the developer would build a 45-floor building; the Hui would build their own adjoining but separate building. The government initially limited their building to five floors but after another two years of negotiation, they increased the height to nine floors. The older building was demolished in 2010 and the new building, at the time of this writing, had just been completed.

The Hui estimate the monetary value of their property in 1980, at the beginning of the 'opening and reform' period, when properties were assigned market

tudishang fangwu zhengshou yu buchang tiaoli), promulgated 21 January 2011 by the State Council, Arts. 13 and 14. Their legal argument was that the basis of their usufruct rights was their status as a 'religious group' (*zongjiao tuanti*). The Religious Affairs Regulations (*Zongjiao shiwu tiaoli*), issued by the State Council on 30 November 2004, Art. 30, afford religious groups procedural protection in the event of demolition for city redevelopment. However, the 2002 government notice failed to recognize them as a religious group.

[26] Interviewees were not uniform in their assessment of this process; some Hui stated that their property actually increased as a result of this negotiation.

value, to be several hundred RMB per square metre. Following the increase in real estate value, in 2010, the price of real estate in the city intersection was RMB 50,000 per square metre for a street-facing shop and RMB 6,000 per square metre for interior parcels. Thus, a conservative estimate of the market price of their property is over RMB 8 million, a sizable increase from its price at the outset of the reform period. Nonetheless, the Hui refused to assign a market value to their property. One member referred to the property as the home of their 'spiritual family' (*xinling jiating*). The property was inviolable and, in their eyes, priceless. The site was tied to their contested history as a legitimate religious community during China's transition from empire to nation state.

As Andrew Willford writes in his study of the proposed demolition of a Tamil temple on Kuala Lumpur's last plantation, 'the violence of the law, its arbitrary and performative quality, had been laid bare to the residents in a manner that allowed for its critique in the name of justice' (2014: 4). The Hui mobilized state law and other extralegal channels (e.g. petitioning) but found these wanting. The Hui rejected market valuation of their property, an objectifying category of state legalism, and instead, esteemed their property in a different register, that of their religious community, which they still recognized as embedded in state law (i.e. their need to gain official status as a religious group). They claim their success rested on their tenacity, connections with officials, and, ultimately, 'grace from God'.

For the Hui, the sacredness of their land was a result of their group's marginality; their long struggle to gain official religious status in the decades after the founding of modern China and be recognized as an orthodox version of Islam; and their fights within and outside Chinese courthouses to gain that recognition. For this particular group that emphasizes commercial as well as spiritual flourishing, the property in question, which is now located in the urban core of one of the largest cities in north-west China, was *prima facie* evidence that they could succeed—and should be recognized for their achievements. Although the legal basis of their claim in the land was uncertain until they obtained usufruct rights in the early 1990s, they dated their ownership of the site to the start of the twentieth century.

Their arguments were based less on formal law,[27] and more on appeals to justice, anchored in their centurial self-mythologizing. Along these lines, I was told that the new building consists of several *waqfs* (pious endowments under Islamic law), one for each of the nine floors.[28] Although knowledge

[27] PRC land law does not recognize adverse possession or 'prescription' (*zhanyou shixiao*). Nonetheless, even in the absence of the legal right, government officials in places like Shenzhen have experimented with recognizing *de facto* possession (Qiao 2015: 306–7).

[28] Some Hui I spoke to did classify the earlier six-floor building as a *waqf*. The Announcement on Fixing Problems Related to Religious Groups' Real Estate Policies (*Guanyu luoshi zongjiao tuanti fandichan zhengce deng wenti de baogao*), issued by the State Council and the Religious

of Islamic law among Hui is thin, *waqfs* have been growing in importance in recent years following China's Islamic revival. While some would question whether the Hui donations are truly *waqfs*,[29] Hui framing of their rights as such demonstrates another aspect of their 'value pluralism' (Alexander 2011; Laidlaw 2014: 166) in property.

ALMOST INVALUABLE PROPERTY

Sacred property may not always be priceless, however, as competing valuations between legalisms may force property holders to make hard choices. Hui tack back and forth between the 'socialist market economy' and the shadow economy, outside the state sphere, based on Islamic law, kinship, and solidarity. Their comparisons across these economic domains suggests that while real property may be formative of Hui communities, families, or selves, they are also ready to alienate part, or all, of it—for the right price. In other words, the weakness of their position often forces them to engage with formal law's quantitative assessment of their rights.

Marilyn Strathern (1990; see also 1999) suggests in her concepts of the 'dividual' or 'partible person', that Melanesians think of persons not as defined isomorphically by pre-existing values, but, rather, as comprised of any number of potential personhoods that depend on the social context. Strathern's ethnographic theory opens up ways to think about value and the constitution of the self via property, one that is predicated on potentials instead of givens, comparison rather than holism, and evaluation in the place of embodiment with particular reference to overlapping legalisms.[30]

Most people, Chinese (Hui or Han) or non-Chinese, for that matter, are not in the position of the Hui described above who had the collective resources to wait out a decade-long property dispute. For many, their attachments to land and home are balanced by their need for a livelihood, and if the

Affairs Bureau on 3 July 1980, recognizes that the expropriation of property owned by religious groups during the Cultural Revolution brought economic hardship to such groups when they generated income from such property. It resolves to 'return, in its entirety, the property rights in housing owned by religious groups to those groups, and where return is impossible, to give a monetary sum' (*jiang zongjiao tuanti fangwu de chanquan quanbu tuigei zongjiao tuanti, wufa tui de ying zhejia fukuan*) (Policy and Law Department of the Bureau of Religious Affairs 1995: 25).

[29] Minimally, the *waqf* requires that, one, the founder (*waqif*) obtain full ownership rights and, two, that the *waqf* be given in perpetuity for a social good. Neither requirement is met in China where citizens cannot have full property rights and their usufruct rights are limited in time.

[30] In making this assertion, I note that Strathern herself would most likely disapprove of such cross-cultural comparison. I believe it is possible to compare without importing wholesale western (or Melanesian, for that matter) categories.

expropriation of the former delays, or worse, threatens the latter, then they must make difficult decisions. Whereas the examples above are instances of already expropriated property, an ongoing dispute shows how the life of property becomes an afterlife through alternative legalisms. To use the archaeology metaphor, rather than examine the end result of its formation, an ongoing dispute demonstrates the processes that form the artefact.[31]

As China embarks on a massive urbanization drive, one of the sites of highest contention is the peri-urban zone that surrounds cities. Such property is increasingly subject to urban sprawl and the often violent conversion of 'rural' land to 'urban' land.[32] This problem may be compounded in ethnic minority areas, particularly where organized religions such as Tibetan Buddhism or Islam or popular religions such as animism and shamanism, have conferred upon the land the nature of sacred obligation.[33] In these peri-urban areas, conflicts among plural legalisms are laid bare, namely those between a state legalism driven by economic prerogative and religious legalisms that stress obligations outside market rationality. This problem is apparent in a city in north-west China that is unique even among predominantly Hui enclaves for its large number of Sufis, who self-identify as Muslims and instead of following literal understandings of *sharīʿah*, as do many modernist Muslims, incorporate *sharīʿah* into their particular 'path' (*tariqa*).

The path is defined both doctrinally and ideologically through a master who is usually based in a tomb complex and who traces his teaching back through a chain of spiritual guides to the founder of the order, usually outside China, in Central Asia, the Arab peninsula, India, or North Africa. There are a number of such orders based in this city with tens of thousands of followers living throughout north-west China and beyond. For these Sufis, a range of sites are sacred: the property of the Sufi tomb (the land it occupies and the interior space, particularly the tomb and surrounding secondary or tertiary tombs); any land where a master was born, died, or received instruction from a foreign missionary; sites where there are any buried relics relating to the master; and land donated by a master such as a *waqf*. As a result, the city is an urbanizing community that is also a sacred landscape dotted with such Sufi shrines.

Beginning in 2009, over a period of eight years, I observed a dispute on the borders of this city in Gansu that highlights how property may possess

[31] William Rathje famously applied this approach in excavating the contents of landfills in Tucson to understand patterns of consumption (and site formation processes) in what has been called 'garbology' (Rathje and Murphy 2001).

[32] The government must convert rural or collectively owned land to urban or state-owned land to expropriate it for commercial purposes (Erie 2012: 40).

[33] See, e.g., Sturgeon (2004), Yeh (2004), and Da Col (2007).

different values, namely, one based on a religious communities' legalism and another one based on state legalism and market economics that commoditize land. The dispute has taken place in an area that consists of two villages of about 700 people in total, 80 per cent of whom are Hui. Each village had its own mosque where villagers prayed and there was a third across a multi-lane avenue, where some Hui prayed as well. Most lineage heads date their families' history in the area to the 1700s when their ancestors were forced to migrate there from Beijing as punishment for allegedly committing crimes, although a few Hui I spoke to said one of the mosques dated to the Yuan period (1271–1368).

In addition, the area has two Hui cemeteries that also date to the late Qing. Almost all of the Hui made their living by farming and sold their vegetables to city dwellers at a local market. Most of the Hui are Sufi and belong to the Qadiriyya order, one of the oldest in China. The city contained two sprawling Qadiriyya tombs in the north of the city, one of which, according to Hui legend, dates to the arrival of an Arab missionary in the Tang dynasty (618–907). The Sufis who congregate at the two tombs originally belonged to the same *menhuan* (Chinese Sufi collectivity), but split due to historical differences. The former master of one of the Qadiriyya Sufi tomb complexes was born and grew up in one of the villages, which bears his lineage's surname (as does one mosque). Although the former master was buried in the tomb complex north of the city in 2009, his family members are buried in one of the Hui cemeteries in the village. Most members of that village share the same surname and share kinship. Members of the *menhuan* beyond the village regularly prayed and read the Qur'an at the gravesite in commemoration of the passing of the former master's kin.[34]

The dispute began in the early 2000s. When, in 2004, plans to expand the city westward encountered violent resistance by rural Hui, the government turned to the east, including the villages in question. In that same year, urban planners constructed a major boulevard immediately south of the Hui villages, and moved the city's major governmental buildings, including the courthouse, the police headquarters, and the prosecutor's office, to this boulevard. Such planning was, in part, an attempt to pre-empt resistance as the seat of the government had moved to the eastern district before the adjacent villages would be razed to expand the city. While the sites of the new governmental buildings were south of the centres of the villages,

[34] Pursuant to Art. 4 of the Regulations on the Administration of Funeral and Interment (*Binzang guanli tiaoli*), issued by the State Council, 9 November 2011, in most areas of the country, the deceased must be cremated and cannot receive a ground burial, however, for those minorities (such as Muslims) that live in 'autonomous areas', according to local regulations, they may be exempt from this requirement. Islam has clear protocol regarding proper burial, of which interment is one.

nonetheless, many Hui homesteads were demolished in the process. Family heads were kidnapped and forced to sign 'demolition and relocation agreements' (*chaiqian xieyi shu*). By 2007, it was clear that the Hui villages would be destroyed too. The municipal housing authority along with ten other government offices, including security forces, a total of 200 cadres, began negotiations with three Hui villagers who were also Party cadres.

In an exercise of collective action, the Hui villagers had already by that time decided to refuse to move or receive any compensation. A usual strategy of developers had been to approach individual households, offering compensation and pitting neighbours against each other. As early as 2007, however, village leaders, namely, senior Qadiriyya Sufis, were harassed by thugs hired by the municipal government. One elderly villager was detained for six hours at the municipal police station. Nearly 700 villagers marched to the police station to set him free, which the authorities did. Most of these early incidents resulted in temporary kidnappings, but not in serious bodily harm.

To defend their property rights, the Hui, as in the other cases mentioned, began by resorting to formal legal measures. As with the Hui group described above, the villagers applied to the township-level people's government for an administrative decision (*xingzheng caijue*) on 16 February 2008. They applied again a week later and had a governmental hearing, but failed to reach a settlement. Village representatives began petitioning all levels of government, including, the township, municipal, prefectural, provincial, and national governments; only the last responded and stated that they had to consult lower levels of administration. The representatives studied the law, researched on the Internet, and reached out to media outlets, demonstrating a willingness to mobilize legal and extralegal means, and developing their own consciousness of state legalism. Initially at least, they believed that the legal system would ensure justice.

Yet the Hui villagers' belief was short-lived as the attacks on them became more intense and violent. In early 2008, two more leaders were detained at the police station, and pressured to sign documents for the demolition of the villages, which they refused to do. Two villagers, including an administrator at one of the mosques, who had not previously been active in the dispute, were attacked by six masked men at one of the mosques and brought in an unmarked car to the police station where they were handcuffed to a desk and told to sign demolition and relocation agreements. They were not allowed to contact family and were missing for seven hours. Again, some 600 villagers marched to the police station, demanding their release. Subsequently, the police, including plainclothes officers, kept the leaders of the mosques under surveillance. Over the course of 2008, the government sent, at different times, officials and personnel from nineteen governmental bureaus, over a thousand people in total, including the armed police (*wujing*), to the villages to pressure the farmers into moving. The villagers pasted notices throughout their villages decrying the injustices; security forces tore them down. In their place, security forces put up large banners around the village, proclaiming the 'rule of law'.

The specific legal dispute was over compensation for the land of the villages, but related to this was the question of which land was to be compensated. The villagers had both land on which their houses were built (*zhaijidi*) and contracted farmland (*chengbao gengdi*). In the summer of 2008, officials offered the villagers monetary compensation for their house-site property only. The government did not offer compensation for the farmland saying that it was owned not even by the collective, but rather, by the CCP. The farming land is a contract for usufruct rights between the individual farmers and the collective, usually for thirty years. Many villagers had documents for rights in the farmland valid until 2028.

One Hui farmer I spoke to (to whom I refer here as Yusuf) was offered compensation for the loss of his house-site property. This calculation was based on a ratio of 1:1.5, meaning one and a half times the current market value of the land. The policy rationale for the additional 50 per cent is that it compensates the house owner for the hardship of moving. According to my interviews, the base value depended on a calculation that considered the quality of the house and the number of occupants, and so could vary from RMB 200 to 500 per square metre for house-site land. Yusuf received a sum of RMB 60,000, based on the calculation RMB 333/sq. m. (as market value) x 120 sq. m. (total area of house-site property) x 1.5.

For the farmland, despite an initial refusal to pay anything, the government eventually offered Yusuf a sum calculated by the price for rural land at a 1:1 ratio. The value of the farmland remained unclear. Most of the farmland occupied the liminal 'suburb' (*jiaoqu*) that depended on the discretion of local government regarding its categorization as urban or rural land. At first, the government offered Yusuf RMB 50,000 for 7 *fen* or 0.7 *mu* of farmland (at a rate of RMB 71,429/*mu*). In April 2010, the government increased this compensation to RMB 81,550/*mu*. Nonetheless, Yusuf argued that the land in question should be valued according to the price for urban land. Yusuf cited the market price for the land across the street from his home at RMB 700,000/*mu*.

Yusuf was able to assign a monetary value to the land: a sceptic may interpret such behaviour as acceptance of the commodification of sacred property, signalling an attempt to maximize individual material benefit. However, such negotiations occurred in a broader context of loss, both of livelihood and of religious tradition, and of being obliged to operate in a particular legal framework however much he might contest its underpinnings.

Over the course of my visits to Yusuf, I saw the strain of the protracted negotiations. As early as 2009, after the government drained the village well to build a nearby road, the villagers had no water. This water was crucial for not only drinking but also for daily ablutions. While the government did not initially respond to their complaints, it did eventually turn the well water back on; however, the water was polluted. They then had to cycle to carry water in from a dispenser in the city centre at a cost of RMB 10 per family for an amount that lasted a month. Yusuf injured his back as a result of the labour, and thus could not attend the fields. Many villagers could not farm under these conditions.

Whereas the monthly income for a village household was about RMB 1,000 (below the poverty line in China), they now struggle to make even this because they are losing their land. As of 2010, 1 kilogramme of produce sold for only RMB 1.10 in the markets. Yusuf complained to me, 'they absolutely do not care about the people's livelihood; they do not care about their right to subsist (*shengcun quan*)'. His injury resulted in his wife having to work overtime as a construction worker in the city. For those families that could still farm, their crops were often bulldozed at night by thugs apparently hired by the government. In February 2012, cabbage was just appearing in a lot across from that of Yusuf when men ploughed it over. The next day, the government went to the affected farmers, whose economic livelihood had been taken from them, to negotiate.

The religious life of the village had similarly come under assault. One of the three mosques was demolished in 2015, although villagers told me that the developer promised to build a new one in the same spot. Additionally, as of 2015, developers were in talks with families of the deceased in one graveyard. It seems the developer planned to erect a high-rise building on the spot of the graveyard, where some 300 Muslims were buried. Initially, the plan was for the developer to give RMB 8,000 to each family who had a deceased member in the graveyard, obliging them to relocate the body to the larger Muslim cemetery north of town. However, these talks were stalled and only a smaller number of bodies were moved. The graveyard that contained the bodies of the Qadiriyya master's family was intact, as of my last visit. However, the developers had sought some land (5 *fen* of house-site property and 0.5 *mu* of farmland) around this cemetery that was owned by a family of a student studying at a major mosque in the city. The developers persuaded the cleric and teacher of the student to convince the student to sell off the land, which he did for RMB 25,900.

The property dispute is ongoing. For Yusuf, whose family had owned the property for four generations, it was evident to me as I sat with him on a bench in his single-room home that the decade-long conflict had worn him down. Yusuf talked about the senior administrator of his nearby mosque, the man who had been detained. He was a successor to the Qadiriyya master by both blood and teaching, and the villagers saw him as a kind of moral exemplar. The stress of the negotiations had impacted on his health, and he died in 2015. Yusuf also talked about how the commodification of land had led to corruption in his own village—their village committee head received some RMB 3,800 in bribes (*hongbao*) from the city mayor in 2009. He has seen some twenty families move to high-rise apartments but lose contact with their village neighbours, and struggle to adapt their means of income without their farmland. The demolition and relocation process had eroded the kinship ties that connected the villagers and, further, linked them to the Qadiriyya Sufi tomb complex.

For Sufi Hui like Yusuf, the natal village is not only a kinship network but also a spiritual community. He told me in 2010:

> For us Muslims, our neighbours are sometimes more important than extended family.[35] We've lived here for generations and everyone around us, we know like brothers and sisters. If we move to one of the apartments, neighbours become strangers. No one will come to our funeral.

Just as the living remember the dead by building tombs and making visitations, so do the dead, and the holy properties that commemorate them, sustain the value of life.

For Strathern, Melanesian wealth items are composed of elements that reflect different sets of social relations (Strathern 1990: 171–2). Melanesians harmonize the functional and symbolic through design, reflecting a notion of personhood that is also composite. Hui may also view their property as composed of values that reflect different social relations (e.g. between members of families or lineages, co-religionists, or participants in the market). These values, unlike the Melanesian case, however, are not the result of design, but rather of political circumstance. Consequently, there may be a higher degree of internal tension between the diverse values. In short, resolving conflicts between and among legalisms is far from straightforward and may result in the disintegration of communities as individuals make tough choices.

Those who determine the value of land must negotiate between property as sacred obligation and property as marketized commodity: this can be difficult and painful. It is precisely because of the corruption of legal practices that they are forced to accept its parameters. Muslims in particular, whether in the Middle East, western secular states, or transitional China, have to negotiate between piety and calculated self-interest (Schielke 2009,

[35] I have heard this same expression used by Uyghurs, the Turkic Muslims that live in China's westernmost area of Xinjiang, and by non-Muslim Han Chinese.

2015; Fadil and Fernando 2015; Khan 2012; Erie 2016). That property can be sold through forced expropriation does not invalidate its capacity to constitute Hui selves, rather, such alienation marks the beginning of its afterlife. Seemingly irresolvable conflicts between property that is priceless, as held by an ethno-religious group, but that can, at the same time, be the basis for monetary compensation, echo value dilemmas in other legalistic settings, for instance, honour societies. From medieval Icelandic kinsmen (Miller 1990; McKinnell 2009) to Arab tribes in northern Yemen (Dresch 1989) to pastoral Tibetans in Amdo (Pirie 2014), groups often must reconcile an affront to an individual or collective honour (e.g. a sheep stolen or household dependent harmed) that may warrant retaliation, with compensation, that is, the exchange of something (money, goods, or kin exchange like marriage) of equal value.

Non-state legalistic systems may have different rules for the appropriate response to honour sullied—revenge versus compensation—but this question is complicated when such systems are subsumed within the law of larger polities. Outcomes depend on not just how far actors are willing to go in protecting their honour, at the expense of fungible rewards, but also the degree to which the encompassing legal system recognizes non-state legalisms. For Hui whose sacred land is being expropriated, they experience such takings as affronts to their dignity as much as to their livelihood. Many (but not all) agree to accept compensation because the state legal system, which in this instance, is principally concerned with assigning a monetary value for the exchange of the right to use, does not value their property based on the same categories as their religion does. In the end, exigencies of food, water, and shelter, the basic means of sustaining life, often win out over prolonged property battles. But sometimes they do not, as cases of self-immolation dramatically demonstrate.

THE LIFE AFTER SELF

Value-oriented approaches to property, such as Hanoch Dagan's 'structural pluralism' helpfully move beyond efficiency as the raison d'être for property rights, but nonetheless adhere to values espoused by classical liberalism (e.g. autonomy, rule of law, liberty, and democracy) (Dagan 2014) which can be unhelpfully western-centric. Similarly, Radin's 'property as personhood' makes a shift from a conception of property as that which is acted upon, to conceptualizing, from a subjective perspective, its capacity to constitute the self; nevertheless, she too develops her thinking through liberal theory, with an emphasis on Hegelian 'occupancy', that is the owner's will as present in property (Radin 1982: 973). Naturally, all these scholars, even with nods to pluralism, assume that the state is both the legislator and guarantor of property rights.

Despite the limits of its philosophical orientation, Radin's interpretation of personal property has been widely accepted in property law scholarship (see, for a review of the literature, Jones 2011). If it is true, then, that 'Most people possess certain objects they feel are almost part of themselves', as Radin asserted (1982: 959), then the question remains: what does it mean for people who experience the loss of irreplaceable property, and what can be learned about property ownership and possession, more generally, through such relationships to lost property?

This chapter has explored the intertwining of persons and things through reference to the anthropology of value and especially neo-Maussian interpretations thereof. It has further suggested that property theories have inadequately considered subjective perceptions of time, and the ways these may shape legal framings of property. This becomes clear, at least in the case of expropriation of property in China case, only in hindsight. The Chinese Party-State has transformed property rights, from collectivization to a form of neoliberalism dressed up as 'market socialism' through time, but without successfully imposing uniformity on people's perceptions of property. As the Party-State defines property rights through these periods, those would-be property owners who either have alternative understandings of rights or claims based on prior property regimes encounter structural obstacles in their attempts to assert these claims. Hua, Ma, the Hui with the multi-floor *waqf*, and Yusuf, each contest current state definitions of property either by reframing rules of property with reference to family lineage or religious group, or by contesting the legality of state action—or both. In distinguishing these cases, Hua's property claim is rooted in the idea that property law should be unchanging. This is underpinned by her sense of family: an intensely personal and individualistic sense of right buttresses her claim. For the Hui, to differing degrees, their claims reverberate in registers beyond the familial, as religious minorities whom the state has historically marginalized. Their contestation of law is more explicitly framed in a local–central dynamic of claims of corruption. Ironically, because the Hui have experienced the violent corruption of law collectively (and sometimes, systematically), they are more willing to work with—as opposed to against—the Party-State. Such accommodations include fixing a monetary amount to their priceless property.

In addition to the criticism that holdouts are mere interest maximizers (which some may be), sceptics may label this problem one of de-temporalized property claims or property rights 'frozen in time'. Anthropologists have long tried to situate time in understanding their interlocutor's notions of causality, agency, and change. Concurrently, scholars have been criticized for relativizing 'social time', as Durkheimian collective representations, in their representation of others (Gell 1992; Greenhouse 1996; Fabian 2014).[36] What property rights defenders in China offer, however, is not an argument for a naturalized view of time, but rather, a problematization of the Party-State's own appropriation of time. When Hua or the Hui ground the legitimacy of their property ownership claims in pre-Communist property regimes or draw attention to the unrecognized injustices of the Cultural Revolution, they point to the arbitrariness of official time. As 'property outlaws' their actions and words do not simply attempt to freeze property law in a past regime, but rather 'broadly reflect ... evolving community values' (Peñalver and Katyal 2007: 1101). Ultimately, the afterlife of property that animates their rights defence haunts the Party-State. Indeed, the current anti-corruption campaign in China, one that has defined the current leadership, shows that it is because of corruption, exposed in part by rights' defenders, that the Party-State must cannibalize itself as it fights for its own life.

[36] Durkheim's 'social time' is hardly the only approach anthropologists have taken to time. Other approaches include phenomenological, 'practice theory', symbolic analyses, and intersubjective approaches, to name a few. For a helpful, if dated, review, see Munn (1992).

5

Jurisdiction as Property in England, 900–1100*

TOM LAMBERT

In the year 2000 the UK government held an auction to sell usage rights for the radio spectrum bandwidths required by third generation (3G) mobile phone technology. This auction was staggeringly successful: the sale of five twenty-one-year licences raised £22.5 billion for the treasury (Binmore and Klemperer 2002). This act of privatization made clear just how lucrative the state's rights over the radio spectrum could be. But where exactly did this extraordinarily valuable state property come from? An easy assumption would be that radio spectrum usage rights naturally belong to governments: before they were sold off to private companies these rights had always been the property of the British state, and therefore do not have an origin in any meaningful sense. Medieval kings held a monopoly of such rights on this logic, even while unaware of the fact. When the UK parliament first made a law on the subject—the Wireless Telegraphy Act of 1904—it seems to have done so partly on this assumption: though regulatory laxity had permitted the proliferation of private wireless stations, the right

* Anglo-Saxon and Anglo-Norman laws are cited using the standard system of abbreviations established in Liebermann 1903–16 (which remains the authoritative edition for many texts). This material is best accessed through the online text indices of the Early English Laws project (http://www.earlyenglishlaws.ac.uk/laws/texts/index), which provides comprehensive information on each text, including references to all editions and translations (some of which are digitized) and facsimiles of the relevant manuscripts. (The texts cited here are most readily available in English translation in Attenborough 1922; Robertson 1925; Downer 1972; O'Brien 1999.) Anglo-Saxon charters are cited by their 'S' (or 'Sawyer') numbers. These originally referred to Sawyer 1968, a comprehensive printed catalogue and bibliography, but more up-to-date information is now available through an online database: www.esawyer.org.uk. Domesday Book is cited by folio.

Jurisdiction as Property in England, 900–1100. Tom Lambert. © Tom Lambert, 2017. Published 2017 by Oxford University Press.

to make use of the airwaves naturally pertained to the state (particularly in view of its potential military applications), so it was legitimate to insist that private radio operators secure appropriate usage rights in the form of licences issued by the Postmaster-General (Hozier 1906). Nonetheless, it is important to distinguish early twentieth-century cultural assumptions from the law as it actually stood. In fact, before 1904 there were no rules about the radio spectrum. The right to make use of it did not belong to the state or to anybody else. If radio spectrum usage rights did exist, they were not state or private property but communally held; any entrepreneur or radio enthusiast who could afford the equipment was entitled to make use of the radio spectrum as he or she liked. If we were to characterize the property regime in operation it would have to be 'open-access commons' but we should recognize this for the imposition that it is; it probably did not occur to contemporaries to conceptualize the matter in terms of property at all. Though it would clearly be wrong to minimize the significance of their legal evolution across the intervening decades, in an important sense the radio spectrum usage rights which the UK government sold in 2000 were first claimed as state property—and indeed were first constituted as 'property objects' which could be possessed and transferred—in the Wireless Telegraphy Act of 1904.

This chapter is not about radio spectrum usage rights in twentieth-century England, but jurisdictional rights in the tenth and eleventh centuries, for which they provide a potentially helpful analogy. Jurisdiction is a notoriously difficult issue in this period of English legal history. 'Jurisdiction' itself can be a malleable term—potentially an unhelpfully vague one—but this is not the source of the difficulty here, as within the literature on this topic the term is (at least some of the time) used with more precision than in ordinary usage. The key distinction is between 'fiscal' and 'jurisdictional' legal privileges. A fiscal privilege is a right to receive the revenues (fines and goods forfeitures) associated with a particular offence or set of offences: it is a financial right only. A jurisdictional privilege, by contrast, entitles the holder not only to receive certain legal revenues but also to perform the legal functions associated with those revenues: to hold their own private courts and to enforce the law through their own agents. Jurisdiction might thus be defined as 'the power of legal administration' (Murray 2010: 915); it could be granted over a specific set of offences, and glossed as 'power to inflict these punishments, power to use these modes of procedure' (Pollock and Maitland 1898: i.695). This is the sense in which 'jurisdiction' is employed in this chapter, but while definitions framed in terms of 'power' capture something of what has been at stake in the literature—jurisdiction as emblematic of the state's sovereignty—the waters are less likely to become muddied if we stick with the language of rights. 'Jurisdictional rights' might accurately, if inelegantly, be rendered 'legal-function-performance rights'.[1]

The historiographical controversy about jurisdictional rights in the tenth and eleventh centuries is rooted in the evidence base. Were we to focus on the later medieval period—from, say, the late twelfth century—things would be simpler. In this later period, it is clear that jurisdictional rights were bound up with landed property. To extend the conventional metaphor, a standard part of the bundle of rights that constituted aristocratic property in land was a sub-bundle of legal privileges, which (though its precise contents varied) always included a number of jurisdictional 'sticks'. These jurisdictional rights had symbolic as well as economic significance (Crouch 2011: chs. 9–10). The right to hold a manorial court where peasants were fined for minor infractions, for example, was a standard prerogative of lordship over land: it entitled those who held it not just to receive legal revenues but to perform a role that forcefully asserted their status as lords. The right to maintain a private gallows and perform executions, by contrast, was a much rarer and more exalted privilege that demonstrated its holder was a figure close in status to the king within his own lands, with authority extending even to matters of life and death. Between these poles lords might exercise or claim a wide range of privileges, which were often explicitly jurisdictional in that they were framed as rights to perform functions associated with royal officials: the right to carry out the procedure known as 'view of frankpledge' instead of the sheriff, for instance; the right to execute royal writs instead of the sheriff; or the right to employ one's own official to perform the duties of the coroner. (For overviews of jurisdictional privileges in this later period, see Pollock and Maitland 1898: ch. 3.5; Sutherland 1963: ch. 1.) Jurisdictional rights might thus be seen both as part of various distinctively aristocratic bundles of property rights in land, and—because they could be separated from these bundles and disputed individually—as a form of property in themselves. Before the late twelfth century, however, the evidence is hazier. It is apparent that by about 1100 lords routinely held their own courts, and had been doing so for some time (Hn 9:4), but before the Norman conquest of 1066 evidence for aristocratic possession of jurisdictional rights of any sort is extremely vague. There can be no doubt that 'fiscal' legal privileges—rights to receive legal revenues—were commonplace, but pre-conquest sources never explicitly attribute rights to perform legal functions to lords, nor do they ever explicitly deny them such rights (Hudson 2012: 60–2).

[1] Because 'jurisdictional' rights include the rights to perform legal functions beyond judgement, they form a more capacious category than 'judicial' rights, a term sometimes also employed in contradistinction to 'fiscal' rights in the literature (where court-holding rights often serve as the focus of analysis).

The bundle of rights that constituted aristocratic landed property in the late Anglo-Saxon period thus included a sub-bundle of legal privileges, as it would continue to do after 1066, but our sources never make clear whether this sub-bundle included 'jurisdictional' sticks. This ambiguity has allowed for a long-running debate, in which historical opinion has been divided between what amount to two basic interpretations. For most of the twentieth century the mainstream view was that espoused by Frederic William Maitland. The following quotation encapsulates the logic of his case:

> As a general rule, the person in whose name the court is held, be he king or lord, gets the profits of the court. No one in the middle ages does justice for nothing, and in the ninth century the days when national officers would be paid by salary were far distant. ... When [a church held the right to receive legal revenues from an entire hundred] ... it was almost of necessity the lord of the court as well as the lord of the land. Why should the sheriff hold that court, why should he appoint a bailiff for that hundred, if never thereout could he get one penny for his own or for the king's use? (Maitland 1897: 277)

Maitland thus reasoned that because the Anglo-Saxon evidence clearly shows lords were entitled to legal revenues it is only logical to infer that they were entitled to perform legal functions as well. After all, once a king had alienated his rights to revenues from a particular area, his local officials would have no incentive to perform the functions associated with those revenues in that area: 'no one in the middle ages does justice for nothing'. Those functions would fall to lords by default, and so we must imagine Anglo-Saxon lords holding what are sometimes termed 'jurisdictional immunities'[2] in much the same mould as their thirteenth century successors, complete with private courts and private gallows. This interpretation was part of a broader narrative emphasizing the decline of the Anglo-Saxon kingdom through its gradual feudalization. Maitland believed that kings had routinely granted rights of 'low' justice to lords throughout the eighth, ninth, and tenth centuries but understood the eleventh as the point at which this feudalization process reached its apogee, with Cnut (1016–35) and Edward the Confessor

[2] On the notion of the 'immunity' in modern scholarship on early medieval law, see Rosenwein (1999), Murray (2010). Its roots are in the use of the term *immunitas* in Frankish charters. In a Merovingian context Murray defines it as 'an institution of public law that, like its Roman predecessor, conferred on a beneficiary exemption from state obligations of various kinds' (915); this is a sensibly capacious definition which avoids the term's more specific and unhelpful conceptual baggage. Anglo-Saxon legal privileges rarely make explicit use of the language of immunity and I therefore try to avoid employing it other than when referring to 'immunity clauses' in charters, as this is the accepted term for those passages where the transferred land's future exemption from royal obligations is defined. It should be noted that, though the phraseology rarely makes this explicit, the point of exempting land from royal exactions was almost invariably to transfer the right to receive those exactions to the beneficiary, not to free its inhabitants from unwelcome burdens.

(1042–66)—'the latter with reckless liberality'—responsible for the alienation of 'high' jurisdiction as well. As Maitland put it, 'the result is that the well-endowed immunist of St Edward's day has jurisdiction as high as that which any palatine earl of after ages enjoyed. No crime, except possibly some direct attack upon the king's person, property or retainers, was too high for him' (1897: 282–3).

The alternative interpretation was dominant before Maitland wrote (Adams 1876) but was generally discredited until the 1990s (in spite of Goebel 1937: ch. 6), when it was revived by Patrick Wormald ([1995] 1999). It has been the mainstream view ever since. The basic argument here is even simpler. Our Anglo-Saxon evidence cannot show a single lord holding the exclusive right to perform legal functions on his land; rather than trying to reason our way around this fact, as Maitland did, we should respect what the sources are telling us: aristocratic legal privileges in this period may have been widespread, but they were fiscal rather than jurisdictional, and always had been. As Stephen Baxter put it, summarizing the modern consensus view, before 1066 privileged English lords 'were probably empowered to collect the profits of justice administered through royal courts in the presence of royal officials' (2009: 417). The historiographical context for this is a broader positive reassessment of the Anglo-Saxon kingdom. In a period when the feudalization of Carolingian society brought the West Frankish kingdom to the point of disintegration, English kings were strong enough to resist such centrifugal pressures; their ability to prevent any alienation of jurisdictional rights to lords might be read as a key indicator of the more general vitality of royal government. To quote Wormald:

> One should no longer be satisfied with a simple equation of governmental health and lack of immunities. But even if immunities were still to be seen as germs of decline in the king's capacity to fulfil his judicial responsibilities, the Anglo-Saxon picture would give us no grounds for finding a further key to the collapse of 1066 in the debilitation of royal justice. Its profits may have been alienated, but the signs are that its servants were intrusive and its arenas monopolised ([1995] 1999: 332).

The master narrative behind this reading, it should be noted, is the same as that underlying the one it opposes. Both explain later medieval aristocrats' possession of jurisdictional rights as the result of a process of feudalization in which rights that had previously been the exclusive property of the state were in effect privatized. The debate is about chronology: whereas Maitland saw this as a prolonged process which culminated in the last fifty years of the Anglo-Saxon period, for Wormald it only began after 1066.

This chapter takes a different approach to the problem, aligning with and informed by Alice Taylor's recent reappraisal of the mechanisms of enforcement implied by early Scottish, Welsh, and Anglo-Saxon legislation (Taylor 2013, 2014). It picks up a lead given by Helen Cam (1957: 427–33) in questioning whether kings 'actually possess[ed] the powers and duties which, it seems, they are charged with relinquishing' (1957: 429), and argues for a third interpretation, roughly analogous to the example of radio spectrum usage rights with which it began. That is, the absence of explicit evidence for aristocratic possession of jurisdictional rights before the Norman conquest is essentially equivalent to the absence of licences permitting use of the radio spectrum before the Wireless Telegraphy Act of 1904: it should be taken as a sign that jurisdictional rights did not exist as things to be possessed or transferred. Just as any radio enthusiast could legitimately attempt to make use of the airwaves in the late nineteenth century, in the tenth century any Anglo-Saxon free man could legitimately attempt to perform, or to participate in the collective performance of, almost any significant legal function. The absence of aristocratic jurisdictional rights does not, then, testify to the presence of an unbroken royal monopoly of jurisdictional rights. Rather, it reflects the fact that nobody in this society, not even the king, made any claim that would exclude other free male adults from performing legal functions.[3] Rights to perform legal functions were neither royal ('state') nor aristocratic ('private') property; if they were property at all they were the collective property of the free community. But even this may be to over-theorize a simpler reality: it is probably more accurate to say that 'jurisdiction' did not exist in a meaningful sense. People would have usually have been able to predict which of their neighbours would be involved in the performance of legal functions locally, of course, and they may have been able to articulate 'rules of thumb' as a guide to patterns of behaviour, but at this point in the Middle Ages their expectations would not have been informed by a legalistic discourse which assigned exclusive legal-function-performance rights to specific figures.

In a medieval historiographical context, this is significant because it allows us to escape the feudalization narrative that has shaped both sides of the debate as it stands. Instead of explaining the complex jurisdictional landscape of the thirteenth century as the result of a period in which an

[3] The extent to which women, children, and the unfree were excluded from the performance of legal functions is hazy. We know that free women could participate in collective oaths, at least in support of a female principal (Hough 1997: 6–7), but it is unclear whether they were routinely involved in assembly judgements; it is not entirely implausible that some were (especially widows who were heads of their own households) but we cannot know. Children and the unfree are very unlikely to have been. It is improbable that any of these figures were expected to participate in collective enforcement expeditions against thieves and defiant wrongdoers, but this is not to say it would have been illegitimate for a woman, child, or slave to kill a proven thief, especially if they caught him red-handed. This would almost certainly have been a commendable act.

early medieval royal jurisdictional monopoly was unevenly privatized, we can think about it as the product of an era in which jurisdictional rights emerged as a form of property. Such a process need not have affected the balance of power between the king and the aristocracy at all: historians would no longer be faced with the problem of trying to locate a period of royal weakness—an episode of recklessly liberal feudalization—in their long-term narratives. Indeed, as we shall see, one way of understanding the emergence and proliferation of jurisdictional rights is as a symptom of administrative changes which increased royal officials' capacity to intervene beyond the boundaries of the king's own landed property. In the present context, I hope, this will provide an interesting case study, which might be taken as either the emergence of a new form of property (i.e. jurisdictional rights) or as the introduction of a new type of stick into the bundle of rights that constituted aristocratic landed property. The focus of the analysis in this chapter is the tenth and eleventh centuries: it begins by establishing the absence of jurisdictional rights in the tenth, then makes an argument for locating the start of the process by which they emerged in the early eleventh century. The twelfth century—the period in which jurisdictional rights emerge firmly in our evidence—is thus left to be considered at another time.

THE ABSENCE OF JURISDICTION IN THE TENTH CENTURY

The first thing to establish is that jurisdictional rights did not exist as a form of property in the tenth century. That is to say, this was a legal environment in which nobody possessed exclusive rights to perform particular legal functions, and this is why our evidence does not show kings and lords transferring these rights to one another or disputing their ownership. The point is not that nobody had the right to perform legal functions but that virtually everybody did. A good modern analogy might be the right to pick up litter. Everybody has this right. To the extent that there is a problem with this situation it is that too few people are public-spirited enough to exercise it of their own accord. Because of this local communities sometimes mobilize themselves for collective litter-picking efforts following exhortations from their more active members, but most of the time litter either remains undisturbed or people have to be incentivized to pick it up (either through paid employment or as an alternative to more unpalatable forms of punishment). For the state, or anyone else, to claim an exclusive right to pick up litter in a given area, such that anyone else who picked up litter there would be committing an offence, would be absurd. This is why litter-picking rights do not exist as a form of property: they cannot become valuable commodities in the way that fishing, grazing, or mining rights can. Tenth-century Anglo-Saxon laws suggest a similar situation applied for the performance of legal functions: while everyone had the right to perform legal functions, nobody owned legal-function-performance (i.e. jurisdictional) rights, and this was because the performance of legal functions was understood to be more of a burden than a privilege.

This situation is most readily apparent if we consider the laws' assumptions about enforcement. Several tenth-century laws discuss situations in which wrongdoers needed to be confronted in force, and either killed on the spot or made to find sureties to guarantee their compliance. The solution the laws imagine is communal expeditions: all the men of an area gather together and set out to find the wrongdoer. This passage from a law of King Æthelstan (924–39) is the most detailed:

> If, however, he [a man who has failed to attend an assembly three times and therefore owes a fine] will not do justice nor pay the fine for disobedience, the most senior men are to ride thither, all who belong to the fortification [*burh*], and take all that he owns and put him under surety. If, however, anyone will not ride with his fellows, he is to pay the fine for disobedience to the king. And it is to be announced in the assembly that everyone is to be at peace with everything with which the king will be at peace, and to refrain from theft on pain of losing his life and all that he owns. And he who will not cease for these penalties—the most senior men are to ride thither, all who belong to the fortification, and take all that he owns. The king is to succeed to half, to half the men who are on that expedition. And they are to put him under surety. If he knows no-one to stand surety for him, they are to take him prisoner. If he will not permit it, he is to be killed, unless he escapes. If anyone wishes to avenge him or carry on a feud against any of them, he is to be at enmity with the king and all the king's friends (II As 20:3–20:7).

The basic assumption here is that enforcement expeditions against wrongdoers are unwelcome and potentially dangerous communal duties. In addition to the time and effort involved there is the possibility of violence, with both its obvious immediate risks and longer-term anxieties about vengeance. The laws assert that everyone has a theoretical duty to participate in these expeditions, but they also recognize that in reality they may be reluctant to do so, hence the share of the proceeds used to reward those who participate and the threat of punishment for those who refuse.

An important consideration for the present argument is the identity of those expected to lead these collective expeditions. It is significant that they are the most senior local men (*yldestan men*) of the locality rather than royal officials, or 'reeves'. ('Reeve' is the standard rendering of *gerefa*, the most common contemporary term for an official tasked with exercising a superior's rights on his behalf; see Stafford 2014.) In laws from the second half of the tenth century the collective expected to mount these expeditions shifts from the men of the *burh* (a military and commercial centre)[4] to the hundred, a term that could equally be used to refer to a local district (a subdivision of a county), the men who lived in it, and the four-weekly assembly in which they resolved their legal business (see Molyneaux 2015: 153–4). In these laws (Hu 2, quoted below, p. 137; IV Eg 8:1) the figure expected to lead communal enforcement expeditions is referred to as the hundredman (*hundredes man*) or hundred *ealdor* (a generic term for someone in a position of authority). This figure has often been taken to be a royal reeve by another name but there is no solid basis for this. In fact, the first text to explain the hundredman's identity in any detail, the early twelfth-century legal treatise known as *Leges Henrici Primi*, suggests exactly the opposite: 'one of the better men [*unus de melioribus*] shall preside over the whole hundred and be known as the alderman' (Hn 8:1a; Lambert 2017: 243–50). That is to say, the expectation seems to have been that prominent local men be in charge of enforcement expeditions, not royal officials (unless we stretch the meaning of that term so far that it ceases to be useful). There is certainly no reason to suppose, at least on the basis of tenth-century evidence, that royal agents claimed an exclusive right to gather bands of armed men and confront, or even kill, those who had committed offences.

Our relatively detailed evidence for the theory of collective enforcement expeditions reflects tenth-century legislators' continuing desire to promote participation in them, which presumably stemmed from concern about communal apathy. The laws' discussion of enforcement in other contexts is briefer but underpinned by the same assumptions. This is most striking in discussions of the execution of thieves. It was every man's right to kill a thief he caught in the act. Indeed, it was his duty at least to attempt to capture any such thief and, if he was unwilling to execute him personally, to hand him over to someone who would. Men who spared thieves in such circumstances were threatened with punishment (II As 1–1:1), whereas those who did their violent duty with zeal could be thought worthy of financial reward (VI As 7). Finally, it is worth emphasizing that Anglo-Saxon laws consistently recognize the legitimacy of vengeance against those who refuse to pay the compensation that they owe, at least in cases of homicide. Lawmakers were generally much more concerned about theft than violence so this is not a prominent theme, but we occasionally find laws stating that killers must either pay compensation with the help of their kinsmen or 'bear the feud'

[4] The word *burh* means 'fortification' and reflects their original military role, but they are also discussed as centres of commerce and many of them evolved into market towns. *Burh* is sometimes rendered 'town', but the point at which *burh*s acquired sufficient urban features to warrant this translation is uncertain. See Holt (2010).

(II Em 1; I Cn 5:2b): that is, accept that their intransigence meant their opponents could legitimately attempt violent action against them. This, clearly, was not a world in which the right to enforce the law was restricted to a limited group of royal agents and privileged lords. Law-enforcement was not an exalted privilege but rather a potentially onerous duty, something that offended families or communities were expected to organize for themselves (see Taylor 2013, 2014).

A similar case can be made for processes of judgement. A dominant strand in the literature looks at judgement in institutional terms. The question that has preoccupied historians is whether the assemblies in which judgements were made were 'royal courts' or 'private courts', and it has generally been assumed that the way to distinguish between the two is to identify the figure who presided; an assembly in which a royal reeve is found presiding is thus interpreted as a royal court, whereas if a lord (or his reeve) were to be detected in this role, the assembly would be classified as a private court. Maitland (1897: 277; see above, p. 118), as we have already noted, proceeded from the assumption that assemblies had to be 'held' by an authority figure: if a royal agent such as a sheriff had no incentive to perform this role, it would fall by default to whichever lord had the right to receive local legal revenues. This same logic underpins Wormald's case. His assertion that the servants of royal justice were 'intrusive' and its arenas 'monopolised' ([1995] 1999: 332; see above, p. 119) was not, in fact, the conclusion of an analysis of the legal role of royal agents. Rather, it flowed from his (wholly justified) argument that the absence of evidence for aristocratic possession of jurisdictional rights ought to be taken seriously: his finding that lords did not 'hold' their own assemblies was the key justification for his contention that royal agents monopolized this role. The debate thus operates within a binary interpretative framework that allows only for 'royal courts' and 'private courts'. One significant problem with this is that the person the laws envisage presiding in hundred assemblies was the hundredman who, as has been noted, seems to have been neither a royal agent nor a privileged lord but 'one of the better men' of the hundred. The binary model simply cannot accommodate this.

The problem with the established approach is more fundamental than this, however. The basic assumption underlying it is that assemblies were administrative institutions whose judgements were controlled by the figures who presided in them. (This is subtly implied in the scholarly language conventionally used to describe them: whereas a community might 'assemble' in an 'assembly' for its own purposes, a 'court' is something that convenes around a powerful figure who 'holds' it.) This assumption cannot withstand close scrutiny. Theoretically at least, the right to contribute to formal legal decision-making was widely dispersed. There are two categories of decision to consider. On the one hand, there were decisions about guilt and innocence, which—if disputed—had to be resolved by means of formal proof procedures: various forms of collective oath and ordeal. On the other hand, there were matters of technical legal interpretation: decisions about which type of proof was required, and what consequences should follow after a defendant either succeeded or failed in his proof.

The first of these types of decision, proof itself, is easily dealt with. The standard form of proof in Anglo-Saxon law, to which all free men were meant to be entitled providing they were of good reputation, was collective oath (see Hudson 2012: 81–4). To prove themselves innocent of a charge, defendants needed to find a number of other people—eleven may have been a customary figure—willing to swear on their behalf. The basic theory seems to have been that any free person was entitled to participate in a collective oath. In some circumstances, we do find more specific requirements: it might be demanded that one or more of the oath-helpers be of noble rank, for instance, or hold a certain amount of land (this way of assigning value to oaths could imply that oath-helpers were normally expected to be heads of landholding households). There is nothing, however, to suggest that in normal circumstances the presiding figure in an assembly had control over the outcome of decisions about proof by virtue of his institutional position. This is not, of course, to imply that the system was invulnerable to manipulation by the powerful. In fact, one of the most detailed accounts of an Anglo-Saxon legal case to survive, the document known as the Fonthill Letter, at one point involves an ealdorman (a high-ranking magnate) agreeing to help a client win a land dispute by mobilizing men to make the supporting oaths he required (Brooks 2009). The decisiveness of this intervention from on high is apparent from the high price the ealdorman exacted for it: the deal was that he would receive title to the disputed land and then lease it back to his client for the rest of his life. The powerful could influence decisions about guilt and innocence, but they did so through networks of patronage rather than by occupying the position of assembly president.

Technical decisions about legal interpretation are more complex. As Wormald pointed out in the 1980s, the vast majority of Anglo-Saxon dispute records contain verbs of judgement in the plural and this permits the inference that judgement was formally undertaken collectively by assemblies ([1986] 1999).[5] This state of affairs was not to change until the second half of

[5] Both this fact and its problematic implications for the concept of jurisdiction were explicitly noted by Maitland (1897: 277–8): 'We must once more remember that even in the days of full grown feudalism the right to hold a court was after all rather a fiscal than a jurisdictional right. We call it jurisdictional, but still, at least normally, the lord was, neither in his own person, nor yet in the person of his steward, the judge of the court. His right was not in strictness a right *ius dicendi*, for the suitors made the judgement.'

the twelfth century (Brand 1990). This fits well with legal passages such as the following:

> And he who in an assembly tries to protect either himself or one of his men by bringing a counter-charge shall have wasted his words, and shall meet the charge brought by his opponent in such a way as seems right to the hundred (II Cn 27).

It is the assembly—the hundred in this context—which collectively rules on procedural issues such as how many oath-helpers a defendant needs to deny a charge. However, the idea was not that assemblies would simply make up whatever procedural rules seemed just for every case; the point of legislation was to instruct assemblies on the judgements appropriate to various specific circumstances. Kings appear to have expected both royal reeves and 'landed' (*gelandod*) thegns—lords who had been granted royal land rights and the legal revenues that went with them—to attend their local assemblies and guide them on the proper application of the law. They threaten these figures with punishment for failing in this duty, for guiding their assemblies to unjust judgements through either ignorance or self-interest (IV As 7; V As 1:3–1:4; VI As 11). This suggests that both royal agents and privileged lords were expected to be able to influence technical legal judgements, but it does not follow that they had absolute authority over them in the way that a modern judge has the authority to rule on issues of legal interpretation within his or her own court (see Lambert 2017: 136–47).

This passage from Asser's *Life of King Alfred* (893) draws out some of the ambivalences that have made it difficult to establish exactly where authority lay on issues of legal interpretation:

> King Alfred used to sit at judicial hearings for the benefit both of his nobles and of the common people, since they frequently disagreed violently among themselves at assemblies of ealdormen or reeves, to the point where virtually none of them could agree that any judgement reached by the ealdormen or reeves in question was just (Stevenson 1904: ch. 106; Keynes and Lapidge 1983: 109).

The assumption here that assemblies in some sense belonged to ealdormen and reeves, who were responsible for their judgements, has been highly influential. It led Wormald to suspect the widespread rhetoric of collective judgement in other sources obscured a situation in which assembly presidents exercised substantial control ([1986] 1999: 306). It should be noted, however, that the situation described here is far from one in which royal officials enjoy absolute authority over assembly judgements. On the contrary, it is one in which their attempts to shape such judgements have been rejected by assemblies, necessitating personal appeals to the king.

Crucially, the issue the text identifies here is not what we might expect—that local assemblies are disobediently rejecting the king's authority as mediated through his officials—but the inadequacy of these local figures. This is apparent from Alfred's solution to the problem: a programme of education for reeves, ealdormen, and privileged lords. He was trying to bring about a situation in which these figures' wisdom was such that assemblies would accept their guidance. In spite of the superficial attribution of control over assemblies and judgements to ealdormen and reeves (which perhaps reflects the ideological ambitions of Alfred's immediate circle), a key assumption underlying this story is that assemblies had considerable autonomy on matters of legal interpretation. Reeves and privileged lords were expected to contribute to their decision-making processes, and if they were sufficiently well educated they would be in a good position to persuade assemblies to defer to their authority, but it was a matter of persuasion in the context of collective decision-making and they did not always prevail.

It seems, then, that decisions about legal interpretation were formally collective decisions, to which all members of an assembly could theoretically contribute. Again, it is important to emphasize that this is not to say assemblies were democratic. Being at liberty to speak up in a debate is not the same thing as having a realistic expectation of affecting its outcome. It is plausible that in practice such collective decision-making was dominated by men of wealth and status. The important point in the present context is that there is little reason to think that occupation of any particular office conveyed full control over an assembly's technical legal decisions. Rather, we should envisage an environment in which numerous factors affected an individual's ability to influence such decisions: for instance, gender, age, status, wealth, local reputation and connections, rhetorical ability, and indeed the specifics of the legal issue in question.[6] Being a reeve or an assembly president may have given additional weight to an individual's views, but it was one factor among many. It may well have been possible for great magnates such as bishops and ealdormen to descend upon hundred assemblies with their retainers and overawe the locals, resolving procedural quandaries (such as which party in a land dispute has the right to prove his case through a collective oath) in ways that favoured their clients' interests. But their ability to do so would have depended primarily on their local political

[6] Procedure in land cases appears to have been much less clear-cut than in those involving accusations of wrongdoing, and is thus likely to have been much more open to debate. In the latter, it is clear that the accused had to respond to the accusation with a form of proof, usually an oath, whereas in land disputes the decision as to which party had the right to swear an oath (and thus usually win the case) seems to have rested on a judgement of their claims' relative merits. See Hudson (2012: 70).

influence—on the crudest level, the rewards they could offer to supporters and the trouble they could cause for opponents—not on any legalistic framework of rules and categories that gave holders of particular offices the authority to impose legal interpretations on assemblies.

The available evidence again suggests the decision-making processes that underpinned final judgements—both those of formal proof and those relating to legal interpretation—were theoretically open to everyone who attended assemblies. It is not immediately apparent in our (primarily tenth-century) sources that participation in these processes was regarded as an onerous duty in the way that enforcement so evidently was. However, there are hints in that direction. Post-conquest evidence suggests that collective participation in hundredal judgements came to be the preserve of a richer stratum of the free peasantry, able to bear the burdens it imposed. The early twelfth-century treatise known as *Leges Henrici Primi*, most notably, exempts the poor from the duty seemingly on the logic that those involved needed to be able to afford the fines for defective judgement that might arise (Hn 29–19:1b).[7] While it is unclear how this relates to pre-conquest realities, one possible reading of the laws' insistence that assemblies at all levels meet at specified intervals (II Ew 8; Hu 1; III Eg 5; II Cn 17–18) is as a sign that established practices could be rather more apathetic.[8] As to matters of formal proof, it is possible that participating in collective oaths carried temporal as well as spiritual risks; in addition to the prospect of divine retribution, men who could be shown to have knowingly sworn false oaths would, at least in the ideal legal world imagined by the laws, suffer grave procedural

[7] The meaning of Domesday Book's (1086) statement that in the manor of Fersfield (Norfolk) it was only those men with more than 30 acres whose sake and soke lay 'in the hundred' (*Domesday Book* ii. 130v) is obscure, but it is possible it refers to a property qualification for participation in hundredal judgements and, if that is so, it is the earliest reference to such a situation of which I am aware. The late twelfth-century chronicle of Ramsey abbey refers to the 'assembly-worthy' (*motweorþ*) men of the hundred-and-a-half of Clacklose when reproducing a supposedly Anglo-Saxon document, but whether this permits us to push a concept of 'assembly-worthiness' back into the pre-conquest period is debatable (Macray 1886: 162). I am grateful to Richard Purkiss for drawing my attention to these passages.

[8] The rhetoric of the Anglo-Saxon laws is inclusive—the obligation to attend local assemblies is presented as universal (e.g. Hu 1)—and the only threats of punishment relating to judgement in tenth-century laws are directed at reeves and privileged lords (e.g. V As 1:3–1:4), either for neglecting their duty to guide assemblies appropriately or for attempting to do so unjustly. The piece of Anglo-Saxon evidence that bears most directly on the question of whether there were formalized barriers preventing poor freemen from participating in tenth-century communal legal practice is the statement that only those with property worth more than 30 pence were expected to pay the annual dues of the London 'peace-guild' (VI As 2). It is not clear that this meant the poor were exempted from participation in the guild's activities, however. Indeed, the passage may imply nothing more than that only the property-owning members of the guild needed to contribute to its collective insurance scheme, the main purpose of which was to compensate the owners of stolen property.

disadvantages for the rest of their lives (I Ew 3; II As 26; I Atr 1:1–1:4; II Cn 30–30:3).[9]

The tenth-century evidence, and indeed much of what comes after, thus suggests a legal environment in which the performance of functions relating to both judicial decision-making and law enforcement was theoretically open to all. It gives us little reason to suppose royal agents, privileged lords or anyone else wished to assume exclusive responsibility for these legal functions. Indeed, the overwhelming impression is that this was a society in which the performance of legal functions was not an exalted privilege or royal prerogative, but a communal duty. The symbolic significance of assuming responsibility for these functions is thus most likely to have been linked to a sense of public-spiritedness: a willingness to undertake burdensome and even dangerous tasks for the benefit of all. (Though we should perhaps also suspect that enthusiastic virtue on this front could be resented as self-satisfied busy-bodying by the more cynical and apathetic.) In practice, the people who took the lead in such matters would usually have been the local elite, those referred to as the 'most senior men' in Æthelstan's laws, their active involvement—perhaps rooted in a sense of *noblesse oblige* and very probably framed as such—a way of demonstrating their status as men of influence. But that is not to say that others were unable either to speak up in judicial debates or to volunteer for enforcement expeditions, still less that they were prohibited from doing so by formalized rules. Exclusive legal-function-performance rights (i.e. jurisdictional rights) simply would not make sense as a form or property in this environment. Yet over the eleventh and twelfth centuries these rights came into existence. Why should this have been?

ECONOMICS: ABUNDANCE TO SCARCITY

One possible way of explaining this is essentially economic. We need to begin by characterizing jurisdiction in economic terms: as the exclusive right to exploit a particular type of resource within a given area. To do this, we need to adopt a term to denote the resource in question: 'performable legal functions' will have to do. From this perspective, the tenth century was a time of abundance. As we have seen, our evidence suggests that there were plenty of

[9] The existence of a rather obscure form of collective oath in which a group of potential oath-helpers is selected in advance, the defendant then being required to persuade a specified proportion of them to swear in his support (IV Atr 7:3; II Cn 22–22:1, 65; Hn 31:8a, 64:9a; Leis Wl 14:1; 14:3, 15–15:1) could perhaps be taken as a sign of general reluctance to become involved in proof procedures. Rather than being given the opportunity to disclaim responsibility for a difficult decision by avoiding participation, this procedure compelled a selected group of men to accept the task of deciding the accused's guilt or innocence, rather like a jury.

performable legal functions available and relatively few people who wanted to perform them, hence the threats, inducements, and exhortations we find in the laws. Supply so far exceeded demand that there was no call for the establishment of a property regime to allocate rights relating to the exploitation of this resource. A possible explanation for the emergence of jurisdiction as a form of property in the eleventh and twelfth centuries would be that this period saw a transition from abundance to scarcity. Changes took place such that demand for 'performable legal functions' increased and came to exceed supply: more people now wanted to perform legal functions than there were legal functions available to perform. Competition for this increasingly scarce and valued resource necessitated the establishment of a property regime to allocate rights over it and resolve conflicts peacefully. Our early eleventh-century evidence is consistent with this essentially economic explanation for the emergence of jurisdictional rights. It implies this was a period which saw a sudden increase in competition for legal revenues, and offers strong hints that this phenomenon was intimately bound up with the performance of associated legal functions.

First, let us consider the evidence for a sudden increase in competition for legal revenues. Up to the late tenth century both the key source-types for aristocratic legal privilege—the laws themselves and the charters in which kings transferred their property rights to lords—imply the existence of a fundamentally very simple set of arrangements for the division of legal revenues between kings and privileged lords. A typical royal charter would define the bundle of rights it conveyed to the beneficiary in a brief 'immunity clause' such as this one from 958: 'this land is to be free from all tribute, great and small, and from royal service, except the construction of bridges, the building of fortifications and military expeditions' (S 677; translated in Whitelock 1979: no. 109). If we take this literally (which we should) it implies that when kings transferred their rights over land to favoured aristocrats, they routinely granted all of their rights except the three that are explicitly reserved, known in the literature as the 'common burdens'. That is, kings wished to keep the right to call upon their people for military purposes, either as soldiers or as labourers on military infrastructure projects, but they were happy to transfer their non-military rights to aristocratic recipients. Although this is not made explicit in most charters, this suggests that all legal fines and forfeitures relating to non-military forms of wrongdoing were included in royal grants as a matter of course.

Crucially, in sources up to the tenth century there is very little to indicate that these rights to receive legal revenues were contentious. When legal revenues are mentioned in charters it is always to confirm that they are part of the bundle of rights being transferred to the beneficiaries in perpetuity. No charter shows a king retaining legal revenues alongside their military dues, which suggests that they had no great interest in them. This contrasts with rights to receive annual renders of agricultural produce from the local population, which we can—albeit rarely—find kings excluding from the standard bundle (Wickham 2005: 321). The absence of any direct allusion to legal revenues in the vast majority of charters should thus be read as a sign of their contemporary insignificance, and those few charters in which they do appear understood as the work of draftsmen with an unusually low tolerance for ambiguity. This immunity clause from a charter of 770 is a particularly extreme example:

> Let everyone know that this land is free from every tribute, small or great, of public matters, and from all services whether from king or ealdorman except for the building of bridges or the necessary defences of fortresses against enemies. Also in every way we forbid in the name of God Almighty that if anyone in this aforenamed land steals anything from outside it, anything be paid to anyone except specifically 'price for price' [*pretium pro pretio*] as settlement, nothing outside as fine [*ad penam nihil foras*] (S 59; translated in Whitelock 1979: no. 74).

The first sentence is an early version of what would become the standard charter immunity clause (the very earliest charters make no effort to define the rights being conveyed); it is the second that is of interest here. It envisages a situation in which someone living within the land being transferred steals from someone living outside it. Tendentiously interpreted, the initial immunity clause could be taken to exempt the land in question from all external dues except the military ones mentioned, meaning that the thief in this scenario would not have to compensate his victim. The second sentence pre-empts this potential misreading. Theft victims must be compensated to the value of the stolen goods (i.e. 'price for price'); it is only the thief's punitive fine that is not to leave the beneficiary's land (i.e. the beneficiary alone has the right to claim it). This should be understood as pedantry: few contemporaries can possibly have regarded the idea that the king intended theft victims to be deprived of compensation as a viable interpretation. This charter and the small number of others which explicitly discuss legal revenues should thus be read as intricate, and therefore valuable, dissections of the standard bundle of rights that constituted lordship over land in this period.[10]

[10] I am deliberately skirting the question of whether this standard bundle of rights over land constituted ownership because the issue is contentious. It certainly involved the right to receive various services and renders from resident householders, but it is not clear that all such figures were understood as tenants and that their dues constituted rent (though this was certainly the case for some). See Faith (1997); Wickham (2005: 347–50). There is also an important distinction to be drawn between the bundle of rights conveyed to lords in written charters and the rights over land that lords might hold by other means. The former was

The laws suggest a similar situation. There are frequent references to punitive fines and forfeitures of various sorts being paid to lords and no explicit statements that any of them are reserved to the king alone before the eleventh century. The overall impression in the tenth century is of sloppiness. Generally, the laws are inconsistent and often rather imprecise in the way they discuss the destination of legal revenues. So, some laws state that fines are payable to the king, others that they are payable to the *landhlaford* (literally, 'land-lord') or to the lord who is 'worthy of the fine', but there is no underlying pattern to their choices of vocabulary.[11] The most plausible reading is that they are all referring to the same situation: fines and forfeitures belong to the relevant *landhlaford*, who was either the king himself or whichever figure had been granted his non-military rights where the offender lived. The laws' inconsistency and imprecision should be taken as a sign that this reality was well understood and uncontroversial. Rights to legal revenues were not a contentious issue that needed to be handled carefully; they were so securely part of the bundle of rights which conventionally pertained to the local *landhlaford* that the drafters of laws did not envisage the possibility of their being unbundled and claimed separately.

In the early eleventh century, however, we find significant changes which suggest certain legal revenues had been detached from this bundle and become a focus of contention in their own right. The most obvious evidential shift is the emergence of a new format of royal grant, the writ, with radically different conventions for the description of legal privilege. (See Sharpe 2003; Keynes 1980: 142–5; Harmer 1952; the old form of royal charter, known as the 'diploma', gradually died out across the eleventh century.) Whereas traditional charters defined the rights transferred to beneficiaries by first liberating their land in all-encompassing terms and then listing a handful of exceptions, the implication being that that any

known as 'book-land' (*bocland*), a charter being a 'book' (*boc*), and much ink has been spilled over how this differed from other forms of landholding. The most plausible interpretation, in my view, is that aristocratic landholding involved essentially the same bundle of rights however it was conveyed, the key distinction being that a grant by charter meant the recipient could enjoy that bundle in perpetuity, passing it on to his heirs, whereas other forms of grant would at some point revert to the grantor. This is set out in Lambert (2017: 126–7, 312–13); for an overview that surveys the range of interpretative options and provides references to the relevant literature, see Hudson (2012: ch. 5).

[11] The key terms used to identify recipients of fines are as follows. *Hlaford*: Hu 2:1, 3; III Eg 7:1; Duns 6:2–6:3; I Atr 1:5, 1:9; II Cn 25:1. *Landhlaford*: II As 10; VI As 1:1; II Eg 3:1;IV Eg 11; I Cn 8:2. *Landrica*: IV Atr 8:1; I Cn 8:2. Someone identified as 'worthy' of a punitive fine (*wites wyrðe*) or wergild forfeiture (*weres wyrðe*): I Atr 1:7; II Cn 30:3b, 30:6. Circumlocutions such as 'he to whom it is due': II As 1:5, 21; II Cn 24:1, 73a:1. The absence of any coherent pattern underlying vocabulary choices is argued in Baxter (2009: 405–6), with references to scholarship that takes the opposite line.

royal right not explicitly reserved had been granted, writs adopted the opposite approach. They listed by name the rights that the recipient was to enjoy, the principle being that a right was not conveyed unless it was explicitly included.

The most important term to occur in this context is 'sake and soke' (*sac* and *soc*), a label for a package of rights which entitled its holder to receive the vast majority of punitive fines. This was the most basic bundle of royal rights available in the eleventh century. All lords who held legal privileges seem necessarily to have possessed sake and soke over their own land; the less common rights appear in writs as additions to it. The pool of such possible additions was limited: *toll* and *team* (which have distinct meanings but always come as a pair) and *infangenþeof* are relatively common, whereas *hamsocn, mundbryce, forsteal,* and *flymenafyrmþ* occur relatively infrequently.[12] We will come to these terms' meanings later; the most important point at present is that they are precise. The emergence of writs and their associated vocabulary of legal privilege implies a legal environment in which lords needed documents that placed their rightful possession of a handful of named rights beyond dispute. This suggests that there was a realistic prospect of their enjoyment of these rights—those not safely bundled within sake and soke—being challenged individually. Legal revenues were now a source of conflict, and perhaps because of this it was no longer the case that all the fines and forfeitures from a given area belonged to a single figure, the *landhlaford*. The issue of who had the right to receive legal revenues was no longer simple and unimportant; it had become complicated and contentious.

Were we reliant solely on the emergence of a new genre of legal document for this impression we would have good reason to doubt it. An obvious alternative reading would be that the complexity and contentiousness implied by the precise legal terminology used in writs was a well-established feature of the legal landscape; it is simply that we are unable to see it before the emergence of this new form of evidence. However, we do not have to rely on writs alone; early eleventh-century laws convey a similar impression. Like writs, and markedly unlike their tenth-century predecessors, they include passages concerned to assert royal and ecclesiastical claims to legal revenue in unambiguous terms. Right at the beginning of the eleventh century, for instance, we find King Æthelred asserting his right to receive fines paid by all men who held land granted by charter (I Atr 1:14). This is the first time we hear of this royal right but on its own this is not particularly significant. This passage from the laws of his successor, Cnut, is much more striking:

[12] Harmer (1952: 73–82) provides a helpful review of authentic pre-conquest writ terminology.

> These are the rights which the king possesses over all men in Wessex, namely, *mundbryce* and *hamsocn*, *forsteal* and *flymenafyrmþ*, and the fine for neglecting military service, unless he desires to honour anyone further. If anyone commits a deed punishable by outlawry, the king [alone] is to have the power to grant him peace. And if he has land granted by charter [*bocland*] it is to be forfeited into the king's possession, no matter whose man he may be. And whoever feeds or harbours the fugitive is to pay five pounds to the king, unless he clear himself, that he did know him to be a fugitive. And in Mercia he possesses just what is written here above, over all men (II Cn 12–14).

Not only is this entirely unprecedented in the laws, it also directly contradicts the formal provisions of earlier charters, which explicitly convey all royal dues saving the three 'common burdens' to their beneficiaries.[13]

Moreover, early eleventh-century laws—most of which have been identified as the work of Archbishop Wulfstan II of York—are also noteworthy for the care with which they distinguish the rights of the king from the rights of the Church. This is particularly visible in cases where a church's protection (*ciricgrið*) was breached. Killing someone 'within church walls' carried the death penalty unless the king was willing to grant the killer his life back in return for his wergild (the compensation that would be payable for killing him). If the king allowed this, however, or if *ciricgrið* was violated in some other way (various offences short of homicide are mentioned, and it is possible that killings within ecclesiastical precincts but outside 'church walls' are implicitly included) the church itself was to be compensated in proportion to its rank and the severity of the offence (VIII Atr 1–5:2; I Cn 2–3:2; see also Grið 2; EGu 1; VI Atr 14). The detail of this scheme, which appears in several laws written by Archbishop Wulfstan for both Æthelred and Cnut, is extraordinary: no earlier laws show a similar concern to delineate the legal revenues pertaining to the king and the Church. Another of Wulfstan's passages may be relevant here too. It explains that previously secular laws had been established to uphold the just laws of God, with the revenues shared between Christ and the king, but rather obscurely complains that since King Edgar's day (959–75) these revenues had been separated, causing much woe in matters both spiritual and secular (VIII Atr 36–38). Like the passages in Cnut's laws defining the king's rights, and like the newly detailed language used in writs, these passages on ecclesiastical rights suggest that the distribution of legal revenues had become an issue of contention in the early eleventh century, and that interested parties were keen to protect their revenues by defining their established rights in precise terms.

[13] Dissatisfaction with this development could well underlie the Archbishop of Canterbury's complaint, recorded in a writ dated 1017–20, that 'he had charters of freedom in plenty, if only they were good for anything': S 985; Harmer (1952: no. 26).

Our evidence, then, suggests that the early eleventh century witnessed a sudden increase in competition for legal revenues, though given the limitations of the available source material the possibility that this reflects developments that began in the final decades of the tenth century should be taken seriously. Why should this have happened? There are several interconnecting factors to consider. First, there are good grounds for thinking that rights to receive legal revenues increased in value at roughly this point, making them more desirable and thus a resource worth competing for. It is possible that legal reforms initiated in the reign of King Edgar increased the value of fines and forfeitures in absolute terms. Specifically, it appears to have been at this point that the system of compulsory suretyship for punitive liabilities which evolved into what later centuries knew as 'frankpledge' first emerged (see Morris 1910: ch. 1; Hudson 2012: 170–1, 391–5). Whereas earlier laws (e.g. Ine 22; III Em 3; Hu 6) assume men will have sureties to guarantee their liabilities for compensation payments should they commit an offence and flee the area, or simply be unable to pay, in Edgar's and subsequent laws all men are ordered to find sureties to guarantee their punitive liabilities as well (III Eg 6–6:2; I Atr 1:7, 1:10–1:11; II Cn 30:6, 31–31:1; see Lambert 2017: 277–82).[14] How effectively this was implemented is uncertain, but in theory it should have made it much easier to extract punitive fines in full: if the offender fled, a lord or reeve could claim the entire fine from his sureties rather than having to make do with whatever remained of his moveable property. Perhaps even more importantly, we might speculate that the period of strong economic growth that began in the late tenth century, and the associated emergence of a network of market towns where farmers could reliably sell their produce, for the first time made it realistic to demand that legal fines be paid in cash rather than in kind, significantly reducing the practical obstacles to making use of the unpredictable windfalls legal privileges generated (Dyer 2002: chs. 1–2; Fleming 2010: chs. 9, 11; Holt 2010; Sawyer 2013: chs. 2, 5). Even if the value of the legal revenues themselves remained unchanged in absolute terms, this shift would have made them much easier to exploit effectively: the right to receive them would thus have become more valuable.

[14] The main purpose of Edgar's suretyship reforms appears to have been to force local communities to police themselves more effectively. His measures placed the burden of ensuring wrongdoers were caught and made to face punishment on the men who had stood surety for them, whose responsibility for an offender's punitive liabilities applied only if he was not produced for trial within a year (III Eg 6:2). A subsidiary aim may have been to isolate and thus firmly identify men regarded as untrustworthy by their peers: those believed responsible for various offences but who had not been caught in circumstances where their guilt was manifest. Inability to find sureties was theoretically punishable by death (III Eg 7–7:2; I Atr 4–4:2).

Additionally, and relatedly, this was a period which saw a marked increase in English kings' general capacity to extract revenue. The clearest indication of this is the emergence of a kingdom-wide system of taxation. From 1012 it seems that a tax known as the *heregeld* ('army-payment') was levied annually until it was temporarily abolished following political pressure in 1051 (Lawson 1984). The two decades before its establishment as an annual levy may have seen one-off taxes imposed to fund the tribute paid to Scandinavian raiders. The *Anglo-Saxon Chronicle* gives figures for such tributes in 991, 994, 1002, 1007, and 1009; we cannot be sure that a forerunner to the *heregeld* was involved in raising any one of these payments but it is plausible (Lawson 1984: 736, 752–6). The *heregeld* is significant because it shows that kings had both the political will and the administrative capacity to claim new and valuable forms of revenue in this period.[15] They imposed these new exactions not just on their own lands but across the kingdom as a whole, including lands that had been granted by charter and thus formally been freed from all royal dues. It is likely that two late tenth-century developments enabled them to do this: the emergence of a major Scandinavian military threat and the establishment of a new tier of royal officials known as sheriffs. The former provided motivation and justification for the imposition of new royal dues, while the latter were central to the administrative apparatus that enabled their extraction: a sheriff was a 'shire-reeve' (*scirgerefa*), a figure responsible for the practical implementation of the king's commands across an entire county (Morris 1927: ch. 2; Hudson 2012: 38–40; Molyneaux 2015: 179–82). Both these developments are germane to the emergence of conflict over legal revenues in early eleventh-century sources. It is not just that the right to receive legal revenues became more valuable, and thus a more likely focus of competition; we also see the emergence of a new and powerful species of royal official with a strong motivation to secure as much revenue as possible for the king. The emergence of evidence for conflict over legal revenues fits well in this wider context.

All these considerations, however, only serve to explain why legal revenues became a focus of conflict in the decades around the turn of the eleventh century. This is significant in itself—rights that had once been part of the standard bundle that constituted lordship over land were now being claimed individually—but its relevance to the emergence of jurisdictional rights is not immediately obvious. Why should conflict over legal *revenues* have anything to do with the emergence of rights to

[15] The *Anglo-Saxon Chronicle* figures for the sums raised by this tax are remarkably high but they gain a certain verisimilitude from their precision. This has led to debate about their accuracy. For a recent reassessment with references to the extensive earlier literature, see Harvey (2014: 211).

perform legal *functions* as a form of property? Tenth-century laws provide a clue here: they suggest the existence of a broad principle that those who invest effort in the performance of legal functions ought to share in any profits that arise from those functions. This comes up most frequently in the context of laws on communal enforcement expeditions, such as that of Æthelstan, quoted above (II As 20:3–20:7, see p. 122). This is a mid-tenth-century equivalent:

> If the need is urgent, the hundredman shall be informed ... and all are to go forth, where God may guide them, until they succeed in coming upon the thief. And justice is to be done on the thief as [King] Edmund decreed previously [i.e. he is to be killed]. And the value of the [stolen] livestock is to be paid to their owner, and the rest [of the thief's forfeited goods] is to be divided in two, half for the hundred and half for the lord. Except the men [i.e. slaves]—the lord is to succeed to the men (Hu 2–2:1).

It is only in this sort of communal context that tenth-century laws show any interest in specifying precisely who is entitled to legal revenues. The point, of course, is not to assert a royal claim to these revenues (indeed, there is no explicit royal claim at all here) but to provide a financial incentive to encourage participation in enforcement expeditions. Those who do their communal duty and risk their lives hunting down thieves are entitled to half the thief's moveable property, excluding any slaves.

One later law shows that this principle was applicable in a different, though still communal, context. The law code known as IV Edgar sets out an elaborate (perhaps rather over-ambitious) scheme designed to ensure that thieves will be unable to dispose of stolen property (IV Eg 3:1–11). This scheme relies fundamentally on communal vigilance: it requires people to monitor their neighbours' livestock so as to ensure that formal notice is given of any new acquisitions, including a declaration of the names of the men who witnessed their legitimate purchase. The idea is that if every acquisition of livestock must henceforth be accompanied by such a declaration about witnesses, men who have in fact stolen their new livestock will be forced to make false declarations. Should they then fall under suspicion these declarations could be investigated—the supposed witnesses located—and shown to be false, proving beyond doubt that the men who made them were knowingly involved in theft and thus removing all procedural obstacles to their immediate execution. At one point (IV Eg 8:1) the law states that livestock forfeited as a result of these procedures should be split between the hundred and the relevant lord. The most natural reading of this is that it recognized the fact that the existence of any profits relating to this scheme depended utterly on the diligent performance of the hundred's collective legal duty of neighbourhood surveillance.

This evidence suggests a hypothesis: when conflict arose over legal revenue, a potentially decisive way of asserting a moral claim to receive it was to perform legal functions associated with it. That is, at least some 'performable legal functions' were an important resource because performing them created a valuable claim to revenue. We might envisage sheriffs, under pressure to extract as much revenue as possible because of the Scandinavian threat, seizing responsibility for the most promising performable legal functions available, and thereby coming into conflict with the privileged lords who had previously been entitled to receive some or all of the associated revenue. The list of rights beyond sake and soke that appear in writs offers considerable support to this hypothesis. These are the specific revenues that were contentious in the early eleventh century and it is notable that they fall into two categories, each with features that would have made them promising targets for revenue-hungry sheriffs.

The first of these categories—revenues which could be argued to pertain personally to the king—is marginal to the present argument. The rights of *mundbryce, hamsocn*, and *forsteal*, relatively rare privileges in pre-conquest writs, can be understood as the king's right to compensation for breaches of the protection he extended to, respectively, favoured individuals, all people within houses, and all people travelling on major roads. Though our one relevant tenth-century law insists that offenders face execution, probably assuming their forfeited goods would be divided like those of slain thieves (II Em 6), in the eleventh century compensation is demanded instead (IV Atr 4–4:1; VIII Atr 5:1; I Cn 3:2; II Cn 62; Hn 12:2, 35:2, 79:4, 80:2) and explicitly reserved to the king alone (II Cn 12). It would, presumably, always have been possible to argue that those who breached royal protection owed the king (and only the king) compensation, but it is only in the eleventh century that this logic seems to have been exploited in a bid to maximize revenue. In the tenth century, the emphasis was firmly on vengeance, the king foregoing his potential compensation claim so as to deter potential offenders with the threat of a violent death. *Fyrdwite*, the fine for neglect of military service, which is also occasionally conveyed by writ is similar, in that charters' long-standing insistence that grants of land did not prejudice the king's right to extract military service would always have provided a solid argument for any royal representative seeking to collect this fine on the king's behalf. Such arguments may not have been made with any frequency in the tenth and earlier centuries, when legal revenues appear to have been of no great concern to kings, but they had always been possible. It seems likely that conditions in the decades around the millennium led to their increasingly rigorous exploitation.

The second category of contentious legal revenues is more pertinent in the present context: revenues associated with performable legal functions.

It must be stressed that most forms of legal revenue were *not* associated with legal functions that a sheriff could plausibly perform. It is likely that cases of wrongdoing generally came to the attention of local assemblies through accusations made by their victims; judgements would duly arise which could involve the payment of a punitive fine. Providing offenders complied with such judgements there would be no legal functions available for a sheriff or anyone else to perform in order to claim this fine. Apart from the four exceptions just noted (*mundbryce, hamsocn, forsteal*, and *fyrdwite*), which are explicable by their strong royal associations, all such fines appear to have remained bundled together within sake and soke in the eleventh century, never being disputed individually. By contrast, the other rights to legal revenues that appear in writs—*team, infangenþeof*, and *flymenafyrmþ*—are notable for their close association with specific legal functions. This is highly suggestive. It is exactly what our hypothesis would lead us to expect: if sheriffs and their subordinates were claiming legal revenues by taking responsibility for legal functions, the specific revenues that became a focus of controversy would of course be those vulnerable to such methods. Those with no directly linked legal functions would be safe unless there was some other compelling logic by which they could be claimed for kings.

Let us take *team* first. *Team* was the right to receive fines paid by thieves who were identified through the legal procedure known to legal historians as 'vouching to warranty' (see Hudson 2012: 155–9). A theft victim would claim to have identified his stolen goods in someone else's possession; the accused then had the option of vouching someone else to warranty—asserting that he had bought the goods legitimately from a third party and that he could call upon witnesses to the transaction to prove it. This third party could then do the same and the process could go through several iterations. One tenth-century law expresses concern about the time and effort required to follow up these claims, verifying a chain of purchases that would in theory lead back to the original thief (II Atr 8:3–9). We might well imagine that theft victims would have welcomed sheriffs' assistance in pursuing such cases—tracking down witnesses and compelling them either to confirm or deny their knowledge of the various transactions—and that having done so sheriffs would have had a strong moral claim to the punitive fine that arose, a claim they were in a strong position to press. Explicit references to *team* in writs would have allowed their aristocratic beneficiaries to resist such claims.[16]

[16] The right of *toll*, which always appears alongside *team* in writs, appears to be the right to receive tolls paid at markets, which are of course where many of the transactions in vouching

The right of *flymenafyrmþ* is analogous: it is the right to the fine of the same name, for the offence of knowingly harbouring fugitives. Tracking down men who fled rather than submit to punishment was, of course, an onerous task. The men engaged in it—either the offender's original victims or his former sureties, who had one year to capture him and reclaim the punitive fine they had been forced to pay on his behalf (III Eg 6:2)—were likely to welcome the assistance of powerful figures such as sheriffs. And having provided this assistance, locating the fugitive and the people harbouring him, sheriffs would again have had a strong moral claim to the fine owed by the fugitive's erstwhile protectors, a claim to which a writ explicitly referencing *flymenafyrmþ* would be the ideal riposte. Finally, there is the right of *infangenþeof*; this is the right to receive the property forfeited by thieves who had been caught in the act and executed or mutilated. The associated legal function here is obvious: catching and executing thieves. As we have seen, tenth-century laws regard this as a communal duty, and characteristically divide the forfeited property between those who took part in the thief-catching expedition and the local *landhlaford*. The emergence of the right of *infangenþeof* in the early eleventh century would make sense if sheriffs were assuming responsibility for the dangerous and possibly even sinful business of killing thieves, thus establishing a claim to their goods forfeitures. A writ explicitly entitling its beneficiary to *infangenþeof* would have protected a *landhlaford* against any such claim.

The specific rights to receive legal revenues that emerge as a focus of conflict in our early eleventh-century evidence are thus consistent with the hypothesis suggested here. Indeed, the idea that performing legal functions served as a way of claiming valuable revenues efficiently explains kings' sudden development of distinct claims to rights of *team*, *infangenþeof*, and *flymenafyrmþ*. Meanwhile, their interest in the remaining privileges listed individually in writs (*mundbryce*, *hamsocn*, *forsteal*, and *fyrdwite*) is readily explicable by the established logic of the king's personal protection and the long-standing reservation of military service from the bundle of rights that constituted lordship over land. The potential implications for the development of jurisdictional rights are significant. There is every chance that sheriffs' attempts to claim legal revenues by seizing responsibility for legal functions—executing or mutilating thieves, following up chains of warrantors through *team* procedures, hunting down fugitives—led to conflicts with

to warranty claims would have taken place. The strong association between *toll* and *team* suggests that the right to resist sheriffs' claims relating to *team* in some way rested on market-holding rights, perhaps because markets were the locations where vouching to warranty procedures were usually held. There are striking parallels with the procedures discussed by both Scheele and Charles-Edwards, this volume—see Chapters 1 and 3.

lords concerned to defend both their revenue streams and their preeminent positions within their own lands. It would not be surprising if some attempted to repel sheriffs and their subordinates by assuming responsibility for these legal functions themselves, and from there it is only a small step to disputes which focused on who was entitled to perform those functions, and thus to the establishment of local customary rules delineating who had the right to do what where. That is, in time we might imagine lords framing their rights in explicitly jurisdictional terms, perhaps as the exclusive right to execute thieves on their land, or to oversee vouching to warranty cases. Or perhaps these rights could be expressed negatively: the right to prevent royal officials from entering their land to seek out fugitives, to seek out witnesses to transactions, or to pursue thieves. However, it is well established that such legalistic representations of jurisdictional rights cannot be discerned in our evidence until after the Norman conquest of 1066. How significant a problem does this absence represent for the interpretation presented here?

I would suggest that it is relatively insignificant. Our evidence for contemporary assumptions about routine legal practice in the period between Cnut's law code, issued in the winter of 1020–21, and 1066 is very slight. No pertinent laws can be dated to this period, and as ever we lack good evidence for legal practice beyond high-stakes aristocratic disputes over land. We have writs, of course, but they are unhelpful for this question: how can we detect when their references to *infangenþeof* stopped meaning simply the right to receive a thief's forfeited goods and began to connote the right to perform executions? That such a shift was taking place beneath our evidence cannot be proven, of course, but there are no strong grounds for dismissing the possibility either. The process I am suggesting, moreover, would have been messy and localized, with different arrangements arising in different places as different lords responded to attempts to claim what had once been their legal revenues in different ways. The long-term durability of the customary arrangements that emerged as solutions to specific conflicts over revenue—whether or not they ripened into what we might reasonably represent as property regimes that distributed jurisdictional rights among a number of local figures—would have depended heavily on contingent factors. The available sources simply cannot provide the sort of textured understanding of evolving local legal arrangements which we would need either to chart jurisdiction emerging in this way or to rule out the possibility that this was occurring.

There is perhaps one exception to this statement. Domesday Book—the great survey of aristocratic landholding throughout all of England carried out in 1086—contains the following description of the legal customs of Dunwich in Suffolk.

> In Dunwich the king has this custom: that two or three [men] will go to the hundred if they have been correctly notified; if they do not do this they are made to forfeit 2 *ora*. If a thief is caught there, he will be judged there; corporal punishment will be exacted in Blythburgh and his goods stay with the lord of Dunwich. At the time of King Edward there was no money changer there but [there was one] in Blythburgh (*Domesday Book* ii. 312r–v).

This shows the existence of what might be described as a jurisdictional rule: corporal punishment of thieves must take place in Blythburgh—a significant royal centre with its own mint—presumably under the supervision of either the sheriff or a subordinate royal official based there. Moreover, it implies the existence of a rather jurisdictional assumption: that thieves' forfeited property would normally pertain to whoever was responsible for their execution. However, it also shows that local realities did not conform to jurisdictional expectations: the royal officials of Blythburgh may have been entitled to execute thieves, but they were not entitled to profit from doing so. A plausible reconstruction of the events that led to this situation would involve royal officials associated with Blythburgh at some earlier point asserting their right to execute thieves, presumably at least partially in the hope of claiming the associated revenues. This claim met with a firm response from the lord of Dunwich who resisted its financial implications, successfully asserting his right to receive the goods of slain thieves. This example is certainly not sufficient to confirm the interpretation offered here but it is rather suggestive. It looks like a legalistic discourse on the performance of legal functions—a discourse articulating explicit jurisdictional rules—emerging rather messily out of conflict between a lord and a royal official over legal revenues, which is precisely what we would expect to see if the processes suggested here were taking place.

CONCLUSION

To summarize, the model proposed here is as follows. Traditionally legal revenues had not been a focus of contention. Rights to unpredictable windfalls from the punishment of wrongdoing, probably usually rendered in kind, were difficult for kings to exploit effectively and they were thus invariably included in the bundle of rights over land that they transferred to favoured aristocrats (and which wealthy magnates themselves often granted to lesser lords). Exclusive rights to perform legal functions, by contrast, did not exist: these functions were understood as duties rather than privileges, and little legalism was applied to the question of who performed them. Tenth-century laws appear concerned about apathy but in theory everyone—all free men at the very least—was entitled to participate in the performance of legal processes, including both judgement and enforcement. Actually doing so signified public-spiritedness: a willingness to step forward and accept potentially onerous, even dangerous, tasks for everyone's benefit. To be actively involved in communal legal processes as a matter of routine was probably to be a member of a local elite that self-consciously took up the burden of maintaining order in a spirit of *noblesse oblige*.

However, this situation changed in the late tenth and early eleventh centuries. The key obstacles to royal exploitation of legal revenues were removed: economic changes meant that they (like other dues) could much more readily be extracted in coin and the introduction of sheriffs gave kings a network of officials capable of intervening even on other lords' land. The extended military crisis caused by renewed Scandinavian raiding created an urgent need for revenue, placing additional pressure on sheriffs and their subordinates to claim whatever fines and forfeitures they could. This led them to seize responsibility for the performance of legal functions, as the principle already existed that those who did so should share in whatever revenues their actions produced. This, however, drew a defensive response from lords, some of whom were able to repel sheriffs' attempts to take revenues from their lands by asserting their own rights to perform legal functions. That is, 'performable legal functions'—the resource which 'jurisdictional' (or 'legal-function-performance') rights would allow one to exploit—shifted from being an abundant to a scarce resource around the early eleventh century. Though our evidence very rarely allows us to glimpse it happening, there is good reason to suspect that competition for this scarce resource prompted the establishment of localized property regimes governing access to it. Gradually and unevenly—and perhaps initially not very legalistically—jurisdictional rights were probably emerging as a form of property in the decades before the Norman conquest. These rights would eventually be incorporated as emblematic 'sticks' in the bundle of rights that characterized aristocratic landed property at a certain social level,[17] as well as being disputed and negotiated individually.[18]

At this point it is important to enter some major caveats. It would be wrong to imagine that the process examined here constitutes a satisfactory explanation for jurisdiction's emergence as a form of property in

[17] An early twelfth-century hint of this is Hn 20:2, which asserts that all archbishops, bishops, earls, and *alia potestates*—presumably meaning other magnates of similarly high rank—possessed *toll, team*, and *infangenþeof* over the lands associated with their positions (though not necessarily over any new acquisitions).

[18] For example, a plea roll of 1204 records a dispute settlement in which 'the gallows and ordeal pit [*furca et fossa*] which the aforesaid Adam claimed to have in Sedburgh he has remitted, quit from him and his heirs, to William Mowbray and his heirs so that neither Adam nor his heirs shall have any there for ever' (Stenton 1952–67: iii. no. 926).

English law. First and foremost, it should be noted that imagining 'performable legal functions' as a once abundant resource that rapidly became scarce around the year 1000 helps us understand the emergence of some forms of jurisdictional right more than others. Crucially, it is hard to see how it applies to the emergence of 'private courts'—the main focus of historiographical discussions of jurisdiction. This, as has been noted, is a rather opaque process as traditionally conceptualized: we probably ought to break it down into more concrete developments. But even if we do, our model does not get us very far. It cannot really explain how and why lords came to demand that their men settle their disputes in assemblies at which they presided and which consisted solely of their own dependants; nor does anything discussed here obviously bear on the much later process by which itinerant royal justices came to have absolute authority to make decisions about legal interpretation in their courts; and there is likewise no clear connection between this argument and the erosion of the free man's right to deny charges brought against him using a collective oath. The process by which various judicial rights were incorporated into the bundle of rights that constituted lordship over land warrants close examination, but not here.

Moreover, it is important to stress that this explanation for the emergence of a property regime governing the performance of legal functions cannot readily be extrapolated to the post-conquest period. Its key feature is its prioritization of economic over cultural factors: sheriffs are driven to take responsibility for legal functions by their desire for revenue, which prompts lords to defend their traditional privileges. Importantly, sheriffs were not, at least initially, motivated to claim responsibility for legal functions because of any symbolic association with the king—some notion that these functions *ought* to be royal property. There is little to suggest such an association in contemporary or earlier evidence. As we have seen, the cultural significance of performing legal functions seems rather to have been bound up with an ethos of public-spiritedness, the sort of communal good-citizenship that fed into local elites' collective identity. When sheriffs first started tracking down fugitives and warrantors, and executing captured thieves, these would have been the resonances their acts had: they were public servants doing what needed to be done in the interests of justice. They probably understood their actions at least partially in those terms; it would be naively cynical to imagine them as the utterly amoral and rapacious predators they are sometimes made out to be by ecclesiastical writers. Nonetheless, an urgent need for revenue provides the most compelling explanation for the unprecedented phenomenon under discussion here: royal agents successfully claiming fines and forfeitures even in lands supposedly freed from all royal exactions.

The significant point here is that there is little reason to think that sheriffs pursued fugitives, administered *team* procedures, and executed thieves because these actions had something of the lustre of sovereignty about them. This would be easy for us to assume because they later acquired this lustre, and the naturalness of the state's responsibility for the performance of legal functions is firmly embedded in our own culture. It is an important part of the model presented here that such assumptions were not a feature of late tenth-century Anglo-Saxon culture, but later developments. Legal functions began as communal duties performed by public-spirited individuals; the king's officers then took responsibility for them, primarily because they desired revenue. Legal functions thus ceased to be communal duties anyone could perform and instead became prerogatives of the king's officers. It is easy to imagine how their position as highly prized rights would in time have ensured that performing them became a marker of status, with connotations of something akin to sovereignty. Economic concerns are the main drivers in the late Anglo-Saxon process identified here, the symbolic associations between the performance of legal functions and kingship are a by-product that emerges only once it is well under way. Yet though it would perhaps have some merit as part of a wider overall picture, this cannot on its own be a convincing model for post-conquest England. It does not allow for the possibility that the significance of performing legal functions altered as a result of cultural shifts unrelated to competition for legal revenues, and this is problematic. It is justifiable for the late tenth and early eleventh centuries because there is no obviously pertinent cultural shift to be accommodated,[19] but the same cannot be said for the century and a half following 1066.

Indeed, it would be extraordinary if the wholesale replacement of the English aristocracy with a new francophone elite in the wake of the conquest did not have a fundamental effect on the emergence of jurisdiction. Jurisdictional rights do seem to have been a familiar form of property in contemporary French legal culture. On the continent legal privileges had been articulated in jurisdictional terms for centuries, with emphasis placed on their holders' rights to perform functions and exclude royal officials (Rosenwein 1999; Murray 2010). It is likely that this new ruling class arrived with their own engrained assumptions about the symbolic significance of performing legal functions and that this ultimately had a transformative effect on the way legal privileges were articulated. To return to the radio

[19] A shift resulting from the Scandinavian conquest of 1016 is only superficially plausible. We know so little of Danish kingship at this time as to be unable to rule out the notion that the rights at issue here were potent symbols of royal authority, but there is no reason to think this likely. Nor does the chronology marry up well: our best evidence for conflict over legal revenues does come from after 1016, but enough precedes it to raise significant doubts about a Scandinavian explanation.

spectrum analogy with which we started, if the process by which jurisdiction emerged as a form of property in medieval English law had an equivalent formative moment to the Wireless Telegraphy Act of 1904, it was almost certainly the Norman conquest. But it is far from being the only cultural shift worth considering. The idea that the later medieval jurisdictional landscape which emerges clearly into view around the turn of the thirteenth century was significantly shaped by the prominence of Roman Law within twelfth-century intellectual culture is surely also worth pursuing, as is the possibility that the late eleventh- and early twelfth-century investiture controversy, in precisely delineating functions that temporal and spiritual authorities might legitimately perform, prompted contemporaries to conceptualize secular legal practice in similar terms. Indeed, once it is accepted that a key legal development of the eleventh and twelfth centuries was the emergence of a property regime governing the performance of legal functions, these essentially cultural explanations for the shift are by far the most obvious. It would be all too easy to view jurisdictional rights in later medieval English law as a little more than the product of a colonial property regime implanted in 1066 and subsequently fortified by the sustained period of cultural imperialism known to historians as 'the making of Europe' (Bartlett 1993). The argument presented here provides a counterpoint to such an interpretation, suggesting that native English legal developments had already begun to provide the impetus for the emergence of jurisdictional rights as a form of property; the fact that these developments were overtaken by rather more momentous events ought not to detract from their significance.

There is a great deal more to be learnt about the process by which jurisdiction became bound up with landed property in England. The narrative of feudalization which has shaped legal historians' approach to the subject for over a century has encouraged the assumption that jurisdictional rights had always been 'property objects', and that the most significant historical questions relating to them are about the dates of shifts in whose property they were: at what point they stopped belonging solely to the king and entered the bundle of rights that constituted aristocratic landholding, giving it a characteristically feudal form. This chapter has attempted to show that the process was actually rather more interesting. Perhaps narratives of the 'feudalization' of property relationships need to be abandoned entirely, the concept now having accreted so many layers of meaning that it is difficult to employ without sowing confusion, but whatever we call the process we need to recognize its complexity. It involved not just transfers of ownership but more fundamental changes to property regimes. This aspect of feudalization appears, in England at least, to have been rather more a matter of propertization than privatization. Indeed, the conventional analogy seems particularly ill-suited to the process described here, which saw a property regime governing the performance of legal functions emerging not as a result of governmental weakness or the short-sighted generosity of kings, but in response to the aggressive extension and intensification of royal legal exactions.

6

'Everything Belongs to God'

Sayyid Qutb's Theory of Property and Social Justice

WALTER RECH

PROPERTY AND SOCIAL JUSTICE IN THE MODERN ISLAMIC AND EGYPTIAN CONTEXT

Sayyid Qutb published *Social Justice in Islam* in 1949 (Qutb [1949] 1996).[1] He finalized the book soon before leaving his native Egypt for a study tour that took him to the United States as well as England, Switzerland, and Italy from 1948 to 1950. As a teacher and a long-term employee of the Egyptian ministry of education, he was sent to visit western institutions, including Stanford University, to gain insights into an advanced education from which the ministry could benefit (Qutb [1949] 1996: xvi; Moussalli 1992: 24). Most likely, the ministry organized the trip with the aim of bringing Qutb closer to the West (Moussalli 1992: 25). The result, however, was just the opposite: Qutb was disappointed by what he saw of western society, in particular its wealth imbalance under the capitalist system, widespread racism, and relations between the sexes.

Economic and political injustice had been a major concern for Qutb since his youth. Born in Musha, in Asyut Province, in 1906, he was brought up in a family of political activists committed to supporting their impoverished neighbours financially: as a youngster, he felt sympathetic to the cause of destitute seasonal workers. After moving to Cairo, where he studied and worked from the late 1920s, he drifted away from the Wafd party towards the Muslim Brotherhood. This was

[1] The book was re-edited several times until Qutb was executed under the Nasser regime in 1966. William Shepard's translation of *Social Justice in Islam* carefully takes into account variations between the different editions (Qutb [1949] 1996).

'Everything Belongs to God': Sayyid Qutb's Theory of Property and Social Justice. Walter Rech. © Walter Rech, 2017. Published 2017 by Oxford University Press.

not least because of the nationalists' alleged failure to tackle inequality and corruption (Akhavi 2013: 160). He was especially worried by governments' inability to take care of the weakest in society, and to free Egypt from subjection to the great powers. As Qutb turned away from Arab nationalism towards Islamism, he reconceived social justice as part of an all-encompassing Islamic system that he thought would provide guidelines for addressing any human and societal dilemma, including the equitable redistribution of wealth, within an ideal 'Islamic state' to be established by an enlightened vanguard. This commitment to radical social transformation would become most visible after the Egyptian Revolution of 1952 as Qutb, despite playing an important role in the uprising, was sidelined by Gamal Abd al-Nasser and became disillusioned with the possibility of carrying out Islamist reform through legal means (Musallam 2005).[2]

As Qutb was not the only Islamic writer of his generation who took a position on social and property issues, his intellectual and political context needs to be discussed in order to make sense of his ideas. Questions about property and social justice had spread throughout the late Ottoman Empire and the newly independent Islamic world since the late nineteenth century. Intellectuals and elites across the political spectrum found it a suitable language for rallying popular support around an ideal of collective harmony which seemed to avert the threat of class warfare (Hourani 1991; Kennedy 2006; Tripp 2006).[3] In Islamist, Arab nationalist, and left-wing circles alike, the politics of the social was underpinned by discursive tensions around property. Islamist scholars attempted to balance and overcome this by embedding the notion of property in a 'total' Islamic system of life that provided guidelines for just and equitable relationships between human beings. This effort was visible, for instance, in the work of the authoritative Islamist scholar A'la Mawdudi, who developed the field of 'Islamic economics', the forerunner of today's Islamic finance (Kuran 2004). Mawdudi, who inspired Qutb among others, strove to demonstrate that the Islamic tradition boasted just and effective economic doctrines, and he used this claim to prove that Islam was a total religious system that did not need to rely on foreign ideologies (Mawdudi 1947). In Mawdudi's work, Islamic economics was characterized (indeed, all

[2] On political utopias in modern Arab thought more broadly, see Bouzid (1997).

[3] In the Arab world, this turn to a western political vocabulary had been prepared since the nineteenth century by a massive effort of conceptual translation from European languages. This work, amplified by increasing media communication and the rise of nation states in the Arab world, resulted in the transformation of classical concepts of Islamic politics. The term *ummah*, for instance, was increasingly used to denote nation states and not only the larger Islamic community (Ayalon 1987: 28).

but defined) as a golden mean between the excessive individualism of western capitalism and the oppressive character of the Soviet economic system. Qutb would partly rely on this 'third way' approach to articulate his theory of property and social justice, though he took a more radical, redistributive line than Mawdudi.

Property and wealth redistribution became especially thorny issues in Egypt, a country affected by deep social cleavages as a result of colonial rule and nineteenth-century land tenure reforms. While pursuing his project of state centralization Muhammad Ali Pasha (1769–1849) had imposed direct taxation through state officials to sideline tax-farmers who, having secured life tenure of lands (*malikāne*), acted virtually as landlords (Cuno 1980: 251). Although Muhammad Ali's reform diminished the status of local landlords, it simultaneously exposed the peasantry to the coercive power of the state, which peasants could no longer negotiate with or challenge through occasional revolts as they had been accustomed to do in earlier periods. From the 1850s, as a new landed class of high state officials secured its ascendancy through legislative measures, peasants were largely reduced to wage labourers and tenants (Cuno 1980: 268). This was the point at which Ottoman law took a turn towards individualized property rights in land and a western understanding of private property spread in the Empire by means of mixed courts, liberal law school education and increasing trade with European countries in the Mediterranean. In old Ottoman law, the Sultan had been conceived as the ultimate owner of land to which subjects might hold a usufructuary right (*miri*), but the Land Code of 1858 turned *miri* into something more akin to ownership (Mundy 2007: 48).[4] The formation of large estates and the related decline of the peasantry, accompanied by sustained demographic growth and migration, created the conditions for the social and economic distress to which Qutb and other social justice theorists would react. By the 1930s and 1940s, Egyptian society was markedly polarized, with a growing gap between the masses and the landowning elite (Thompson 2014); land ownership largely defined formal political life, since access to parliament was dependent upon payment of high fees that only the wealthiest could afford. In the interwar

[4] The situation was rather complex, since in practice the rights of the Sultan had been confined to taxation and coercive irrigation, and *miri* did not exclude individual rights to dispose of property rather freely (*mulk*). Nevertheless, the late nineteenth century saw an increasing individualization of property rights and the development of a more unified and less hierarchical concept of property compared with earlier periods, also as a result of cadastral registration that contributed to detaching property from social relationships (Mundy 2007: 235).

period the fall of cotton prices, along with a very slow increase in the arable land-area, worsened the condition of peasants; concomitantly, urbanization, high demographic rates and unemployment resulted in the expansion of urban slums and paved the way for political radicalization in secular as well as Islamist circles (Bechor 2007: 22).[5] This was the environment in which the Muslim Brotherhood rose to become one the major political forces in Egypt.

THE MUSLIM BROTHERHOOD AND THE GOAL OF SOCIAL JUSTICE

The founder of the Muslim Brotherhood, Hasan al-Banna, was born in the town of Mahmudiyyah in 1906. The son of Shaykh Ahmad Abd al-Rahman al-Banna, who himself wrote on Islamic tradition and jurisprudence, Hasan soon devoted himself to religious learning and to Sufism (al-Banna 1978). As a youngster, he became leader of the Society for Moral Behaviour and was active in the Hassafiyya Society for Charity, which aimed, among other things, to restrain the influence of Christian missionaries in Mahmudiyyah (Mitchell [1969] 1993; Lia 1998: 112). In 1923 al-Banna moved to Cairo, where he studied at Dar al-Ulum, which offered courses based on western educational models. It was precisely as a result of coming into contact with Christian and western worldviews that al-Banna, like Qutb, developed his political vision, in which ideas about property and attitudes to wealth accumulation were key. While at Dar al-Ulum, al-Banna defined what he deemed the major problems of Egyptian society, namely internal political factionalism and the impact of foreign materialistic doctrines on the people's faith and mores (Mitchell 1993: 5; Lia 1998: 27). To address these issues, he organized groups of engaged students to provide religious teaching in public places and to counter the spread of foreign ideas, through bringing young people back to the path of Islam and promoting an Islamic critique of the negative impact of wealth accumulation on Egyptian social life. Al-Banna maintained and even increased this commitment in later years.

After graduating, he worked as a primary schoolteacher in Ismailiyyah, which hosted British military camps, the Suez Canal Company, and the residences of wealthy foreigners, all of which he believed symbolized the continuing 'economic occupation' of Egypt under the British Protectorate and the dire conditions of the local labour force. This experience

[5] The constitutional experiment of the interwar period, undermined by internal struggles between the monarchy and party elites and by the persistent intervention of western powers, failed to provide social reforms. For more on Egypt at the period, see Issawi (1954).

prompted al-Banna to found the Society of the Muslim Brotherhood. Upon the Society's foundation in 1928 the Brothers established a number of mosques, schools for boys and girls, as well as small industries like workshops, carpet, and embroidery factories. This social commitment increased during the 1930s as the Brotherhood's branches proliferated in rural areas as well as Cairo, setting up clinics, hospitals, pharmacies, programmes for fighting illiteracy, and committees for the orderly collection of *zakat* (Lia 1998). Charitable activity seemed all the more urgent where corrupted or authoritarian governments failed to tackle social issues effectively. In the summer of 1935 al-Banna denounced the desperate condition of the Egyptian countryside and the lack of governmental action as follows:

> Nobody can escape noticing the vast chasm between the comfortable, exciting and boisterous city life of luxury, entertainment and pleasure, and the life of the countryside where people have sunk into the deepest misery. . . . O ye Ministers and Senior Officials! These miserable peasants are sons of Egypt . . . For these subjugated and wretched of the earth God will summon you to a difficult and scrupulous account! (Lia 1998: 109).

In the famous tract 'Toward the Light', which he sent to King Farouk in 1936, al-Banna laid out a plan for improving the economic condition of the poor, based partly on Islamic tradition and partly on modernist notions of state intervention. His proposal centred upon ideas about the distribution of property, whether financial or landed. It included the prohibition of usury, 'the organisation of *zakat* in terms of income and expenditure', the encouragement of economic projects involving unemployed citizens and the transfer of economic activities 'to the purely national sector', 'the protection of the masses from the oppression of monopolistic companies; keeping these within strict limits, and obtaining every possible benefit for the masses' (al-Banna 1978: 130), all of which would be taken up by Qutb in *Social Justice*. In 'Toward the Light' al-Banna also promoted health-related reforms for the benefit of the disadvantaged, including 'the dissemination of health information through all media; increasing the number of hospitals, physicians, and mobile clinics; facilitating the means of obtaining medical treatment', and providing cleanliness and purification of water in villages (al-Banna 1978: 129). By blending Islamic principles with an interventionist state programme, al-Banna reasserted a typical reformist discourse whose roots went back to the likes of Jamal al-Din al-Afghani (1839–97) and Muhammad Abduh (1849–1905). Following in their footsteps, he maintained that Arab countries should appropriate important achievements of modernity in science, technology, and standards of living, while rejecting western doctrines incompatible with authentic Islam.

INSTITUTIONALIZING A 'SOCIAL' VIEW OF PROPERTY RIGHTS: SANHURI'S CODE

In the 1930s and 1940s a value-laden approach to property and its attendant legalism was taken not only by emerging Islamist activists, but also by influential voices in the Egyptian establishment, notably by the main drafter of the New Egyptian Civil Code, Abd al-Razzaq al-Sanhuri. Born in Alexandria in 1895, he attended Cairo Law School at the age of eighteen and then moved to France to write his dissertation at the University of Lyon (Bechor 2007: 34). Under the mentorship of Edouard Lambert and François Gény, two major representatives of the sociological approach to law, Sanhuri developed an anti-formalist legal theory: he advocated the use of law for the sake of social engineering, in particular for addressing inequalities and strengthening social cohesion, yet he remained averse to European socialism (Shalakany 2001: 215). His greatest hope, like Mawdudi's and Qutb's, was that his country would find a middle way between the excesses of the socialist and capitalist approaches to wealth accumulation and property rights.

Back in Egypt, Sanhuri was appointed in 1936 to the committee for drafting a civil code and later became head of the supreme administrative court, from 1949 to 1952. After the fall of the monarchy in 1952, Sanhuri, like other liberals, was confident that the Free Officers' revolution would promote progressive reform. He thus supported the revolution and even obtained a post of legal advisor to the Revolutionary Council. Yet his call to establish the rule of law in Egypt soon clashed with the politics of Gamal Abdel Nasser, who had him beaten and put an end to his political career (Bechor 2007: 41). From 1954 onwards, Sanhuri devoted himself to composing his voluminous commentary on the civil code.

The New Egyptian Civil Code, initiated in 1936 and entering into force in 1949, was drafted under the same political and economic circumstances that prompted Qutb to write *Social Justice*. During the Second World War, the Egyptian economy was caught up in the British war effort, resulting in massive post-war unemployment. The war also adversely affected social life: there was a growing public perception that moral and sexual standards were being relaxed, due to western influences, in particular as a result of the arrival of western soldiers, who were seen to encourage prostitution and other practices that many Egyptians found immoral (Bechor 2007: 23). In the meantime, the Palestinian situation had worsened, which led to increasing commitment by Egyptian parties and movements, including the Muslim Brotherhood, to contribute large numbers of volunteers to fight there. In a climate of unrest and violence several political and government leaders were assassinated and the Muslim Brotherhood was dissolved by the Egyptian government in 1948. Prime Minister Ibrahim Abdel Hadi Pasha, and probably King Farouk as well, signed off on the assassination of al-Banna, who was killed by secret police officers in 1949 (al-Banna 1978: 71).

Fully aware of the growing political implications of civil law in a time of social tensions, Sanhuri shaped the New Egyptian Civil Code protecting, as far as possible, collective rights and the rights of the weakest, in contrast to the former Code of 1873, which had inherited the individualist focus of the 1804 French Code. In his later commentaries, he explained that in his Code the right of property was no longer to be seen as 'absolute and limitless': owners were protected by the law only as long as they fulfilled a social function (Bechor 2007: 13). In his view, general interest took precedence over the right of property, and judges should keep in mind the goal of social balance even in disputes between individuals not directly involving public interests. Among the most important changes introduced by Sanhuri under the banner of social justice were restrictions on the freedom of contract, largely justified through conceptual imports such as doctrines of abuse of right, discriminatory treatment, and exploitation, which applied to contracts allocating disproportionate benefits and burdens to the parties. In light of the difficult economic situation and increasing borrowing by impoverished Egyptians, the Code reduced legal interest rates from 5 per cent to 4 per cent in civil matters and from 6 per cent to 5 per cent in commercial matters (Bechor 2007: 198). Norms on unlawful enrichment were also introduced.

While some of Sanhuri's most radical proposals were amended during the review process, both the upper and lower houses of parliament approved the Code, largely out of concern that failure to meet popular demands would cause a revolution. Social justice thus became a legitimate political language, sanctioned by conservatives too. Muhammed al-Wakil, the president of the Senate Civil Code Committee, found no difficulty presenting the Code to the plenum as a text following 'contemporary trends in its social and economic goals, striking a balance between individual liberty and the interests of society', and indeed in line with 'the modern trends of social justice' (Bechor 2007: 317). While Sanhuri's Code did not prevent Egypt from plunging into a revolution,[6] it did remain an authoritative text, later imitated by Syria, Lybia, Jordan, Yemen, and Kuwait (Bechor 2007: 57). It is still mandatory reading for many lawyers in the Arab world.

[6] The revolution, when it came, turned on very much the issues al-Banna and Qutb had highlighted. Frustration with governmental failures to tackle poverty and foreign 'economic occupation' was epitomized by the Cairo Fire of 1952, which destroyed large parts of the quarters in which foreigners and wealthy Egyptians lived.

'EVERYTHING BELONGS TO GOD': QUTB'S VIEW OF PROPERTY AND THE CALL FOR REDISTRIBUTION

While starting from Islamist instead of liberal assumptions, Qutb followed Sanhuri in critically scrutinizing the right to property ([1949] 1996: 47). While Qutb respectfully admitted that private property occupied an important place in the Islamic legal tradition, he placed the need for social justice ahead of the protection of property, in particular the property of the wealthy and those in power. He wished to articulate a novel and yet 'authentically' Islamic theory, moving beyond formalist jurisprudential ways of conceptualizing property that failed, he claimed, to engage with both the genuine spirit of Islam and the political challenges of modernity. Qutb thus advanced a view of property as embedded in a broader and meaningful social and religious context, a thesis with striking echoes of Karl Polanyi's book *The Great Transformation*, which had been published in 1944, just a few years before *Social Justice* (Polanyi [1944] 2001).

Traditionally Islamic law had endeavoured to maintain a balance between redistributive duties towards the community—which took the form of obligatory and voluntary alms-giving (*zakat* and *sadaqah* respectively) and the institution of charitable trusts (*awqaf*, pl. pf *waqf*)—and the right of property, whose violation potentially entailed harsh penalties (Islam 1999; Yanagihashi 2004; Hallaq 2009). Islamic jurists also elaborated careful distinctions of property into, for instance, value-laden (*mutaqawwim*) and value-less (*ghayr mutaqawwim*); or moveable (*manqul*) and immoveable (*aqar*). They distinguished between complete (*tamm*) and incomplete (*naqis, daif*), voluntary (*milk ikhtiyari*) and involuntary (*milk qahri*) ownership. Rights to usufruct were divided into rights of enjoyment (*milk intifa*) and rights which could be shared with other people (*milk manfa'a*) (Hallaq 2009: 296). In addition, jurisprudential schools debated a variety of definitions of the concept of property itself (*al-Mal*). Hanafi scholars held that usufruct and rights are not material and therefore cannot be defined as *mal*, whereas other schools adopted a broader definition stating that *mal* is anything that yields benefits (under the Shafi'i view), or anything that yields specifically lawful benefits (in the Hanbali view), or something over which the owner has exclusive possession (according to Maliki jurists) (Islam 1999: 363).

Yet Qutb rarely engaged with such jurisprudential debates: this is not an accident (Tripp 2006: 153). Like al-Banna and other Islamic modernists, Qutb saw the learned jurists, the *ulamā'*, as a largely conservative class acquiescent in existing power relations and thus as an obstacle to realizing social justice.[7]

[7] For a discussion of allegedly conservative attitudes in Islamic jurisprudence, see El Fadel (2001).

Qutb lamented that it was precisely 'the interpretation of the professional "men of religion" in the ages of tyranny [which lulled] public awareness and [kept] it from demanding social justice' ([1949] 1996: 52). Instead of entering subtle jurisprudential disquisitions that left large-scale wealth redistribution unaddressed, al-Banna and Qutb called for a return to the Qur'ān and the prophetic Sunnah, which they interpreted according to their egalitarian agenda (al-Banna 1978).[8] This was not meant to delegitimize the institution of private property, which was explicitly justified in numerous qur'ānic verses, but rather to reassert the 'authentic', restrained understanding of ownership contained in the Qur'ān and thereby critique the accumulation of wealth in the hands of a few privileged individuals in contemporary Islamic societies. Anti-jurisprudential Qutb may have been, but anti-legal he was not. He never denied that property, if properly understood, could contribute to the economic and moral development of society.

Qutb's critique of wealth accumulation resonated with the theories of Sanhuri and other theorists of the social who argued that property rights must be subordinated to community interests and not be regarded as unrestrained. Qutb maintained that profit, while in principle allowed and even beneficial to society as an incentive for entrepreneurship, must have boundaries, and that wealth must to some extent be redistributed. This was not a matter of philanthropy but law. That is why he defined *zakat* squarely as 'a right *against* property' and as 'a right of the community *over* and *against* the individual' (Qutb [1949] 1996: 162). Such statements refer to a tension between the protection of property rights and social justice, a tension he clearly felt in contemporary Egypt.

To redress current wealth imbalance, Qutb claimed that authorities in an ideal Islamic state should be granted broad discretion to tax the rich, since 'Islam does not leave the right of private property absolute, without restriction or limitation—as does the capitalist system' ([1949] 1996: 128). The notion of limited property rights is also visible in *In the Shade of the Qur'an*, an extensive qur'ānic commentary Qutb began to publish serially in 1951–2 and completed in 1959. Commenting on verses 38–9 of the *Surah al-Rum*, which urged Muslims to distribute surplus wealth for charitable purposes, Qutb affirmed:

> [s]ince all wealth belongs to God and it is He who grants it to some of His servants, He, the original owner, has determined that a portion of it should go to certain groups, to be given to them by those who are in actual possession of

[8] For instance, al-Banna noted that *zakat* must today be organized to carry out 'necessary benevolent projects such as homes for the aged, the poor, and orphans, and strengthening the armed forces' (al-Banna 1978: 130).

> it. Therefore, He calls it a right due to these groups, of which the sūrah mentions here 'the near of kin, the needy and the traveller in need'. ... Since all money and wealth belong to God, it is subject to what He, as the original owner, determines with regard to how it is owned, invested or spent. The person who is in control of it does not enjoy absolute authority in this respect ([1964] 2005: XIII, 306).

This notion of restrained property lay at the basis of Qutb's understanding of social justice as harmonious relationship between individuals, social groups, and public authorities. He claimed that, within an Islamic framework, justice rested on three pillars that were absent or misconceived under capitalism and socialism: absolute liberation of the soul, complete human equality, and firm social solidarity (Qutb [1949] 1996: 40). Absolute liberation of the soul, one of the principal benefits of Islam, stemmed from the recognition of God as the only sovereign and lawgiver, which relativized all earthly authority. This allowed humans to free themselves from deference to despotic rule, from social conditioning and from desire for wealth and material values beyond that which is permitted by God. Qutb contrasted this existential and political liberation with the narrower forms of economic emancipation promised by communism and capitalism ([1949] 1996: 36 and 42). In particular, Qutb criticized the communist insistence on the formal equality of wages and labour conditions: he argued that the paradoxical reversion of communist systems into oppressive regimes was precisely due to a lack of a common understanding of the good shared by elites and masses, an insight which purportedly only religion could provide.

On Qutb's assessment the ideal of striving for absolute liberation 'allows the poor man who is seeking his livelihood to confront forcefully and courageously the person who appears to have that livelihood in his hand' and to seek assistance from authorities for that purpose, since Islam 'makes the individual's right to his basic needs an obligation on the state or on those in power in the community (*ummah*)' ([1949] 1996: 47 and 55). For him the absolute liberation of the soul represented the first step towards a true and 'complete human equality', the second pillar of social justice in Islam. Equality went beyond the balance of social wealth and also attested to

> the unity of the human race in origin and destiny, in life and death, in rights and duties, before the law and before God, in this world and the next, with no preference except for righteous works and no honor except for piety (Qutb [1949] 1996: 57).

It also included equality between men and women, which Qutb tried to demonstrate at length from an Islamic perspective ([1949] 1996: 61–6).

Egalitarianism had to be complemented by the third pillar of social justice, solidarity, which differentiated the Islamic way of life from individualist capitalism (Qutb [1949] 1996: 69). Solidarity naturally grew within the family, which in his view had regrettably been attacked by both western and Soviet modernist ideologies, but which should again flourish in a true Islamic society. This solidarity grounded the Islamic social norms stated in the Qur'ān and the Sunna, including those on inheritance, welfare, and punishment, all of which, he argued, are rooted in human nature (Qutb [1949] 1996: 72–82). Thus, *Social Justice* was not intended as a proposal for normative change or reform, but as a powerful restatement of the established norms of the Islamic tradition as inherently rational and suitable for modern life. The main goal of the book was to demonstrate that Islamic teaching could fully address contemporary challenges, and that social justice, one of the key components of modern politics, could best be understood as part of an Islamic way of life (Qutb [1949] 1996: 24). To this end, Qutb felt it necessary to articulate a novel understanding of property rights as fundamentally restrained and, to use Polanyi's words, as deeply 'embedded' in the social and the religious.

QUTB'S METHODOLOGY: AN EXISTENTIALIST APPROACH TO THE QUR'ĀN[9]

Although Qutb linked the Islamic conception of property and social justice to concrete public interests, such as the avoidance of conflict and the prevention of immorality, his argument for Islamic law was not utilitarian, consequentialist, or rationalist. For him, social justice was not about constructing legal rules through reasoning or based on empirical data, but rather about discovering the legal norms of rightful government in the letter of the Qur'ān. Traditional norms only needed better implementation and enforcement, which could be provided by the tools of modern statehood, including centralized political and economic administration, and tax collection. Thus, the principal task of the modern Islamic state was to fully implement *sharīʿah*. Importantly, however, Qutb did not thematize the relationship between the state and the *ulamā'* in this context. While he criticized their speculative exegetical work he never explicitly called for limiting their legal functions and reducing their social status. It is hard to tell whether Qutb's silence on the issue stemmed from political prudence or simply unwillingness to elaborate on the concrete features of the Islamic state. One might

[9] Here the term existentialism is used to define Qutb's concern with the ultimate religious meaning of human life and existence, as opposed to the utilitarian or materialist approach of western and Soviet thinking on social justice. Obviously Qutb's religious existentialism substantially differed from coeval European existentialism (be it religious or atheist), notably because he rejected the latter's thick notion of human freedom.

assume that in his social utopia both the state and the *ulamā'* should cooperate to implement *sharīʿah* properly and effectively. However, how jurists and their law can be integrated within modern state apparatuses without losing their 'genuinely' Islamic character and social role would beg questions to which Qutb offered little answer.

What counted most for Qutb was the underlying religious project of the Islamic state rather than the latter's concrete form. Accordingly, he defined the ongoing struggle between the Islamic, capitalist, and socialist systems as primarily a clash of beliefs, not of cultures, mentalities, civilizations, or rationalities (Qutb [1964] 2005: 110). Those systems certainly produced their own specific forms of rationality and social and institutional practices including contrasting doctrines of property as either absolute (under capitalism) or restrained (in 'authentic' Islam). Yet such doctrines, he argued, were bound up in people's acts of faith towards a particular system. By rendering this a matter of faith rather than of political or economic 'rationality', Qutb could argue that those who strive in the path of God do not, and should not, choose Islam over western ideologies merely in so far as Islam provides more efficient answers to concrete problems, but simply and essentially because Islam is the truth. No other argument must or can be provided. Any rational or pragmatic reason for the believer to subject themselves to God would contaminate the purity of their intention to adhere to Islam. This position reflected the inadequacy of human rationality and the existential character of human decision, a conclusion Qutb drew after studying different systems of thought. He tellingly noted that the right attitude to truth was shared by believers and 'true atheists' alike: while rationalist Islamic philosophers had attempted to demonstrate the existence of God and the utility of faith by rational and eventually groundless arguments, both believers and 'true atheists' did not bother to pose the question of 'why' things are as they are and instead confined themselves to asserting their own belief in the existence or non-existence of God ([1964] 2005: 110). In Qutb's view no rational argument for any kind of truth added to the persuasiveness of that truth.

Qutb's existentialism had important consequences for his approach to the qur'ānic text and the normative content the text conveyed. He wished to stick to a literal reading of the Qur'ān, which on his assessment had historically been distorted by layers of misinterpretation, yet he conceded that the variation of circumstances and needs over time inevitably led different readers of the Qur'ān to emphasize diverse aspects of the text. He noted that every Muslim generation faced unique challenges and therefore implemented the qur'ānic message in particular and ever-changing ways ([1952–9] 2008: xv.194). Admitting that his own reading was subjective, he made clear that his books were not meant to replace revealed truth but simply to motivate readers to 'seek in [the Qur'ān] the great truth of the Islamic concept for themselves' ([1962] 1991: 6; Moussalli 1992: 82).

Qutb expressed scepticism towards exegetic and jurisprudential literature that intellectualized divine revelation and thus extinguished the pathos of the qur'ānic text. Both theology and jurisprudence of the sophistic kind alienated the believer from the original Islamic 'spirit' and drove him or her into a human world of artificial, abstract reasoning, one in which the powerful ideas of charity and social justice, but also jihad, might forfeit their existential appeal.[10]

> The real problem in grasping the significance and the spirit of the Qur'anic teachings does not lie in understanding its words and sentences, that is to say, its exegesis, as is often claimed. This does not constitute a problem at all. The problem lies in the capacity of our minds to reconstruct feelings, ideas, and experiences like the feelings, ideas, and experiences of the first generation of Muslims when they received these revelations from the lips of the Prophet (peace be upon him) in the thick of the struggle (Qutb [1962] 1991: 4).

Understanding Islam meant experiencing the urgency of the struggle of Islam against barbarism and ignorance (*jahiliyyah*) first carried out by the Prophet and his followers. This does not mean that the believer should literally transfer him or herself to an earlier stage of history but rather live the present *as if* it were a time of original and authentic existential struggle for life or death. Qutb's theory is primarily a theory of praxis in the present, a theory concerned with the contemporary loss of religious and communitarian values and the rise of individualism, materialism, and an absolute understanding of property ([1964] 2005: 1). Yet he assumed that the present must be redeemed in light of an original and truthful divine message uncontaminated by intermediate, multiple layers of human exegesis (Moussalli 1992: 160), which is to say the established tradition of Islamic law and doctrines of property. The doctrines of the *ulamā'* were problematic for Qutb precisely because they watered down the essence of the qur'ānic message, and its potential for total liberation, through casuistic and purportedly conservative legal reasoning. While the *ulamā'* focused on painstaking discussions of what Qutb perceived as the merely technical side of the law of property, he wished to articulate a visionary and politically committed theory of property that would underpin sweeping social reforms.

[10] As Moussalli notes, Qutb clearly distinguished jurisprudence as a human endeavour liable to error from *sharī'ah* as the truthful message of God (Moussalli 1992: 161). This, of course, did not prevent Qutb from praising Islamic jurists whose thought was in line with his own, such as Ibn Qayyim al-Jawziyyah (1292–1350) (Qutb [1964] 2005: 33).

GOD AS THE LORD OF THE WORLD

Qutb's theory of social justice and the right of property is rooted in a political theology. Examining this political theology is key to an understanding of the way Qutb theorized the fundamental and mutual link between property and power, a link allegedly missing in traditional jurisprudential debates that focused on the technical issues of the law of property. For Qutb it was impossible to think of property without linking it to a broader understanding of just social and political relationships between human beings and between humans and God, from whom all ownership and power derived.

A caveat is in order. As someone faithful to the letter of the Qur'ān, Qutb opposed 'theological' speculation in Islam ([1962] 1991: 7) and attempted to focus his analysis on God's will as expressed in revealed truth instead of discussing God's essence. He was convinced that non-literal, speculative readings would inevitably turn the reader away from the plain meaning of Revelation and end in empty sophistry and dangerous questioning of God's will. However, Qutb's reflections on the Qur'ān eventually did go beyond a mere rendering of the text and resulted in what can be called, in the broad sense, a 'theological' discourse, though one opposed to the rationalist theology he despised.[11] A case in point is his examination of the fundamental attributes of God, such as supreme power, authority, and ownership of the whole world. He thereby established an analogy between the divine and the human, since he defined both God and human individuals as able to enjoy lordship and ownership, if to essentially different degrees. This analogy between theological concepts and those belonging to the sphere of earthly politics and law allowed commentators to read Qutb's theory as a political theology in the sense of a theory grounded on structural analogies between the political and the theological.[12]

Qutb expounded his position on God's lordship in *Social Justice* and then in writings of the 1950s–1960s such as *In the Shade of the Qur'an, The Islamic Concept and Its Characteristics*, which dealt with Islam as a holistic way of life, and *Milestones*, which partly summarized earlier statements and became the most popular of Qutb's books ([1952–9] 2008; [1962] 1991; [1964] 2005). The theoretical starting point of Qutb's political theology was the affirmation of monotheism as expressed in the Islamic confession of faith, 'there is no god but God' ([1962] 1991: 122; [1964] 2005: 29). This affirmation is central to the Islamic doctrine of sovereignty as it entails that there is only one

[11] In his discussion of *kalam*, Halverson (2010) has also maintained that theological assumptions are still behind much modern Islamic scripturalist thought.

[12] One of the clearest examples of this historiographical approach is the analogy between monotheism as a religious creed and monarchy as a form of government (Schmitt 1985).

transcendent divinity that is recognized as highest Lord, as confirmed by qur'ānic verses positing that all power in the heaven and on the earth belongs to God.[13] The principle that 'there is no deity but God', which Qutb defines as the core statement of the whole Qur'ān:

> has only one meaning, which is that sovereignty in human life, and indeed in the entire universe, belongs only to God alone. It is He who rules over the universe as He exercises His will, and it is He who controls the lives of human beings in accordance with the law He has laid down and the way of living He has prescribed ([1952–9] 2008: vi.21; viii.18).

The concept of God's sovereignty (*hakimiyyah*, a concept already used by Mawdudi) over man and the world is loaded with practical meaning. By asserting humans' total dependence on God, divine *hakimiyyah* implies that humans must fulfil His will and live according to the message revealed in the Qur'ān, and that only by doing so humans act justly and become worthy of God's mercy and reward. This notion of divine *hakimiyyah* entails important corollaries in terms of political power and the understanding of ownership. First, man is essentially defined as God's vice-regent on earth, not as a self-referential and autonomous being, which gives rise to a set of social rights and obligations while according humanity a special status among all creatures (Qutb [1962] 1991: 46). Vice-regency also constitutes the key rationale for social justice, as all human beings without exception must equally be regarded as God's vice-regents and therefore as worthy of decent treatment. Qutb thus notes that in Islam, as a consequence of man's vice-regency, there is 'no material value on earth that can be raised higher than the value of man or for which man can be sacrificed' ([1962] 1991: 46). On his assessment, the Islamic system thus differs from capitalist and socialist systems that tend to sacrifice some individuals for the benefit of the majority or, worse, of an oppressive elite. This links back to Qutb's call for wealth redistribution and for restraining property rights through zakat and additional taxation. Because not even the life of the most ordinary of Muslims can be sacrificed for the sake of profit (as under capitalism) or production (as under socialism), measures must be taken to protect the poor and those in need.

A further important claim of Qutb's political theology is that compliance with *sharī'ah* is not a form of subjection but an experience of liberation at all levels, spiritual, economic, social, and political ([1962] 1991: 133). The

[13] This confession of faith also entails that God is entirely separated from His creation and is therefore truly 'ab-solute' (in the literal sense of being detached from and completely free from any external boundaries, limitations, or dependence). This neat separation from God and creation allows Qutb to make a distinction between Islam and other religions, for instance Christianity, which attributes both divine and human historical nature to the person of Jesus.

believer's choice to live in accordance with the Qur'ān releases them from their servitude to earthly rulers and materialist worldviews and thereby accords them the highest form of human freedom. This notion of liberation might have far-reaching political consequences, as illustrated by the radical course of action taken by later Islamist militants inspired by Qutb's writings (Musallam 2005; Calvert 2010; Halverson 2010). Since the task of all humans is 'the worship of Allah, in the sense of complete obedience to Allah alone' (Qutb [1962] 1991: 46) rulers must be held accountable for failing to implement *sharīʿah* and, Qutb argues, genuine Muslims are entitled to topple corrupt regimes to set up true Islamic governments (Qutb [1952–9] 2008: vi.103). In fact, Qutb's emphasis on resistance might sound questionable in light of some qur'ānic passages that require believers to comply with the commands of authorities. *Sura al-Nisa*, verse 49, famously states: 'You, who believe, obey God and the Messenger, and those in authority among you.' Yet Qutb reads this verse as meaning that obedience is due not to any prince but specifically to those in authority '*among you*', where *you*, in his restrictive reading, means the members of the Muslim *ummah*. Therefore, he argues, obedience is not necessarily due to non-Muslim and pagan rulers, including purportedly impious leaders of Muslim countries like Nasser, the modern 'pharaoh' (Qutb [1952–9] 2008: v.166).

THE ISLAMIC STATE AND THE MEANS TO REALIZE SOCIAL JUSTICE

Qutb argued that rebellion against impious authorities was the first step in a path towards overcoming the condition of *jahiliyyah* and establishing an Islamic state in which the laws of God would truly be obeyed. Here Qutb noted that the institution of a state is a necessary condition for implementing and securing compliance with Islamic law, as shown by the example of the Prophet who first set up a state in Madinah ([1952–9] 2008: ii.265; iii.59). Now as then, the full realization of the Islamic way of life rested on 'a regime, an authority, and a system of government to implement the Islamic law and constitution' and redistribute wealth (Qutb [1952–9] 2008: iii.171). Yet Qutb did not spend many words on the concrete features of the Islamic state since, as an existentialist thinker, he assumed that '[t]he important thing is not the precise form of the [legal and political] system; the important thing is its spirit' ([1949] 1996: 169). Based on his few remarks on the topic, what strikes the reader is that the Qutbian ideal state was equipped with what appear like distinctively modern features: a centralized administration, a treasury and a system of wealth redistribution, an advanced economy, institutions devoted to scientific and technological research, and a constitution (though Qutb did not insist on the latter item). Yet these characteristics do not have to be defined as peculiarly 'modern' and 'western'. Indeed, redistribution has been a trait common to all 'premodern' societies, and centralized administration is not exclusively a western phenomenon. In Egypt, the project of centralized statehood pursued in the early nineteenth century might have led less to 'westernization' than to a (temporary) return to the strong model of political and administrative organization of the early Ottomans (Mundy 2007: 40). One should not forget that, back in the sixteenth and seventeenth centuries, the centralized political, bureaucratic, and military structures of the Ottoman Empire provided an important model for European (absolutist) statehood itself (Kammel 2001).

To be sure, by Qutb's lifetime what had dramatically changed since the early Ottoman period was the state's reach into society. Thus, Qutb's ideal of the state as an entity capable of enforcing wealth redistribution came closer to Soviet Russia or western interventionist states than to the early Ottoman Empire. Yet Qutb entirely rejected the ideological underpinning of Russian and western statehood. For him, political legitimacy and internal cohesion did not rest on general happiness, universal equality, national identity, or the procedural rationality of democracy, but rather on the citizens' shared belief in Islam (and the simultaneous submission of the non-Muslim minority to the law of the state). In Qutb's opinion this shared belief allowed the Islamic state to avoid the pathologies of modern western statehood, most notably internal class struggle—which he thought had unmasked democracy as a tool for partisan politics instead of a means to seek the common good—and constant hostility towards foreign countries.[14] While the western 'welfare' state emerged as a political and social compromise, social justice in the Qutbian Islamic state was, he argued, religiously embedded in one of the pillars of Islam, the duty to give alms to the poor, orphans, and all those in need. Qutb noted that '[l]ife in the view of Islam is mutual love and respect, cooperation and solidarity' ([1949] 1996: 33), and these were not intended to be empty words: 'when it is feared that wealth may accumulate too narrowly in private hands, the means exist for the Muslim leader (*imām*) who governs by the *sharī'ah* of God to rectify the situation' by legislation and taxation ([1949] 1996: 74 and 86). Once again, modern statehood and sacred law merged in the Qutbian social justice discourse.

Qutb made clear that alms-giving in the Islamic state was a matter not only of charity in the moral sense (that exists primarily in the form of voluntary

[14] Nonetheless, the Qutbian state itself would likely enter into conflict with neighbouring countries, since its mission was to protect and expand the Islamic faith while all other countries still lived in the condition of *jahiliyyah*. The duty to expand Islam, apparently, might require the Islamic state to topple the hostile government of a foreign country so that the latter's population would listen to the message of the Quran (Qutb [1964] 2005: 35).

charity or *sadaqah*) but also of legal duty, as in the case of obligatory charity or *zakat*, which he reckoned could be collected by civil servants ([1949] 1996: 5). *Zakat* was a legal duty for the wealthy, and correspondingly, from the perspective of the poor, it qualified as an actual 'right to share in the wealth of those who are well off, a right which the Muslim state enforces by virtue of *sharīʿah* and by force of its authority' (Qutb [1949] 1996: 88). Further, in Qutb's view the authorities' duty to ensure social justice entitled them to set up a taxation system going beyond the collection of *zakat* and having broad distributional aims. In support of this policy Qutb quoted a *hadith* reported by Al-Tirmidhi stating that in Islam there was 'a claim on wealth other than Zakat' ([1949] 1996: 169). Based on *Surah al-Nisa*, 75 and *Surah al-Fajr*, 89 Qutb reminded the reader that 'the nation is responsible to protect the weak within it and to take care for and defend their interests', and that 'if one individual spends the night hungry, then the whole nation spends the night in sin so long as they do not bestir themselves to feed him' ([1949] 1996: 78 and 79). As the Muslim nation (*ummah*) was conceived as one body, every member of it should feel affected by evils and misfortunes befalling fellow members. This is quite different from the traditional view of non-canonical taxation (*maks*) as lying beyond law. From a Qutbian perspective, charity was a matter of strict law, a law that, lacking enforcement by local authorities, should be imposed by a centralized disciplinary state run by a vanguard of enlightened believers.

While Qutb backed his argument for wealth redistribution through scriptural evidence, he remarked that, like many other principles of Islamic law, it could additionally be justified by the broader 'interests of the community' and to 'assure the avoidance of all harm'. Here he was not thinking of western utilitarianism but rather of the classical Islamic doctrine of *maslaha* (meaning 'well-being' and 'welfare'), which early Islamic jurists had developed to deal with legal matters on which revelation was silent, and which nineteenth- and twentieth-century reformers had revived to adapt Islamic law to modern conditions (Opwis 2005). Based on this tradition Qutb mentioned some of the ways through which community interests can be legally protected. He referred to the notion of 'unrestricted benefits', that is, important benefits not mentioned in authoritative text and yet worth being preserved, and to 'blocking the devices' (or *hiyal*), i.e. outlawing permissible acts to prevent them from resulting in illegal conduct. Qutb, who had no jurisprudential background and little interest in technical legal matters, did not delve into these concepts and confined himself to providing the reader with a long explanatory quote from a work of al-Azhar jurist Muhammad Abu Zahra (1898–1974).[15] Qutb concluded his argument by remarking that

[15] A conservative scholar, Abu Zahra taught at al-Azhar's faculty of theology and Cairo University. He published a number of intellectual biographies of authors such as Abu Hanifah, Malik, Shafii, and Ibn Hanbal, as well as writings on legal matters, including property (Esposito 2003: 6).

Islamic principles properly address all concerns of modern life, including redistribution.

> It has been necessary to explain all of this [concerning wealth redistribution] to expose the collusion that takes place when all the discussion is focused on Zakat, as if that were the only claim on wealth in Islam ... Also, it is to expose those who underrate the safeguards in the Islamic order and claim that they are not adequate, so that they can then claim that the Islamic order is inadequate for modern life ([1949] 1996: 176).[16]

A striking absence in Qutb's theory of property and social justice is the notion of charitable trust (*waqf*), which had traditionally played an important role in shaping economic and social life in Islamic countries. The *waqf* was a legal means by which men or women would set up a revenue-bearing asset managed by chosen beneficiaries to provide public services, including hospitals, orphanages, and water delivery, in perpetuity (Kuran 2001). The *waqf* played a significant historical role in Islamic societies, since public services would not be provided by centralized municipalities until the modern era. Admittedly, it could also be a means for well-off Muslims to shield their and their families' wealth from confiscation by greedy authorities. Several legal stratagems were deployed to circumvent restrictions on the management of the *waqf* and basically turn it into private property, and many trusts were founded by rulers with the main aim of securing political legitimacy (Hourani 1991: 163; Kuran 2001; Hallaq 2009: 143). The ambivalence of the economic and social role of the *waqf* may explain Qutb's apparent unwillingness to mention it as a tool for ensuring social justice and large-scale redistribution. Indeed, among Islamic scholars, critiques of the *waqf* were already widespread in the 1930s and 1940s. Egyptian liberals like Sanhuri explicitly opposed this institution, which was reformed by Law 48 of 1946 and eventually nationalized under the Nasser regime (Coulson 1964: 199; Bechor 2007: 224).

THE TENSE RELATIONSHIP BETWEEN PRIVATE PROPERTY AND SOCIAL JUSTICE

In Qutb's argument on property the reader can detect an 'economic theology' that runs parallel to his political theology, and that had its starting point in the notion of God's absolute power stemming from the principle 'there is no god but God'. This absolute divine power is precisely manifested in the qur'ānic statement, frequently recalled by Qutb, that '[i]t is to God that

[16] Al-Banna in 'Toward the Light' had only mentioned zakat, not additional taxation, as the main financial resource for social reform (al-Banna 1978).

everything in the heavens and the earth truly belongs' (10: 55). Interestingly the Qur'ān does not, and does not need to, distinguish between the role of God as lawgiver and proprietor, since He has absolute power of command as well as effective control over His creatures and creation as a whole. This is visible, for instance, in the fact that one of the principal attributes of God, *al-Malik* (meaning 'king' or 'sovereign') encompasses both the idea of absolute ruler and absolute owner of the world (Khatab 2006: 18).

This doctrine of divine ownership and absolute power rests on three main tenets: that God originally created the world and mankind; that He keeps control over them after creation; and that He exercises this control and oversees the historical development of humanity in the best and most just way, which further legitimizes His possession of, and power over, the world. It is by creating and controlling the universe and mankind in this providential manner that God can fully be conceived as their absolute and rightful sovereign and owner. In Qutb's theory, this dynamic was mirrored at the level of human society, as individuals' right of ownership stemmed from activity, work, and production, that is, from instances of creation and control on a small scale. Thus, in the Islamic state '[p]rivate property arises from the particular effort expended by the individual to acquire title to part of the general property over which God has delegated stewardship (*istakhlafa*) to the human race' (Qutb [1949] 1996: 129). Qutb maintained that, as vice-regents of God on earth, individual owners were additionally supposed to improve what He has mercifully allowed them to possess, and to use their wealth virtuously and charitably to contribute to the material and moral development of the broader society, thereby giving back to the community the benevolence that God had bestowed on them in the first place. The community indeed played an important role in *Social Justice*, and in some passages Qutb defined it as the actual subject of the right of property granted by God, a right the community then delegated to individuals.

> The first principle established by Islam—alongside the right of private ownership—is that the individual is virtually the community's agent in relation to his property, and that his tenure of it is more like employment than ownership, and that ownership in general is fundamentally the right of the community and that the community has this as a delegation (*mustakhlafah fihi*) from God, who is the only true owner of anything ([1949] 1996: 129).

The community in turn constituted an ideal entity that could only act through its actual lawgiver, so 'all permission to distribute [property] in particular ways must issue from the Lawgiver either in reality or in terms of legal judgement' (Qutb [1949] 1996: 129). Here, again, one finds parallels between Qutb's economic theology and his political theology. Both narratives rested on a two-step model in which God originally delegates power and authority to the community and the latter transfers it to the ruler. Curiously, this model also had some analogies with the early Ottoman idea of the Sultan as ultimate owner of the land. This latter was a political and economic theology too, though a secularized one, which Qutb could not accept.

THE RIGHT OF OWNERSHIP AND THE LABOUR THEORY OF APPROPRIATION

While Qutb's aim in justifying property was not the same as that of classical western authors like Grotius and Locke, his argument rested on similarly theological reasoning with common monotheistic roots. Grotius, Locke, and Qutb shared the presupposition that property originally rests on divine legitimacy but they took it in radically different directions. The theological vocabulary of property is highly flexible, and has been put to a variety of uses, including the justification of colonial occupation in Grotius and Locke (Tuck 1999; Van Ittersum 2006; Fitzmaurice 2014) and the advocacy of wealth redistribution in Qutb. In *Two Treatises of Government* Locke argued that

> [t]he Earth, and all that is therein, is given [by God] to Men for the Support and Comfort of their being. And though all the Fruits it naturally produces, and Beasts it feeds, belong to Mankind in common ... there must of necessity be a means *to appropriate* them some way or other, before they can be of any use, or at all beneficial to any particular man ([1689] 1988: 286).

This means of appropriation was labour. Several western philosophers, most importantly Hegel and Marx, would elaborate on Locke's intuition by arguing that through labour individuals humanize nature, put their mind and spirit into it and thus fully appropriate it. Humans first dominate matter through their hands and intellect and then establish property rights to secure continuous control over what they have apprehended through the efforts of their bodies and minds.

Qutb agreed with Locke that God had given man the earth as a gift to be taken advantage of, and man was consequently mandated to develop it. This was attested to by qur'ānic passages, such as *Surah al-Baqarah*, 29–30, stating that God 'created all that is on the earth' for man, who acts as His 'successor on earth', or *Surah al-Najm*, 48, saying that 'it is He who gives wealth and possessions'. Yet, in Qutb's reading, the notion of God's absolute ownership operated as a tool for *both justifying and contesting* human property rights, since he retained a much more important and permanent role for God as the absolute owner than Locke was willing to concede. In Locke's narrative God only initially and briefly entered the stage as the owner of the world and benevolent gift-giver and then disappeared from the scene, allowing humans to establish unrestrained property rights based on economic activity and entrepreneurship. For Qutb instead God remained an absolute owner in full control of the world and mankind at all points in history. If truly 'everything belongs to God', human ownership was necessarily relative and derivative, a mere form of trusteeship, and on Qutb's view this notion had important practical ramifications. It entailed that the human property rights in the Islamic state could be invalidated when used in a manner contrary to the purpose of the trust, that is, the improvement and development of the material and spiritual resources that God had generously bestowed on mankind and individual owners ([1952–9] 2008: vol. 1, 344). Commenting on *surah al-Baqarah* in *In the Shade of the Qur'an* Qutb claimed that

> [Humans] are bound by the terms of that custodianship, as set out by God Almighty, the ultimate owner, in the divine code of living revealed to mankind. Any violation of these terms leads to disqualification and censure of the trustee ... Once the belief is firmly established in our consciousness that everything in this world belongs to God and that what we own is merely on loan for a limited period of time, greed and lust to accumulate wealth and worldly possessions by any means will not be difficult to hold in check ([1952–9] 2008: i.345).[17]

What Qutb meant by misuse of property becomes clear in light of his argument that the right to property stems from work and activity, which in Locke gave rise to unrestricted human ownership. In contradistinction to Locke, Qutb argued that because ownership rested on effort and labour all, say, 'inactive' ways of acquiring and controlling property that created wealth *ex nihilo*—notably through usury, i.e. charging interests on loans, and the setting up of monopolies—were unjust and illegal.[18] As seen above, these items had already been listed by al-Banna in 'Toward the Light' and targeted by Islamist critique. Moving beyond al-Banna, however, Qutb attacked usury and monopolies not only at the local or national level but also globally.

> The disaster that has come to completion in the modern age—and did not exist in this repugnant form in the [early] Jahiliyyah—is that these usurers—who were represented in the past in the form of individual and banks but now are represented in the form of the founders of modern financial institutions—have been able, with their terrifying and fearsome power within the institutions of government world-wide and beyond them, and with their means of propaganda throughout the world, whether newspapers or books or broadcasting

[17] This restriction of property rights based on theology substantially echoed Sanhuri's secularized claim that the right of property was subordinated to higher public interests. In both cases it was up to the 'community', be it represented by an Islamist vanguard or by the jurist, to decide whether property had been misused or unlawfully accumulated.

[18] There are striking similarities here with late medieval objections to usury: see, e.g. Armstrong (2016: 3–36).

> stations or cinemas or universities and their professors or other means, to create a certain general mentality among the impoverished masses of humanity whose flesh and bones those usurers consume and whose sweat and blood they drink in the shadow of the system of usury: This general mentality has submitted to the vicious and poisonous suggestion that usury is the natural and reasonable system and the only sound basis for economic growth, that the cultural progress of the West is one of its blessings and benefits, and that those who would abolish it are a group of impractical idealists who base these views of theirs merely on ethical theories and imaginary ideals which have no practical value and which would guarantee the ruin of the whole economic system if they were allowed to have any effect on it ([1949] 1996: 149).

Qutb here put forward a radically alternative view of the evils of international political economy to the explanations offered by free-market liberals. Economists in the latter mode tend to argue that the major cause of international financial trouble is fiscal mismanagement by national governments and the ensuing risk of sovereign default, which must then be fixed by recourse to international creditors and austerity measures. Conversely Qutb believed that the culprits of international economic distress are financial institutions that impose intolerable burdens on Third World countries and thrive on these countries' debt. Interestingly, Qutb also denounced financial institutions' capacity to hegemonize public discourse and thus rationalize and normalize their practices.[19] From his viewpoint, opposing their public rhetoric and their system of 'usury' both internationally and domestically qualified as an act of resistance analogous to rebellion against tyrannical rulers.

QUTB'S LEGACY AND BEYOND: PROPERTY, CHARITY, AND SOCIETY

Qutb's radical ideas were echoed by the nascent doctrine of Arab socialism which, while ideologically antithetical to Qutb's Islamist view, would promote a redistributive social agenda similar to his. Throughout the 1950s and 1960s Nasser in Egypt, as well as Muammar Gaddafi in Libya, pursued social and economic programmes redistributing land and nationalizing private enterprise.[20] 'Social justice', as we saw, was a concept used both by liberals like Sanhuri and by Islamists like Qutb, and its attractions extended beyond

[19] For a critical view on the modes of operation of international institutions and the politics of economic development, see Chimni (2004), Anghie (2005), and Pahuja (2011).

[20] Nasser's nationalization policy seemed so radical to some pro-western scholars that they felt urged to argue that his agenda actually clashed with Islamic law which, in their view, provided strong protection for property owners (Habachy 1962).

any one political project. While Sanhuri's harmonious vision of social justice encouraged both the wealthy and the poor to contribute to common progress, Qutb, Nasser, and Gaddafi all took a revolutionary approach to changing Arab society. However, Qutb felt more hostile to Nasser, whose social agenda he shared but whose Islamic faith he questioned, than to the liberals like Sanhuri, who was religiously closer yet politically distant from Qutb.

The appeal of Arab socialism and nationalism faded in the aftermath of the Six-Day War of 1967,[21] and radical Islamism emerged as the most powerful language of political struggle. While a number of Islamist intellectuals and activists from the 1970s to the 1990s still looked back at Qutb for inspiration, their focus was on his theory of jihad, not on projects of wealth redistribution. In the ideologies of Qutbists like al-Jihad's Muhammad Abd al-Salam Faraj, al-Qaeda's Ayman al-Zawahiri and Ansar al-Islam's Fateh Krekar, social justice has played little to no role compared with the perceived need for armed struggle against 'Zionism' and imperialism. In moderate Islamist circles, too, the theme of social justice has lost ground to other concerns, and the Muslim Brotherhood itself, once the bulwark of the social, has adopted a largely neoliberal economic agenda (Shabi 2012).

However, it would be hasty to declare social justice a forgotten ideal in the Arab world. For the last thirty years, major Islamist movements such as Hamas and Hezbollah have grounded much of their legitimacy and popular support on their ability to provide social services in contexts where state institutions appear unable or unwilling to address the population's basic needs. It has been estimated that around 95 per cent of Hamas's 70 million USD annual budget is devoted to social programmes, including medical and educational institutions and workers' unions (Robinson 2004: 127). The charity *Mujama Islamiya*, founded by Sheikh Ahmed Yassin and linked to Hamas, finances schools, kindergartens, clinics, hospitals, nursing schools, and sports clubs. As for Hezbollah, its main declared goal is the fight against Zionism, yet it has built much of its popularity on its social projects. The Hezbollah project even started with charitable institutions like *al-Shahid* and *al-Jarih*, which were set up to provide financial aid to families of 'martyrs' and those wounded in 1982. Hezbollah's Jihad al-Bina, active since 1985, 'took in hand the reconstruction of many buildings that had collapsed during the war, the repair of flood damage, the treatment of household waste, the transport of potable water, the installation of electricity (power stations and lines), and roadwork' (Avon and Khatchadourian 2012: 60). Hezbollah also provides low-cost housing and scholarships. In addition to Hezbollah, other Lebanese parties, such as Amal, the 'movement of the disinherited',

[21] On the ramifications of that event for Arab thought see Kassab (2010).

founded in 1974 and still an important Shia political force in Lebanon, have addressed the concerns of the poor and built their own networks of social welfare.

Notions of social justice meanwhile flourish in other domains, most notably Islamic finance. An outgrowth of the Islamic economics once established by the likes of Mawdudi, Islamic finance has developed rapidly from the 1980s and has now turned into a global phenomenon, with most major international banks now supplying *sharīʿah* -friendly products (Iqbal and Mirakhor 2011: 16). The main characteristic of contemporary Islamic finance is that it prohibits the charging of financial interests (*riba*) and encourages risk-and-profit sharing, allegedly promoting social justice and restraining unfair enrichment.[22] In fact, because there are many ways of legally circumventing *sharīʿah* prohibitions by making interest appear like sale or rent in contracts, some scholars have claimed that 'despite the good intentions of its pioneers, Islamic finance has placed excessive emphasis on contract forms, thus becoming a primary target for rent-seeking legal arbitrageurs' (El-Gamal 2006: xi). Still, the recent global expansion and popularity of this brand of finance even among ordinary Muslim customers illustrates that the Islamic notion of property as subject to religious norms still has purchase among believers. Whether this conception has been hijacked to develop a business model that barely differs from standard 'capitalist' banking remains, of course, a legitimate question (Tripp 2006: 146), but it does not diminish the relevance of the Islamic discourse on property in the contemporary world. Quite the contrary, the ambivalent practical outcomes of that discourse attest to the need for engaging with it further, devoting increasing attention to the way it has interacted with and accommodated established economic and financial practices.

CONCLUSION

This chapter has shown that the notions of social justice and charity, underpinned by a critique of the right of property, have occupied a central place in a large strand of twentieth-century Islamic thought from al-Banna through to Sanhuri, Qutb and contemporary Islam. In this strand property is not conceived as absolute and exclusive, but rather as subordinated to public interest and restrained by religiously grounded social obligations. Within this framework, property's key attribute is that it should be redistributed: there

[22] Nevertheless, Islamic finance remains grounded in the full respect of property rights. In that respect, it resonates with Mawdudi's position and is less radical than Qutb's theory, which demanded the subordination of individual ownership to social needs.

is no right of property without a simultaneous duty to redistribute. This way of viewing property as socially embedded and restrained certainly had predecessors in 'pre-modern' societies (Polanyi 2001), including in the Jewish and Christian religious traditions, as well as modern parallels in western and Soviet forms of state interventionism. Yet this doctrine of property limitation has followed a particular trajectory in Islamic contexts, a trajectory largely under-examined in many contemporary studies focusing on jihad and therefore worth retracing and studying on its own terms.

For contemporary readers Qutb's theory begs a variety of questions, notably about the potential for *sharīʿah* to restrain the abuse of property rights and advance social justice within the structures of the modern nation state. He assumes that *sharīʿah* can operate within the state without forfeiting its original social purposes and therefore promote social justice in a 'genuinely' Islamic way. Still, Qutb did not discuss the details of the Islamic state's system of wealth redistribution, the concrete ways taxation should be enforced, or the prospective role of the *ulamā'* in advancing social justice. He believed that his main task was to revive the Islamic 'spirit' rather than focus on specific legal and political arrangements (Qutb [1949] 1996: 169). His was an interest in law minus complex and, in his view, elitist jurisprudence which betrayed its spirit. Yet it seems that an 'authentic' Islamic law can thrive only when shaped and negotiated in everyday relationships within communities held together by established norms, recognized practices, and local institutions. In these contexts, jurists, not the state, have final authority in interpreting God's will, while central powers claiming ultimate authority, like the Sultan of old, rarely interfere with the local operations of jurists' law. Although novel and hybrid forms of *sharīʿah* will continue to develop and remain at the centre of political contestation (Hallaq 2009), the immediate revival of authentic *sharīʿah* is thus a political myth. Qutb himself largely supported strong statehood and was adamant that the whole state apparatus should be put at the service of *sharīʿah*,[23] but that would imply the creation of new, hybrid forms of law and administration with little historical precedent.

[23] For Qutb the agency of the vanguard was essential to the transition from 'ignorance' to Islam. Although some have seen this educational reform as utopian, it has had a strong appeal to many Muslim Brothers and other Islamists, and has been a driving force in the early Qutb reception and in more recent revivals of his thinking by moderate Islamist groups (Cakir 2015).

7

A Sea of Profit

Making Property in the Western Indian Ocean

JATIN DUA

'What we do is different. In Asia they make whole ships disappear; in Africa [i.e. here the Gulf of Guinea] they steal oil. We [in Somalia] just catch fish' (interview with 'Farah',[1] February 2011). Farah was explaining the uniqueness of Somali piracy, one that made the practice of taking ships at sea permissible and distinct from theft. 'Many of us used to be fishermen', he continued:

> I'm from Eyl [a fishing village on the Indian Ocean coast]. I grew up catching lobster, tuna, and snapper. One night a trawler cut our nets when we were fishing not far from the coast. A few of us decided enough was enough and we boarded the boat. We made the captain pay $1,000 as a tax to fish in our waters. We went back to the village and told everyone about it. Soon the boys started getting on the fibre boats and chasing trawlers to get money from them. This is how we became pirates. After a while, we started going after bigger boats. As a fisherman, I used to capture small fish, now I capture a different kind of fish, a bigger fish (ibid.).

'Now I capture a different kind of fish, a bigger fish': while minimizing the role of violence in the hijacking and the ransoming of ships and seafarers in the Western Indian Ocean—a practice that occurred with unprecedented frequency between 2007 and 2012 when over 150 ships and 3,500 seafarers were held hostage—this slippage between fish and ships is more than a mere rhetorical ploy to justify piracy. It helps explain, as this chapter will show, the transformation of fishermen into pirates. Specifically, far from being in

[1] For reasons of confidentiality all names and locations in the chapter have been changed.

A Sea of Profit: Making Property in the Western Indian Ocean. Jatin Dua. © Jatin Dua, 2017. Published 2017 by Oxford University Press.

contradistinction to ideas of legalism, capture is a framework of action with its own ideologies of redistribution and responsibility embedded within, what appear initially as, simple acts of taking. Through highlighting principles of legalism within forms of taking, this chapter points to the centrality of capture in the making and unmaking of property at sea.

Somalia's twenty-plus plus years of state collapse is routinely cited as explaining the rise of maritime predation in these restive waters. Jeffrey Gettleman observes that off the coast of Somalia 'the perfect conditions for piracy prevail: anarchy, a cold war legacy that left Somalia armed to the teeth, and a 1,900-mile coastline abutting the Gulf of Aden, which 20,000 ships traverse each year. The pirates of Somalia have an entire country the size of Texas to use as a sanctuary' (quoted in Dua and Menkhaus 2012: 756). The logic is clear: the proximity to a major shipping lane provides opportunity and the ungoverned space removes deterrents: piracy will therefore flourish. This story of failed states and criminality obscures the fact that piracy in Somalia tended to be concentrated in the north-east coast in Puntland and in several fishing villages in central Somalia (see Figure 7.1) where a weak but functional local administration held power rather than in the relatively lawless south-central coastal region. Furthermore, this narrative of state failure has been critiqued for ignoring the forms of governance and order without government (Menkhaus 2006) that continued to exist in Somalia after 1991. Somalia lacked a central government but it did not lack governance.

Several scholars have sought to avoid a narrative of failed states by situating maritime piracy within a world of marine exploitation and overfishing (e.g. Hansen 2009; Samatar et al. 2010; Weldemichael 2012; Bueger 2013; Dua 2013). The dramatic upsurge in maritime piracy off the coast of Somalia, perhaps inadvertently, drew global attention to fishing, specifically to the problem of illegal fishing in the Western Indian Ocean. While reports highlighting the prevalence of illegal, unreported, and unauthorized (IUU)fishing vessels in Somali waters date back to the early 1990s when large-scale foreign trawling first made its appearance in the Western Indian Ocean, this renewed emphasis on illegal fishing can be directly linked to the spectacular rise in incidents of maritime piracy and international efforts to curb this practice since 2007. Critiquing a simplistic tale of piracy as criminality, these scholars have argued for pluralizing and contextualizing the rise of maritime piracy. Samatar, Lindberg, and Mahayni, for example, reach beyond the legal definition of piracy as the illegal capture of ships in international waters, instead describing the different forms of piracy operating off the coast of Somalia. Illegal fishing in this narrative is a form of 'resource piracy' that emerged in 1991 and led to a response from Somali fishing communities, a response they label 'defensive piracy':

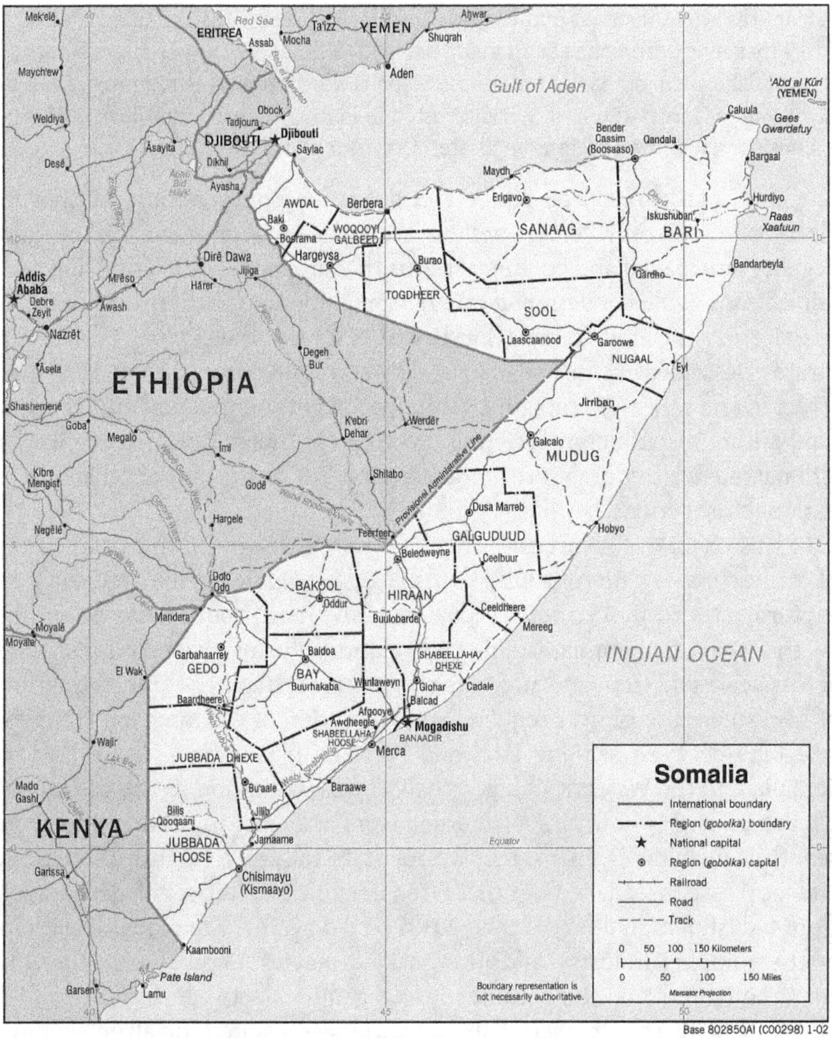

Figure 7.1 Map of Somalia with Puntland
Source: Open Source-CIA Factbook

The second type of piracy appeared along the Somali coast after the political disintegration of the country in 1991. Two sub-groups of pirates constitute what we would like to call 'resource pirates'. They include companies from Asia, Europe and Africa who are driven by the lure of Somalia's unprotected rich fish resources, and others who are motivated by the search for unguarded territories where Europe's surplus trash and toxic waste could be dumped … in the absence of any state authority that could fend off resource pirates, fishing communities along the coast have watched factory ships anchor short distances

> from the shore for days and ransack Somali resources. Consequently some of the former government's coast guard decided to challenge the predators before local fishermen joined the fray. These Somalis were attempting to protect their marine resources and were not interested in looting the merchant marine. We consider these to be 'defensive pirates' (Samatar et al. 2010: 1379).

The concepts of resource piracy and defensive piracy remind us that in global coverage only certain actions are labelled as piratical: 'piracy' and 'legality' are loaded and polemical terms that are modes of legitimizing certain actions while condemning others. Somali piracy for these authors, like practices of 'social banditry' (Hobsbawm 1959) and the exploits of Atlantic pirates described by historians such as Marcus Rediker (2004) is a constructed and contested category. While importantly contextualizing the rise (and fall) of maritime predation in the Western Indian Ocean, these works still narrate a story of failure—of governance, of states, and of other international institutions.

In this chapter, I recast the story of piracy through Farah's description of 'captur[ing] a different kind of fish'. By emphasizing the centrality of capture—and notions of bounty, payment, and redistribution nested within it—this chapter illuminates shifts in relationships of property and profit across scale and time and suggests that to understand the transformation of fishermen into pirates requires an exploration of the long and complex interplay between sea and land and between fishing and pastoralism in Somalia and the Western Indian Ocean. A close attention to the genealogy of capture shows how piracy emerged from attempts to make property at sea, thus pushing against narratives of state failure, foreign exploitation, and local response: narratives that often imagine a ragtag set of 'desperados from a dysfunctional land' (Lane 2013) pitted against the global leviathan of the shipping industry and international navies. Capture expands this frame to understand the contingent engagements between fishermen and pastoralists, fish and camels, fishing trawlers and state officials in shaping concepts of property and profit that have implications for how we understand maritime piracy and property regimes more generally. As the legal scholar, Carol Rose has noted, a fundamental puzzle for property scholars remains: 'how do things come to be owned?' (Rose 1985: 73) Through the framework of capture, this chapter highlights the various ways littoral societies in northern Somalia have come to understand, justify, and contest forms of taking as well as locating these within broader national, regional, and global modes of making property at sea.

I begin this story on the Somali coast and explore the role of fish and fishing within a pastoral world. The focus then shifts to the heyday of the Somali state and the period of scientific socialism (1969–75). The argument tracks shifting claims to property and access and the transition from artisanal fishing to a 'sea of fish' (Dua 2013) as the Somali government, other states and private actors sought to exploit and harness the resource-rich sea. I highlight the remaking of property and the development of licensing regimes that were at the heart of fishery development in Somalia from the 1970s onwards. Rent seeking through a form of licensing was crucial to the establishment of fisheries and constituted a central logic of statecraft in Somalia more generally. In this view the contemporary upsurge in maritime piracy off the coast of Somalia is not a moment of rupture resulting from the absence of a centralized government, but rather an extension and transformation of this licensing regime now pursued by non-state actors in the guise of 'piracy'. Throughout this narrative, and in keeping with the spirit of the volume, the chapter emphasizes an understanding of property as contingent, contested, and imbricated within more general questions of obligation and reciprocity in the global system.

PIRATES IN A LAND OF PASTORALISTS

What does it mean to make property at sea? In the classical world, Roman jurists divided the universe into things over which individual human beings could have patrimony and things that were seen to lie outside this system (*res extra nostrum patrimonium* or *res extra commercium*) (Buckland 1963: 180–6; Mousourakis 2012: 120–1). Land could be fenced in and enclosed, and so was fair game for conquest and control.[2] Things outside the threshold of human patrimony and ownership included those that belonged to the gods and those over which no single being, divine or human, could lay claim. This latter realm of law included the air, flowing water, and the sea. This elemental distinction was the basis for a young Dutch jurist's defence of acts of seizure at sea by the Dutch East India Company (VOC). Writing in the aftermath of the capture of the Portuguese carrack *Santa Catarina* in the Straits of Singapore in 1603, Hugo Grotius sought to justify Captain Jakob van Heemskerck's action through recourse to natural law and divine will. Grotius sought to locate van Heemskerck's actions within a wider context of freedom of trade and navigation. Property (or what we would term a property right in contemporary parlance) could only be derived from physical possession and use. Given the fluidity of the ocean and its seeming inexhaustibility, no one could possess and thus exclude others from the sea. As he notes in his *Mare Liberum*, '[t]he sea therefore is in the number of things

[2] For Roman law of land ownership, see also Kantor (Chapter 2, this volume). For the basics of this classification in Roman–Dutch law, see Lee (1925: 123–8).

which are not in merchandise and trading, that is to say, which cannot be made proper' (Armitage 2004: 30). Thus, the Portuguese attempt to exclude Dutch shipping from the Indian Ocean was an act of aggression justifying van Heemskerck's seizure as a legitimate act of reprisal. As David Armitage has noted in his discussion on Grotius's *Mare Liberum*, '[t]his fundamental contrast between the properties of sea and land would remain central to later conceptions of property within the natural-law tradition up to and beyond John Locke's agriculturalist argument for appropriation, which similarly exempted "the Ocean, that great and still remaining Common of Mankind" (Locke, *Second Treatise*, §30) from the possibility of exclusive possession' (2004: xvi). The vision of capture that emerges from the Somali case discussed below is one that befuddles this elemental distinction and mediates between land and sea and the worlds of pastoralism and fishing.

With one of the longest coastlines in continental Africa, Somalia is home to some of the world's richest marine resources. During the months of June to September, the warm southwest monsoon churns the waters off the coast of northern Somalia. Merging with the Findlater jet, a narrow low-level atmospheric jet stream that blows diagonally across the Indian Ocean, these currents combine to create a coastal upwelling that brings nutrient-rich waters to the surface attracting tuna, snapper, and other coveted piscine delights. The north-east monsoon, which occurs from December to February, causes a reversal of the Somalia current, moving the coastal waters southwest. As air from the north cools the water, more nutrients arrive to the surface creating one of the most productive marine ecosystems in the world.

In 1962, a British businessman named William Travis arrived in Mogadishu, the capital city of newly independent Somalia, with a 'plan to open up the world's first turtle cannery' (Travis 1967: 5). In his memoirs, *The Voice of the Turtle*, one of the few twentieth-century English-language accounts of the Somali coast, Travis wrote in vivid detail of his travels along the Somali coast and the fecundity of the waters offshore. At one point in his journey, Travis spent the night on a beach in the ancient port city of Merca and was regaled by tales of the coast from *Mzee* (elder) Ibrahim, whom he described as a 'net-maker, arbitrator and fable weaver extraordinaire' (1967: 130). After recounting a particularly gruesome set of stories involving face-eating hyenas, Ibrahim began reminiscing on his travels to the Red Sea coast, 'now you [Travis] have never been further than the Jubba river and so you do not know what goes on outside. But in my youth I went far, by boat and by land, even as far as Alula and Berbera in the north and distant M'kullah, Socotra [in Yemen]. I know the abode of djinns and Ras Haafun, where the fish and the bounty of the sea is so plentiful it casts itself onto the shore' (ibid.). At this point, Travis remarked 'I thought this a great lie, till I visited the north and found it all to be true' (1967: 131).

Despite the riches of the sea, Somali society, like a number of East African societies is one defined through the rhythms and idioms of pastoralism. 'A person who owns a camel is a man, someone who owns a goat is half a man and a fisherman is no man at all', announced Hassan, one of the most successful camel traders in Bosaso, a semi-bustling port on the Red Sea coast of northern Somalia. He had a satisfied chuckle as he laid out the hierarchy of Somali masculinity, in which he clearly enjoyed an exalted status. Within the anthropological archive, pastoralists and their relationship to livestock occupies a central focus in writings on East Africa. Beginning with Hershkovitz's (1926) 'cattle complex' to Evans-Pritchard's (1940) classic ethnographic account of the Nuer, anthropologists have long emphasized the 'bovine mystique' of livestock (see Scheele, Chapter 1, this volume). Through ethnographically nuanced accounts, this scholarship has highlighted the role of livestock as a storehouse of value in multiple registers (Hutchinson 1992); a means for forging sociopolitical ties (Kuper 1982); and a mode of linking economies of production and exchange across local–regional, and precolonial–colonial scales (Ferguson 1985; Comaroff and Comaroff 1990). Somalia's 'camel complex' fits neatly within this literature on pastoralism. In their oral histories, poetry, and encounters with visiting ethnographers, Somalis emphasize the centrality of livestock in shaping the rhythms of everyday life. As a marker of prestige and status, livestock is a key element in the formation and transformation of property relations.

I had met Hassan at the customs office in Bosaso port where he was waiting for an export certificate from the quarantine office for his herd of camels destined for Saudi Arabia. Following the establishment of Aden in 1839 as a major coaling station for British shipping, Bosaso and neighbouring Berbera became ports of call for the British Indian Navy eager to secure supplies, primarily livestock—camels and goats—to feed booming Aden. Then, as now, ships regularly plied across the salty *Badda Cas* (Red Sea), connecting these small port-cities with worlds of exchange far beyond their hazy shorelines. Once Hassan had secured his export certificate, we ended up sitting in the hold of his boat, an MSV (motorized sailing vessel) class *dhow* built in Mandvi, India. As he explained the hierarchy of livestock ownership in Somalia, Hassan noted that unlike sheep and goats, camels constituted both his individual wealth and a joint stock of his lineage (*summad*). As Hassan explained, while the prestige of ownership belonged to him, it came with an obligation to share the milk and meat with his *summad*. This kin group was in turn obligated to assist him in raising and maintaining his camel herds. The anthropologist I. M. Lewis has emphasized that this shared property claim, in addition to the ecological needs of pastoralism in a harsh and unforgiving climate, is integral to social solidarity and clan cohesion (Lewis 1994): he highlights the central role of property in shaping institutions like clans, and their forms of sociality and moral engagements. What is often occluded in this understanding of wealth and property is the coexistence of capture. The shared wealth in camels has historically also led to the emergence and perpetuation of raiding economies built around capture and other systems of violent redistribution and incorporation (Laitin and Samatar 1987; Lewis 1994). Capture, then, is not the failure of solidarity but tied to modes of maintaining and indeed transforming social structures and hierarchies. Systems of property and capture also traverse specific geographies, connecting land and sea.

The communities that inhabit the Somali coast, known locally as *sab* or 'occupational castes', are often understood (by both anthropologists and local communities) as removed from the world of lineage, clan, and property. Hassan, like a number of his compatriots, repeatedly emphasized this distinction through his distaste and even revulsion for fish. 'I am not *afkalluun*' (lit. fish mouth) he reminded me, referring to the disparaging way of describing fishermen and other coastal residents. Most coastal communities exist at the physical and social periphery of Somali society, traditionally intermarry only within their group, and speak dialects of Somali distinct from the standardized Af Soomali. However, they remain deeply intertwined within pastoral worlds and wider national and regional markets. Systems of patronage and the shifting seasonal demands of labour in the interior and the coast create a constant movement of people and livestock between the coast and the hinterland (with pastoralists arriving on the coast during dry season to work on fishing boats and fishermen moving inland to pastoral camps during the monsoons to tend goats and camels). Additionally, pastoral idioms of ownership and the prominence of capture, collection, and redistribution shape the world of the coast as well. Livestock and fish mediate relationships between pastoralists and coastal *sab*, particularly through ideas of property and wealth.

A SEA OF FISH

In addition to rich fishing resources, the monsoonal waters of the Indian Ocean also bring pieces of ambergris jettisoned from whales up into the northwest corner of the ocean, in the bottleneck formed by Somalia and the peninsula of southern Arabia. Historical accounts of the ambergris trade and the moral economy of artisanal fishing along the northern Somali coast underline the importance of exchange between the coast and the pastoral hinterland. Ambergris is one of the more unusual flotsam of the sea. Produced in the digestive tract of sperm whales in order to ease the passage of hard, sharp objects—such as squid beaks—that the whale may have ingested, ambergris was valued for its medicinal properties and as a fixative for perfumes (allowing scents to last much longer). By the early nineteenth century, a boom in the global ambergris trade led to the establishment of 'ambergris villages' along the northern Somali coast where communities earned their livelihoods by collecting the valuable wax as it is deposited on their doorsteps by the obliging waves.

Ambergris was seen as a 'gift from the ocean' whose bounty tied these coastal villages to wider economies in the region. Indian and Arab merchants routinely visited these villages to purchase the substance and the resulting cash provided villagers with access to livestock and other commodities. Echoing rules regarding the distribution of salvage from shipwrecks in the nineteenth century,[3] this ambergris economy was built on a mix of capture, collection, and redistribution. Few restrictions existed at sea for its appropriation, and chance and risk were crucial to the acquisition of this bounty. Once the flotsam washed onto shore, rules regarding property and ownership were strictly, and often violently, enforced within the local community. As Travis notes in his description of the ambergris villages, village elders (*oday*) allocated to each family in the village 'a section of the beach, with the sole right to collection. Like plots of precious farmland they [were] zealously tended and handed down from father to son' (1963: 183). The transformation of profits from ambergris into livestock or payments for labourers, such as *askaris* (guards) or cleaners for the sea frontages, created a redistributive network built around clan payment groups. In the nineteenth century, the opening of the Suez Canal and British imperial expansion into the Red Sea and the Indian Ocean transformed northern Somalia's incorporation into currents of global capitalism.[4] Within the world of ambergris collection, possibilities for profit and potential access to a wider world of consumer goods greatly increased alongside a rise in violence during this period. Ambergris, like the world of shipwreck salvage in nineteenth-century Somalia, brought together land and sea: capture and redistribution.

[3] In the nineteenth century, the northern Somali coast had become infamous for shipwrecks due to whirlpools and other treacherous conditions as ships moved from the relative calm of the Red Sea to the Indian Ocean. As a result of these shipwrecks, an economy of plundering vessels and ransoming those who had the misfortune to be stranded along this desolate coast developed, at the same time as these waters were becoming key to British, Ottoman, French, and Italian imperial designs. See Cruttenden (1846) for an account of this shipwreck economy from the perspective of a British Navy officer. Durrill (1986) and Dua (2013) locate this shipwreck economy within wider Somali engagements with colonial powers in the nineteenth century.

[4] For an analysis of the shifting nature of this incorporation of northern Somalia within global capitalism in the immediate aftermath of the opening of the Suez Canal, see Kapteijns (1995), Samatar (1989), and Reese (1999). For a broader discussion of the role of the British in the Red Sea, see Marston (1961).

With the development of synthetic substitutes, demand for ambergris decreased as the perfume industry was able to use cheaper substances to fix scents. Additionally, from the 1970s, the possession and trade of ambergris was prohibited by numerous countries as part of a wider ban on the hunting of sperm whales. While ambergris continues to enjoy a niche market, mostly for its reputed properties as an aphrodisiac, the ambergris economy is no longer a mainstay in coastal Somalia. But crucially, understandings of property implicated within the practice of ambergris capture and collection, and the circuits of redistribution that this engendered, continue to be key in framing the practices of a variety of actors in this littoral space, from artisanal fishermen to pirates.

'Fish are fugitive', explained Ali, a fisherman with a fabled reputation for catching shark. 'You and I can go into the ocean right now in the same area and I can guarantee we will come back with very different catch, actually I will come back with fish and you will come back with saltwater on your face!' (Ali, interview with the author, April 2011). As with the collection of ambergris, within the world of artisanal fishing capture at sea creates property. As Ali and other fishermen explained to me, chance, risk, and 'personal enskilment' (Palsson 1994) are crucial in transforming fish into property. The mobile and migratory nature of fish requires an engagement with the materiality of the ocean: fishing, by its very nature, is built around practices of capture. Fish (like camels and ambergris) are fugitive in another sense also, as qualified forms of property: in this sense, these processes that resonate with idioms of property making far beyond the shores of Somalia.

The notion of 'fugitive property' has a long history in the annals of property law, especially concerning the status of foxes, whales, and in the early twentieth century, oil and subsurface natural resources.[5] In a now classic case, *Hammonds* v. *Central Kentucky Natural Gas Co.*, the Court of Appeals in Kentucky turned to the rule of capture from common law doctrine in England in order to decide the ownership over natural gas extracted from the ground. In 1930, the Central Kentucky Natural Gas Company leased tracts of land above a depleted natural gas stratum and used this land as an underground storehouse of gas. But the geological dome of natural gas lay only partly under the land they were leasing and partly under someone else's land. When the company began extracting the gas they were storing, Hammonds, one of the other landowners, sued for trespass, claiming that some of the gas was stored under her property without her consent.

[5] The concept of fugitive property extends back to Roman law and continental legal tradition that influenced American jurisprudence on capture and rights in fugitive resources. See Donahue (1986) for an exploration of this history, specifically a discussion of *Pierson* v. *Post*, an iconic case in US property law and legal pedagogy.

Hammonds asserted that the defendant made illicit use of her property by introducing natural gas into the dome beneath her land. In order to adjudicate liability, the court had to decide whether the natural gas was still owned by the company once it was injected back into ground. Through analogy to classic common law doctrine on hunting, specifically fox-hunting cases from the nineteenth century, the court held:

> In seeking for an analogous condition in the law, the courts, since the early Pennsylvania case, have compared natural gas and oil to that of animals *ferae naturae*. The analogy, as we have seen, formed the basis of the all but universal doctrine of property in these wandering minerals. So we may look to that analogous law. From the beginning, wild animals have been regarded as quasi property of the entire human race. It is the recognition of land titles rather than of any individual property in the game that prevents its pursuit, and, barring all questions of trespass, exclusive property in birds and wild animals becomes vested in the person capturing or reducing them to possession. But unless killed, this is a qualified property, for when restored to their natural wild and free state, the dominion and individual proprietorship of any person over them is at an end and they resume their status as common property. [similar for fish, foxes, and water] We are of opinion, therefore, that if in fact the gas turned loose in the earth wandered into the plaintiff's land, the defendant is not liable to her for the value of the use of her property, for the company ceased to be the exclusive owner of the whole of the gas—it again became mineral *ferae naturae* (*Hammonds* v. *Central Kentucky Natural Gas Co.*: 1314).

By analogizing the status of natural gas to that of wild animals (*ferae naturae*), the court upheld a principle of 'first possession' or the rule of capture in making property claims for fugitive property. First possession is a key concept in the realm of property law. The discussion of how 'things become property of individuals' in the *Institutes* of Justinian, for example, begins with the example of 'wild animals, birds and fish, i.e., all animals born on land or in the sea or air, [which] as soon as they are caught by anyone, forthwith fall into his ownership by the law of nations: for what previously belonged to no one is, by natural reason, accorded to its captor' (*Institutes of Justinian* 2.1.12, transl. in Sandars 1876). Enlightenment scholarship followed Justinian, and treated animals *ferae naturae* as the paradigm of an unowned thing. John Locke famously proclaimed, 'In the beginning, all the world was America': in the state of nature all the world was apparently unowned and available for the taking. As Patricia Seed (1995) has noted, this vision of *ferae naturae* was central in European colonial expansion and the expropriation of native land. But, as the *Hammonds* case also highlights, wild animals (and natural gas), unlike continents, are a form of qualified property. As the court noted in *Hammonds*, 'When gas is ... brought under dominion and into actual possession at the surface, it, of course, becomes the personal property of the one who has extracted it under a right so to do' (*Hammonds v. Central Kentucky Natural Gas Co.*: 1314). Yet, this right is limited, for once the gas is released back into the earth it returns to *ferae naturae* and once again becomes common property. Capture and possession, far from being absolute, are contingent practices. This contingency lies in what happens to property after capture.

Whereas the vision of qualified property envisioned in *Hammonds* is ultimately about the balance between public and private property, the moral economy of capture in Somalia is a mode of socializing and embedding property: in other words, it addresses what happens to the property after it has been caught. This is framed within a wider Islamic moral universe. The celebration and exaltation of the livestock rustler and raider: '*xalaal iyo xaaraan, hadow xera galo midna kuma xuma* (whether through licit or illicit means, it matters most that you possess the camel)', paradoxically articulated alongside a critique of ill-gotten wealth: '*hal xaaranihi nirig xalaal ah ma dhasho* (a stolen she-camel will not beget a licit calf)' (quoted in Ahmed 1996: 23), works to regulate capture and embed rules framing property. In Somalia and across fishing communities in the Western Indian Ocean the sea is the 'gift of God' and cannot be owned or enclosed. In contrast, camels, wells, fish, and boats can be owned, stolen, or captured, and the boundaries of this ownership are often violently policed through references both to idioms of Islamic law—*xaalal iyo xaaraan* (licit and illicit)—and customary norms. Mobility as opposed to a fixed idiom of territory is central in making and justifying claims to property. Fish, camels, and boats are constantly on the move; grazing areas transform through drought and other vagaries of nature. This mobility and contingency means that property claims tend to be based on the capture of objects and routes. Yet, capture is always a form of qualified property: in order to be legitimate and lasting it has to be embedded within a social world of obligation and reciprocity.

In his classic text *Stone Age Economics*, Marshall Sahlins proposed a typology to understand gifts, capture, and other forms of credit–debit relationships (1972). For Sahlins, theft and capture constitute an attempt to break the credit–debt relationship by seizing the credit and disavowing the debt. In contrast to this neat typology, the capture of fish is always already located within pre-existing ideas about reciprocity and return. 'Fish are the bounty of the sea', Ali explained. 'This means that I share with others, but also that my prize gives me the right to demand and expect things and respect from others' (Ali, interview with the author, April 2011). Capture, then, is akin to Karl Polanyi's 'embedded economy' and entails a politics of recognition: as Ali noted, capture gave him 'a right to demand and expect things and respect from others'. Capture thus usefully intervenes in understandings of common resource management and provides a way of thinking about the sea that brings together international property law with local responsibilities that include redistribution.

RETHINKING REGULATION

By highlighting a logic of property that continues to shape engagements with the ocean across the Western Indian Ocean littoral, the above discussion on capture allows us to reimagine the relationship between overexploitation and shared resource management: a relationship central to the ways in which global commons such as the oceans are conceptualized and regulated.[6] In his now classic treatise on fisheries off the coast of California, Arthur McEvoy outlines the fisherman's problem as the failure of the fishing industry to 'respect the biological limits of its resource's productivity' and argues:

> Fishing industries ... do not generally manage their affairs in a rational way. This is primarily because fishery stocks are common property resources; that is, although many different individuals or firms may compete with each other for fish, no one of them owns the resource so as to keep others away from it. As a result, everyone has an incentive to keep fishing so long as there is money to be made in the effort, whereas no one has an individual incentive to refrain from fishing so as to conserve the stock (1990: 9–10).

As McEvoy notes, one of the first scholars to stress the importance of institutional and legal arrangements in managing fishery resources was the economist H. Scott Gordon. In a 1954 article, Gordon criticized the sustainable yield theory of fishery management. For Gordon, the fisherman's problem was the direct result of the industry's legal and economic organization as opposed to a problem of biology or population dynamics. Gordon's solution sought to transform fisheries from a common property resource to a limited entry regime, making fisheries into 'private property or public (government) property, in either case subject to a unified directing power able to exclude outsiders and adjust harvesting efforts to maximum advantage' (1954: 125).

In 1968, the biologist Garrett Hardin published 'The Tragedy of the Commons', expanding and canonizing Gordon's argument about private

[6] This focus on imaginaries draws from Carol M. Rose's (1994) scholarship on property, narrative, and vision. In *Property and Persuasion*, Rose highlights the centrality of 'storytelling' in naturalizing concepts of property. While Rose's emphasis is on the power of stories about private property and propriety, this idea is equally relevant to the framing of discussions on the commons around ideas of scarcity and overexploitation. See also Raffles (2010), for an imagining of air outside the notion of the commons by exploring the vantage point of insects.

property and common resource management. For Hardin, the tragedy of the commons, namely ecological degradation is located in free and unregulated access to scarce resources. Hardin argued that freedom becomes tragic because individuals would rather maximize their own use of a shared resource than protect it from overuse. The solution to this tragedy implicit within Hardin's thesis was privatization because individuals can only be expected to protect their own property. While admitting that this solution might be draconian and, at times, unjust, Hardin defended his findings by noting that the alternative was 'too horrifying to contemplate'. 'Injustice', he wrote, 'is preferable to total ruin' (1968: 1247). As Ian Angus has noted, 'since appearing in *Science* in December 1968, "The Tragedy of the Commons" has been anthologized in at least 111 books, making it one of the most-reprinted articles ever to appear in any scientific journal' (Angus 2008). Despite its popularity, Hardin's thesis has been subjected to many critiques and revisions.

In their analysis of Hardin's work and influence, McCay and Acheson highlight the individualistic bias central to Hardin's approach. The tragedy of the commons, they argue, 'fails to distinguish between the commons as a theoretical condition in which there are no relevant institutions (open access), and common property as a social institution' (1987: 12). They argue that Hardin's mistake is to conflate these two, and thus to ignore or underestimate the presence of regulatory institutions that manage the use of collectively shared resources. McCay and Acheson also point to the absence of a clear concept of 'community' in Hardin's analysis: 'Hardin assumed only a collection of individuals using a common resource. He did not recognize the existence of communities that dealt with conflicts and ecological problems associated with the commons by creating and enforcing rules about their use' (1987: 12). A further rich interdisciplinary literature has developed in recent years highlighting multiple systems of governance, including polycentric forms of governance that complicate and indeed challenge Hardin's original tragedy of the commons (see Wheeler, Chapter 8, this volume, for a related discussion on the tragedy of the commons).

However, both these framings of the problem of the commons: overexploitation on the one hand, and a communitarian management of resources (i.e. an enclosure within limits) on the other—fail adequately to speak to the Somali case. Both approaches are underpinned by a notion of the commons as a distinct property regime, and by the question of scarcity. Additionally, both Hardin and his critics operate within a system that presumes dichotomies between public and private, capture and redistribution. In Somalia, by contrast, the sea is neither an overexploited commons nor one managed through egalitarian modes of shared access. Rather, it is a commons framed by interwoven maritime and land property regimes. At sea, capture creates property. But this property, like Hassan's camels and boats, is embedded within claims that can be made by others on land. Capture thus works alongside redistribution and connects the coastal world to the pastoral hinterland through a shared idiom of property and ownership, but also through the economic exchange of fish for goats and camels.

Land and sea, like capture and redistribution, are not incommensurable: capture allows one to make property at sea and to embed it within worlds of pastoralism. Fish and ambergris turn (metaphorically) into goats and camels, creating systems of interdependence as one moves through the porous spaces between onshore and offshore. The next section focuses on how shifting claims to the sea brought together a host of actors from the state to fishermen and trawlers in contests over property and profit.

SCIENTIFIC SOCIALISM AND THE REMAKING OF PROPERTY

Fish and other seafood have rarely occupied centre stage in the culinary traditions of the majority of those who inhabit the Somali peninsula. In the 1970s, during the heyday of scientific socialism in Somalia, the Siyad Barre regime sought to address this dietary aversion. Joole, a former government employee working in Mogadishu in the 1970s and 1980s, recalled listening to radio jingles exhorting Somalis to eat fish:

> We used to listen to Radio Mogadishu back then [in the 1970s]. One afternoon, the presenter started talking about eating fish and selling fish as important to the project of *hanti-wadaagga cilmi ku dhisan* [scientific socialism]. This was surprising to us at first because most Somalis don't like to eat fish. The Ogaden, my mother's family, have a saying, 'don't trust a man whose mouth smells of fish'. Siyad Barre tried to change all that. When he was president we used to hear a jingle on the radio saying, 'let us fish and make a profit'. There was lots of opportunity in fishing for many people including my family (Joole, interview with the author, March 2011).

Property regimes are seldom stable categories. Ambergris, camels, fish, and even the ocean acquire meaning and substance within specific historical, political, and economic contexts. The previous section highlighted the centrality of capture in making property in ways that complicated boundaries of land and sea as well as those of public and private. This section turns to postcolonial Somalia. We will need to discuss the various attempts of making (and unmaking property) on land in order to highlight the temporalities and scales of property regimes more widely, turning then to the specific case of fish. Temporalities and scales that bring together a range of actors from local fishermen and state officials, to South Korean trawlers, are central to understanding the transition from capturing fish to capturing ships.

On 15 October 1969, almost a decade after attaining independence, the President of the Somali Republic, ʻAbd ar-Rashid ʻAli Shirmarke, was assassinated by a disgruntled soldier. While the Somali parliament debated the election of a successor in the days following the assassination—a debate that revealed the 'deep sores in the Somali body politic' (Laitin and Samatar 1987: 43) divided along clan and regional lines—a group of army officers staged a coup. In the early hours of 21 October, the army occupied key points throughout the capital, and members of the government and other leading politicians and personalities were placed in detention. The Constitution was suspended, the Supreme Court abolished, the National Assembly closed, political parties declared illegal, and rule by Supreme Revolutionary Council (SRC) established. The membership of the SRC was announced on 1 November 1969 and the new president, as widely anticipated, was General Muhammad Siyad Barre. According to David Laitin and Said Samatar, the early days of the SRC were focused on decrying the corruption of the old regime:

> Drawing on an onomatopoeic expression from the poetry of the Sayyid, the SRC accused the politicians of *musuq maasuq*—of going in different directions at the same time. Politicians were also accused of *afmishaarism*—literally, acting like 'saw mouths'—because they put praise singers on the government payroll. Government cars were being used as private taxis; government medicine was on sale in local pharmacies. The new government helped mobilize people's support through its campaign of *hisaabi hil male*, an 'accounting without shame'. The use of these colloquial political expressions lent a populist aura to the military junta's image (Laitin and Samatar 1987: 53).

Additionally, to bolster this populist sentiment, the SRC engaged in a discourse of anti-Americanism that resonated with a large segment of the Somali population who saw the United States as anti-Muslim and hostile to the unification of 'Somalia's dismembered nation'. This anti-Americanism was also fuelled by closer alignment to the Soviet Union, and within a year US Peace Corps volunteers, along with other remnants of American foreign interest, were ordered to leave Mogadishu to be replaced by Soviet technical assistance and expertise. This realignment towards the Soviet Union was completed when on the first anniversary of the coup (now reframed as a revolution) Siyad Barre proclaimed on Radio Mogadishu that Somalia would henceforth be dedicated to *hanti-wadaagga ʻilmu ku disan* ('scientific socialism').

Somalia's cold war shift towards the Soviet Union occurred within a broader chessboard-like trading of loyalties across the Horn of Africa and the Middle East in the period immediately following decolonization. From Libya to Somalia, newly independent countries moved back and forth between the

Soviet bloc and the United States. These movements had significant political repercussions within the region and for the broader balance of power in the cold war era, allowing local elites to consolidate and centralize their political power through arms transfers and economic subsidies funded by their patrons. Within popular memory and the scholarly archive on Somalia, scientific socialism is largely remembered for the ways in which the promise of the Revolution unravelled and as a precursor to the process of dissolution of the Somali state. My interest here lies in the rescaling of the economy, and the remaking of property, during this period: the relationship between fish, property, and profit was transformed, even while retaining continuities with, and echoes of, the past. Given the broader context within which Somalia's experiments with scientific socialism occurred, this section also seeks to locate this rescaling of property within a wider mode of imagining property under socialism.

Following the proclamation of scientific socialism, Barre's regime sought to quell criticism regarding the un-Islamic nature of the ideology. The criticism was not simply a theological critique of socialism as atheism, but one that focused on the compatibility of scientific socialism with an Islamic moral economy and communal rules regarding property and redistribution. Barre's socialism framed property at the crossroads between socialist and Islamic moral economies. In a speech marking the end of the Muslim holy month of Ramadan, Barre declaimed:

> Our Islamic faith teaches us that its inherent values are perennial and continually evolving as people progress. These basic tenets of our religion cannot be interpreted in a static sense, but rather as a dynamic source of inspiration for continuous advancement ... If we decide to regulate our national wealth it is not against the essence of Islam (1974: 24).

But more was at stake than moral economies. Property regimes and their associated legalism were powerful political and economic tools for nation-building. Barre described the attempt to regulate national wealth as essentially a project of rescaling (i.e. shifting the locus from community to the nation) rather than a complete transformation: 'to help our brethren and our fellows, we must go beyond the concept of charity, and reach the higher and more altruistic concept of cooperation on a national scale' (1974: 24). Scientific socialism thus echoes similar projects of postcolonial refashioning of national economies across the globe. Indian nationalists on the eve of independence sought not to dismantle developmentalism altogether but to scale it to the nation. As Goswami and others have highlighted in the Indian case, nationalists criticized a drain of wealth by colonial economic practices while sharing a broader epistemology with their colonial adversaries that emphasized the universalistic promise of development as part of national reconstruction (2004: 240). The developmentalist project of Siyad Barre's scientific socialism involved a similar rescaling[7] of a set of divergent local, regional, and transregional economic practices into the national frame as part of a project of Somali nation building.

Legalism was a central framework through which Barre sought to rescale these economic practices into a national framework. Somalia's economy at the time of independence consisted of a thriving livestock trade centred primarily in northern Somalia and a small but profitable plantation economy in the inter-riverine areas of southern Somalia. While trade in the north was controlled by the Berbera trading community and consisted mainly of Indians, Arabs, and Somali middlemen, the southern economy was dominated by Italian interests (the Filonardi and the Benadir companies) who established a monopoly over property, export, customs, and tariff regulations. It was through property, then, that scientific socialism after 1970 sought to rescale this transregional economy, an economy that had been underdeveloped by both Italian and British colonial authorities, into the frame of the nation. Bolstered by Soviet assistance and technical advisers, Barre's regime initially nationalized a number of institutions such as banks, petroleum distribution firms, and schools. Imports and exports were also controlled by government agencies with the exception of livestock on the hoof. All grain grown privately was bought by the national Agricultural Development Corporation and sold at government regulated prices. At the same time, government officials reassured pastoralists that livestock would not be nationalized and continued to allow the private ownership of banana plantations, although bananas were marketed and exported solely through government agencies. They thus ensured that the two major export sectors remained firmly in private hands. Nationalization was not simply a straightforward transformation of 'private' property into 'public' property, but 'a process of making and unmaking certain kinds of relationships', as Katherine Verdery has argued in the context of socialist and post-socialist Romania (2003: 14).

Verdery's observations on property regimes in socialism are key to understanding property transformations in socialist Somalia. The definition of property under socialism in Romania contrasted with the distinctions between real and personal property, tangible and intangible property, and state commons and private property upon which western economic and

[7] Neil Brenner's rethinking of scale-making as inherent to the 'continual deterritorialization and reterritorialization that has underpinned the production of capitalist spatiality since the industrial revolution of the early nineteenth century' (1999: 42) is a useful frame for thinking through the transformations that occurred in the scientific socialism moment. At the same time, as this chapter highlights, scale-making needs to be historicized beyond the nineteenth century.

legal systems are based: 'Socialist property categories by contrast emphasized a different set of property types based on the identity of the owners and the social relationships among them' (Verdery 2003: 49). In Romania, these property types included the state, socialist cooperatives and individuals or households: the role of socialist transformation entailed the distribution of property according to these three ownership patterns. In addition, and crucially for Verdery, what defined property and a theory of socialist property was not the status of ownership but rather 'patterns of use, administrative rights and social networks of exchange and reciprocity' (2003: 70).

In Somalia, the attempted transformation of a transregional precolonial and colonial economy into one scaled to the space of the nation state entailed the redistribution and appropriation of pre-existing forms of property and the creation of new structures and ownership regimes. Yet as anthropologists working on property relationships in socialist and post-socialist Europe remind us, these transformations are always contingent and open-ended. In Somalia, scientific socialism's remodellings of property relations defy the easy teleology of 'private' to 'public' or 'clanism' to 'developmentalism'. The primary export economy remained in private hands, including key sectors, such as livestock exports and the ownership of banana plantations. This private economy was organized according to the lineage and clan logics, so that 'clanism' was smuggled back in even as the state sought to eradicate clan and lineage as a basis for political authority and legitimacy. And even the state itself, which quickly transformed itself into an extension of Barre's lineage, captured rents from this private economy, creating a clan-based patronage system while simultaneously disavowing the possibility of claim-making or access to property and resources through the language of lineage and clan. As Abdi, a businessman based in Mogadishu during the Barre years, explained:

> Siyad Barre used to make speeches about evils of clan all the time. He made clannism a crime and the government even policed how we addressed each other. Before Barre, a polite form of addressing a stranger was to say 'cousin' (*ina'adeer*). Since this is a clan terminology we were banned from using it and instead told to say 'friend' (*jaalle*). But nationalization was completely done in clan logic with everything divided between MOD [MOD was the acronym used to surreptitiously refer to the three clans that were beneficiaries of the Barre regime: the Marrehaan (Barre's patrilineage), the Ogaden (his mother's clan) and the Dulbahante (his son in law's lineage)] (Hassan Abdi, interview with the author, Mombasa, Kenya, October 2010).

State appropriation was not simply a matter of seizure, but embedded, as Abdi notes, within structures of patronage and redistribution. In addition to rescaling economic practices on land, this attempt at appropriation/channelling had a significant impact in shaping the development of fisheries and transforming claims to the ocean. Beginning in the 1970s a licensing regime sought to transform the capture–redistribution system highlighted earlier to a regime built on state appropriation. Yet, as I will show, state licensing was also a form of capture, where now the licence instead of fish became the coveted form of 'fugitive property'.

RESCALING CAPTURE

In 1972, the Barre government decreed in Law No. 37 on the Territorial Sea and Ports that the Somali territorial sea extended to 200 nautical miles as opposed to the traditional designation of 12 nautical miles. This move was followed by the launch, primarily through Soviet assistance, of a deep-sea trawling fleet and the construction of fish factories and processing plants along the coast. The drought of 1974 that devastated large portions of the livestock throughout the region also created a new impetus for the establishment of fishing cooperatives along coast. By 1975, new settlements along the coast were built for the resettled nomads at Eel Haamed, Eyl, Adale, and Barawa, stretching from the Red Sea to the Indian Ocean. With Soviet and later Australian and Italian capital and advisers, these settlements attempted to transform nomads into fishermen and create a vibrant fishing sector. Prior to the settlement programme, fisheries accounted for less than 1 per cent of the country's GDP. The Food and Agricultural Organization of the United Nations (FAO) noted in its 2005 report on fisheries in Somalia that:

> with the introduction of 500 mechanized boats in the early 1970s, the annual catch increased from about 5,000 tonnes to a peak of 8,000 tonnes in 1975. However, due to the lack of maintenance and spare parts for the new boats that had been distributed to the fishermen, about two-thirds were out of operation after only two years, and, as a direct consequence, by the late 1970s annual fish production was back to 5,000 tonnes (FAO FID/CP/SOM 2005)

This short-lived development enterprise nonetheless created a pattern of licensing[8] and concessions. As the FAO report notes, Somali fisheries were both a small part of the country's GDP and from the perspective of an emergent maritime regulation regime considered 'underexploited'.

Primarily emerging out of fishery management in the North Atlantic from the 1930s (see Rose 2007 for a critical analysis of fishery management in this

[8] While Ferguson (2005) and Mbembe (2000) locate licensing, i.e. the transformation of sovereignty in sub-Saharan Africa into a rubber stamp for resource extraction, as a central feature of the neoliberal post-cold war state, the Somali experience highlights the centrality of licensing during the heyday of the socialist moment, with wider consequences for thinking about state and sovereignty in cold war Africa.

region), the concept of maximum sustainable yield (MSY) was developed to manage global fisheries. A fundamental tenet of MSY is the assumption that it is possible to calculate the largest yield that can be taken from the stock of a species over an indefinite period of time.[9] As long as stocks were being exploited under the MSY threshold, anyone had the right to fish off any coast, a principle enshrined within the international MSY treaty and the United Nations Convention on the Law of the Seas (UNCLOS). Within this management system, coastal states like Somalia were now obligated to promote 'optimum utilization' of marine resources by giving third states access to the excess 'allowable catch' (Art. 62 UNCLOS) through a system of licensing. Alongside the development of fisheries, the Somali government created a licensing regime based on principles of MSY that gave access to Somali coastal waters to long-distance trawlers in return for a licensing fee. Even as equipment broke down and production in fish factories dwindled, this licensing regime continued to expand at a robust pace. Initially, Italian and Soviet trawlers were granted exclusive licences and concessions by the state to fish in Somali 'territorial waters' in return for a fee. By 1986 the virtual monopoly of Soviet and Italian trawlers was disrupted with the entrance of Norwegian and Japanese trawlers. Responding to the establishment of regional fishery management systems in the Northern Atlantic and the Pacific and a growing global appetite for seafood, these trawlers utilized the MSY ethos of fishery management to force an entry into the Western Indian Ocean. Specifically, licensing created 'jurisdiction as property' (see Lambert, Chapter 5, this volume) where now the licences rather than simply fish were targets of capture. At the local level, this form of licensing was mirrored in the interactions between newly resettled pastoralists and fishing communities that traditionally inhabited the coast. A large number of pastoralists resisted the transformation into fishermen and instead loaned out fishing equipment and boats to *sab* and other coastal fishing communities creating redistributive networks that were similar to the wider jurisdictional and property claims established over the sea by the Barre regime. Local fishermen also created informal agreements with fishing fleets, often selling fish directly to trawlers or providing protection guarantees to keep fishing areas clear from Yemeni fishermen and other interlopers. This system both worked within and transformed pre-existing understandings of fishing, bounty, and pastoral property relationships.

[9] See Larkin (1977) for an influential critique of the idea of maximum sustainable yield (MSY). Even as MSY has been critiqued for its failure to take into consideration a holistic view of fish stocks, including mobility and ecological transformation, this principle continues to shape regulatory policy at regional and international levels.

Benderbeyla, on the north-eastern tip of Somalia, has been at the centre of the recent upsurge in maritime piracy. A fishing village that was also the site of a major fishing cooperativc in the 1970s, Benderbeyla is the perfect vantage point from which to understand the complex relationship between fishing, licensing, and piracy. Mohamed Hershi, a clan elder explained the licensing system that his village developed with the state-backed fishing cooperative SOMFISH in the early 1980s.

> When SOMFISH wanted to fish near our village, they agreed to pay us $1000 a month so that we stayed out of their way. They also hired a number of men from here to give protection to the trawlers and make sure no other vessels came into the area. Most of the time we were just keeping the area free from fishermen from Bossaso or other places around the coast (Mohamed Hershi, Benderbeyla, interview with the author, March 2011).

Villagers recalled that the trawlers began to arrive from other countries around 1986. While most of these vessels stayed away from the coast or were chased away by the local protection group, many interviewees recalled Norwegian trawlers attempting to make similar protection deals with the local community. A number of these trawlers had obtained licences from the regime in Mogadishu and hired groups such as the local protection group in Benderbeyla to keep other fishing boats out of the water. As with the world of capture described in the previous section, appropriation and redistribution were intimately related in this system of making property at sea. This is not to suggest that this was a harmonious system or one geared towards sustainability or benefit for Somali fishermen. Violent confrontations between local protection groups and foreign fishing vessels, especially those that attempted to fish in the area without official or unofficial 'licences' grew increasingly commonplace in the 1980s, especially after the fall of the Barre regime in 1991. In addition, foreign trawlers, in particular those using bottom trawling techniques, greatly harmed local fishing grounds and impacted the artisanal fishing communities along the coast. Following the collapse of the Somali state, with the intensification of foreign trawling, this system was transformed and rescaled when semi-autonomous regions, such as Puntland, turned to private security companies to extract rents for licensing and protection at sea. This shift to multiple security companies and the aftermath of these attempts to extract revenues underpinned the transition from licensing to piracy.

FROM LICENSING TO PIRACY

The national rescaling of economic practices engendered new modes of property regime, but also bolstered inequalities structured on clan and other divisions. Licensing became increasingly problematic. Siyad Barre's regime was built on a territorial logic of 'Greater Somalia' (*Soomaaliweyn*). This vision of a unified country encompassing all the Somali-speaking regions in the Horn of Africa emerged in the colonial era and was mobilized by Barre in justifying conflicts with neighbouring Ethiopia and Kenya. By the mid 1980s, the damage wrought by these conflicts and the regime's increasing authoritarianism led to the emergence of numerous insurgent groups that sought to challenge the Somali regime. An increasingly violent counter-insurgency created 'networks of dissolution' (Simons 1995) and by January 1991 Siyad Barre's regime was toppled. From the vantage point of the coast, the collapse of the state in 1991 and the subsequent 'privatization of the maritime economy' (Marchal 1996: 38) accelerated and reconfigured systems of licensing and protection that had emerged following the establishment of fishery cooperatives in the 1970s.

The aftermath of state collapse was characterized by tremendous population upheaval creating large refugee communities in countries as widespread as Norway to Kenya, as well as significant internal displacement. A number of these population movements occurred along clan and kinship lines with many 'returning' to ancestral homelands to establish subnational regions. The region of Puntland in north-eastern Somalia abutting both the Red Sea and the Indian Ocean is one such subnational entity that emerged in 1998 through a process of cohesion and concession among the Harti, one of the major clans within Somalia's kinship system. The semi-autonomous region of Puntland was part of a 'building blocks' approach to reconstituting the Somali state. As the International Crisis Group (2009) notes, this approach was built on the argument that any attempts to recreate a unitary centralized Somali state were bound to fail. Instead, each of the four major Somali clans were to build a 'block' within a loose federal or confederal structure. The charter of Puntland recognized the in-between status of Puntland as a placeholder for a yet-to-come Federal Somali Republic.

Beginning in 2000, the government of Puntland, especially under the administrations of Abdullahi Yusuf Ahmed and Adde Muuse, turned to fisheries as an additional source of revenue. In addition to developing small-scale fish and lobster processing plants, the government attempted to exert Puntland's sovereignty over the ocean. Roland Marchal's (1996) study of the post-civil war private sector has highlighted the continued operation of Somalia's small fishing fleet in the aftermath of the civil war. But this privatized fishing fleet alongside the foreign trawlers complicated the Puntland government's attempts to collect revenues and develop a primarily export-oriented fishery sector. In order to exert its sovereignty over the sea, the Puntland government, beginning in 2000, contracted private security companies to regulate the ocean.

This was a key moment in the shift from catching fish to capturing ships. Licensing itself became a matter of contestation. The private coastguard initiatives of the newly emergent Puntland regime transformed the maritime world of licensing and rent-seeking, bringing with them a host of new technologies, including mobile phones, global remittance systems, the proliferation of small arms, and access to skiffs with powerful outboard motors. Privatization, associated technologies, and violence, were key to the growth of piracy. The arrival of private security helped with mixed results to deal with illegal fishing, but crucially, it also impacted the informal licensing systems that already existed in coastal communities throughout Puntland. While a few coastguard initiatives attempted to create an inclusive and salaried employee pool, most attempts at coastal regulation were built on logics of capture tied to existing patronage networks and often led to violent confrontations at sea. As explained at the beginning of this chapter, armed skiffs would intercept fishing trawlers and 'sell' a licence to boat captains. The fees from this licence would then be divided among the crew and authorities on land. Often, these licensing regimes came into conflict with pre-existing systems. In Benderbeyla, Mohamed Hershi noted that starting from 2001, official coastguards consisting of militia groups with ties to the government in Garoowe, the capital of Puntland, attempted to shut down their informal licensing system. Conflicts over jurisdiction sparked often armed confrontations between competing coastguards over the 'right to tax and issue licences'.

> When the Puntland government started issuing fishing licences, the Thai trawlers that used to pay us to fish in our area stopped paying and said they would deal with the Hart people [Puntland Coastguard which was trained by a British private security firm Hart Security Maritime Services Limited] instead. Since this was our right to issue licences we fought the Hart boats if they came close to our area. This was a time when even a fisherman had to take a gun when he went out to sea because everyone was trying to become a coastguard (Mohamed Hershi, Benderbeyla, interview with the author, March 2011).

The rise and fall of various coastguard initiatives was deeply tied to contestations over political power on land and they underscore the close relationship between profits from a 'sea of fish' and political authority in Puntland.

Conflictual in themselves, the short-lived coastguard initiatives also had a major consequence that is linked directly to the upsurge in maritime piracy. As official coastguards fell in and out of favour depending on their connections with the ruling elite in Garoowe, these multiple and scattered attempts at regulation left behind a well-trained, unemployed labour force along the coast that took to the seas in order to extract revenues from fishing vessels, *dhows*, and cargo ships.

Hashi, a former private coastguard, exemplifies the experience of a number of Somali coastguards from the early 2000s, who found themselves without a salary when shifting political alliances left their employers (in this case Somcan)[10] out of political favour.

> Many of us had been trained in GPS and also to do boarding of ships. When the Taar brothers lost their contract, I decided to join another group and we became our own private security. At some point we decided to move from *capturing fishing vessels to capturing even bigger fish and we moved to capturing oil tankers and other vessels.* At this point, this is our work. Why would anyone go back to catching tuna when you can catch an oil tanker? (Hashi, Eyl, interview with the author, March 2011).

Hashi's transformation from coastguard to pirate; from capturing fishing vessels to *even bigger fish*, like the 2009 hijacking of the *Sirius Star*—a Saudi-flagged oil tanker and the largest ship ever to be hijacked—highlights the scalar transformations of idioms of capture and bounty that this chapter has sought to narrate. Far from a story of failed states or disgruntled fishermen, acts of maritime predation are extensions and breakdowns of contestations over property, access, and wealth in this oceanic space. Focusing on the historical and scalar transformations of property regimes not only provides an alternative narrative for understanding the emergence of piracy in its current guise, but also a story of the development of a 'sea of fish': a space for harnessing the bounty of the ocean. Finally, capture is central to the contingent and contested modes of making and unmaking property. In opposition to 'taking without giving' capture entails forms of relationality, crafted often through violence, across scale and time. In the conclusion, I reflect briefly on capture as a way of thinking about the broader global debts and credits within which Somalia's relationship to the world is embedded.

[10] Somcan was one of the numerous private maritime security companies that were involved with the Puntland government in providing licensing to foreign fishing vessels and 'anti-piracy activities'. Unlike its predecessor Hart Security, Somcan was locally owned, although registered in the UAE. The Taar family who had close personal relationships with the former president, Abdullahi Yussuf, ran the company. It was this personal connection that has been seen by many as resulting in rapid deterioration in relations between the company and the administration, following the election of Mohamud Muse Hersi. See Kinsey et al. (2009), which focuses exclusively on political connections or lack thereof as determinants of efficacy. My focus on private companies concerns specific claims to the ocean and rent-seeking. The coastguard projects of Puntland in my account are tied to a longer history of protection as highlighted in this chapter. Protection, in this sense, then, is a source of resource extraction and also a modality of governance as opposed to reflecting corruption or nepotism.

CONCLUSION: THE RESONANCE OF CAPTURE

In 2011, spurred by the sudden popularity of all things camel in the Arabian Gulf and Kenya, from camel milk chocolate to camel burgers, the price of camels reached an all-time high in the livestock markets of northern Somalia. At the same time, a rumour started circulating in the port-cities and the 'pirate towns' of northern Somalia: a tale about raiding and capture. Sheikh Yusuf narrated this story to me one night as we were walking back from an evening session spent drinking tea and watching the Manchester derby:

> On nights like this we must be very careful, especially if we are near a *geelher* (camel camp). My cousin's son Osman disappeared from a camp about a week ago. He was guarding his camels when all of a sudden he heard a loud noise in the sky. It was a helicopter that had come from the navy ships out in the ocean. All of a sudden some marines jumped from the helicopter and quickly tied camels with ropes. Then they climbed back into the helicopter and Osman could only watch as helicopters came one after another and stole four camels. When the fifth helicopter came, Osman tried to fight the marines and I think that's when they captured him as well. This is why the navies are here. Pirates are an excuse ... they are here to steal our wealth (Sheikh Yusuf, Bosaso, interview with the author, March 2011).

Marines in Blackhawk helicopters, livestock raids, the disappearances of young men. These are not strange images in Somalia. Before *Captain Philips*, the Hollywood blockbuster *Black Hawk Down* sought to render an earlier violent encounter between the US Marines and young Somali men, an encounter framed yet again by a narrative of state failure and chaos. Those recent and not so recent histories—of violence, of dispossession, of intervention—frame the ways in which maritime piracy is understood within Somalia. As Bruce Grant (2009) has reminded us, capture is always central to the forms of violence that shape colonial encounters. Yet recent accounts, particularly those that emphasize the 'freakonomics' or the 'business models' of piracy tend to focus on the 'rationality' and the almost 'victimless nature of the criminal enterprise' (see Leeson 2012; Percy and Shortland 2010). Sarah Percy and Anja Shortland highlight what they call the absence of violence as one of the successes of the business model of Somali piracy. When violence appears in scholarly accounts, it is usually in the figure of the hostage and the seafarer on whose behalf a multi-billion-dollar intervention off the coast of Somalia is supposedly being waged. The stories told within Somalia—of stolen livestock, of the disappearance of young men—refuse this erasure.

Since the recent upsurge in incidents of maritime piracy, numerous young Somali men have been detained and killed, and many others have disappeared or drowned. By openly describing the violence of the world of piracy, these narratives are at one level a way of working through personal distress. As the mother of one disappeared pirate reminded me: 'we don't know whether to laugh or cry. My son could be in Kenya buying a big house, he could be in jail in Denmark where he will get asylum and bring me to Europe, or he could be at the bottom of the ocean.'

But there is also a wider logic at stake. By locating piracy within idioms of capture (and exchange), these stories highlight the resonance of piracy as a frame for thinking through global credits and debts, and the role of Somalia within this global order. Far from opposing a world of legalism, capture is a socialized practice with its modes of reciprocity and distribution and, additionally, a frame to reflect on the ethics of giving and receiving in an unequal world. A few days after my late-night stroll with Sheikh Yusef, I heard the same story told by different people at a *khat* chew. But this time at the end of the story one of the participants refused to condemn the theft of livestock and blamed the pirates for initiating this cycle of raiding. 'The pirates stole their [navy] ship, so why shouldn't they come and try and steal our camels? The problem is that piracy is *haram* [illicit] and they [pirates] bring this problem to us. Now the navies have captured our livestock and this cycle will only continue.'

In a provocative rereading of American Indian captivity and UFO abduction narratives, Susan Lepselter highlights the 'resonances of capture' and the ways in which images and stories of captivity highlight anxieties about power and containment in the United States. Working through Freud's idea of the uncanny, Lepselter notes

> how familiar but repressed material reappears in altered forms, how the half-forgotten won't stay down. And it suggests as well a poetics: it gets in to the ways that inexplicable repetition and reiteration create a specific sensation. Noticing the weird patterns between various things in everyday life produces anxiety but also a sense of meaning that is never totally explained, a half-dreaded conviction that some undiscovered agency lurks behind the scenes, creating the reiterative pattern (2012: 86).

Stories about capture, camels, and helicopters in Somalia, similarly produce a sense of meaning, and gesture to a longer history of interventions and engagements with the outside world. These narratives reference sediments of an older and ongoing process of making and unmaking property in the Western Indian Ocean. In opposition to the pirates, who appear suddenly and without warning over the horizon of the azure-blue ocean, this chapter has emphasized a longer history and logic from which forms of rent-seeking emerged in Somalia under the guise of piracy. Maritime piracy in this narrative then is a story of land and sea, of the ocean as a space of profit and property and the scalar and temporal movement from collecting ambergris to hijacking ships.

8

Fish as Property on the Small Aral Sea, Kazakhstan

WILLIAM WHEELER

Since Hardin's (1968) influential thesis of the 'tragedy of the commons', property institutions have often been seen as a means to ensure sustainable use of natural resources: if property is a bundle of rights and obligations concerning things, these rights and obligations may be distributed so as to ensure the future of the things in question. However, as property relations are embedded in a range of social and economic relations (Hann 1998; von Benda-Beckmann, von Benda-Beckmann, and Wiber 2006), there tends to be a gap between formal property rules, and practices, which may follow other sorts of rules and logics. Such at any rate is the case on Kazakhstan's Small Aral Sea, where, although a postsocialist property regime predicated on scarcity is designed to secure the future of the fishery, the future is very much in question: above-quota fishing is ubiquitous and environmental regulations are flouted. This chapter asks why this is.

Unpicking this question throws up three further questions. First, is above-quota fishing simply a matter of failed institutions resulting in a free-for-all? If not, what is the status of formal rules in the regulation of the fishery? Second, intensive fishing needs to be explained through examination of how fishermen think about the resource: if the Aral fisherman views the resource as abundant and, as a local proverb goes, 'dreams for the day', is this in spite of, or because of the formal rules based on scarcity? Finally, as fishing practices also depend on the social lives of fish out of the water, I ask what sort of property object fish are in Aral villages.

In addressing these questions, like other contributors to the volume, I pay close attention to the materiality of the resource under examination, which, I argue, inflects practices to a large degree. If at one extreme, property in people is conceptually and ethically problematic because it collapses the

Fish as Property on the Small Aral Sea, Kazakhstan. William Wheeler. © William Wheeler, 2017. Published 2017 by Oxford University Press.

boundary between persons and things (Skoda, Chapter 9, this volume), and if cattle are personalized, their biographies intertwined with those of the persons who hold them (Scheele, Chapter 1, this volume), fish by contrast tend to resist individuation: they are fungible and impersonal; the span of a fisherman's engagement with them is brief, hence a certain immediatism in practices surrounding them (see also Dua, Chapter 7, this volume).[1] I also contextualize the current property regime in the longer history of the fisheries, suggesting that the materiality of the resource inflects practices in different ways in different historical contexts.

THE ARAL SEA

The Aral Sea, once the world's fourth-largest inland body of water, is no stranger to resource mismanagement and depletion (see Figure 8.1). Soviet authorities expanded irrigation systems for cotton and rice across the vast and arid Aral basin, with the result that inflow into the sea was drastically reduced and from 1960 the sea began to retreat. As salinity levels rose, the native freshwater fish died out, and by the late 1970s, the valuable fishery based in the ports of Aral'sk (Kazakh SSR) and Muinak (Uzbek SSR) was devastated. The population of the region suffered from polluted drinking water and toxic dust storms from the dried-up seabed.[2]

Less well known is the recent recovery of the Small (North) Aral Sea, located exclusively in Kazakhstan (see Figure 8.2). In 2005, the Kökaral dike, part of a World Bank/Kazakhstan project, was built to prevent the waters of the Small Sea from flowing into the doomed Large Sea to the south; the level of the Small Sea has risen slightly and stabilized; crucially, salinity levels have fallen, leading to the rapid recovery of many freshwater species (Micklin and Aladin 2008). Over the last decade, catches have risen dramatically, and there is a growing commercial fishery based mainly on bream, roach, asp, and zander, although sturgeon has not recovered. In 2008 a major new fish-processing plant was opened in Aral'sk, capable of processing 6,000 tonnes a year. Infrastructural problems remain. The sea is still 10–20 km from coastal fishing villages and there are no roads or refrigeration units on the shore, so in summer, when fish spoil quickly, fishing is impossible. Because fishing is banned in May when fish are spawning, and dangerous in late autumn and early spring when ice is forming and melting, fishermen

[1] This chapter is based on ethnographic and archival research carried out for an ESRC-funded PhD between December 2012 and May 2014 in Aral'sk and surrounding fishing villages, particularly Bögen. Many thanks to the participants at the Legalism workshop for their feedback; thanks also to Tommaso Trevisani, Pauline von Hellermann, and Frances Pine for their comments on an earlier draft of this chapter.

[2] See Micklin (2007) for a comprehensive account of the causes of the desiccation.

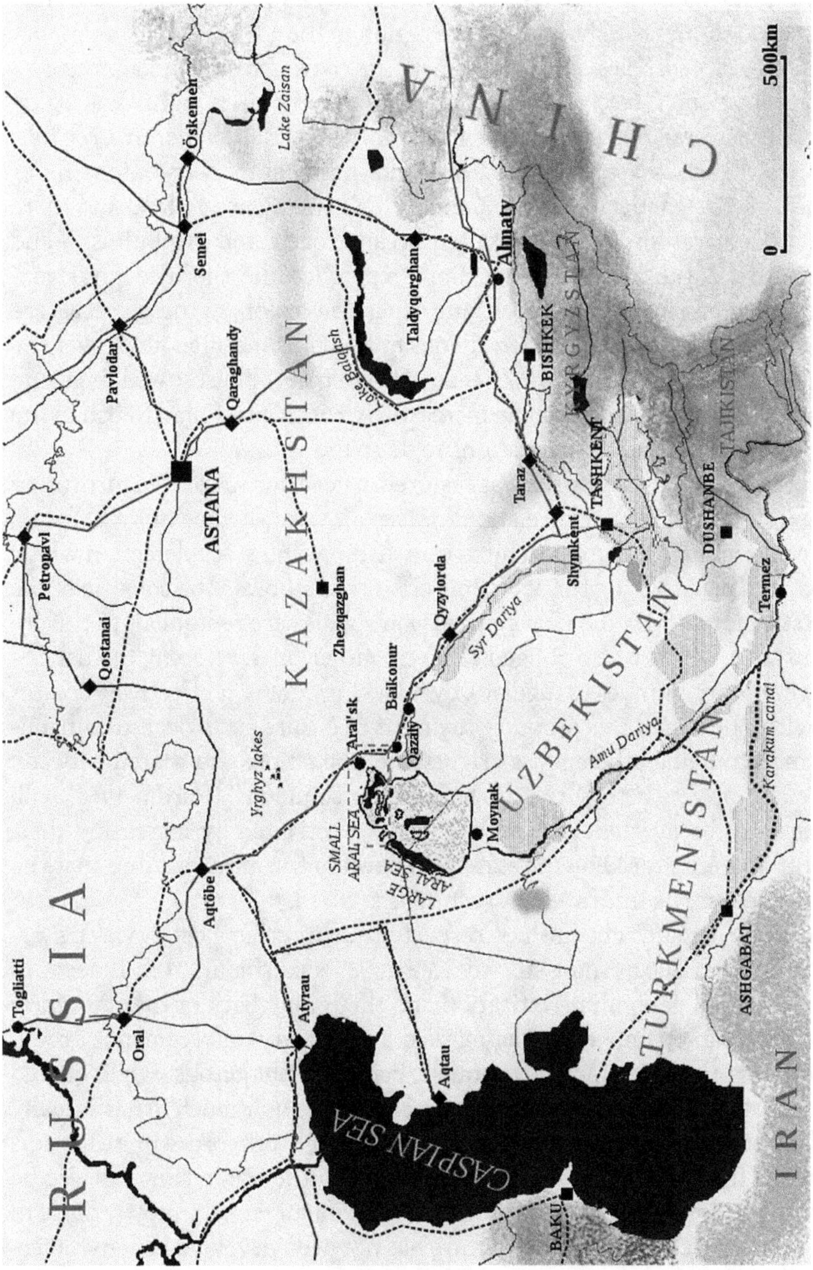

Figure 8.1 Map of Central Asia

work only about six months of the year. But when I was conducting fieldwork in 2012–14, recorded catches in the Small Aral Sea stood at about 4,000 tonnes, and unofficial catches were considerably more, though still less than the 20,000 tonnes caught in the same region in the 1950s.

After years of hardship, fishermen are now earning good money—generally about 150,000KZT (*c*.1,000 USD) a month, often more, in a region where the average salary is about 45,000KZT (*c*.300 USD) a month. Crucially, the Aral fisheries are integrated into international markets extending as far as the EU—zander fillets are popular in Germany and Poland and there is high demand for smoked or cured bream, roach, and asp in Russia and other parts of the former Soviet Union. In practice, there is little infrastructure for processing bream, roach, and asp in the region, so these species are much less valuable than zander: thanks to zander, fishermen have, over the last ten years, invested in UAZ jeeps and built new houses; weddings and other celebrations have become increasingly lavish. Most plan to fish in the future, and want future generations to do so too.

At the same time as the sea was restored, a new law was passed instituting a new system of property relations across all water-bodies in Kazakhstan, aimed at ending years of poaching, over-fishing, and stock depletion which had taken place during the economic crisis that followed the collapse of the Soviet Union. Under the new system, waterbodies are rented out to private companies, who are also obliged to invest money in developing the fishery. But the state continues to regulate: by imposing quotas, it effectively creates scarcity. The aim of this property regime is to ensure ecological sustainability and economic efficiency: as rights and obligations are shared between state and private actors, the 'tragedy of the commons' (Hardin 1968) will, apparently, be averted, and private actors, motivated by increasing their profits and monitored by the state, will develop the infrastructure that the region needs. The future will, it seems, be secured.

However, regulations are not respected—as in other post-Soviet fisheries (E. Wilson 2002; Knudsen and Toje 2008; Nakhshina 2012). Indeed, in Kazakhstan in general, privatization and the rolling back of the state have resulted in an opaque economy marked by arbitrary enforcement of regulations. On the Small Aral, over-quota fishing is ubiquitous: while official catches stand at about 4,000 tonnes, no one knows how much fish is actually caught; some estimate more than twice that, while others are more conservative. If fish are hard to see and know while in the water, they can also be hard to pin down out of the water. Illegal monofilament nets, mostly made in China, are widely used. Infrastructure has not been developed as envisaged. The above-quota fish which are caught do not make it either to the shiny new factory in Aral'sk, which stands idle most of the time, or even to the market in the town, but mysteriously disappear out of the region—causing

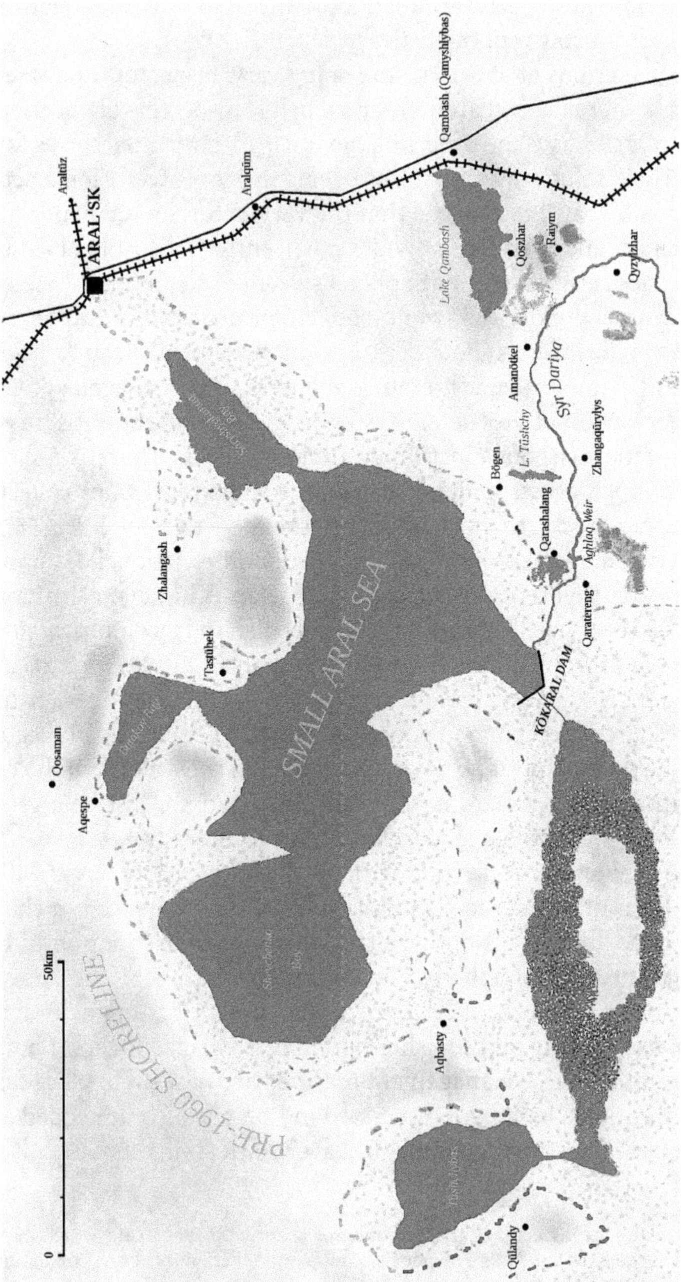

Figure 8.2 Map of the Aral Sea region

considerable resentment among townspeople. This is not to say that the system has failed: there are those who have profited from it, including many fishermen. But the formal dysfunction of the system casts doubt on the long-term sustainability of the fishery.

Local explanations of above-quota fishing vary. Inspectors and scientists argue that laws are inadequately enforced (while inspectors blame their lack of resources, scientists and others blame the inspectors themselves for corruption). Their solution is better enforcement. By contrast, some activists in a local NGO, Aral Tenizi, argue that the very nature of regulations alienates fishermen, and therefore provides no incentive for sustainable fishing; they have tried, unsuccessfully, to pilot a system of community-based management, whereby more rights and obligations are devolved to fishermen themselves in the interests both of equity and sustainability. Such diagnoses echo debates in the academic literature about resource management. In calling for enforcement of the current system, inspectors and scientists assume, like Hardin, that without functioning property rights, there is a free-for-all, de facto open access: individuals seeking short-term gains collectively deplete the fish stocks, to the detriment of the collective long-term good. By contrast, co-management—widely promoted in international development today—rests on theoretical perspectives developed in new institutionalist economics (see especially Ostrom 1990) and bolstered by empirical findings of anthropologists and others (e.g. McCay and Acheson 1987) which suggest that, while both state and private control can create incentives for unsustainable resource use, common pool resources can be successfully regulated by individuals cooperating to devise rules both in their own and the collective best interest.[3] *Pace* Hardin, the commons need not just be a group of individuals who are unable to identify collective interests.

Since co-management has not been tried, and probably never will, and since the current system looks unlikely to be fully enforced in the near future, it is not my intention here to assess which distribution of rights and obligations is preferable for securing the future of the Aral Sea's fishing resources. Instead, I anatomize the current system as it actually functions, by focusing on the fishermen in one village, Bögen. If both the approaches to resource management outlined above seem to place faith in formal institutions, I am here interested in how socially embedded actors negotiate formal institutional rules (Cleaver 2001; Steins 2001). I will argue

[3] There are also strong ecological arguments for adaptive management which integrates fishers' knowledge so as to be more responsive to the unpredictability of fish populations: see Wilson et al. (1994), Johannes et al. (2000), J. Wilson (2002). Anthropologists' assessments of co-management have ranged from cautiously positive (Li 1996; Caulfield 1997; Tsing 2005) to sympathetically critical (Agrawal and Gibson 1999; Li 2002; Acheson 2006); success or failure seems to be largely based on contextual factors.

that over-quota fishing is not about an absence of rules; rather, legal categories are selected, adapted, and meshed with informal categories, to suit the constraints of social, economic, and environmental contexts, most importantly the constraints deriving from tensions in the formal property regime itself.

Over-quota fishing also depends on fishermen's conceptualization of the resource as abundant, which undermines the official creation of scarcity in the form of quotas. Indeed, property institutions which are designed for sustainable resource use rest on particular assumptions about how people think about resources: if regimes inspired by the tragedy of the commons thesis rest on the economistic assumption that individuals seek to maximize their short-term advantage and must be restrained, community-based property regimes assume that resource dependence makes people good ecological stewards (Agrawal and Gibson 1999). Empirical evidence could be deployed to query both sorts of assumption—and I shall return to this point in the conclusion. However, my ethnography suggests that we should turn the question round: can property regimes themselves shape conceptualizations of natural resources? After all, if property relations are relations between people with respect to things, in different property regimes, both people and things are constituted differently. I therefore explore how understandings of persons and things are (re)constituted within particular property regimes, arguing, paradoxically, that the short-termism itself stems, in part, from formal property regimes past and present.

Finally, any answer to explain why above-quota fishing happens is incomplete without asking what fish mean to villagers, and what roles they play in village life. After all, property-oriented approaches to resource management tend to ignore the 'social life' of things as they enter different sets of human relationships (Appadurai 1986; cf. Richardson and Weszkalnys 2014). The final part of this chapter, then, unpacks the various meanings of fish as commodities of various values and foodstuffs. In particular, I contrast the short-term relationships with fish with the long-term meanings of the other forms of property which they enable—up to and including the reproduction of cultural property attached to place.

Before proceeding, a caveat. The 'social life' of fish spans thousands of kilometres and radically different social worlds. Although my focus here is on fishermen themselves, there are many factors behind above-quota fishing, and it would be reductionist to prioritize any one—or to cast any one group as responsible. In so far as the market, particularly the lucrative demand for zander in Europe, provides strong incentives for intensive fishing, and the formal property rules engender tensions with above-quota fishing, agency is distributed across the social worlds fish pass through in their journey from sea to table.

PAST PROPERTY REGIMES ON THE ARAL

The property regime on the Small Aral was not, of course, imposed on a tabula rasa. This section, therefore, contextualizes the current system in a history of the Aral Sea fisheries, in which relationships between fish and livestock have been reconfigured by state interventions and integration into markets at different scales—with suggestive parallels to the history of the Somali fisheries charted by Dua (Chapter 7, this volume). Indeed, the fortunes of the Aral fisheries have fluctuated dramatically as property regimes and environments have changed, and as different sorts of value have been ascribed to fish in nomadic, colonial, socialist, and postsocialist economies.[4]

Prior to Russian colonial expansion, fishing was marginal to the nomadic economy of the steppe. The property that mattered was livestock and access to pastures; camels and horses in particular signified wealth and prestige (Tolybekov 1959: 95–6; Khazanov 2012). Society was organized around patrilineal clan groupings; practices of exchange were intertwined with kinship practices. Fishing, like cultivated agriculture, was practised with rudimentary technologies by the poor—those with few or no livestock (Beknazarov 2010). Proverbs testify to what sort of activity this was: *balyqshynyng bailyghy etek zhengï kepkenshe*, 'the fisherman's wealth lasts until his sleeve dries'; *egenshï zhylda armanda, balyqshy künde armanda*, 'the sower dreams for the year, the fisherman dreams for the day'. This was then, about immediate returns: fish were not property objects suitable for long-term accumulation or exchange with a view to future increase in material or social capital. Nor was it about the careful husbandry of scarce resources, as livestock demanded. *Aulau*, 'to fish', also means 'to hunt', deriving from the noun *au*, trap/net.[5] This may be related to the relative abundance of fish: while the economy of livestock herding in harsh, arid conditions was premised on scarcity, when they fished, employing basic technologies, Kazakhs were faced with a natural abundance—lakes and rivers teeming with fish.

There are, therefore, some informative comparisons to be made with hunter-gatherer societies, which are dominated by presentist ideologies of immediate consumption and egalitarian sharing practices rather than reciprocal exchange (e.g. Woodburn 1982; Ingold 1986: ch. 5). Such ideologies are reflected in a now defunct Kazakh tradition that you should not invite someone to eat fish with you (which would imply some sense of

[4] My narrative is woven from archival data drawn from the Central State Archive of the Republic of Kazakhstan (hereafter TsGARK), fond 759, fond 1130, and the Aral'sk branch of the state archive of Qyzylorda oblast (hereafter AFGAKO), fond 4, fond 5, fond 7. For the most part, this tallies with oral accounts that I heard, though with one major exception, as we see below.

[5] This is not to say that there were not rights to certain pieces of water, particularly where semi-fixed traps would be set. I have found no evidence about this question.

reciprocity)—they should join you of their own accord (Beknazarov 2010). There is also a custom which more or less survives today, as we see below, that fish ought to be given to anyone, whether kin or not, who visits you while you are fishing, with no obligation to reciprocate or exchange.

Russian colonial expansion marked a cataclysmic upheaval in property relations, with a disastrous impact on the pastoral economy of the steppe (Tolybekov 1959; Beknazarov 2010). As settlers encroached on the best pastures and migration routes were curtailed, impoverished Kazakhs increasingly turned to fishing. After a group of Ural Cossacks was deported to the region in the 1870s, bringing new technologies for processing and curing fish, Kazakhs began to fish for the market. At the same time, the sea began to be regulated, with access regulated by licences from 1886 (Plotnikov et al. 2014: 56). Initially, fish could only reach imperial markets in winter, by caravan to the railhead at Orenburg, but the Tashkent railway, completed in 1906 to pass the north-eastern corner of the Aral Sea, opened up wider, more lucrative markets. There was widespread immigration into the region. Icehouses and processing workshops were established around the sea, particularly in Aral'sk, which was growing rapidly around the port and station. Within this rapidly developing infrastructure, fish became a new sort of property object, acquiring monetary value within debt relations: fishermen would be advanced food and equipment for the season by Russian entrepreneurs, to whom they would be obliged to sell their catch. Ever since, there has been a close association between fish and money.

All this collapsed during the First World War as the provisioning of the region fell apart: non-Kazakhs left the region, many were conscripted into the army, while Kazakhs returned, as far as possible, to pastoralism. During the 1920s, the industry was reconstructed gradually.[6] In 1925 the Aral State Fishery Trust (Aralgosrybtrest) was established, which later became Aralrybokombinat and finally Aralrybprom. The socialist fishery was at first also founded on debt: the Trust would advance equipment and foodstuffs to independent fishermen or cooperatives, who were then obliged to sell their catch to the Trust. Cooperatives also played some role in processing fish and managing lakes.

However, although catches were growing rapidly, they were not sufficient for the gigantism of the Stalinist period. Thus, the authorities sought to harness the natural abundance in the sea through sedentarization and collectivization of the semi-nomadic population and deportations into the region. As much labour was to be mobilized as possible, including female labour—women would fish until the fishery contracted in the 1960s. As elsewhere

[6] See Pianciola (forthcoming).

in Kazakhstan, sedentarization policies were accompanied by confiscation of Kazakhs' most important property, their livestock. The result was widespread famine, which was exacerbated when the provisioning of the region with grain failed in the early 1930s.[7] While planned catches were enormous, far exceeding the likely capacity of the sea, actual catches crashed.

However, many older people in the region today deny that there was a famine: the sea, they insist, sustained human life with its fish—alluding to the motif of natural abundance. Other narratives about this period stress that the situation improved when the fishery was constructed and—as one elderly informant put it—'Lenin–Stalin brought money'. Indeed, chaotic as the process was, collectivization instigated a new set of property relations, whereby equipment was owned by collective farms (*kolkhozy*), which themselves were provisioned by state organs; fishing was carried out in brigades according to a plan dictated by higher authorities, and was remunerated with money, with various deductions to the *kolkhoz* accounts. This tendency towards centralized control of the means of production was accelerated in the late 1950s, when most of the *kolkhozy*, which were struggling financially, were dissolved and incorporated into Aralgosrybtrest as state fishery bases (*bazy goslova*).

The distribution of rights, obligations, and entitlements in this property regime constituted fish and fishers in particular ways. 'Extraction' (*dobycha*), the work of the *kolkhoz*, was distinct from processing (*obrabotka*); improvement measures (*meliorativnye mery*) to clear lakes and spawning grounds, to keep them free of weeds, to deepen channels were dictated by a separate body, Aralrybvod. Although there were sometimes tensions between scientists and industry, fishing plans were, in principle, guided by science. The role of fishers was simply to fish, according to the plan laid down by higher authorities: their knowledge was not valorized. The Soviet system also reinforced the effects of the colonial market economy in the transformation of fish into property objects valued according to their exchange value.[8] However, fish signified more than just exchange value: the practice of fishing, as a form of labour, also enabled access to rights and entitlements as Soviet citizens.[9] These rights and entitlements were limited: the rising living standards which underpinned the legitimacy of the Soviet system were unevenly distributed between the metropolitan centres and remote

[7] AFGAKO f. 7, op. 1, d. 32, l. 37 describes the failure in provisioning; AFGAKO f. 7, op. 1, d. 12, l. 3 describes the flight of hundreds of households from around the sea; for a detailed study of the famine in the region, see Pianciola (forthcoming). More generally, on the famine in Kazakhstan, see Pianciola (2001) and Payne (2011).

[8] Similarly, Lampland (1995) argues that socialism in Hungary paradoxically accelerated the inculcation of ostensibly capitalist values.

[9] See Verdery (1996) on the social contract of state socialism.

peripheries such as the Aral, where villages lacked housing, electricity, and drinking water well into the 1960s and 1970s. Nevertheless, fish mediated the relationship between fishers and the state—and entitlements grew gradually. In such a property regime, the state was, as Alexander (2004: 271) puts it, 'an over-arching structure of connection'. Although there were incentives for over-fulfilling the plan, there was little incentive to fish without limit, since prices were low and the monetary value of fish was only part of the web of relations and entitlements connecting fishers and the state. In effect, the aggregate demand embodied in the plan was finite.

While the Soviet system consolidated the role of professional fisher, this did not exhaust the repertoire of roles played by the inhabitants of fishing villages. After collectivization, villagers were allowed to buy limited amounts of livestock with their earnings from fishing: distinct from the 'collectively' held property of the kolkhoz, this was classed as personal property, officially connected to household consumption rather than production. Furthermore, although production was no longer organized around patrilineal groupings, kinship remained important for organizing and negotiating social relations, and livestock again mediated kinship practices. Crucially, the state-socialist economy could not function according to the formal rules: although the planned economy was predicated on total state control of production, pervasive shortages at all levels imposed constraints (Kornai 1980; Verdery 1996; Humphrey 1998). Formal tensions in fulfilling plans thus necessitated hoarding supplies, falsification of accounts, and exploiting informal connections so as to acquire materials or to bargain with superiors over plans and allocations.

Formal hierarchies were thus, in practice, open to negotiation: claims could be made according to informal categories such as kinship, patron-client obligation, and so on. The difficulty of regulating an activity carried out over large spaces outside the purview of agents of the state exacerbated such tensions. Even getting people to fish so as to fulfil the plan was a question of negotiation, as workers could not be fired for poor discipline. The brigade system was often ignored, and most fishing was conducted on easily accessible inshore waters rather than across the sea. Regulations about keeping *kolkhoz* property, like nets, in centralized stores were routinely disregarded. According to one document, fishers, who were permitted 100–120 kg of fish per year for their families, often took home that quantity every month without paying for it.[10]

Fish played their part in these informal negotiations: I was once shown a now desiccated pool which was, apparently, used to store large

[10] AFGAKO f. 4, op. 2, d. 8., ll. 125–7.

sturgeon—when a gift was needed for a minister, the sturgeon would be dispatched by train to Kazakhstan's then capital, Alma-Ata; on a more local scale, I heard about a fisherman tethering a carp by its gills to a reed, which could be given to passing dignitaries. Such practices depart from the usual immediatism involved with fish: in such cases, highly valued fish became rather more individuated than usual and mediated personal relations with superiors.

From the 1960s, as the sea dried up and native fish died out, the fishery was severely curtailed. In the 1970s, several villages were entirely relocated, and parts of the enterprise were closed down. Thousands left the region altogether—either to work on rice farms upstream on the Syr Darya, or on other enterprises in the region or beyond. But many refused to leave, and the fishing industry limped on: acting on instructions from the ministry, fisheries bosses established fish farms on the depleted delta lakes, and sent the remaining fishermen to fish for months at a time on other lakes in Kazakhstan. Local narratives about this period thus oscillate between a sense of rupture—'the sea went away, everybody left'—and a sense of continuity provided by the ongoing practice of fishing. After all, wherever you fished, you had to fulfil the plan, and you received money and entitlements in exchange for fulfilling the plan. But in neither sort of narrative is there any sense of agency: narratives about the sea's regression place the blame, quite rightly, either in Moscow or Tashkent, while narratives about fishing stress that the factory or the minister sent them—after all, the right to fish on other lakes depended on centralized control over the means of production, a factor which was also crucial to the sea's regression (see Wheeler 2016). However, when people today account for why they did not leave, another form of property becomes evident: they express their attachment to *tughan zher*, or 'land of birth', the place where the ancestors are buried—an attachment which persisted despite the ecological devastation. This notion of cultural property constitutes persons through their connections with the land, with their ancestors and with their kin.

After the collapse of the USSR, deep economic crisis ensued, exacerbating the environmental crisis: the gridded economic infrastructure of Soviet space disintegrated, and subsidies dried up. Although there was no immediate change in the formal property regime, there was a gradual breakdown in the functioning of the industry as Aralrybprom's assets lost their value, which had depended on the infrastructure of the planned economy (Alexander 2004; Verdery 2004). More people left the fishing villages. People today explain that it was a bad time: no water, no fish, no money. Indeed, fishermen did not even see money for several years, as they would be paid in kind in the dying years of Aralrybprom—with boats, livestock, even cheap foodstuffs like margarine. Though pastures were depleted and the cost of feed had risen dramatically, livestock became a crucial form of property to fishing families.

However, by the time Aralrybprom finally went bankrupt in 1997, there was a new source of hope in the region. In 1991, some visiting Danish ecological activists heard that there was flounder in the remains of the sea. Flounder had been introduced in Soviet times as a saltwater fish, and by the 1990s it was thriving; but it could not be exploited owing to lack of equipment amidst the economic crisis. The Danes launched a project to provide nets and other equipment and repair boats. When Aralrybprom collapsed, they set up an NGO, Aral Tenizi, to organize fishermen into cooperatives. They also installed refrigeration units in some villages, and, in 2004, opened a small fish processing plant in Aral'sk. In their short-term goals of getting people fishing again, the Danes were successful—and are fondly remembered today, as I found when I was taught to say *Skål!* over a measure of vodka. The Danes also had long-term utopian goals of establishing a sustainable and democratic fishery in which fishermen would take responsibility for themselves, their equipment and the resource; they sought to realize these goals by establishing small cooperatives and limited liability partnerships managed directly by fishermen.

However, the legal context was not conducive to these goals: according to new property laws, cooperatives were obliged to purchase quotas, with which they could fish anywhere on the sea. In practice, most would purchase a quota for a few tonnes and then fish as much as they could. Regulation and management of the resource was still formally in the hands of the fisheries inspectorate, but, amidst lax regulation, poaching was rife. Furthermore, the small companies and cooperatives were also saddled with paperwork and compliance with regulations which ordinary fishermen were unused to. In practice, the pattern of formal hierarchy and informal negotiation remained.[11] Because of the obvious problems with the system, NGO workers came to place their hope in new property relations, seeking to test a system of co-management when the sea returned, with World Bank support. Instead, when the sea returned, the current system was implemented, to which we now turn.

THE PROPERTY REGIME TODAY

Formally the North Aral Sea remains state property. However, it has been divided into eighteen plots (Kaz.: *uchäske*/Rus.: *uchastok*), each of which is

[11] See the World Bank report (World Bank 2004), drafted by western consultants and Kazakhstani ichthyologists with input from the NGO workers in Aral'sk.

put out to tender for ten years to a 'nature user' (Kaz.: *tabighat paidalanushy*/ Rus.: *prirodopol'zovatel'*),[12] usually a limited liability partnership (LLP) or, more rarely, a cooperative. The use rights which the state has devolved to the nature user are limited: the nature user may only fish within the quota for each species, defined by the state inspectorate on the basis of data from a research institute, KazNIIRKh. So, in addition to property rights over the sea, the nature user also holds another form of property, a quota—a quasi-commodity, which Minnegal and Dwyer (2011) term 'virtual fish'. Compared to actual fish in the sea, 'virtual fish' are scarce. Quotas therefore limit present exploitation with a view to securing the future of the resource. Unlike transferable quotas in European fisheries, these quotas are inalienable, and can only be exploited on the relevant plot of sea. Furthermore, there are regulations about sizes of fish that may be caught, and there is a banned season in May, when carp spawn, and a banned zone in the spawning grounds around the mouth of the Syr Darya.[13]

The nature user also holds the right to employ fishermen to turn 'virtual fish' into real fish, paying them according to how much they catch at the prices he sets. There are no rules as to how many fishermen should be employed, or how many nets or boats they should use. Crucially, although fishermen's formal right to fish depends on receiving a licence from the nature user, this right does not limit how many fish they can catch: the quota itself is only the concern of the nature user, who should limit his catch either by licensing fewer fishermen or adjusting his prices. Only the nature user, then, deals directly with the scarcity instituted by quotas. The nature user also mediates between fishermen and the state by paying pension contributions and social security tax, and, in theory, a sales tax on fish. Whereas previously the base, as a state enterprise, provided fishermen with nets, boots, and special clothing, the nature user only provides boats and engines; and while fish also embody some connection with future entitlements in the form of pension contributions, this is far from the full range of future *and* everyday social entitlements under the Soviet system. Since the state no longer provides 'an over-arching structure of connection', it is unsurprising that fishermen describe the system as 'private' (Kaz.: *zheke*).

[12] Though nature users are also obliged to act as environmental managers, the term, dating from Soviet times, captures a vision of nature as a source of economic benefit.

[13] It is not my intention to assess the scientific basis of the management system. Quota-based management has been widely critiqued by ecologists and anthropologists alike (e.g. Larkin 1977; Ludwig et al. 1993; Wilson et al. 1994; Pálsson 2006). Such authors suggest parametric management, e.g. of conditions for reproduction, food base, species interactions. In theory, KazNIIRKh scientists, as in Soviet times, take such parameters into account; furthermore, there is regulation of spawning times and zones. However, KazNIIRKh is severely underfunded, and there are therefore question marks over the quality of its research.

However, the state is not wholly absent. Nature users are no longer constrained by higher bodies setting the plan, but by their relations with the fisheries inspectorate. As a property object, each plot of sea also carries a number of obligations detailed in a 'fisheries development plan' drawn up during the tender process: nature users should pay KazNIIRKh for their research, and spend money 'to increase fish stocks'; they should also invest in infrastructure to improve working conditions, such as roads to the sea, pontoons, a receiving station on the shore, refrigeration units, accommodation for fishermen by the sea. Formally, the sea as an object of property is not only an economic resource to be exploited: it is also, as in Soviet times, to be managed and improved.

If practice does not match formal rules, this is first and foremost because of formal tensions in the system itself. After all, actual nature users are more than an abstract category: they are real companies, operating under difficult economic constraints, run by human beings who are more or less embedded into local social and political relations. In Soviet times, enterprises were constrained by shortages of materials, while money was relatively abundant. Today the constraint is the reverse: the necessary goods are available, but money and credit are not, such that it would be impossible to fish within quotas and fulfil all obligations.[14] On one small plot, if the nature user fishes within the quota, zander, the source of most profits today, brings in about 1.5m KZT profit per year—only one-third of all the expenditure in the development plan. So, it is not surprising that in practice, obligations are not fulfilled. Some aspects of the development plan are more likely to be fulfilled than others. It is suspected that improvement works largely take place on paper. There is very little investment in infrastructure, except for refrigeration units, which directly and immediately increase profitability. Since a refrigeration unit can cost 9m KZT, credit is necessary—which means that the fishery can quickly become a liability. Given the difficulty in fulfilling the plan, it is unsurprising that several nature users have, over the years, gone bankrupt and had their plots confiscated. Those who survive must juggle their legal obligations with debt repayments, which carry more immediacy than the future of the fish stocks—hence the compulsion to fish above quotas, especially zander. The divergence in profitability also means that fishing practices are wildly uneven: while quotas exist for all species in the sea, nature users in practice are only interested in zander, asp, roach, and bream, and offer more than five times as much for zander as for other fish. Although they hold virtual carp, virtual flounder, virtual catfish, and so on, they tend not to turn these into commodities.

[14] See Visser (2006: 137–8), for similar dynamics in rural Russia.

Better enforcement of regulations would only exacerbate such financial tensions. To the extent that rules are flouted, this therefore derives in no small part from the tensions within the rules themselves. Nevertheless, over-quota fishing is certainly facilitated by lax regulation. As inspectors complain, they themselves are constrained: the inspectorate is understaffed, with neither the manpower nor sufficient vehicles to patrol the shoreline and to monitor the receiving stations. However, their own behaviour is marked by considerable arbitrariness. The tender process itself has been widely criticized for its lack of transparency. Furthermore, enforcement of regulations is uneven: informal connections between inspectors and nature users can be exploited to avoid punishment, while inspectors may also pursue someone they do not like on the basis of a technicality.

The general tendency over the last ten years has been for small-scale operators to go out of business, and large-scale operators, with good relations with inspectors, to consolidate more plots—as in other postsocialist agrarian settings (Perrotta 2002; Shreeves 2002; Toleubayev et al. 2010). Crucially, when a fishery looks healthy from the outside, over-quota fishing is tolerated. Thus, rights and obligations which are legally bundled together, are dissociated in practice (Sikor 2006). If by state law the sea is constituted as an object of economic value *and* of environmental management, in practice, nature users treat it first and foremost as an object of economic value. This context shapes the relations between nature users and fishermen: if virtual fish are supposed to regulate through instituting scarcity, this is not translated into practice.

BÖGEN

I turn now to the relationship between formal rules and practice in Bögen, whose fishermen work on one of the more successful fisheries, based mainly at a site called Shaghalaly. Bögen is a village of about 140 houses, 12km from the sea, 150km from Aral'sk, and 20km from other villages in either direction. Most families depend on one or more family members who are fishermen; there is some limited, low-paid work for women in the school and kindergarten. Most fishing families also keep some livestock—sheep, goats, one or two camels, one or two horses, and there are also a few full-time commercial livestock herders. Livestock graze on the steppe and dried-up seabed around the village, all unregistered land and thus, in official terms, an open-access resource; camels and horses owned by different households form herds, while sheep and goats are tended on a household basis. Most fishing takes place on the sea, though there is also a nearby lake, Tūshchy. Whereas in Soviet times, fishing brigades were comprised of up to twelve people, fishing units today are considerably smaller, because fishermen use fixed gillnets which can be laid by two or three people, and because the influx of UAZ jeeps has facilitated access to the sea (previously fishermen would have camped in large groups for several days). Usually fishing units consist of three to five people, operating in two boats, or one vehicle in winter. A typical unit may be a father, sons, and maybe a brother, or a friend or neighbour. Those without a UAZ will generally team up with those who do have one. Fishing units are extremely flexible, and in spring in particular, family members from Aral'sk or even further afield, as well as non-fishermen in the village, are hired informally.

The nature user is Baqyt, an LLP run by Amanbai Erkhatov, a businessman who lives in the town of Qazaly, about 100km upstream on the Syr Darya, outside the Aral *raion*. Until he won the tender, he had no connection either to the village or to fishing in general—he made his money in rice in the 1990s. He has a factory for processing zander fillets in Qazaly, and has recently, on credit, installed a refrigeration unit and sorting plant in Bögen itself. Initially, poaching was common, and Amanbai faced competition from illegal traders, *kommersanty*, in the village (the Russian word *kommersanty* can mean any traders but in this context was used negatively). Today however there is very little poaching on the sea, and Amanbai's formal rights are broadly enforced. This relates in part to security along the shore and heavy fines, but compliance also stems from the fact that the fishery is relatively well organized: fishermen are paid in cash daily; most are provided with boats and radios; fuel and (illegal Chinese) nets are sold at the receiving station; weather forecasts are provided. Although Amanbai has not fulfilled all his obligations, such as building a pontoon and receiving station, during my fieldwork the inspectors rewarded him with two more formerly empty plots which were put out to tender, one near Aral'sk itself, the other near the village of Tastübek.

Amanbai's formal right is negotiated by his local representatives, the fish receivers (Rus.: *priëmshchiki*), whose role it is to receive fish and check for poachers, their authority marked by state-issued camouflage uniforms. In return for their obligations, they have the lucrative right to extract value as they transfer fish from shore to factory. Their legal property right both strengthens and is strengthened by their status in the village. One receiver, Meirambek, is Amanbai's nephew and is also from Qazaly; he moved to the village in 2006. The other, Zhaqsylyq, who is in his late fifties, is a local fisherman who started working as a receiver in 2012. Zhaqsylyq is a well-respected figure in the village: while beneficiaries of postsocialist property regimes have usually been former socialist managers, Zhaqsylyq was initially an ordinary fisherman, and later worked tending the base's livestock. His authority stems from the Danish project, when he was selected as a leader who could organize fishermen into brigades, as he had a reputation for hard work and honesty, he did not drink, and he could mobilize his extensive kin connections in the village. His family has benefited considerably from this support, and from his most recent position: they now own thirty valuable angora goats, and some horses and camels, including a prestigious *nor* camel.

In 2009 Zhaqsylyq's youngest daughter Danagul married Meirambek, thus connecting the two families through ties of affinity (Kaz.: *qūda*), with concomitant reciprocal obligations. Indirectly, the marriage of Meirambek and Danagul is also a connection between Amanbai and all Zhaqsylyq's fellow clan members (Kaz.: *rulas*) in the village, such that the relationship between employer and employees is more than purely economic. However, Meirambek's authority within the village goes beyond both the formal legal rights and his kinship relation to Zhaqsylyq: it is remade through his active participation in village life. Whatever is going on in—camel-slaughtering, housebuilding, drinking at a wedding—Meirambek puts himself at the centre of the activity. Often in quiet periods at the receiving station, he will command attention through lengthy anecdotes. In a context where people are always laughing about something, Meirambek's sense of humour asserts his central position within the group, at the expense of weaker members or outsiders—drunks, fishermen from other villages, me.

THE RIGHT TO FISH

These then are the social relations in which property relations are embedded. Unsurprisingly, rules may be negotiated or worked around: indeed, there is a sense of complicity between receivers and fishermen. Formally, fishermen must obtain permission from Meirambek to go to the sea; so long as the weather conditions are good and it is not the banned season, Meirambek will grant permission. In April 2014, as spring was late, there were still ice floes and strong winds: Meirambek was not giving permission to fish. However, when Aikeldï, a fisherman in his forties, announced that he was going to lay his nets anyway, Meirambek did not try to dissuade him. Although Aikeldï is not related to Zhaqsylyq's family, he lives nearby and sometimes fishes with Zhaqsylyq's sons. Given these relations, Meirambek was confident that Aikeldï would hand in his fish to the factory in the village.

Formal legal categories, however, are far from irrelevant. Lake Tūshchy was restored at the same time as the sea, but it is poor in ichthyofauna, which consists mainly of low-value pike. When I met some Bögen fishermen fishing there, they were planning on selling their catch to local *kommersanty*, and were dismissive of any punishment from Meirambek—as a distant relative, he would not punish them for fishing on Tūshchy, although, they stressed with a lewd gesture, fishing on the sea would be another matter. However, when on another occasion I accompanied Meirambek on a trip to the lake, we found two men laying their nets through the ice beside an ancient Ural motorcycle. Meirambek did not know them. Meirambek puffed himself up in his uniform and demanded their documents. As they did not have any, he announced that they should have requested permission and took a photo of them, to their discomfort. One of the men was elderly, and had an air of quiet dignity. He negotiated rather than argued, addressing Meirambek as *sen* (the form of address for an equal or junior). He talked quietly, slowly, and extensively. Various phrases asserted their right to fish: *bïz qazaqpyz*, 'we are Kazakhs'; *men aqsaqalmyn*, 'I am an *aqsaqal* (white-beard/elder)'; *bïz tengïzde auladyq, bïz dariiada auladyq*, 'we have fished on the sea, we have fished on the river'; *kölïmïz*, 'our lake'. But most of the conversation was taken up with the old man telling Meirambek about his various kin across the region. Meirambek's demeanour altered: he listened patiently, nodding, occasionally raising his head slightly and asking for clarification as the man reeled off his kinsmen, addressing him with the respectful *sïz*. At one point, he asked what the man's clan was, before lapsing again into deferential silence. However, the old man was unsuccessful: he could not find a connection. After about fifteen minutes of this, Meirambek read out an official statement about how they were fishing illegally and would have to pay a fine, though with more patience and respect than he had at first shown. He also said he would give them his phone number so they could get his permission in future. The old man was made to write out a confession; inspectors would then impose a fine.

Meirambek, bolstered by the authority of the camouflage uniform, appealed to the legal rules. But the old man, drawing attention to his white beard, challenged the authority of the camouflage uniform and appealed to different normative frameworks—ethnicity, seniority, and kinship. In narrating past fishing experience, establishing a relation between persons and places through story, he laid a claim to the right to fish based on quite different categories from the formal legalism underpinning Meriambek's position. Had the old man found a kinship connection, I suspect that this normative framework would have trumped the formal rule. As it was, the formal authority of the camouflage costume won the day.

Although in this case official rules governing access to the fishery *were* enforced, if it suits the nature user, formal legalism may be drawn upon more selectively. At Shaghalaly, and at Amanbai's other fishing sites, there are a number of fishermen from other villages working informally as hired workers. They do not receive boats or pension contributions, and are invisible to the state. Such informal labour is strictly speaking forbidden, but Amanbai needs to fish as much as possible. There is thus a differentiation between the fishermen who are formally employed and those who are informally hired: in winter, so long as they have UAZ jeeps, hired fishermen can fish as much as anyone else. When the ice has melted, however, they must use their own boats, which are often small 'lake boats' made of metal sheets, sometimes without motors. Besides being dangerous in the open sea, these boats cannot travel far, and cannot hold so much fish.

In sum, the fishery is neither open-access nor simply a negation of the formal property regime: legal categories may in some contexts be negotiable, but, through selective application of legal categories, Amanbai's representatives can regulate access to the fishery.

AT THE RECEIVING STATION

The cooperative labour of laying nets, involving skill and local knowledge, in which tasks are assigned according to seniority, stakes out a temporary claim to a particular part of sea as the property of a group of fishermen; so too are the fish caught held collectively by the unit. However, these rights are limited by the obligation to sell to the fish receivers, who, formally, have a monopsony. At the receiving station, other sorts of negotiation become evident, which are neatly encapsulated in a proverb: *Balyqshy aitpaidy rasyn, künde alady bïr asym*, 'the fisherman doesn't tell the truth, every day he takes one portion'. This proverb is told with a smirk, defining the fisherman's compliance with rules as flexible, and the nature user's ability to realize his legal monopsony as limited. Not telling the truth is legitimated—within reason. I shall discuss this proverb further below.

The 'receiving station' is simply a set of Soviet-era scales and a Soviet-era ZiL truck. During the first part of my fieldwork, in winter, Zhaqsylyq would be dressed in smart clothes and fur hat, while Meirambek wore the camouflage uniform with camouflage cap; later Zhaqsylyq too donned the uniform, but never quite looked comfortable in it, and tended to wear a rather incongruous leather flat cap with it. As fishermen come in, Zhaqsylyq chats affably with the older ones; Meirambek jokes with all and sundry. As fish enter relations between the fishing unit and the fish receivers, there is a tension between what is and is not seen. Just as inspectors cannot monitor whether recorded catches match actual catches, it is also difficult for fish receivers to know for certain what they are receiving. Fishermen may haul in their nets in the morning and take their boat to some reedy shoreline a few kilometres from the receiving station, where they put the fish into sacks. One or two sacks go into their UAZ which is parked nearby—a sack of bream, and maybe some asp; and a sack of non-commercial fish like carp or catfish. They then take the commercial catch by boat to the receiving station. Zhaqsylyq and Meirambek are busy all day receiving fish and cannot patrol the entire shore. Furthermore, they cannot check that every sack contains what it is supposed to contain. A sack of zander is generally quite obvious because the zander's pointy heads tear the sack and stick out of the sides. But a sack of bream will almost certainly also contain some small flounder or young carp not worth eating. The difficulty of monitoring in this sort of environment thus imposes constraints on the receivers.

As the fishermen unload the sacks of fish onto the scales, fish become a new sort of property: as they are known by weight, they acquire value as commodities. The production of this knowledge depends not only on the technology, but also on the social relations involved. The receivers ask what is in the sack, but do not check. They also do not enquire about what is in the fishermen's UAZ. When the scales are fully loaded, Meirambek or Zhaqsylyq adjusts the balance and reads off the weight. Although the fishermen are keen to hear the result, in general, they do not watch to check that it is being read correctly. Meirambek operates the scales deftly and efficiently, whereas Zhaqsylyq is clumsier. But only once did I see the result challenged. Zhaqsylyq was operating the scales, and sliding the measure slightly too far, aroused an angry shout—but there was no one else about, and Zhaqsylyq ignored the fisherman. On another occasion, a zander was rejected from the lorry as it was found to be mangled; it was reweighed and deducted from the fisherman's pay. Another fisherman was watching, and, although it was not his catch, he shouted 'It's just one!', to which the response was 'Yes, but that's 500KZT!'

Because everyone knows that what is visible is partial, the production of knowledge must be to some extent negotiated. The minor incidents above show the forms of 'social pressure' (Hivon 1998) involved: the receivers' authority is limited by the need to maintain the fishermen's trust. Though in these very minor cases the social pressure did not work, I did not see more serious challenges to the receivers' authority in Bögen—indeed, it was striking how rarely fishermen would even monitor the operation of the scales. If the Bögen fishery was thus relatively free of major conflict, this is arguably key to the relative success of Amanbai's fishery. In other villages such as Zhalangash on the other hand, relations are considerably more fractious—and it is, perhaps, not surprising that the nature user has had the plot confiscated. Trust, rather than official rules, is key here.

If there are social pressures on the receivers, there are also limits to what fishermen themselves can get away with: not telling the truth may receive censure. One day, Zhaqsylyq was outraged to learn that a sack of zander had been rejected by the directors of the factory, because it was full of young zander, some 20cm long. This is illegal, as juveniles should be put back, but Zhaqsylyq's outrage was financial: the fish were too small to be filleted, so had been rejected by the factory. Zhaqsylyq pays fishermen with his own money, so he was out of pocket: his right to extract value in mediating between fishermen and nature users had become a liability. When the receiving station was set up for the day, this sack was left near the scales, a few fish spilling out, and as fishermen arrived, Zhaqsylyq drew their attention to it. Eventually the man assumed guilty came in, and was given a stern dressing down by Meirambek and Zhaqsylyq—on the basis that the factory would not receive fish under 400g. Shamed by the incident, the fisherman did not dispute the cost of the sack being deducted from his day's earnings; when he left, he made a point of saying a cordial goodbye to Zhaqsylyq, who ignored him. No mention was made of the formal legal category whereby juvenile zander under 38cm should be put back; but the unofficial category, defined by the practice of the factory and enforced by men of high social standing in the village bolstered by the authority of their state-issued uniform, was certainly not negotiable.

At the moment of translation into money, the catch is recorded in Meirambek's copybook. Later, this will be re-entered into the official logbook and the figures massaged through creative accounting—zander may be recorded as, for example, a non-commercial fish like sabrefish. Of the fish which have been turned into commodities, only some will be matched up with 'virtual fish' to constitute the official catch for the eyes of the inspectors; the rest will remain invisible to the state, and will remain so as they are packaged and sent for export. Actual property practices, therefore, diverge from the formal rules—especially the quotas. However, this does not constitute an outright rejection of official categories: after all, Amanbai, Zhaqsylyq, and Meirambek are using their authority to realize their legal right to extract value from fishermen's labour. But since they are embedded in social and economic contexts, the rules by which they regulate the fishery may differ from, or even contradict, official regulations.

THE FISHERMAN DREAMS FOR THE DAY

Although, as I have stressed, intensive fishing, especially of zander, is in part driven by the conjunction of lucrative markets with formal tensions in the property regime, it also depends on fishermen's understanding of fish as abundant. This is not universal: some fishermen *are* anxious about the future of the stocks, but they are in a minority. When I asked if intensive fishing might cause a collapse in stocks, I was told again and again that 'every fish lays a million eggs!'; if there is water (and there will be, because of the dam), there will be fish. In this sense, the fisherman 'dreams for the day' because fish are seen as an abundant resource, which do not require management and economizing with a view to the future—unlike livestock.

To this extent, I suggest that the comparison with hunter-gatherer societies is still relevant. Astuti (1999) makes a similar analogy for the Vezo of Madagascar—as fisher people who fish for the market, their presentist orientation to fish as a resource is sustained by images of natural abundance. Astuti's chapter forms part of an edited volume, *The Lilies of the Field* (Day et al. 1999), whose contributors argue that images of abundance and a 'politics of the present' may be found among marginalized people in a wide range of societies, beyond the hunter-gatherer societies with which such practices are often associated. Similarly, while Aral fishermen's presentism has its roots in the specific role of fish within the nomadic economy, it has also been reproduced over the years by the political-ecological history of the Aral region, which is one of marginalization. Of course, villagers have known the resource become scarce, but they know that this was not due to overfishing, but rather to the prioritization of cotton- and rice-growing regions of Central Asia which led to the sea's regression. The marginality of the Aral Sea in this political economy had dire ecological effects; but villagers are well aware that this was nothing to do with their actions, and emphasize indeed that there was nothing they could do about it. Over the last few years, fish populations have been growing rapidly despite intensive fishing, which further reinforces the view that fishermen's actions do not affect the resource.

Paradoxically, this presentist attitude is also indirectly reproduced by the form of the property regime itself, which marginalizes fishermen from the management of fish stocks. In the Soviet system, the sea was a space to be managed and regulated by higher authorities: although labour was valorized, fishermen were constrained simply to extract resources. Under the current system, too, fishermen continue to be constrained only to extract resources, not to manage them. Indeed, according to one old man, it is hierarchical management that guarantees natural abundance: there would, he said, be plenty of zander in the future, because now the government (*ükïmet*) is growing zander in hatcheries; thus, fishermen could, he insisted, fish without end. Fishermen's role is thus limited: although they should obey regulations, it is the nature users who face onerous obligations regarding both the state and the environment. In practice, as we have seen, many of the nature users' rights are dissociated from obligations; nevertheless, the *formal* distribution of rights and obligations has real subjective effects in the constitution of fishermen and fish.

This is illustrated by the issue of Chinese monofilament nets, which are illegal: because they are cheap and readily abandoned, and because monofilament does not decompose, they accumulate on the seabed, continuing to catch fish. However, as they are relatively cheap and effective, they are used by nearly everyone. They are sold at the receiving station—demonstrating the complicity between fish receivers and fishermen in circumventing formal regulations. When I asked why they were illegal, fishermen would respond in indirect statement, as something they had been told. The following conversation is typical:

> WILLIAM: Why don't they give permission [to use them]?
>
> KÜNTUGHAN: I don't know. If they are left in the water they don't decompose, they say, there's a storm or whatever and they can't be pulled out . . . fish come and get stuck, they say, and they rot. When that fish rots, it pollutes the water they say. Then diseases spread from it, they say. Therefore, it's not allowed to lay those nets.

After disavowing knowledge, Küntughan proceeded to give a full explanation, but at one remove, as someone else's knowledge, while he situated himself as agnostic. In fact, I never heard such an explanation from scientists, but presumably this was what he had heard from the inspectors—in any case, Küntughan seemed uninterested in the real reason for the ban. On another occasion, I pressed a fisherman about the issue: did he think they were harmful? He replied with a broad grin: 'Harmful, it's said, but . . . they catch fish well!' He thereby carefully delimited two domains of knowledge: he claimed knowledge about the technology in the practice of fishing, but not about the long-term effects of the technology. There is an instructive contrast to Knudsen's (2008) account of arguments over sonar in his ethnography of the Turkish Black Sea fisheries: while fishers insist that sonar damages fish, scientists insist that it has no negative impact; while the scientists simply see it as a piece of technology, Knudsen argues that fishers' practical knowledge about the sonar represents a moral commentary on technology and social inequality. With Chinese nets on the other hand, there is no clash of knowledge systems, but rather a disavowal of knowledge: for Aral fishermen, Chinese nets *are* just pieces of technology.

At the same time, by distancing themselves from the explanation of why Chinese nets are banned, fishermen create a sense of the arbitrariness of power, a sense that the diktats of the authorities do not relate to everyday life except as a form of control. Thus, while the hierarchical *form* of the current system distances fishermen from resource management, at the same time, their sense of the inherent gulf between form and reality means that these kinds of rules are readily ignored.

There is a similar disavowal of knowledge about quotas. Although creative accounting is essential to conceal above-quota fishing from official eyes, this is not evident at the receiving station itself, where there is no talk of quotas at all. Indeed, in Bögen, I found that this formal alienation, and the distance from the state, was embraced by the fishermen. When I asked about quotas, they would express their indifference with a laugh and a dismissive expletive. However, whereas the official catch translates not only into pay for fishermen, but also into pension contributions, the unofficial catch does not. Fishermen have told me that their pension contributions are 3,000KZT a month, when if they claim to have earned 150,000KZT, the contributions should be 15,000KZT! Their attitude is characterized by not asking questions, and not looking into what is not their business. Since 'virtual fish' are not respected, prices, at least for zander, are relatively high, which carries more immediacy than pension contributions.

The literature on quotas in European contexts, which tend to be transferable, stresses their alienating effects. They represent the shift in the right to fish from labour to capital, and marginalize practical knowledge (Pálsson 2006). In separating the right to fish from the ability to do so, they represent a process of disembedding, which corrodes both the autonomy of fishermen and trust between fishermen (Minnegal and Dwyer 2011). But in the Aral context, there are some continuities between the quota and the Soviet plan: in so far as numbers were imposed by a higher authority, practical knowledge was marginalized and the management of the fishery was already disembedded in Soviet times, even if actual fishing practices were embedded in social relations between fishers and managers. If anything, today's quotas have less direct impact on fishermen than the plan, for while the plan would be assigned to the base, which would pass it down to each brigade, the quota is only the concern of the nature user. This is in stark contrast to the European system, where fishermen are acutely aware of quotas in their daily practices of fishing (Minnegal and Dwyer 2011). It is in this sense that the fisherman dreams for the day: the formal property regime limits his role, as in Soviet times, simply to one of fishing.

SOCIAL LIVES OF FISH

To complete our explanation of current fishing practices, it is necessary to follow the fish into the village. As property objects, fish are quite unlike livestock. Camels and horses are branded with the initials of the male members of the household owning them. Livestock is part of the household economy: gifts may be made to fulfil a ritual commitment between kin; it is a source of social capital, although it can also be translated into money if money is necessary for a ritual obligation. Relations involving fish, by contrast, tend to be impersonal and transitory.

In the first instance, fish are associated, as they have been for more than a century, with money, specifically ready money: as a young fisherman remarked, pointing triumphantly to a heap of fish, 'For us, fish are money!' (Kaz.: '*Bïzge balyq—aqsha*!') This significance of fish became evident outside fishing seasons, when I would be called upon to buy drinks and cigarettes for fishermen: they had no fish, so no money. Money from the commercial fish is divided evenly between the fishermen who caught them, regardless of age or status: at this fleeting moment, fishermen are disembedded economic actors. Like the Vezo described by Astuti (1999), Aral fishermen consume some of this money immediately, in the form of beer, vodka, and cigarettes.

However, if the formal property regime assumes that all fish caught become commodities differentiated by price, in practice different fish enter different regimes of value and are not wholly commensurable. This depends not only on the market, but also on the roles of fish in local cuisine: though not as highly rated as meat, fish is valued as part of the local diet. As we saw above, 'the fisherman does not tell the truth', but the exact wording of second part of the proverb is telling: 'every day he takes *bïr asym*'. *Asym* signifies a pot's worth of food, the amount of meat you need to make a *beshbarmaq*. That is, the fisherman does not tell the truth about his catch because he is taking some home for a meal with his household: it is not the same as taking some home to sell to a *kommersant* (this may happen too, but it is not encoded in the proverb). Fish are not only exchangeable commodities, but also an object of household consumption. According to the proverb, the fisherman's need to feed his family imposes a moral constraint on the ability of the nature user to realize his formal right.

Above all, carp is prized for its fattiness, and a carp *beshbarmaq* is a local twist on the Kazakh national dish—but though some may reach the bazaar in Aral'sk via poachers and *kommersanty*, it does not exist in sufficient quantities to be the basis of a commercial fishery. Other popular fatty fish are bream and catfish, which may form the basis of another local dish, *qarma*. All such dishes are consumed by households and prepared by women. Smoked fish is also popular, especially roach, sabrefish, and asp—prepared by men, and, in general, eaten by men over beer in Russian style. While fishermen describe zander as 'our job/work' (Kaz.: *zhūmysymyz*), it is not prized locally: popular for its leanness in Germany and Poland, it is unpopular for the same reason among Kazakhs.[15]

The non-commercial catch is therefore divided rather differently from the proceeds of the commercial catch. A large carp may go to the oldest

[15] McGuire (2014) explains the importance of fat in Kazakh diet; see also Zanca (2007) on its significance in Uzbekistan.

fisherman in the unit. Catfish is sliced evenly, each household taking a share. Bream and roach are also divided by household. Most of this fish is for household consumption. Furthermore, claims may be made on fish, mostly obviously by relatives or friends, according to affective obligations; but fish like bream or roach, which tend to be caught in abundance, may also be offered to someone completely unconnected, where there is no long-term reciprocity. In such instances, fish enter short-term immediate relations with no expectation of return: the hunter-gatherer ideology of shares, whereby economic value is not assigned to nature's bounty, thus persists where fish have low monetary value on the one hand, and resist individuation on the other.

However, there are important distinctions between Aral fishermen and hunter-gatherers. Hunter-gatherers are famous for their limited needs, so only work to fulfil those needs (Sahlins 1972). But fishermen today work very hard. One reason for this lies in the legacy of Soviet ideologies of labour. The main reason, however, is the role fish play today as alienable commodities, whose conversion into money enables other forms of property (Dua, Chapter 7, this volume). However much money there is, it is perceived to be not enough. Furthermore, hunter-gatherer societies tend not to invest in long-term transactional orders; similarly, the Vezo described by Astuti (1999) spend all the money earned from fishing immediately. But Aral fishermen only consume a small portion of the day's earnings immediately in the form of beer or vodka; most of the money is handed to the wife or mother, who controls the household finances. When I was coaxed into buying drinks in non-fishing seasons, there was plenty of money in the household—but it was earmarked for some future purpose.

High-intensity fishing, then, depends on the value of money in contemporary Aral communities. After all, with the demise of the state as an 'overarching structure of connection', fishing does not carry the entitlements which it carried in Soviet times, resulting in an increasing emphasis on the exchange value of fish, particularly high-denomination fish such as zander. Thus, in addition to expenditure on expensive everyday goods, some of the money from fishing is invested in productive capital like a UAZ. Money from zander also, however, facilitates acquisition of other forms of property such as houses and livestock. In particular, if a wedding is coming up, a new house is required, preferably larger than the previous one, and preferably in *evrotip*, 'Euro-style'—fronted with bricks, with plastic windows, laminate flooring, and so on.[16] The Central Asian institution of *asar*, which enables people to rally other villagers' labour to assist with their projects, persists, but in

[16] Land itself is not a particularly salient form of property: the land on which the house is built is free, though 25,000KZT should be paid to register it.

general changing tastes mean that housebuilding is coming to depend more and more on money. Bridewealth is still sometimes made up of livestock, but it too is becoming increasingly monetized. In such an economy, therefore, money is acquiring increasing value as it facilitates symbolic capital—and so too are zander.

The forms of property which money from fishing enables relate to a long-term order of social reproduction. In this sense, Aral villagers are closer to the Malay villagers described by Carsten (1989) than to the Vezo: Carsten explains how fishermen's wives symbolically 'cook' the money from the day's catch, turning the proceeds of a short-term competitive order into a long-term transactional order which reproduces society itself. However, unlike Carsten's case, the Aral villagers' long-term order is not egalitarian, but highly competitive, and fish are indirectly agents of social differentiation. In Bögen, it is the family of Zhaqsylyq that benefits most: his formal position in the fishery, cemented by and cementing his connections with Amanbai, allows him to extract value from the labour of other fishermen. At the other end of the scale, hired fishermen who lack affective connections with the fish receivers or nature user may access the resource so long as it is abundant and prices good; but, without access to boats, their capacity to extract value from the sea is more limited.

These, then, are the conditions in which fish are increasingly seen as a source of financial value, and in which zander come to be valued above other sorts of fish.[17] If the fisherman dreams for the day, the fisherman's family dreams for the next wedding. The politics of the present is restricted to the exploitation of the resource. As I have mentioned, some fishermen do express anxiety about the future of the stocks: if the dominant view, that fish are abundant, suppresses this anxiety, it is perhaps because it provides a justification for intensive fishing.

CONCLUSION

There would seem to be striking differences between this material and Erie's case study from China (Chapter 4, this volume), where the legal shift in the definition of relationships between persons with respects to things has prompted resistance through appeals to historic claims. On the Aral, there are strikingly few such appeals. One reason for these differences evidently lies in the continuities between Soviet and post-Soviet fisheries: after all,

[17] This competitive monetization of the ritual economy is typical of post-Soviet Central Asia, especially in contexts where migrant remittances have transformed local economies: see Trevisani (2016) on Uzbekistan, and Reeves (2012) on Kyrgyzstan; see also Botoeva (2015).

the Aral fisheries were built on a series of dispossessions going back to the colonial period; what fishermen today remember from the Soviet period is a disjuncture between an official legalism which rigorously separated fishing from management and processing, and unofficial categories through which formal tensions were negotiated. Although relationships between persons with respect to the fisheries have been realigned as the state has retreated, this disjuncture persists today. Its principal result today is that the new form of property created by the postsocialist regime, virtual fish, has little meaning for everyday practices of fishing.

But another reason for the differences with Erie's case study perhaps lies in the differences between the property objects affected by official changes in property law. Erie describes how persons are constituted through their long-term relationships with each other, with respect to family houses and ancestral property, and hence resist their economic valuation. As I have emphasized, fish are a form of property which tend to facilitate short-term, impersonal relations. Particularly in the case of zander, this means that they may be readily commodified. But zander, once translated into money, facilitate the acquisition of livestock and the building of houses—forms of property which emphatically *do* constitute persons over long time periods. From this perspective, there is perhaps a deeper similarity with Erie's case study. Indeed, in the broadest sense, as zander, via money, facilitate social reproduction, the cultural property of *tughan zher*, or homeland, is reproduced, albeit in a new form, as social relations are differentiated.

To return to the question of over-quota fishing, this is not a matter of institutional failure, of a total breakdown of rules: Amanbai, Zhaqsylyq, and Meirambek are, by and large, realizing their formal legal rights, though a degree of negotiation is necessary, embedded as these rights are in local social relations. The fishery *is* regulated—as was made clear to the poachers and to the unfortunate fisherman caught handing in undersized fish. Nevertheless, formal legalism is meshed with other normative frameworks—kinship, moral ideas about fish as an object of household consumption, the market-driven demands of the factory, and so on. If the poachers were picked up for transgressing official legalism, the fisherman who was caught out for not telling the truth had transgressed the unofficial legalism of the factory—though in both cases the points were bolstered by the official authority of the camouflage uniform.

As I have emphasized, if regulations about quotas do not translate to the local context, this derives primarily from tensions in the formal legalism of the property regime. One obvious solution to above-quota fishing—state investment to develop infrastructure, guarantee incomes, and diversify the economy—is politically unconscionable, given the ideological preference for private forms of property in post-Soviet Kazakhstan. The inspectors' solution—better enforcement—might make people fish within quotas, but, given the existing financial constraints, the fishery would be unlikely to thrive. Were co-management to be implemented, fishermen would doubtless negotiate its formal institutions so as to adapt to the various contexts within which fishing takes place: the unbalanced markets, the financial constraints, and the politics of the future which fishing supports. Without these contexts changing as well, it is unclear whether changing property institutions would result in quotas being respected. Critically, if the current system is based on the assumption that fishermen are individuals seeking maximum short-term gain who must be restrained, co-management rests on the assumption that fishermen actively care about the future of the fish stocks. The ethnography here queries both assumptions, suggesting rather an interplay between orientations to the present and to the future, deriving, in part, from property institutions themselves: formal alienation from the current property regime reproduces a presentist orientation to fish which underwrites a future-oriented accumulation of money, livestock, and symbolic capital.

Given the demise of the NGO, co-management is unlikely to be tried on the Small Aral. Instead, the pattern is for consolidation of large-scale operators. Amanbai has built on the success of his Bögen fishery to gain two more plots. Near the end of my fieldwork, when there was a tender for the six plots which had stood empty for years, they were all won by Aimbetov, the last director of Aralrybprom, who is reputed to have enriched himself from the bankruptcy of the state fishery in the 1990s. Today he has a processing plant in Aral'sk, on the site of the old Soviet one, but until recently he only had a small plot upstream on the Syr Darya, and the factory was not working to capacity. There is little doubt that his victory in the tender process was due to manipulation of his extensive connections. But six plots carry with them extensive obligations, and will also require major investment just in establishing the fishery. If he does succeed, it seems more than likely that it will involve over-quota fishing, but also that he will need to find some ways of manufacturing compliance among fishermen.

But does the above-quota fishing matter? There is a high level of uncertainty, not least because there is little transparency around the establishment of quotas: it is unclear either how many fish should be caught or how many are actually being caught. In addition, fisheries scientists today increasingly argue that quotas are an ineffective means of management, unable to cope with the high level of scientific uncertainty involved in fish populations (e.g. Larkin 1977; J. Wilson 2002). Global comparisons are not encouraging: fish populations, particularly in endorheic basins, are unpredictable, but tend not to be resilient (Holling 1973; Ludwig et al. 1993). If stocks were to crash, it may well lead to a paradigm shift in views of the resource (Finlayson and McCay 1998). There are also rumours that oil will be exploited, with negative effects on the local ecology. On the other hand, no one expected that the fish populations would recover so quickly when the sea returned. Many of the Aral fish spawn upstream on the Syr Darya, so much depends on the water quality and quantity hundreds of kilometres away. Furthermore, there are plans to raise the dam higher, or to create a new waterbody, and also to develop fish farming—including of zander. So, I would like to close with this conversation with a young fisherman who was more doubtful than most about the future:

WILLIAM: Will you fish in the future?
NŪRLAN: Time will show.
WILLIAM: Will there be fish in the future?
NŪRLAN: Only God knows.
WILLIAM: Today you're fishing lots and lots of zander—tomorrow will there be zander?
NŪRLAN: *smile, shrug, pause*. That is unknown.
WILLIAM: And if there are no fish . . .?
NŪRLAN: The people will leave.
I mentioned the possibility of oil. He was pessimistic for the fish if oil were found—they will be wiped out.
WILLIAM: Is that possible?
NŪRLAN: Everything is possible.
WILLIAM: The fisherman dreams for the day, yes?
NŪRLAN: *pause, nod*. What you say is true.

9

People as Property in Medieval Dubrovnik

HANNAH SKODA

In 2014, the mayor of Dubrovnik gave a speech to the tourists arriving in the city on one of the many cruise ships. He told them that, in 1416, the first European state to abolish slavery was the Republic of Dubrovnik (known in this period as Ragusa): Dubrovnik was home to a thriving slave market, largely for domestic service, and largely female. The abolition should not be a surprise, he said, given the fact that the Republic of Dubrovnik was at that time one of the most progressive states in Europe and beyond. Apparently, the business of slave trafficking in humans was deemed so abhorrent that a law was created to send a clear message to the world that the people of this city state valued human life.[1]

He was, of course, not making up this statute of 1416: it was a hugely important moment in the history of the city. But it is equally clear that the statute of 1416 was in reality more limited in its effects than he imagined and far more complex in its motivation: the slave trade continued unabated, and the statute itself responded not just to moral unease, but to diplomatic fragility, economic anxiety, and a concern for reputation. The relationship between law and slavery was neither straightforwardly prescriptive nor descriptive, but interwoven with the contradictions and problems of the institution of slavery. It was not the question of freedom or unfreedom which was the problem: medieval people were conceptually accustomed to

I would like to thank Milena Grabacic for generously piquing my interest in the archives of Dubrovnik. The Oxford History Faculty generously contributed towards funding my trip. Vesna Rimać and Zoran Perović at the archives were immensely welcoming and helpful. All archival references are from the State Archives in Dubrovnik.

[1] See <http://www.huffingtonpost.com/regina-fraser-and-pat-johnson/freedom-from-slavery-croatia_b_4905880.html>, accessed 1.6.17. Peter Frankopan claims that slavery was abolished because 'it seemed wrong to hold fellow humans in bondage and not to pay them for their work' (2015: 195).

People as Property in Medieval Dubrovnik. Hannah Skoda. © Hannah Skoda, 2017. Published 2017 by Oxford University Press.

thinking about this on a sliding scale (Helmholz 2012: 17).[2] The problem was the brutal, and frankly, odd, idea that a person could be property.

This chapter is predicated on two assumptions: first, that the concept of property is a defining feature of slavery; second, that law is integral to the construction of the relationship between master and slave as one of property. Neither assumption is uncontroversial, and neither assumption is immune to exceptions. The League of Nations in 1926 described slavery as 'the status or condition of a person over whom any or all the powers attaching to the right of ownership are exercised' (Patterson 1982: 21).[3] Anthropologists and sociologists have challenged this characterization by drawing attention to the relationship of domination involved (Vlassopoulos 2011: 115), and the utter alienation of the slave, as referred to in Patterson's coinage 'social death' (Patterson 1982); such approaches have the advantage of avoiding western-centric ideas about property which may not be appropriate in all cultural contexts (Kopytoff 1982: 220; Meillassoux 1996: 321). At the same time, though, this focus on subjugation and alienation tends to imply that slaves lacked any agency, something which more recent scholars have found problematic: not all slaves have found themselves 'socially isolated and parasitically degraded' (Patterson 2012: 329), and even when utterly subjugated, slaves found ways still to act as individuals (Zemon Davis 2011). In two important ways, the twin concepts of property and ownership can ironically restore the possibility of some degree of agency by slaves: laws of property were obliged to formally acknowledge the complexity of slave status, as legal things, but people with minds of their own; slaves could sometimes use law themselves to contest their position (McKinley 2010).

What is property? Honoré's (1961) 'bundle of rights' is a useful starting point: the right to have exclusive physical control of a thing; the right to personally use a thing; the right to manage; the right to income; the right to capital (to alienate, consume, or destroy the thing); the right to security (for no one to take the thing); the right to alienate or sell the thing; and the

[2] The distinction between unfreedom and being owned is a tantalizing one, unfortunately beyond the remit of this chapter. The concepts are clearly interrelated but distinct. In the Middle Ages, one could be an unfree serf, but not formally owned. Perhaps a striking example nowadays might be ownership of the contract rights of a professional footballer: third party ownership of football players has been described as a form of modern-day 'slavery' by some of the most senior figures in football (<http://www.bbc.co.uk/news/business-37483203>, accessed 30.9.2016). However, their emancipated and empowered personal situation would bear not the slightest resemblance to the lot of medieval slaves. On transfers of sportspeople, see Hickey (2012: 228).

[3] For extensive discussions of the legal implications of this definition, see Allain (2012), Hickey (2012), and Penner (2012). As Penner points out, the paradigm of ownership focuses attention on 'the concentration of the slave's universe in the hands of the slaveowner, i.e. there are no normative relations with others which are de facto respected' (2012: 252).

right to hold the thing over time.[4] Not all slave systems involve all these rights (Meillassoux 1996: 10–11), and slavery in Dubrovnik restricted some of these rights through, for example, limitations to the right to physically abuse one's slave. Honoré's discussion is useful, though, in pointing to a constellation of property-related rights, rather than a single defining feature.

Most basically, property involves relationships between people with respect to things. To make people into property, they need somehow to be stripped of their personhood, and reconceptualized as things. But distinctions between people and things cannot be easily elided or resolved. For classical Roman law, the distinction between people and things was never quite fully realized (Buckland 1908: chs. 2–9). Ragusan law drew on Roman law, but articulated these conceptual problems particularly starkly. The contradictions thrown up by treating people as things are fourfold. First, legal categories, predicated on straightforward distinctions, become problematic. Second, thinking of people as things presents (what should be insurmountable) moral problems. Third, economic processes can be complicated and undermined if the commodities are not passive objects, but individuals capable of exercising agency. Fourth, the categorization of a person as a thing is an act of violence which is likely to be contested. The legal evidence for slavery in Dubrovnik shows law as an effective agent to express and negotiate these tensions.

Making people into property, and defining them as things required law (see Garnsey 1996). This is, after all, fundamentally, the predicate of the Roman law of slavery. Whereas Aristotle had argued that slavery was a natural state (*Politics* 1.3), this view was rejected by the vast majority of ancient philosophers and lawmakers (e.g. Florentinus, in *Digest* 1.5.4; Ulpian, in *Digest* 1.1.4): if slavery could not be essentialized, it must be dependent upon processes of law.[5] 'Slavery is an institution of the *ius gentium*, whereby someone is against nature made subject to the ownership of another' (Florentinus, in *Digest* 1.5.4.3). This position was taken up by early Christian philosophers, with Augustine arguing that 'the law of man' created the institution of property, including that of slaves: 'Humans have accepted the laws of kings so that they can possess just such things' (*In Evangelium Iohannis tractatus* 10.6.25; cited in Harper 2011: 356–7). A similar position emerged in the

[4] Hickey (2012) uses Honoré's 'bundle of rights' theory to unpick what ownership might mean in the context of slavery. While some of the bundle is so capacious as to implicate 'normal' employment relations (e.g. the right to enjoy the income generated by the thing), much of it (e.g. the right to alienate) offers more critical purchase, not least in providing ways to tackle modern-day slavery where *de iure* attention only to claim-rights might make slaving practices hard to identify and to prosecute.

[5] 'The Roman justification of slavery was, in short, based on formalism rather than essentialism' (Mouritsen 2011: 17).

later Middle Ages. Thomas Aquinas's argument was ingenious: he claimed that law itself was only necessitated by the sinful state of the postlapsarian world, and that slavery could therefore be justified by law itself: 'a slave is his master's chattel in matters superadded to nature, but in nature things all are equal' (cited in Brundage 1995: 95). By the fifteenth century, Bishop Antoninus of Florence stated that 'slavery was instituted by divine law and confirmed by customary law, and canon law' (cited in Brundage 1995: 97; Pinelli 2008: 61). The *ius commune*, a blend of Roman law and canon law, followed this position, in accepting the justification of slavery through the *ius gentium*, despite its contravention of the *ius naturale* (Helmholz 2012: 4).

None of these discourses was entirely comfortable with the direct contradiction between *ius gentium* and *ius naturale.* After all, usually the *ius gentium* gains its rhetorical power through the illusion that it is merely a clarification of natural law and morality. The *favor libertatis* of Roman law was an expression of this hesitation. This was the idea that if the law should present any doubts, rulings should err on the side of the slave and his or her claims to freedom (Helmholz 2012: 4). It became an equally strong feature of the medieval *ius commune* and its local variants. So, law was never simply the means by which people were made into property. Acknowledging the contradictions and tensions of people and property was always part and parcel of the law of slavery.

This chapter, then, is an examination of the ways in which law dealt with the problems thrown up by the characterization of slaves both as things, and as people: a tension resurrected by Justinian (Honoré 2012: 1–3). Anthropologists, sociologists, and historians of slavery have debated whether slavery and its tensions are driven by economic prerogatives (e.g. Nieboer 1910); by violence (e.g. Patterson 1982; Graeber 2011); by culture, politics, religion, and morality (Finley 1980); or by law (Maine 1861; Morgan 1877). The Dubrovnik evidence shows that both the practice and theory of slavery was shaped by all these layers, and legal categorizations were attempts to navigate the complexities and demands of these different discourses. Law was, *pace* Patterson, not just 'window-dressing' (Patterson 1982), but both discursive (negotiating the different layers of tension between personhood and 'thing-ness'), and prescriptive (future-oriented and shaping the practice of slavery).

Woven into my discussion will be two further observations. First, slavery in the West has been most obviously shaped by Roman law. But Roman law was subject to processes of adaptation, selection, and hybridization. Customary law, canon law, and ad hoc responses, produced a quite specific flavour in Dubrovnik. Second, we clearly know better than to treat law as straightforwardly hegemonic, but this has proved more than ever tempting in the case of slavery. Nevertheless, there are hints throughout the archives, that slaves were not just subjects of the law, but could interact with, and exercise agency, through the law (McKinley 2010: 757). Law did not simply reduce slaves to things: rather, its acknowledgement of the tension between people and things provided opportunities, however meagre, to slaves.

This chapter adds (I hope) to a very significant body of detailed scholarship on the law of slavery in Croatia (Čremošnik 1947; Krekić 1997; Budak 2000), and the more socio-economically oriented approach of Susan Mosher Stuard (1983; also Čremošnik 1932, 1947, 1949; Vinaver 1953; Dinić 1967; Lucić 1979).[6] It asks new questions about the role of law, and the implications of treating slaves as property. The sources for slavery are in any case largely of a legal nature. Statute law was embodied in the provisions of 1272 (Bogišić and Jireček 1904; Cvitanić, Križman, and Kolanović 1990; Rimać and Lonza 2012). Slave sales were regularly registered at the Ragusan chancery, and provide a set of highly formulaic, but systematic records (Debita Notariae; Diversa Notariae; Diversa Cancellariae).[7] All these types of documents were obviously loaded in favour of the city state and the slave-owners, but even here, slaves appear as both legal things and human individuals. The latter characterization and sense of agency is far more obvious in our third type of source: litigation (concerning e.g. slave status: Lamenta de foris; Lamenta criminalia) and wills (Testamenta de Notaria, Distributione Testamentorum).

Dubrovnik was a thriving city state in the later Middle Ages: situated on the edge of the Adriatic, bathed in golden sunshine, it enjoyed superbly wealth-enhancing commercial links with Italy, managing the trade from the hinterlands of the Balkans (Carter 1972; Mosher Stuard 1992). Dubrovnik imported cattle products, furs, wax, honey, forest products, wool, minerals, and slaves. And it exported manufactured goods, particularly textiles, and slaves. By the later thirteenth century, all these trades were thriving. From 1205 to 1358, Dubrovnik lay under the sovereignty of Venice; in 1358, it broke free from Venice by becoming a vassal state of the kingdom of Hungary, and achieving de facto autonomy. But from 1440, with the expansion of the Ottoman Empire, Dubrovnik was precariously maintaining its position by paying a heavy tribute to the Sultan. Set beside its commercial dominance, then, was a sense of geopolitical fragility which saw the city council legislating repeatedly in the interests of the security of the city.

Slavery in Dubrovnik dates back at least to the ninth century (Budak 2000: 745). By the second half of the thirteenth century, the slave trade in

[6] There have been some significant disagreements, notably regarding the earlier history of slavery: see Budak 2000: 758, n. 43. A useful survey of the literature up to 1984 is Budak (1984). Less detailed, but more up to date, is the literature survey by Pinelli (2008).

[7] These can be accessed in the State Archives in Dubrovnik. Note also the significant published collections of Čremosnik (1932) and Dinić (1967).

Dubrovnik was organized and efficient: indeed, it was bipartite, consisting of the supply of slaves for domestic use in the city, and a flourishing trade with Italy. Budak notes that surviving records covering a total of ten years between 1280 and 1301, detail 269 sales. This may not seem a very high number, and is certainly modest in comparison with other great centres such as Venice: however, it is nevertheless a significant one, since it only covers sales rather than the whole slave population, and may well leave a number of more underhand transactions invisible to the historian (Budak 2000: 750). Most of these slaves came from the hinterlands around Dubrovnik, but as the trade expanded over the centuries, slaves from further afield became more common (Perović 1992: 12–14). The first half of the fourteenth century saw very little evidence of slavery (either there was a genuine decline, or a rise in illicit smuggling: Budak 2000: 752); from the second half of the fourteenth century, the trade became once again more prominent, although increasingly problematized (Budak 2000: 756–7). The status of these slaves was defined, in the first instance, through law.

The status of slaves was effectively set out in the 1272 statute, which drew both on *ius commune* and local customary law (Lonza 2012: 10): it was also articulated in sale contracts—law in practice.[8] The 1272 statute (Latin edition Bogišić and Jireček (1904); Croatian translation Cvitanić, Križman, and Kolanović (1990); edited and translated into English by Vesna Rimać (2012)) was the fundamental legal document of the Ragusan commune; when the Republic became quasi-independent in 1358, at least twelve patricians owned their own copy, and the oldest extant copy dates to the 1340s. Although subject to minor adaptations in the fifteenth century, it remained largely unchanged, and became a crucial symbol of the commune (Lonza 2012: 1–17). Slaves could be used to pay off gambling debts, the 1272 statute tells us (Book III, ch. 12 in Bogišić and Jireček (1904): 62). As presented in many contracts, a slave was property which could be sold, given, or transferred (e.g. Dinić 1967: document 145, p. 57). According to the *ius commune*, anyone could be a slave whose mother was a slave, who had been captured in battle, or who sold him or herself to pay a debt (Budak 2000: 758; Helmholz 2012: 20).

[8] The latest edition of this statute represents a conscious and publicly funded effort to make it widely accessible. Its editor and translator Vesna Rimać tellingly commented: 'In these times when we question Croatia's position towards the EU, as a legal historian, I would like to submit the fact that the statute of Dubrovnik is a reminder of times of common European legal concepts equally shared among the member states. It is of great importance for us as it signifies resurgence of natural boundaries and the continuation of a long tradition, tradition with multi-layered and complex sense of identities, just like the legal order of Dubrovnik Republic used to be' (<http://www.dubrovnik-excursion.com/dubrovnik-info/the-statute-of-dubrovnik-in-english/47>, accessed 12.1.2016). Strikingly, the statute was promulgated in the same year as the Code de Tortosa, which offered similar regulations regarding slavery (Verlinden 1955: 291–2).

Mosher Stuard posits that slavery may have been particularly popular in Dubrovnik as a way of controlling population numbers (Mosher Stuard 1983: 157). Because of its geographical position, the city was dependent on a limited water supply, and immigrants to the city were carefully controlled. A comparative context reveals this to be a problematic argument, as slavery was far more widespread in the later Middle Ages than is often assumed. Since the work of Charles Verlinden (1955–77), historians have become more aware of the prevalence of slavery at least in southern Europe during the later Middle Ages: Venice and Crete have been subject to detailed studies (McKee 2008); slavery in Genoa was highly developed (Epstein 1996); late medieval Tuscany witnessed a thriving slave trade (Delort and Boni 2000); the south of France was not exempt (Verlinden 1955); and late medieval Iberia was a flourishing centre (Blumenthal 2009). It is an uncomfortable fact that the great city states which we like to hold up as birthplaces of European culture and political thought (like those of the ancient Greek and Roman worlds) were also cities whose commercial interests were heavily intertwined with the slave trade.

Christoph Cluse (2007; Heers 1981), working on Genoa, points to what looks like quite a typical pattern: in the thirteenth and first half of the fourteenth century, most of the slaves were from the Black Sea region, with a few also from the Byzantine Empire, or described as 'Sarrasins'; from 1360 or so, more and more Tartars from the Golden Horde were being enslaved. The fifteenth century saw a growing number of slaves from North Africa. Some of these slaves from the Black Sea area were transported on from Italy to the Iberian peninsula: this Iberian trade also relied increasingly on slaves from the West African coast. For the period we are discussing here, most of this slavery was domestic, and the bulk of slaves were women. On the face of it, slavery was not racialized in this period. For Dubrovnik, certainly, since many of the slaves came from Bosnia, there were no straightforward ethnic differences, and comments in the documents on the race of the slaves are minimal (Earle and Lowe 2013: 415).

Most people were enslaved in this period through war. This was the most prominent 'legitimate' reason for enslaving people (based on Roman law and ratified by canon law ideas about just war) (Helmholz 2012: 20). Slave traders, carrying out brutal raids in the Bosnian hinterlands, disingenuously categorized those raids as acts of war and claimed local acts of aggression to justify their intrusions. Once captured, slaves were in a horrific position, lacking support networks and basic rights. Consider the case of one Bratosclava, a war captive, sold by the trader Dragus Drocinus of Rudnić, to Jacominus Caxolus *diffinite ad mortem* in October 1280 (*Debita notariae* I, fol. 26v)—she knew no one apart from her owner and her seller, and she had nothing. As Graeber puts it, a slave is someone who would otherwise be dead (Graeber 2011: 169).

Equally self-sale was increasing: many sold themselves, or their children, or their siblings. This was particularly common in the second half of the fourteenth century when epidemic disease ravaged the countryside and, far from affording new opportunities to the poor,[9] effectively pushed them into poverty so unbearable that selling their own selves was a matter of survival. Interestingly, self-sale was not normally recognized in Roman law (Buckland 1908: 427–36; revisionist view in Silver 2011), and these proscriptions were reiterated in Byzantium (Rautman 2006: 22). The situation in Dubrovnik was idiosyncratic and shaped by local circumstances.

COMMODITIES

There are, of course, conceptual distinctions between commerce and ownership; just as there is a fundamental distinction to be made between slaves captured for trade, and slaves captured for domestic service in Dubrovnik. Nevertheless, the idea of property underpins them both. In any case, several scholars have argued that much of the domestic slavery in Dubrovnik was really a form of training, so that the slaves could then be sold on at a higher price: this was a highly developed trade, often run by professional and specialized slave traders (Stójkovski 2011: 250–4).

Elaborate and rigorous contracts were a fundamental building block of the slave trade. Dubrovnik had exceptionally high rates of literacy in the later Middle Ages, and was a remarkably legalistic society (Krekić 1997: 228). It drew both on local practices, and on wider Italianate notarial culture: I was excited to discover very early examples of a bracket in some contracts from the 1400s (e.g. *Diversa Cancellariae* 33, fol. 229r.), which was most likely an Italian import (Wakelin 2005: 26–46).[10] And if slaves were to be marketized within a commercial economy, efficiency was maximized by formalizing categories. It is hard to have a market which allows for comparison of products, and which goes beyond one-off purchases, without having formal, even legal categories: and this was even more pressingly the case with slaves, who remained, emphatically individuals.[11] Mosher Stuard has argued that categories were fairly fluid, with a wide range of almost interchangeable terms (1983: 162), but this is convincingly refuted by Budak (2000: 758, and n. 43;

[9] It is a common assumption that the Black Death in Europe reduced the labour supply and thus shifted the balance of power in favour of workers. For a nuanced view, see Hatcher and Bailey (2001).

[10] For comparison, the earliest English bracket dates to 1460.

[11] Blumenthal gives some nice examples of ways in which slaves were able to disrupt these categories in fifteenth-century Valencia, showing slaves at market claiming illness, general sluggishness, or even insanity—to the fury of their vendors (2009: 71).

Teja 1942: 33–45). Categories, such as those of gender and ethnicity, allowed pricing to be relatively consistent and predictable. Prices for slaves from the hinterlands were between 28 and 30 ducats in the fourteenth century, varying according to gender: slaves from other backgrounds (Tartar, Circassian, Bulgarian, Russian, or Saracen) tended to fetch higher prices of over 40 ducats, depending on beauty, training, health, and so on (Pinelli 2008: 61).

Notarial contracts described categories, and thus made possible a reduction of people to commodities. They also prescribed. To put it another way, they were future-oriented, assuring the possibility of trade by removing or at least minimizing the risks associated with commerce in things which were not really things. In the first instance, they were important simply because they provided a fetishistic memento of a transaction, which could be produced and cited should ownership be contested at any future point. Second, they took particular steps to attempt to guarantee the quality of the product (Budak 1986: 56). For example, in 1280, a trader called Serdanus sold Tuerdoe of Bosnia with a money-back guarantee if she should run away within three years (*Debita Notariae* 1, fol. 29r; see also e.g. fol. 99r). The sale was for life, the guarantee for three years, as if after that the trader could hardly be held responsible for the long-term usefulness of his product. Contracts then, enshrine property as a relation which lasts into the future and remind us that ownership is a process (Strang and Busse 2011: 1–4).

These kinds of guarantees were underpinned by the assurances of statute law. The community as a whole was supposed to act together to catch the fugitives: the matter was articulated in terms of communal behaviour, in a city whose motto was inscribed above the Rector's Palace: *Obliti privatorum publica curate* ('put public concerns before private ones'). This was liberty, wealth, and prosperity for the privileged who were 'in', and it was reinforced by collective action against those who were 'out'. By statute, owners had the right to punish fugitives, and any who might have aided the runaway. In many cases, owners employed professionals to hunt down the runaways. A typical public announcement about a runaway slave on 12 September 1429 states that citizens are forbidden from giving the fugitive moral advice and support, practical help, or refuge in their own homes (*Diversa Cancellariae* 25/46, fol. 36r).[12] Any citizen who disobeyed was to be heavily punished. These legal rulings were moves to stymy attempts by slaves to act as individuals: law tried to deal with the personhood of slaves and to fix them as property and commodities.

[12] For other examples, see *Lamenta de foris* 2, fol. 63r; 195v; *Diversa Cancellariae* 25/46, fol. 136r; 138v; 139r; 150v; 158v; 160v; 164v; *Lamenta Criminalia* 2, fol. 1v; 2r.

CONSENT

In many ways, legalism is future-oriented: its categories and rules provide assurances beyond the present. This future-oriented dimension may provide the clue to one of the strangest aspects of notarial slave contracts in Dubrovnik: the regular inclusion of phrases such as *presens et consentiens* or *mea bona voluntate*.

It is perhaps unsurprising to find such a clause in a two-party contract of self-sale such as the following of June 1281:

> *Ego quidem Dabrenus filius Zueti Tragurini confiteor quod mea bona voluntate dedi et vendidi me pro servo Elye Blasii de Rasti pro s. dr. grossi quatuor et dimidi diffinite ad mortem, ut dictus Elias de presenta mea velle suum faciat* (*Debita Notariae* 1, fol. 57r).
>
> I, Dabrenus son of Zuetus from Trogir record that I gave and sold myself, of my own free will, as a slave to Elias, son of Blasius of Rastus for four and a half gold coins, valid until my death, so that the said Elias can do with me as he pleases.

It is more surprising to find the slave's consent required when he or she was being traded on as a commodity. A typical contract would state the name of the seller, followed by the name of the consenting slave, followed by the name of the purchaser. For example, in 24 October 1281

> *Juannus filius Clapote presentem et consentientem ancillam suam Constanisclavam de Bosna vendidit Michaeli Lucari c per s. dr. gross. quinque et dimidem diffinite ad mortem. Testis Sersius Clementis Iudex* (*Debita Notariae* I, fol. 28r).
>
> Juannus son of Clapota, sold his slave Constanisclava from Bosnia, who was present and consenting, to Michael Lucaris for five and a half gold coins. Valid until death. Witnessed by Sersius son of Clemens, judge.

This clause is not a feature of classical Roman law, nor does it seem to have characterized the later Byzantine institution, which would have had no room for such a statement, given the rigorous prohibition on self-sale (Rautman 2006: 22). It is very rare to find examples of the *presens et consentiens* formula in other cases of late medieval European slavery (I know of one example from fifteenth-century Valencia: Blumenthal (2009: 39)).[13] This practice seems to be quite specific to the Ragusan context. There are two explanations.

The first relates, once again, to assurance against risk. Owners were afraid of slaves (Origo 1955: 322), partly because they feared violence, and partly

[13] Although Blumenthal only cites one example of the clause, she evokes the wider agency of slaves in their own sales. The sales involved an interview between slave and buyer, the purpose of which was to assure quality: these interviews inadvertently provided an opportunity for slaves to hijack sales by denigrating themselves (2009: 46–61).

because they feared that slaves might contest their status. If the slave, at the point of sale, could be made to affirm that he or she was a willing party to the transaction, then the slave would be in a much weaker position to claim at any stage that he or she had been wrongfully enslaved. Čremošnik (1947: 71) demonstrates that the clause was inserted where no prior document proving slave status was available (a situation common with Bosnian slaves, who were taken from areas without notaries to record their change of status):[14] the phrase acted as legal confirmation of slave status. The fear that slaves could later litigate against their fate might sound far-fetched, but there were a number of reasons why slaves might be able to lodge such a complaint.

One is rooted in the political context, Bosnian rulers regularly complained to the council of Dubrovnik that raiders were unlawfully snatching people from their villages and enslaving them, and that these were not acts of war, but acts of violence and theft (Fejić 2010: 145–58). Embedding the consent of the slave in the contract of sale would preclude any such challenges later on and guarantee the validity of the purchase. Arguably, this was a problem quite specific to the Dalmatian coast, since so many of the slaves came from the immediate hinterlands: it was perhaps not such a problem in Italy or Southern France, where most slaves had been transported from overseas and seemed to lack the means for such litigation.[15]

Additionally, canon law proscribed the enslavement of fellow Christians. The loophole was that slaves could be baptized after the moment of enslavement, and remain slaves. This meant that, if a slave could demonstrate that he or she had been baptized *before* enslavement, the enslavement could be shown to be illegal. For example, in 1393, a slave trader was sued by three girls named Grlica, Stojana, and Tvrdislava: he claimed that they were Paterenes when they were enslaved, but they said that they had already converted prior to this moment. Interestingly, they were found to be correct, and the trader was admonished (Dinić 1967: 63, document 161). Litigation such as this was a very real fear for owners, and again was a problem arguably quite specific to Dubrovnik, since the non-Christians being enslaved

[14] Important in this context is a statute from Trogir: 'We state that whoever in this community wishes to buy a slave, male or female, in perpetual slavery, should buy him or her with a notarial charter; and if someone does not have a charter, and the aforesaid slave or servant-girl wants to bring a suit before the court, he or she will escape from servitude, and the slave or the servant-girl should be trusted, while the buyer should in no way be believed' (cited in Budak 1986, 56 n. 6: *Statuimus, quod si quis hic in civitate voluerit servum vel ancillam in perpetuam servitutem emere, emat eum vel eam cum carta notarii; et qui non habuerit cartam, et dictus servus vel ancilla coram curia questionem movere voluerit, a servitude se retrahent, adhibeatur fides servo vel ancille, et emptori nullo modo sit credendum*).

[15] This could be compared with Valencia where the slaves who did litigate against their enslavement, needed to wait until they were more locally integrated (Blumenthal 2009: 211).

were most often Paterene or Bogomils, whose heretical status was highly contested: the line between Bogomilism and orthodox Christianity was a very fluid one (Lambert 1977). Origo cites a 1413 Luccan lawsuit involving a Bosnian Paterenes slave, presumably traded via Dubrovnik: the purchaser refused to pay because, he said, 'the Bosnian race is Christian, and in that region Christ is worshipped by whose blood all believers are redeemed and radically freed from every yoke of servitude' (1955: 335).[16] From the perspective of traders and owners, then, slavery was a precarious kind of property, and gaining the formal consent of the slaves would stand in the way of future lawsuits.

This anxiety about validity was underpinned by the leaning of the *ius commune* towards *favor libertatis* (Gilchrist 1976: 292–3; Helmholz 2012: 4). *Favor libertatis* was, in itself, an unwilling admission that slaves never shed their essential personhood: the *presens et consentiens* clause paradoxically minimized any recourse to it. The clause integrated personhood into the commoditization of slaves to limit the possibility of agency at a later stage. In other words, legal approaches to slavery could never escape the personhood of slaves: slaves could never be entirely reduced to things and remained a fragile form of property. So, legal discourse provided ways of negotiating the tension in entirely obfuscatory ways. So, on the one hand, the *presens et consentiens* clause is another way in which law was able to deal with the problems of people as property and the tension between persons and things. It provided some kind of future-oriented assurance that the category of property was not as unstable as it might appear.

There is a second explanation. It was a sleight of hand or moral obfuscation to make something acceptable in legal terms which was clearly fraught with ethical and logical problems. Nevan Budak argues that, whereas the phrase originated in a desire to provide a water-tight *carta servitutis*, the moral concern behind the clause became more pressing over the course of the period (Budak 1986: 56–64).

Slavery had to be reconciled with the ideals of liberty which underpinned Ragusan ideology. Clearly, this has never been an insurmountable problem, since so many great slaving societies have been based on ideals of liberty. Nevertheless, discursively, there is a bit of working out to do, particularly when, as in the case of Dubrovnik, so many of the slaves were of almost local origin. The liberty of Dubrovnik's citizens apparently meant the ability to

[16] Origo also argued that the phrase *presens et consentiens* was a legal fiction to circumvent the invalidity of reselling slaves who had been baptized under their first owner (1955: 334). However, there is no canon law prohibition on such sales (it was the moment of first enslavement which counted in relation to baptism), and Dubrovnik presents both cases of unbaptized slaves swearing this clause, and the clause being used at the first moment of enslavement (e.g. *Diversa Notariae* 1, fol. 35r).

control their own jurisdictional, fiscal, and commercial affairs: it was both inspired by, and developed in contradistinction to, Venice, as its imperial overlord for part of the period. But more fundamentally, liberty meant the ability to dispose of one's goods as one pleased: and this might mean one's own body. As Richard Tuck demonstrates, Jean Gerson, chancellor of the University of Paris in the early fifteenth century suggested that one's own liberty was a kind of property, and one had the natural right to dispose of it as one pleased (Tuck 1979: 52–7). So, it was not only perfectly in keeping with a city state powered by ideas of liberty to allow people to sell themselves into slavery, but this little formula 'present and consenting' served in a way to crystallize that political ideal. It is striking that in the autocratic regime of Byzantium, any idea of selling one's own liberty was strictly outlawed: it was not alienable property. Legal discourses were not, then, just about coercion: they articulated the tension between property and personhood in Dubrovnik, and bolstered the ideal of liberty itself by stressing its application to our most fundamental sense of self.

The ethical dilemma was more compellingly present in Christian thought. Indeed, John Chrysostom had argued that slaves should have to consent to their sale (*Commentary on Epistle to Titus* 4.3, cited in Harper 2011: 226). Yet *pace* Fynn-Paul, who claims that Christianity served inevitably to problematize slavery (2009: 17), canon lawyers and theologians had always accepted the presence of slavery, seeking only to regulate and explain it (Gilchrist 1976: 271–302). Indeed, the third Lateran Council of 1179 had actively encouraged slavery. Later papal proscriptions on slavery were not attempts to undermine the institution, but rather complaints about the enslavement of Christians by people of other faiths. However, the general thrust of the fourth Lateran Council of 1215 did nuance the position a little, or at least throw up fresh problems. Lateran IV is famous for the highly legalistic culture of its rulings, and for its attention not only to the systematization of Christian life in Western Europe, but to the spiritual path of the individual. Some of its most significant innovations included the provision of baptism and marriage as sacraments, thus integrating Christians into the wider body of the Church, but also guiding the spiritual journey of the individual. This attention to individual spirituality produced new challenges for the institution of slavery. According to Roman law, as interpreted through the *ius commune*, marriage and children were two areas in which slaves should have no agency (Helmholz 2012: 10). They were, after all, legal objects. Slaves might breed, and the children would automatically belong to the master. However, Lateran IV's emphasis on marriage and baptism was supposed to apply to all Christians. Canon lawyers never really found a straightforward way around the problem (Gilchrist 1976: 288–93), and different cities along the Adriatic coast reached rather different conclusions regarding the possibility of slave marriage. The matter is indicative of the ways in which developments within the Church began, gradually, to throw the contradiction between slaves as persons and slaves as property and things, into still sharper relief (Brundage 1995: 14).

No straightforward conclusion was reached concerning the off-spring of slave parents either, and an ad hoc approach was most common in Dubrovnik (Budak 2000: 758). One striking outcome seems to have been for the master to adopt his own illegitimate slave offspring. For example, on 28 January 1392, a man adopted a girl *seu filiam meam* ('as my daughter'); he pledged 'to instruct and correct her as a daughter and to give her in marriage at the opportune time' (*Diversa Cancellariae* 31, fol. 4v: *instruere, corigere velut filiam et ipsam cadere nuptii temporis habilitate*; another example on fol. 124v). The frequency of adoption in Dubrovnik should be the subject of another article (although, on this, see Römer 2011: 15–32), but it is suggestive in a number of ways for the purposes of my argument. There is Roman precedent for the practice: 'Justinian, to some extent, restored the [Republican] practice: a master who declared in writing that his slave was his son thereby made him free' (Watson 1987: 27–8). Pace Kuehn's claim that many Florentine contracts of adoption were in fact only of legitimization, since there is no evidence of prior manumission (1998: 69–81), free fathers (in particular) seem to have been formally adopting their illegitimate offspring, rather than simply selling them off as another commodity.

Adoption is a striking phenomenon since it makes the slavery of Dubrovnik look a little more like Islamic slavery, where we might expect to find eventual integration of the slaves into the kinship networks of the owners (Amitai 2007: 1–8). In most cases, such integration was out of the question in western slaving societies, but the growing practice of adoption suggests ways in which the care for the individual implied in Lateran IV, began to complicate straightforward assumptions about the positions of slaves as property.

Be that as it may, the growth of a sense that the individual mattered even if enslaved, makes the *presens et consentiens* clause look like a sop to Christian consciences. It was a way to negotiate the moral perils of treating people as objects. If one could claim that the slave had voluntarily allowed him or herself to be subjected in this way, one could rest more assured that God-given humanity had been respected.

The *presens et consentiens* clause brought plenty of contradictions of its own which were nicely passed over in the importance of preserving the legal fiction of consent. Enslaving a child who was below the age of legal consent? No problem: the formula was used anyway. Enslaving a Patarene, who as a non-Christian was not supposed to have legal personhood? Contemporaries simply skated over this problem, since all slaves were, in any case, nominally non-Christian at the point of enslavement. Approving the transfer of a slave who was not really a legal person because of their slave status? The formula was, of course, still there.

It is striking then, that these contracts became increasingly elaborate over the course of the period. Ideals of liberty were ever more central to political discourse and Christian concern for the spirituality of the individual grew in importance into the Renaissance. Law was an important way of inserting slavery into these frameworks. By the late fourteenth century, we find the formula 'present and consenting' amplified with *Et volo quod possit facere de me omne velle suum tamquam de sua re propria* ('And I wish that he may do whatever he wants with me, as with his other property': Dinić 1967: document 91, p. 37).

A late fourteenth century contract attempts to remove all doubt on this score (*Diversa Cancellariae* 33, fol. 129r). This concerns the sale of a girl, rather than a resale. The emphasis on consent is perhaps then even more important.

> *Ego Iuica filia quidam Pricod partium Ussore de Bossina generis patarenorum [...] sponte et ex certa mea scientia et non per errorem, non vi nec metu coacta coram vobis testibus et notario subscriptis confiteor me esse servam empticiam Zanini de Gociis de Ragusio ... de voluntate mea ... Et quod me et servicia mea possit et valeat tam aliis vendere, donare et transferre quam pro se et ejus familia retinere ac de me omne aliud ejus velle facere tamquam de serva sua empticia et eius re propria.*
>
> I Iuica daughter of a certain Pricod, from the land of Usora in Bosnia, born of Patarene parents, of my own free will, and with my knowledge, and not by mistake, pushed neither by force nor by fear, in the presence of these witnesses and the notary, declare myself to be sold as a slave to Zaninus of Gocii of Ragusa, by my own free will. And that he could and would have power to sell, give or transfer my services rather than to keep me for him and his family, and in all other respects to do with me as he pleases, as he would with his purchased slave girl or his other property.

This contract is particularly striking since it goes on to refer to another, whereby Juica was sold by her father. The impulse to show her consent for the transaction was sufficient to generate another contract where she acts on her own behalf without her father. And she was 11 years old.

There is no need to choose between these two explanations for the *presens et consentiens* clause. It was both about moral obfuscation, and about guaranteeing immunity from future litigation. Legal discourse provided ways to deal, at one blow, with the various challenges, economic and moral, which the objectification and propertization of people threw up.

VIOLENCE

The amplification of the *presens et consentiens* clause came at a moment of growing problematization of slavery (Budak 2000: 756–7). The year 1416 saw the promulgation of the famous statute against the slave trade in Dubrovnik (Krekić 1987: 309–17). It contained a tirade against:

> *Mercatores ... eo quia emunt et vendunt ex eorum subditis, considerantes talem mercantiam esse turpem, nefariam et abominabilem et contra omnem humanitatem ... videlicet quod humana species facta ad ymaginem et similitudinem creatoris nostri converti debeat in usus mercimoniales et vendatur tamquam si essent animalia bruta ...* (Dinić 1967: 89–90, document 200).
>
> Merchants, who buy and sell slaves, because we consider such commerce to be disgraceful, wicked, an abomination, and against all humanity ... this is to convert the human species made in the image and likeness of our creator, into a commercial commodity, to be sold like brute animals.

The acknowledgement of a moral problem with slavery could not be more explicit here, and suggests a degree of contemporary discomfort and debate. But the statute only applied to the commerce of slaves rather than straightforwardly condemning attempts to reduce people to property. So here we have a statement of extreme moral distress about slavery, married with a clear sense that domestic slavery is still acceptable. The commerce in slaves continued nevertheless. Later fifteenth-century comments along the same lines manage to preserve domestic slavery while vilifying the Ottoman Turks for enslaving Christians. Papal provisions against slavery vilified non-Christian slave owners, while continuing actively to encourage the enslavement of the 'enemies of Christ'. Indeed, it has been compellingly argued that by the fifteenth century, slave raids by Christians were being conceptualized and even justified in terms akin to those of missionary activity, since these apparently provided for the possibility of conversion (Schiel 2015: 23–45).

If the 1416 statute was indeed a result of a growing sense of moral unease, it was also driven by far more pragmatic considerations. These were twofold. First, as has been argued by Mosher Stuard, the foreign market was pushing slave prices so high as to preclude ownership by Ragusans themselves (1983: 169–71). This is not entirely convincing as a motivation, given that money from slave trading trickled back into the Ragusan economy. Second, this was a period of escalating tension between the rulers of Bosnia and Serbia, and the city of Dubrovnik/Ragusa. Indeed, the situation in Ragusa was increasingly precarious (Fejić 2010: 103–45).[17] No longer able to count on the protection of the powerful Venetians, Ragusan de facto

[17] Here I would like to credit helpful discussions with Marko Pijović.

independence (under the nominal overlordship of the kingdom of Hungary) came at the price of diplomatic fragility. One of the principal bones of contention was frequent enslavement of people from these regions by traders from Dubrovnik. The 1416 statute was, then, a very public statement which attempted to demonstrate the good faith of the Council of Dubrovnik to these other rulers. In this sense, the 1416 statute was not just a moralistic statement of the ineradicable contradiction between slaves as people and slaves as things. It was also an acknowledgement of the potential conflict and violence engendered by treating people, in this staggeringly reductive way, as property.

MANUMISSION

A similar engagement with the problems of propertization at a variety of levels is apparent when we turn to the practice of manumission. Watson (1987: 9–23) has distinguished between 'open' and 'closed' slave societies, as those which regularly freed slaves, and those in which slavery was a permanent and unalterable state. Like Roman society, Ragusan slavery was definitely of the 'open' sort. Manumission was common, if by no means guaranteed, and often slavery was temporary. However, it does not take much to see that dangling the possibility of manumission before the subjugated person, without ever guaranteeing it, is perhaps the most powerful form of domination available. Herein lies what seems to be the most compelling explanation for manumission: that it provided an incentive to slaves (Brunt 2013: 394–404). In this sense, the acknowledgement that people might become things, and then transform back into legal persons at some stage in the future, was deemed the most effective way to ensure that slaves, in their 'thing-ness', were as profitable as possible.

There is more to it than this. Slaves as marketable commodities were problematic because they remained people who would age. Ownership of slaves brought with it a certain responsibility: just as one is expected to care for one's other chattels, so one was expected to feed and clothe slaves and even to care for their health. This was all well and good as long as the slave was economically useful, but disadvantageous when the slave was old and decrepit: slaves could be discarded when they became an economic burden. Cervantes wrote that the freeing of slaves excluded them from the only home they knew, and granted them liberty to starve to death in a hostile world (1987: II, ch. 24, p. 371).[18]

[18] Many thanks to Glyn Redworth for this reference.

Manumission was also a useful way of recovering capital. Strikingly, many slaves in Dubrovnik purchased their own freedom. Purchasing freedom depended upon the slaves having a *peculium*. In this sense, manumission contracts were made possible by a much greater degree of equivocation in the status of slaves in the first place. The practice of *peculium* is well known from Roman law (Papinian, in *Digest* 15.1.50.3; Ulpian, in *Digest* 15.3.3; Javolenus, in *Digest* 15.3.2). It originated from the problems of liability engendered by slaves acting on their masters' behalf in business (Aubert 2013: 192–200). Allowing slaves autonomous control of a fixed sum was an effective way of limiting the liability of the master for transactions undertaken by slaves, while allowing owners to use them effectively as business representatives. Through careful custodianship, slaves could then save up a pot of capital, using it in time for the purchase of freedom. In Roman law, such a sum is known as *peculium*: using it to purchase freedom was extremely rare in classical Rome, but common in Dubrovnik. The sum remained, in law, the property of the master, but de facto, it was in the hands of the slave. Canon lawyers approved the practice (e.g. Rufinus, *Summa* ad D. 54 d. p. c. 8, and Stephen of Tournai, *Summa* ad D. 54. C. 7, cited by Gilchrist 1976: 294).[19] In an extreme example from 1281, a slave named Dubrosta bought her freedom by selling her own slave, Radosta. Slaves owning other slaves was not unknown in Ragusa. Radosta was handed over *diffinite ad mortem*, and if she fled, Dubrosta undertook to pay 12 solidi *sine aliqua questione* or to return to slavery herself (*Debita Notariae* 1, fol. 37r).

The possession of *peculium* was just that: possession not property, for the slave. However, it could be used as though it were property, and thus challenged the thing-ness of slaves. The practice produced many legal conundrums, not least because it was responding to a contradiction itself: the fact that the property of the master was actually administering property on his behalf. In western philosophical terms, possession or still better owning property, is often seen as lying at the heart of personhood (Hegel [1821] 1967: para. 41a; Green [1895] 1941: 219; Kant [1797] 1996: 37); and in legal terms, property can most effectively render one a legal person.

Of course, owners did not need to cooperate. A contract from one Tyse, wife of Nicholas de Roncino, stated that she had freed her slave Drugosti. But this was not out of generosity. Drugosti had carefully saved up to purchase her freedom and had been allowed to do so only on condition that she also purchase a replacement, one Budica de Sana (*Debita Notariae* 1, fol. 75r.).

Many other slaves were manumitted through testamentary bequest. In such cases, the motivation was not economic. It was good for the soul of the

[19] For the style of references to the canon law glosses on Gratian's *Decretum*, a convenient guide in Brundage (1995, 200–2).

owner to manumit a slave. These wills then frame in legal language the tension between the earthly benefits of holding slaves, the equivocal canon law justifications for this, and the overriding sense that it was not quite ethical.[20] The question remains whether the moral good came from respecting the humanity of the slave, or from the general desirability of giving away one's worldly goods. It is hard to tell, but the Dubrovnik evidence does favour the former explanation. In one striking case, Nicholas Mauricenus, count of Ragusa, paid Dimitrius Pradanovich of Canalus in order to manumit a pair of the latter's slaves, a brother and a sister: this was not simply about giving away his wealth, but about focusing that donation on the emancipation of two human beings. The count was motivated *pro bono animae suae* ('for the good of his soul': *Debita Notariae* 1, fol. 34v).

In Roman law, freedmen usually continued to have obligations towards their former owners: manumitted slaves remained under the patronage of their former owners (Mouritsen 2011: 39). Similar concerns were often present in Dubrovnik. Legal things might have become legal persons, but their status remained equivocal. For instance, in the statutes of 1272, book VI, chapter 45 addressed the question of what might happen should a freed slave find that they were no longer in a position to support themselves and need either to sell themselves or contract themselves out (Bogišić and Jireček 1904: 141). If liberty was the ability to sell oneself, then freed slaves were often shown to have a very particular, restrained kind of liberty. According to the statute, they could indeed sell themselves, but their previous owner was to have right of first refusal. And if they had already sold themselves to someone else, the previous owner apparently had the right to purchase the slave back for the same price. So, the statute denied the absolute freedom of a manumitted slave, who was shown to be still bound legally to the original owner in ways which ensured that manumission could not entirely contradict the logic of slavery. Book VI, chapter 47 carried the point a bit further, by laying out the ongoing and very specific obligations of slaves towards their owners, obligations such as a duty, during the grape harvest, to row boats to Ragusa if they were stuck in another port because of the weather (Bogišić and Jireček 1904: 141–2).

[20] Note the interesting comparison here with the *Siete Partidas* of Alfonso the Wise of Castile and Léon, which passed into law under Alfonso XI in 1348. While regulating slavery, Alfonso described it as 'the vilest and most contemptible thing in the world' and only reconciled himself to this through multiple provisions for manumission (McKinley 2010: 752). A manumission of a slave in Perpignan in 1465 stated that: 'on men, whom nature in the beginning produced free, the law of nations, for their sins, imposed the yoke of slavery' (Verlinden 1955: 829: *hominis quos natura ab inicio liberos protulit et postea jus gencium, propter eorum culpas, servitutis substituit jugo*).

However, in other cases, the formula used in the manumission differed significantly from that found either in Roman law, or in other parts of late medieval Europe. The Ragusan freed slave was apparently free to go to the 'four corners of the earth'. For example, one Orbatus of Bosnia, called Radosclavus was freed that he might 'roam free' (*Diversa Cancellariae* I, 102r: *vadat liber*); in October 1280, Blasius de Baoisa freed his slave Premillus 'so that he might wander into the four parts of the world, free and at liberty, wherever he might please, without any hindrance, for ever' (*Debita Notariae* 1, fol. 26r: *ut vadat per quatuor partes mundi liber et francus quorum, que ei placuerit sine ulla contradictione in perpetuum*). Ragusan legal language allowed, then, for the restoration of personhood to slaves in more explicit terms than we see elsewhere. These manumission contracts were extreme statements of the contradiction at the heart of slavery, and suggested that the tension was peculiarly present. To see freedom conceptualized in such spatial terms is very striking: perhaps it reflects the general lack of integration of slaves into their new setting, and the assumption that they would wish to travel home or begin a new life away from the crowded city of Dubrovnik.

In one case of 1282, a slave called Dabraça de Bosna bought her freedom with the financial help of her sister (*Diversa Cancellariae* I, fol. 110v). She became free to *vada[re] per quatuor partes mundi, quocumque ei placuerit, libera et franca in perpetuum* ('wander through the four corners of the earth, wherever it should please her, free and liberated for ever'), but raised the money by promising *omnia servicia ad eius voluntatem facere* ('to serve [another] owner in all ways according to his wishes'). The second bondage was not quite like the first, for instead she sold her labour for four years. After the four years were up, she was apparently, free to go. This looks like a case of one sibling generously supporting another, the emotive bond between two siblings pushing one to act to free her sister, and the other to exercise what little agency and choice she had to limit the terms of her future bondage. It shows how law heightened the tension between persons and things, as these slave women actively engaged with it.

LEGAL PERSONS

The involvement of slaves in criminal activity was an even more problematic area. If slaves were not legal persons, how could they be held accountable for infringements of the law? It was an accepted argument in the *ius commune* tradition that a criminal accusation could be lodged against a slave except where the penalty would normally incur a punishment of property or status (Helmholz 2012: 7, referring to Accursius, *Glossa Ordinaria ad Digestum novum* 48.2.11). The problem remained that if a slave was put to death or banished, the master lost his property and was implicitly punished for a crime he did not commit (Helmholz 2012: 7). One way around this would have been discursively to remove moral accountability from the slave, and to claim that the master was liable for the slave's behaviour and therefore suffered the consequences: in other words, the whole matter could have been conceptualized in terms of property of things. But this was not the solution they opted for. In 1272, the Dubrovnik statute decreed that slaves guilty of murder were to suffer capital punishment. Masters were to be compensated with a fixed sum for the executed slave (Book VI, ch. 42 in Bogišić and Jireček 1904: 140). On the one hand, this underlined the sense that the slave was nothing more than property since a monetary payment apparently did the trick. But it also admitted that the slave was the one morally responsible for the crime committed, and that the slave was therefore to be conceptualized independently from the master.[21] The fixed compensation sum was 12 yperperi. In the latter decades of the thirteenth century, the average price for a slave was around 16 to 20 yperperi. Of course, the value of a slave decreased over time, but nevertheless, the compensation would have left the master out of pocket, implicitly punished, and bound up in the actions of his or her slave.

The lawyers of Dubrovnik went further, and ignored the *ius commune* prescription that slaves could not be punished through removal of property. They were more determined for slaves to be held accountable. In 1272, it was decreed that slaves should be obliged to pay a fine if they struck a free man or woman; if this proved impossible, they were to be flogged and then returned to their master or mistress (Book VI, ch. 42 in Bogišić and Jireček 1904: 140). Interestingly, Bartolus de Sassoferrato (d. 1347) argued that many slaves were indeed in a position to pay pecuniary penalties, pointing to their equivocal position as both objects and holders of property (Helmholz 2012: 7, referring to *Commentaria ad Digestum novum* 49.2.1.1.4 no. 5).

The lawyers also discussed the implications of situations where slaves found themselves as victims of violence: if slaves were not fully legal persons, how might such an offence be conceptualized, and who was the true victim? The 1272 statute of Dubrovnik made it absolutely clear that in such a case, the offence was one against the master of the slave, to whom damages were to be paid (Book VI, ch. 43 in Bogišić and Jireček 1904: 140; on this see Budak 1986: 64): if the master or mistress did not bring a complaint, there was apparently no need for any payment. At the same time, the statute followed the *Institutes of Justinian*, as interpreted

[21] These problems can be sidestepped in other institutions of labour, such as indentures, however exploitative, since they separate the labour from persons: only the former can be bought and sold, leaving the latter more clearly as moral agents.

in the *Ius Commune*, in prohibiting excessive brutality towards one's own slave (*Institutes* 1.8.2): moderation was the key. While such prohibitions drew an analogy between slaves and other subordinate members of the household, the declarations seemed also to reinforce the thing-ness of the slave, and carefully to avoid his or her treatment as a person: excessive brutality was proscribed because 'the public interest requires that no person should make evil use of his property'.

How could a slave bring a complaint if he or she was not a legal person? The *ius commune* got around this by claiming that the slave was just the conduit of the complaint and not actually the accuser. By the fourteenth century, as an inquisitorial system became increasingly prominent and placed the responsibility for responding to criminal acts in the hands of legal officials, it became easier to get around the problem of complainant slaves who were not legal persons. But de facto, slaves were looking more and more like people who could try to protect and defend themselves through the law. Law provided a way not of resolving tensions, but of articulating them and attempting to resist the humanization of slaves, while being implicated in this precarious balance.

The *ius commune* equally addressed questions of whether slaves could be called as witnesses to a crime, evoking similar problems. Slaves, according to Roman law, were precluded as witnesses (Helmholz 2012: 7); but canon law justified this exclusion in terms of personhood rather than its lack. It was argued that slaves would be motivated by their situation to bear false witness against their masters (Accursius, *Glossa Ordinaria ad Digestum vetus* 22.5.3). It is striking then to find a far more equivocal position in practice. Slaves were largely debarred from giving testimony (Čremošnik 1947: 69–73), but exceptions were created by the statutes which effectively left the matter at the discretion of the litigants: *ejus testimonium esse in providencia illorum qui judicaturi sunt inter ipsos* ('they are to decide amongst themselves whether his testimony is to be admitted', cited in Čremošnik 1947: 72; 1272 Statute, book VII, ch. 27 in Bogišić and Jireček 1904: 160).

DEGREES OF UNFREEDOM

The ways in which the legal language of Dubrovnik attempted to deal with the multiple layers of problems produced by attempts to make people into property created a de facto situation of degrees of unfreedom or, in the context of this volume, degrees of 'propertization'. Such an image is not unknown in other slaving societies, notably, of course, ancient Rome (Mouritsen 2011: 11). Such problems become particularly stark in the context of the rapid development of indentured labour.

According to Nevan Budak, slavery all but disappeared during a period of superabundant labour in the first part of the fourteenth century (2000: 752–3). It was so cheap to hire labourers, that there was no need to enslave people. He claims that after the second wave of plague in 1363, the conjunction of famine in the countryside, and higher labour costs in the city, again raised the stakes for slavery. In the work of Susan Mosher Stuard, we find a slightly different chronology, as she claims that the slave trade grew so effectively over the course of the fourteenth century, that the people of Dubrovnik were priced out of the market, benefiting commercially from the demand for slaves in Italy, but no longer able to afford them themselves (1983: 164–8).

I do not propose to enter into this debate. But what is clear is that over the course of the fourteenth century, we see an increasing number of indentured labour contracts, apparently replacing slave contracts (e.g. *Debita Notariae* 2, fol. 4r; *Diversa Notariae* 11, fols 2v, 3r etc.). Indentured labour was practical: you ensured exclusive rights to a person for a fixed term (most commonly twelve years), and handily disposed of the indentured labourer before he or she became more of a liability than an asset. Equally, one avoided the expensive and time-consuming paperwork of a manumission.

But if it was a practical solution, it was also a nice sop to consciences. One got all the perks of slavery without the ethical problems which accompanied the idea of people as property. They certainly were increasingly concerned: in a late fourteenth-century letter to the Bosnian king, quoted by Nevan Budak, the Ragusans wrote that Italian citizens had told them that 'Bosnia sells people, and Bosnia is close to you, and you are all the same' (2000: 757 n. 35).

If we look at the language of the labour contracts, we find the form to be almost identical to that of permanent slavery documents. Here's a fairly typical slavery contract of March 1281, with a mother selling her daughter into slavery:

> *Obellica de Rudine presentem et consentietem filiam suam Pervosclavam vendidit Radosclave, uxori Marini Johannis de Valio pro denariis grossis decem et octo diffinite ad mortem* (*Debita Notariae* I, fol. 44r).
>
> Obellica of Rudine sold her daughter Pervosclava, who was present and consenting, to Radosclava, the wife of Marinus Johannis de Valio, for 18 silver pieces, valid until death.

Here is a fairly typical indentured labour contract, with a father selling his daughter in August 1393:

> *Ego Mevghen Stepoevich confiteor quod loco quondam meam filiam et operas suas nomina Stoycham ibidem presentem et consentientem ad standum cum Dobroslavo Merghich Statoncio usque ad annos octo proxime venturos, prometens pro dictam Steychu et ipsa Stoycha consenciens bene et fideliter serviere dicto Dobroslavo et obedire*

> *eius mandatus cum de stando et redeundo ut ad dictum temporem* (*Diversa Cancellariae* 31, fol. 73r).
>
> I Mevhen Stepoevich declare that I place my daughter, Stoycha, she being present and consenting, and her labour with one Dobroslavus Merghich for the next eight years, and I promise on behalf of my daughter, and Stoycha herself consents, faithfully to serve the said Dobroslavus and to obey his commands and to stay with him and return to him for the whole of this time.

Or in 1393:

> *Ego Juachus Septuvich de Lubomir confiteor quod filium meum Previnec etatis annorum novem vel circha presentem volentem et consentientem et eius operas dedi et locavi ad standum cum Ratcho Prebillovich usque ad duodecim annos* (*Diversa Cancellariae* 31, fol. 82v).
>
> I Juachus Septuvich of Lubomir declare that I place and rent out my son Previnec, aged nine years, or thereabouts, present, consenting and wishing it, and all his labour, with Ratko Prebillovich for twelve years.

Each of these contracts was concluded by a lump sum payment.

There is a fine line between these kinds of contracts and contracts of apprenticeships when most legal rights were also surrendered. However, the latter are clearly differentiated by the stipulation of the learning of a trade, as opposed simply to the promise to obey the master in anything he should wish (e.g. *Diversa Cancellariae* 31, fol. 75r).

The debate about the relationship between slavery and indentured labour in a modern context is an extremely polemical one. Those who dismiss the elision of the two, point out that slavery was an entirely violent phenomenon where the rights and free choice of the individual played no role; whereas indentured labour, however exploitative, depends upon a choice by the labourer who enters into a contract as a legal person. Such a distinction is problematic in Dubrovnik though, since slaves were also supposedly 'present and consenting'. While indentured labour may have been a legal way of manoeuvring around the ethical problems of slavery, that process had already been begun in the formulation of the slavery contracts themselves. Property was not a watertight category.

This seems to be a fairly classic picture of degrees of unfreedom. More importantly here, we have legal degrees of unfreedom which produce almost exactly the same result for the master, while providing new ways of obfuscating moral and ethical problems. Legalism served as a useful way of smoothing out the inconsistencies in the practice of slavery and its place in society.

The chronology of the formula in surviving documents would suggest that the slavery contracts provided the blueprint for indentured labour contracts, rather than vice versa (it is, of course, always possible that documents demonstrating the opposite have not survived). The indentured labour contracts did not fundamentally challenge the concepts of property underpinning slavery. All the while, the tension between slaves as persons, and slaves as things, remained prominent.

CONCLUSION

In conclusion, slavery in late medieval Dubrovnik was driven by moral, economic, and diplomatic prerogatives. All these layers of discourse had continually to deal with the contradictions and tensions produced by a clash of natural and positive law. In order to become property, slaves had to be conceived of both as people and as things. This produced discursive, as well as practical problems. Law was a useful way of negotiating these dilemmas. The idea of property was fragile and problematic, but capacious. Ultimately, this might provide a more effective way of thinking about why slavery was eventually abolished in Dubrovnik. Clearly in part, this was simply a matter of profit: the slave economy ceased to pay. But it was speeded by the contradictions that even laws of property could not resolve.

This kind of equivocation and anxiety is nicely encapsulated in an extraordinary fifteenth-century play, *Robinja*, by Hanibal Lucić (1485–1535).[22] It tells of a young girl, captured by Turks who want to sell her as a slave. After a series of romantic adventures, she is rescued by the man who had once tried to woo her, Ban Derenčin. The play was written in the vernacular, and predicated on classical models. On the one hand, it is a classic adventure story, designed to keep the audience on the edge of their seats. It also plays to stereotypes of evil Saracens, exploiting and enslaving innocent Christians, a growing concern in the late fifteenth century. But it is built on the implicit recognition that slavery as an institution of property has very human victims. The audience is expected to empathize with the plight of the girl, to feel her pain and terror and ultimate relief. All this is rather extraordinary, given that the audience would have been made up largely of slave-owners. That imaginative literature should fulfil such a problematic role is not surprising. That the law should busy itself with articulating and negotiating these kinds of contradictions and tensions is perhaps more so.

[22] Edition available online at <http://www.ss-obrtnicka-pozega.skole.hr/download_zona/lucic_robinja.pdf>.

References Cited

Acheson, James M., 2006. 'Institutional Failure in Resource Management', *Annual Review of Anthropology*, **35**/1: 117–34.

Ackerman, Bruce A., 1977. *Private Property and the Constitution.* New Haven, CT: Yale University Press.

Adams, Henry, 1876. 'The Anglo-Saxon Courts of Law', in H. Adams et al. (eds.), *Essays in Anglo-Saxon Law.* Boston, MA: Little, Brown, 1–54.

Agrawal, Arun, and Clark C. Gibson, 1999. 'Enchantment and Disenchantment: The Role of Community in Natural Resource Conservation', *World Development*, **27**/4: 629–49.

Ahmed, Ali Jimale, 1996. *Daybreak is Near . . . : Literature, Clans, and the Nation-State in Somalia.* Trenton, NJ: Red Sea Press.

Akhavi, Shahrough, 2013. 'Sayyid Qutb', in John L. Esposito and Emad El-Din Shahin (eds.), *The Oxford Handbook of Islam and Politics.* Oxford: Oxford University Press, 159–68.

al-Banna, Hasan, 1978. *Five Tracts (1906–1949): A Selection from the Majmū 'at Rasa'il al-Imam al-Shahid Hasan al-Banna*, trans. from the Arabic and annotated by C. Wendell. Berkeley, CA: University of California Press.

Alexander, Catherine, 2004. 'Value, Relations and Changing Bodies: Privatization and Property Rights in Kazakhstan', in K. Verdery and C. Humphrey (eds.), *Property in Question: Value Transformation in the Global Economy.* Oxford: Berg, 251–74.

Alexander, Gregory S., 2011. 'Pluralism and Property', *Fordham Law Review*, **80**: 101–36.

Alexander, Gregory S., 2013. 'Ownership and Obligations: The Human Flourishing Theory of Property', *Hong Kong Law Journal*, **43/2**: 451–62.

Alexander, Gregory S., 2016. 'The Public Use Requirement and the Character of Consequentialist Reasoning', in B. Hoops, E. Marais, L. Verstappen, H. Mostert, and J. Sluysmans (eds.), *Rethinking Expropriation Law II: Context, Criteria and Consequences of Expropriation.* Den Haag: Eleven International Publishing, 113–36.

Alexander, Gregory S., and Eduardo M. Peñalver, 2012. *An Introduction to Property Theory.* Cambridge: Cambridge University Press.

Alifa, Ousmane, 2000. *Justice officielle et justice parallèle. Cas de l'accord des chefs de race.* Mémoire de fin d'étude du premier cycle, ENAM, N'Djamena.

Allain, Jean, 2012. 'Legal Definitions of Slavery in the Twenty-First Century', in J. Allain (ed.), *The Legal Understanding of Slavery: From the Historical to the Contemporary.* Oxford: Oxford University Press, 199–219.

Alonso, José Luis, 2013. 'The Status of Peregrine Law in Egypt: "Customary Law" and Legal Pluralism in the Roman Empire', *Journal of Juristic Papyrology*, **43**: 351–404.

Amitai, Reuven, 2007. 'Military Slavery in the Islamic World: 1000 Years of a Social–Military Institution', in *Medieval Mediterranean Slavery: Comparative Studies on Slavery and the Slave Trade in Muslim, Christian, and Jewish Societies (8th–15th Centuries).* Online at <http://med-slavery.uni-trier.de:9080/minev/MedSlavery/publications/Amitai.pdf>.

Anderson, David, 1986. 'Stock Theft and the Moral Economy in Colonial Kenya', *Africa*, **56**/4: 399–416.

Ando, Clifford, 2011. *Law, Language and Empire in the Roman Tradition*. Philadelphia: University of Pennsylvania Press.

Ando, Clifford, 2015. *Roman Social Imaginaries: Language and Thought in Contexts of Empire*. Toronto: University of Toronto Press.

Anghie, Antony, 2005. *Imperialism, Sovereignty, and the Making of International Law*. Cambridge: Cambridge University Press.

Angus, Ian, 2008. 'The Myth of the Tragedy of the Commons', *The Bullet: A Socialist Project E-Bulletin*, **133**. Online at <http://www.socialistproject.ca/bullet/bullet133.html>.

Ankum, Hans, 1985. 'Le droit romain classique a-t-il connu un droit de propriété bonitaire relatif?', in *Satura R. Feenstra LXV annum aetatis complenti ab alumnis collegis amicis oblata*. Fribourg: Editions Universitaires, 125–39.

Appadurai, Arjun (ed.), 1986. *The Social Life of Things: Commodities in Cultural Perspective*. Cambridge: Cambridge University Press.

Arditi, Claude, 1993. 'Commerce, Islam et État au Tchad (1900–1990)', in E. Grégoire and P. Labazée (eds.), *Grands commerçants d'Afrique de l'Ouest*. Paris: Karthala, 175–220.

Arditi, Claude, 1995. 'Le commerce des dattes du Borkou (Tchad)', *Cahiers des Sciences Humaines*, **31**/4: 849–82.

Arditi, Claude, 2000. 'Du prix de la kola au détournement de l'aide internationale: clientélisme et corruption au Tchad (1900–1998)', *Les nouveaux cahiers de l'Institut universitaire d'études du développement*, **9**: 249–67.

Armitage, David (ed.), 2004. *Hugo Grotius: The Free Sea*. Indianapolis, IN: Liberty Fund.

Armstrong, Lawrin, 2016. *The Idea of a Moral Economy: Gerard of Siena on Usury, Restitution, and Prescription*. Toronto: University of Toronto Press.

Astuti, Rita, 1999. 'At the Center of the Market: A Vezo Woman', in S. Day, E. Papataxiarchis, and M. Stewart (eds.), *Lilies of the Field: Marginal People Who Live for the Moment*. (Studies in the Ethnographic Imagination.) Boulder, CO: Westview Press, 83–95.

Attenborough, Frederick Levi, 1922. *The Laws of the Earliest English Kings*. Cambridge: Cambridge University Press.

Aubert, Jean-Jacques, 2013. 'Dumtaxat de peculio: What's in a Peculium or Establishing the Extent of the Principal's Liability', in P. du Plessis (ed.), *New Frontiers: Law and Society in the Roman World*. Edinburgh: Edinburgh University Press, 193–206.

Avon, Dominique, and Anaïs-Trissa Khatchadourian, 2012. *Hezbollah: A History of the Party of God*, trans. by Jane Marie Todd. Cambridge, MA: Harvard University Press.

Ayalon, Ami, 1987. *Language and Change in the Arab Middle East: The Evolution of Modern Arabic Political Discourse*. New York: Oxford University Press.

Baier, Stephen, and Paul Lovejoy, 1975. 'The Desert-Side Economy of the Central Sudan', *International Journal of African Historical Studies*, **8**/4: 551–81.

Baldus, Christian, 2016. 'Possession in Roman Law', in P. J. du Plessis, C. Ando, and K. Tuori (eds.), *The Oxford Handbook of Roman Law and Society*. Oxford: Oxford University Press, 537–52.

Baron, Jane B., 2014. 'Rescuing the Bundle-of-Rights Metaphor in Property Law', *University of Cincinnati Law Review*, **82**/1: 57–101.

Barre, Siyad M., 1974. *My Country and My People*. Mogadishu: Ministry of Information and National Guidance.

Bart, Jean, 2013. 'Property, Succession', transl. Philip Stewart, in Catherine Volpilhac-Auger (ed.), *A Montesquieu Dictionary*. Online at <http://dictionnaire-montesquieu.ens-lyon.fr/en/article/1367163276/en/>.

Bartlett, Robert, 1993. *The Making of Europe: Conquest, Colonization and Cultural Change*. London: Allen Lane.

Bartolus de Sassoferrato, 1574. *Bartoli a Sassoferrato in primam partem codicis commentaria*. Turin.

Baxter, Stephen, 2009. 'Lordship and Justice in Late Anglo-Saxon England: The Judicial Functions of Soke and Commendation Revisited', in S. Baxter et al. (eds.), *Early Medieval Studies in Memory of Patrick Wormald*. Farnham: Ashgate, 383–419.

Bechor, Guy, 2007. *The Sanhuri Code, and the Emergence of Modern Arab Civil Law (1932 to 1949)*. Leiden: Brill.

Beknazarov, Rakhym Agibaevich, 2010. *Kazakhi Severnogo Priaral'ja v XIX—nachale XX vv. (Istoriko-Etnograficheskoe Issledovanie)*. Avtoreferat dissertatsii na soiskanie uchenoi stepeni doktora istoricheskikh nauk, Almaty: In-t ist. i etnol. im. Sh. Ualikhanova.

Bell, Abraham, and Gideon Parchomovsky, 2005. 'A Theory of Property', *Cornell Law Review*, **90**/3: 531–615.

Bemmer, Jaqueline, 2013. 'The Types of Pledge in Medieval Irish Law: Form, Function and Context', in A. Ahlqvist and P. O'Neill (eds.), *Medieval Irish Law: Text and Context*. Sydney: University of Sydney Press, 3–23.

Bemmer, Jaqueline, 2016. *The Early Irish Law of Pledging*, unpublished D.Phil. thesis, University of Oxford.

Bencivenni, Alice, 2004. 'Aristodikides di Asso, Antioco I e la scelta di Ilio', *Simblos: Scritti di storia antica*, **4**: 159–85.

Benda-Beckmann, Franz von, Keebet von Benda-Beckmann, and Melanie Wiber, 2006. 'The Properties of Property', in F. von Benda-Beckmann, K. von Benda-Beckmann, and M. Wiber (eds.), *Changing Properties of Property*. New York and Oxford: Berghahn, 1–39.

Bentham, Jeremy, [1802] 1931. *The Theory of Legislation*, ed. with an intro. and notes by C. K. Ogden. London: Kegan & Paul.

Berry, Sara, 2013. 'Questions of Ownership: Proprietorship and Control in a Changing Rural Terrain—A Case Study from Ghana', *Africa*, **83**/1: 36–56.

Bertrand, M., 1990. 'Compromis locaux et concurrence foncière dans deux villes maliennes', *Politique Africaine*, **40**: 21–30.

Besteman, Catherine, 1999. *Unraveling Somalia: Race, Violence, and the Legacy of Slavery*. Philadelphia: University of Pennsylvania Press.

Bikerman [Bickerman], Elias, 1939. 'La Cité grecque dans les monarchies hellénistiques', *Revue de philologie*, **13**: 335–49.

Binchy, Daniel A. (ed.), 1941. *Críth Gablach*. Dublin: Stationery Office.

Binchy, Daniel A. (ed. and trans.), 1955. *'Coibnes Uisci Thairidne'*, *Ériu*, **17**: 52–85.

Binchy, Daniel A., 1973a. 'Distraint in Irish Law', *Celtica*, **10**: 22–71.

Binchy, Daniel A. (ed. and trans.), 1973b. 'A Text on the Forms of Distraint', *Celtica*, **10**: 72–86.

Binchy, Daniel A. (ed.), 1978. *Corpus Iuris Hibernici*, 6 vols. Dublin: Dublin Institute for Advanced Studies.

Binmore, Ken, and Paul Klemperer, 2002. 'The Biggest Auction Ever: The Sale of the British 3G Telecom Licences', *Economic Journal*, **112**: C74–C96.

Birks, Peter, 1985. 'The Roman Law Concept of Dominium and the Idea of Absolute Ownership', *Acta Juridica*, **7**: 1–37.

Birks, Peter, 1987. 'Review of B. W. Frier, *The Rise of Roman Jurists*', *Oxford Journal of Legal Studies*, **7**/3: 444–53.

Blackstone, William, [1766] 2016. *Commentaries on the Laws of England. Book II: On the Rights of Things*, ed. with intro. and notes by Simon Stern. Oxford: Oxford University Press.

Blake, Quentin, 1980. *Mister Magnolia*. London: Jonathan Cape.

Blei, Josephine, 2013. *Dominium populi Romani vel Caesaris* und *causa dominica: Römische Rechtstradition und Fiskalsukzession im bairischen Dukat der Aigilofinger.* Berlin: Frank & Timme.

Bleicken, Jochen, 1974. '*In provinciali solo dominium populi Romani est vel Caesaris*: Zur Kolonisationspolitik der ausgehenden Republik und frühen Kaiserzeit', *Chiron*, **4**: 359–414. [Reprinted in his *Gesammelte Schriften* II (Stuttgart 1998): 722–77.]

Blumenthal, Debra, 2009. *Enemies and Familiars: Slavery and Mastery in Fifteenth-Century Valencia*. Ithaca, NY: Cornell University Press.

Boffo, Laura, 2001. 'Lo statuto di terre, insediamenti e persone nell'Anatolia ellenistica. Documenti recenti e problemi antichi', *Dike*, **4**: 233–55.

Bogišić, V., and C. Jireček (eds.), 1904. *Liber statutorum civitatis Ragusii compositus anno 1272*. Zagreb, JAZU.

Botoeva, Gulzat, 2015. 'The Monetization of Social Celebrations in Rural Kyrgyzstan: On the Uses of Hashish Money', *Central Asian Survey*, **34**/4: 531–48.

Bouchon, Richard, 2014. 'Démophilos de Doliché, Paul-Émile et les conséquences de la troisième guerre de Macédoine à Gonnoi', *Topoi*, **19**/2: 484–513.

Bouchon, Richard, and Bruno Helly, 2015. 'The Thessalian League', in H. Beck and P. Funke (eds.), *Federalism in Greek Antiquity*. Cambridge: Cambridge University Press, 231–49.

Bouzid, Samir, 1997. *Mythes, utopie et messianisme dans le discours politique arabe moderne et contemporain*. Paris: L'Harmattan.

Bozza, Francesca, 1942. 'Gaio II, 7 e la proprietà provinciale', *Athenaeum*, **20**: 66–85.

Bozza, Francesca, 1943. 'Gaio II, 7 e la proprietà provinciale (continuazione)', *Athenaeum*, **21**: 13–20.

Brachet, Julien, and Judith Scheele, 2015. 'Fleeting Glory in a Wasteland: Wealth, Politics, and Autonomy in Northern Chad', *Comparative Studies in Society and History*, **57**/3: 723–52.

Brand, Paul, 1990. '*Multis Vigiliis Excogitatam et Inventam*: Henry II and the Creation of the English Common Law', *Haskins Society Journal*, 2: 197–222.

Brégi, Jean-François, 2009. *Droit romain: Les biens et la proprieté.* Paris: Ellipses Édition.

Brenner, Neil, 1999. 'Beyond State-Centrism? Space, Territoriality, and Geographical Scale in Globalization Studies', *Theory and Society*, **28**/1: 39–78.

Bresson, Alain, 2016. *The Making of the Ancient Greek Economy*. Princeton, NJ and Oxford: Princeton University Press.

Brooks, Nicholas P., 2009. 'The Fonthill Letter, Ealdorman Ordlaf and Anglo-Saxon Law', in Stephen Baxter et al. (eds.), *Early Medieval Studies in Memory of Patrick Wormald*. Farnham: Ashgate, 301–17.

Broughton, Thomas Robert Shannon, 1934. 'Roman Landholding in Asia Minor', *Transactions of the American Philosophical Association*, **20**: 207–39.

Brundage, James A., 1989. 'Usury', in Joseph R. Strayer et al. (eds.), *Dictionary of the Middle Ages*. New York: Scribner, xii.335–9.

Brundage, James A., 1995. *Medieval Canon Law*. London: Longman.

Brunner, Melanie, 2014. 'Pope John XXII and the Michaelists: The Scriptural Title of Evangelical Poverty in *Quia vir reprobus*', *Church History and Religious Culture*, **94**/2: 197–226.

Brunt, Peter Astbury, 2013. 'Marcus Aurelius and Slavery', in his *Studies in Stoicism*, ed. by M. T. Griffin and A. Samuels. Oxford: Oxford University Press, 394–406.

Brynjar, Lia, 1998. *The Society of the Muslim Brothers in Egypt: The Rise of an Islamic Mass Movement 1928-1942*. Reading: Ithaca Press.

Buckland, William Warwick, 1908. *The Roman Law of Slavery: The Condition of the Slave in Private Law from Augustus to Justinian*. Cambridge: Cambridge University Press.

Buckland, William Warwick, 1963. *A Text-Book of Roman Law from Augustus to Justinian*, 3rd edn. rev. by P. Stein. Cambridge: Cambridge University Press.

Buckland, William Warwick, and Arnold D. McNair, 1965. *Roman Law and Common Law: A Comparison in Outline*, 2nd edn., rev. by F. H. Lawson. Cambridge: Cambridge University Press.

Budak, Neven, 1984. 'Pregled literature i objavljenih izvora o problem serva i famula u srednjovjekovnim društvima na istočnom Jadranu', *Radovi Instituta za hrvatsku poveijest*, **17**: 5–34.

Budak, Neven, 1986. 'Pravni položaj serva i famula u komunalnim društvima na istočnom Jadranu', *Radovi Zavoda za hrvatsku povijest*, **19**: 56–64.

Budak, Neven, 2000. 'Slavery in Late Medieval Dalmatia/Croatia: Labour, Legal Status, Integration', *Mélanges de l'école française de Rome. Moyen Âge*, **112**/2: 745–60.

Bueger, Christian, 2013. 'Practice, Pirates and Coast Guards: The Grand Narrative of Somali Piracy', *Third World Quarterly*, **34**/10: 1811–27.

Burbank, Jane, 1995. 'Lenin and the Law in Revolutionary Russia', *Slavic Review*, **54**/1: 23–44.

Busse, Mark, 2012. 'Property', in J. G. Carrier (ed.), *A Handbook of Economic Anthropology*, 2nd edn. Cheltenham and Northampton, MA: Edward Elgar, 111–27.

Buzzacchi, Chiara, 2013. *Lex Rivi Hiberiensis: Per un'indagine sul processo civile nelle province*. Rome: L'Erma di Bretschneider.

Byock, Jesse, 1982. *Feud in the Icelandic Saga*. Berkeley CA: University of California Press.

Cakir, Dunya D., 2015. 'Islamist Texts in Practice: Commemorating Qutb in Turkey before and after the Arab Spring', *Muslim World*, **105**/4: 540–60.

Calvert, John, 2010. *Sayyid Qutb and the Origins of Radical Islamism*. London: Hurst.

Cam, Helen M., 1957. 'The Evolution of the Medieval English Franchise', *Speculum*, **32**: 427–42.

Campbell, Brian, 2000. *The Writings of the Roman Land Surveyors*. London: Society for the Promotion of Roman Studies.

Capogrossi Colognesi, Luigi, 1969. *La struttura della proprietà e la formazione dei "iura praediorum" nell'età repubblicana*, vol. 1. Milan: A. Giuffrè.

Capogrossi Colognesi, Luigi, 1986. *Proprietà e signoria in Roma antica*. Rome: Edizioni La Sapienza.

Capogrossi Colognesi, Luigi, 1998. *Ai margini della proprietà fondiaria*, 3rd edn. Rome: Edizioni La Sapienza.

Capogrossi Colognesi, Luigi, 2016. 'Ownership and Power in Roman law', in P. J. du Plessis, C. Ando, and K. Tuori (eds.), *The Oxford Handbook of Roman Law and Society*. Oxford: Oxford University Press, 524–36.

Carlà, Filippo, 2015. '*Pomerium, fines* and *ager Romanus*. Understanding Rome's "First Boundary"', *Latomus*, **74**: 599–630.

Carsten, Janet, 1989. 'Cooking Money: Gender and the Symbolic Transformation of Means of Exchange in a Malay Fishing Community', in M. Bloch and J. Parry (eds.), *Money and the Morality of Exchange*. Cambridge: Cambridge University Press, 117–41.

Carsten, Janet, 2000. *Cultures of Relatedness: New Approaches to the Study of Kinship*. Cambridge: Cambridge University Press.

Carsten, Janet, and Stephen Hugh-Jones (eds.), 1995. *About the House: Lévi-Strauss and Beyond*. Cambridge: Cambridge University Press.

Carter, Francis W., 1972. *Dubrovnik (Ragusa): A Classic City State*. London: Academic Press.

Caulfield, Richard A., 1997. *Greenlanders, Whales, and Whaling: Sustainability and Self-Determination in the Arctic*. (Arctic Visions.) Hanover, NH and London: University Press of New England.

Cervantes Saavedra, Miguel de, [1605] 1987. *El ingenioso hidalgo don Quijote de la Mancha*. 2 vols., edited by Luis André Morillo. Madrid: Castalia.

Chan, Koonchung, 2011. *The Fat Years (Shengshi Zhongguo)*, trans. M. Duke. London: Transworld.

Chanock, M. 1991, 'A Peculiar Sharpness: An Essay on Property in the History of Customary Law in Colonial Africa', *Journal of African History* **32**/1: 65–88.

Charles-Edwards, Thomas, 1989. *The Welsh Laws*. Cardiff: University of Wales Press.

Charles-Edwards, Thomas, 1993. *Early Irish and Welsh Kinship*. Oxford: Clarendon Press.

Charles-Edwards, Thomas, 1999. *The Early Mediaeval Gaelic Lawyer*, Quiggin Pamphlets on the Sources of Mediaeval Gaelic History 4. Cambridge: Department of Anglo-Saxon, Norse, and Celtic.

Chen, Ruoying, 2010. *Informal Sales of Rural Housing in China: Property, Privatization and Local Public Finance*. Chicago: University of Chicago Law School.

Cheng, Jie, 2015. 'Enforcing Takings Clauses in China', *Tsinghua China Law Review*, **7**: 191–220.

Chimni, B. S., 2004. 'International Institutions Today: An Imperial Global State in the Making', *European Journal of International Law*, **15**/1: 1–37.

Chivakul, Mali, W. Raphael Lam, Xiaoguang Liu, Wojciech Maliszweski, and Alfred Schipke, 2015. *IMF Working Paper: Understanding Residential Real Estate in China*. New York: International Monetary Fund.

Chouquer, Gérard, 2010. *La Terre dans le monde romain: anthropologie, droit, géographie*. Paris: Éditions Errance.

Clanchy, Michael T., 1993. *From Memory to Written Record: England, 1066–1307*, 2nd edn. Oxford: Basil Blackwell.

Clarke, Donald C., 2014. 'China's Stealth Urban Land Revolution', *American Journal of Comparative Law*, **62**/2: 323–66.

Cleaver, Frances, 2001. 'Institutional Bricolage, Conflict and Cooperation in Usangu, Tanzania', *IDS Bulletin*, **32**/4: 26–35.

Cluse, Christoph, 2007. 'Intimate Strangers: Slave Women as Wetnurses in Medieval Genoa', in Laura Guidi and Maria Rosaria Pelizzari (eds.), *Nuove frontiere per la storia di genere*, vol. 2. Salerno: Università di Salerno, 149–55.

Col, Giovanni Da, 2007. 'The View from Somewhen: Events, Bodies and the Perspective of Fortune around Khawa Karpo, a Tibetan Sacred Mountain in Yunnan Province', *Inner Asia*, **9**/2: 215–35.

Coleman, Janet, 1988. 'Property and Poverty', in J. H. Burns (ed.), *The Cambridge History of Medieval Political Thought, c.350—c.1450*. Cambridge: Cambridge University Press, 607–48.

Comaroff, Jean, and John L. Comaroff, 1990. 'Goodly Beasts, Beastly Goods: Cattle and Commodities in a South African Context', *American Ethnologist*, **17**/2: 195–216.

Comaroff, Jean, and John L. Comaroff (eds.), 2008. *Law and Disorder in the Postcolony*. Chicago: University of Chicago Press.

Connolly, Seán (trans.), 1989. '*Vita Prima S. Brigitae*: Background and Historical Value', *Journal of the Royal Society of Antiquaries of Ireland*, **119**: 5–49 (trans., 14–49).

Cordell, D., 1977, 'Eastern Libya, Wadai, and the Sanusiya: A Tariqa and a Trade Route', *Journal of African History*, **18**/1: 21–36.

Cottier, Michel, et al., 2008. *The Customs Law of Asia*. Oxford: Oxford University Press.

Coulson, Noel J., 1964. *A History of Islamic Law*. Edinburgh: Edinburgh University Press.

Cowell, Cressida, 2006. *That Rabbit Belongs to Emily Brown*. London: Orchard.

Crawford, Dorothy J., 1976. 'Imperial Estates', in M. I. Finley (ed.), *Studies in Roman Property*. Cambridge: Cambridge University Press, 35–70.

Crawford, Michael Hewson (ed.), 1996. *Roman Statutes*, 2 vols. London.

Crawford, Michael Hewson, 2010. 'Review of O. Sacchi, *Regime della terra e imposizione fondiaria nell'età dei Gracchi*', *Journal of Roman Studies*, **100**: 250.

Čremošnik, G., 1932. *Kancelarijski i notariski spisi 1278–1301*. Belgrade: Srpska kraljevska akademija.

Čremošnik, G., 1947. 'Pravni položaj našeg roblja u srednjem veku', *Glasnik Zemaljskog muzeja u Sarajevu*, **2**: 69–73.

Čremošnik, G., 1949. 'Izvori za istoriju roblja i servicijalnih odnosa u našim zemljama srednjeg vijeka', *Istorijski glasnik*, **1**: 151–62.

Crone, Patricia, 1987. *Roman, Provincial and Islamic Law: The Origins of the Islamic Patronate*. Cambridge: Cambridge University Press.

Crook, John, 1976. 'Classical Roman Law and the Sale of Land', in M. I. Finley (ed.), *Studies in Roman Property*. Cambridge: Cambridge University Press, 71–83.

Crouch, David, 2011. *The English Aristocracy 1070–1272: A Social Transformation*. New Haven, CT: Yale University Press.

Cruttenden, C. J., 1846. 'Report on the Mijjertheyn Tribe of Somallies, Inhabiting the District Forming the North-East Point of Africa', *Transactions of the Bombay Geographical Society*, **7**: 111–24.

Cuno, Kenneth M., 1980. 'The Origins of Private Ownership of Land in Egypt: A Reappraisal', *International Journal of Middle Eastern Studies*, **12**/3: 245–75.

Cuomo, Serafina, 2007. 'Measures for the Emperor: Volusius Maecianus' Monetary Pamphlet for Marcus Aurelius', in J. König and T. Whitmarsh (eds.), *Ordering Knowledge in the Roman Empire*. Cambridge: Cambridge University Press, 206–28.

Cvitanić, Ante, Mate Križman, and Josip Kolanović (eds.), 1990. *Statut grada Dubrovnika, 1272*. Dubrovnik: Historijski arhiv Dubrovnik.

Dagan, Hanoch, 2011. *Property: Values and Institutions*. Oxford: Oxford University Press.

Dagan, Hanoch, 2014. 'Property's Structural Pluralism: On Autonomy, the Rule of Law, and the Role of Blackstonian Ownership', *Brigham-Kanner Property Rights Conference Journal*, **3**: 27–41.

Dahl, Roald, 1964. *Charlie and the Chocolate Factory*. London: George Allen & Unwin.

Dalla Rosa, Alberto, 2014. 'Prolegomeni allo studio della proprietà imperiale in Asia Minore: La questione dell'imperatore come acquirente', *Scripta Classica et Orientalia*, **60**: 329–48.

Daube, David, 1969. *Roman Law: Linguistic, Social, and Philosophical Aspects*. Edinburgh: Edinburgh University Press.

Davies, R. W., Mark Harrison, and S. G. Wheatcroft (eds.), 1994. *The Economic Transformation of the Soviet Union, 1913–1945*. Cambridge: Cambridge University Press.

Davies, Wendy, and Paul Fouracre (eds.), 1986. *The Settlement of Disputes in Early Medieval Europe*. Cambridge: Cambridge University Press.

Davies, Wendy, and Paul Fouracre (eds.), 1995. *Property and Power in the Early Middle Ages*. Cambridge: Cambridge University Press.

Davis, John, 1973. *Land and Family in Pisticci*. London: Athlone Press.

Day, Sophie, Evthymios Papataxiarchis, and Michael Stewart. 1999. *Lilies of the Field: Marginal People Who Live for the Moment*. (Studies in the Ethnographic Imagination.) Boulder, CO: Westview Press.

Debos, Marielle, 2008. 'Tchad. Index chronologique 1900–1960', in J. Semelin (ed.), *The Online Encyclopedia of Mass Violence*. Online at <http://www.massviolence.org/Tchad-1900–1960>.

Debos, Marielle, 2011. 'Living by the Gun in Chad: Armed Violence as a Practical Occupation', *Journal of Modern African Studies*, **49**/3: 409–28.

Debos, Marielle, 2013. 'La guerre des préfets. Répression, clientélismes et illégalismes d'Etat dans l'entre-guerres tchadien', *Politix*, **104**: 47–65.

Delort, Robert, and Monica Boni, 2000. 'Des Esclaves toscans', *Mélanges de l'Ecole francaise de Rome. Moyen Âge*, **112**/2: 1057–77.

Demsetz, Harold, 1967. 'Toward a Theory of Property Rights', *American Economic Review*, **57**/2: 347–59.

Devreker, John, 1971. 'Une inscription inédite de Caracalla à Pessinonte', *Latomus*, **30**: 352–62.

Dilke, Oswald Ashton Wentworth, 1971. *The Roman Land Surveyors: An Introduction to the Agrimensores*. Newton Abbot: David and Charles Press.

Dinić, M., 1967. *Iz Dubrovačkog arhiva, vol. III*. Belgrade: SANU.

Diosdi, György, 1970. *Ownership in Ancient and Preclassical Roman Law*. Budapest.

Djian, G., [1915–6] 1996, *Le Tchad et sa conquête, 1900–1914*. Paris: L'Harmattan.

Donahue, Charles, 1986. '*Animalia ferae naturae*: Rome, Bologna, Leyden, Oxford and Queen's County, N.Y.', in R. S. Bagnall and W. V. Harris (eds.), *Studies in Roman Law in Memory of A. Arthur Schiller*. Leiden: Brill, 39–63.

Donaldson, Julia, 2011. *The Highway Rat*. London: Alison Green.

Downer, L. J., 1972. *Leges Henrici Primi*. Oxford: Oxford University Press.

Dozhdev, Dmitry, 1996. *Osnovanie zaschity vladenija v rimskom prave*. Moscow: Institut gosudarstva i prava.

Dresch, Paul, 1989. *Tribes, Government, and History in Yemen*. Oxford: Clarendon Press.

Dresch, Paul, 1998. 'Mutual Deception: Totality, Exchange and Islam in the Middle East', in N. Allen and W. James (eds.), *Marcel Mauss: A Centenary Tribute*. New York and Oxford: Berghahn, 111–33.

Dresch, Paul, 2006. *The Rules of Barat: Tribal Documents from Yemen*. San'ā': Centre français d'archéologie et de sciences sociales.

Dresch, Paul, 2012a. 'Legalism, Anthropology, and History: A View from Part of Anthropology', in P. Dresch and H. Skoda (eds.), *Legalism: Anthropology and History*. Oxford: Oxford University Press, 1–38.

Dresch, Paul, 2012b. 'Aspects of Non-State Law: Early Yemen and Perpetual Peace', in P. Dresch and H. Skoda (eds.), *Legalism: Anthropology and History*. Oxford: Oxford University Press, 145–72.

Dresch, Paul, 2015. 'Written Law as Words to Live By', in P. Dresch and J. Scheele (eds.), *Legalism: Rules and Categories*. Oxford: Oxford University Press, 53–78.

Dresch, Paul, and Judith Scheele, 2015. 'Rules and Categories: An Overview', in P. Dresch and J. Scheele (eds.), *Legalism: Rules and Categories*. Oxford: Oxford University Press, 1–27.

Du Plessis, Paul, 2015. 'Property', in D. Johnston (ed.), *The Cambridge Companion to Roman Law*. Cambridge: Cambridge University Press, 175–98.

Dua, Jatin, 2013. 'A Sea of Trade and a Sea of Fish: Piracy and Protection in the Western Indian Ocean', *Journal of Eastern African Studies*, **7**/2: 353–70.

Dua, Jatin, and Ken Menkhaus, 2012. 'The Context of Contemporary Piracy the Case of Somalia', *Journal of International Criminal Justice*, **10**/4: 749–66.

Dubouloz, Julien, 2011. *La propriété immobilière à Rome et en Italie (Ier–Ve siècles). Organisation et transmission des praedia urbana*. Rome.

Durrill, Wayne K., 1986. 'Atrocious Misery: The African Origins of Famine in Northern Somalia, 1839–1884', *American Historical Review*, **91**/2: 287–306.

Dyer, Christopher, 2002. *Making a Living in the Middle Ages: The People of Britain 850–1520*. New Haven, CT: Yale University Press.

Earle, T. F., and K. J. P. Lowe (eds.), 2013. *Black Africans in Renaissance Europe*. Cambridge: Cambridge University Press.

Eberle, Lisa Pilar, 2014. *Law, land, and territories: The Roman diaspora and the making of the provincial administration*, unpublished Ph.D. thesis, Berkeley.

Eberle, Lisa Pilar, 2016. 'Law, Empire, and the Making of Roman Estates in the Provinces during the Late Republic', *Critical Analysis of Law*, **3**: 51–69.

El Fadel, Khaled Abdou, 2001. *Rebellion and Violence in Islamic Law*. Cambridge: Cambridge University Press.

El-Gamal, Mahmoud A., 2006. *Islamic Finance: Law, Economics, and Practice*. Cambridge: Cambridge University Press.

Ellickson, Robert C., 1993. 'Property in Land', *Yale Law Journal*, **102**/6: 1315–1400.

El-Tounsy, Mohamed b. Oumar, 1851. *Voyage au Soudan oriental. Le Ouadây*. Paris: B. Duprat.

Epstein, Richard A., 2016. 'The Economic Structure of Roman Law', in P. J. du Plessis, C. Ando, and K. Tuori (eds.), *The Oxford Handbook of Roman Law and Society*. Oxford: Oxford University Press, 513–23.

Epstein, Steven, 1996. *Genoa and the Genoese, 958–1528*. Chapel Hill, NC and London: University of North Carolina Press.

Erie, Matthew S., 2007. 'China's (Post-)Socialist Property Rights Regime: Assessing the Impact of the Property Law on Illegal Land Takings', *Hong Kong Law Journal*, **37**/3: 919–49.

Erie, Matthew S., 2012. 'Property Rights, Legal Consciousness, and the New Media in China: The Hard Case of the "Toughest Nail-House in History" ', *China Information*, **26**/1: 34–58.

Erie, Matthew S., 2016. 'Shariʿa, Charity, and Minjian Autonomy in Muslim China: Gift-Giving in a Plural World', *American Ethnologist*, **43**/2: 311–24.

Erie, Matthew S., forthcoming 2018. 'The Traveling *Waqf*: Property, Religion, and Mobility beyond China', *Islamic Law and Society*, **25**/1: 1–35.

Erie, Matthew S., and Allen Carlson, 2014. 'Introduction to "Islam in China/China in Islam" ', *Cross-Currents: East Asian History and Culture Review*, **12**: 1–12.

Esposito, John L. (ed.), 2003. *The Oxford Dictionary of Islam*. Oxford: Oxford University Press.

Evans-Pritchard, E. E., 1940. *The Nuer: A Description of the Modes of Livelihood and Political Institutions of a Nilotic People*. Oxford: Clarendon Press.

Evans-Pritchard, E. E., 1951. *Kinship and Marriage among the Nuer*. Oxford: Clarendon Press.

Ewart, Elizabeth, 2015. 'Rules and Consequences in Amazonia', in P. Dresch and J. Scheele (eds.), *Legalism: Rules and Categories*. Oxford: Oxford University Press, 205–29.

FAO FID/CP/SOM 2005. Online at <http://www.fao.org/fi/oldsite/FCP/en/SOM/profile.htm>.

Fabian, Johannes, 2014. *Time and the Other: How Anthropology Makes Its Object*. New York: Columbia University Press.

Fadil, Nadia, and Mayanthi Fernando, 2015. 'Rediscovering the "Everyday" Muslim: Notes on an Anthropological Divide', *HAU: Journal of Ethnographic Theory*, **5**/2: 59–88.

Faith, Rosamond, 1997. *The English Peasantry and the Growth of Lordship*. London: Leicester University Press.

Famularo, Julia, 2015. 'Chinese Religious Regulations in the Xinjiang Uyghur Autonomous Region: A Veiled Threat to Turkic Muslims?', Project 2049 Institute website. Online at <http://www.project2049.net/documents/Famularo_PRC_Religious_Regulations_Xinjiang.pdf>.

Fang, Lizhi, 1990. 'The Chinese Amnesia', *New York Review of Books*, 27 September. Online at <http://www.nybooks.com/articles/1990/09/27/the-chinese-amnesia/>.

Fang, Qiang, 2009. 'A Hot Potato: The Chinese Complaint Systems from Early Times to the Present', *Journal of Asian Studies*, **68**/4: 1105–35.

Favre, Johanne, 2007. 'Marginalité de l'Etat et violences sociales au Far East (Tchad oriental)', *Bulletin de l'association des géographes français*, **84**/3: 357–65.

Favre, Johanne, 2008. *Insécurités. Une interprétation environnementale de la violence au Ouaddaï (Tchad oriental)*, Ph.D. thesis in geography. Paris 1/Sorbonne.

Feenstra, Robert, 1968. 'Duplex dominium', in J. A. Ankum, R. Feenstra, and W. F. Leemans (eds.), *Symbolae iuridicae et historicae Martino David dedicatae*, vol. I. Leiden: Brill, 55–71.

Feenstra, Robert, 1971. 'Les origines du dominium utile chez le Glossateurs avec un appendice concernant l'opinion des Ultramontani', in J. H. A. Lokin and N. van der Wal (eds.), *Flores legum H.J. Scheltema antecessori Groningani oblati*. Groningen: Wolters-Noordhof, 49–93.

Feenstra, Robert, 1989. '*Dominium* and *ius in re aliena*: The Origins of the Civil Law Distinction', in P. Birks (ed.), *New Perspectives in the Roman Law of Property*. Oxford: Oxford University Press, 111–22.

Feenstra, Robert, 1992. 'Law', in R. Jenkyns (ed.), *The Legacy of Rome: A New Appraisal*. Oxford: Oxford University Press, 399–420.

Fejić, Nenad, 2010. *Dubrovnik (Raguse) au Moyen Age: Espace de convergence, espace menacé*. Paris: L'Harmattan.

Ferguson, James, 1985. 'The Bovine Mystique: Power, Property and Livestock in Rural Lesotho', *Man*, **20**/4: 647–74.

Ferguson, James, 2005. 'Seeing Like an Oil Company: Space, Security, and Global Capital in Neoliberal Africa', *American Anthropologist*, **107**/3: 377–82.

Finlayson, A. Christopher, and Bonnie J. McCay, 1998. 'Crossing the Threshold of Ecosystem Resilience: The Commercial Extinction of Northern Cod', in Fikret Berkes and Carl Folke (eds.), *Linking Social and Ecological Systems: Management Practices and Social Mechanisms for Building Resilience*. Cambridge: Cambridge University Press, 311–37.

Finley, Moses I. (ed.), 1976. *Studies in Roman Property*. Cambridge: Cambridge University Press.

Finley, Moses I., 1980. *Ancient Slavery and Modern Ideology*. Cambridge: Viking Press.

Fitzmaurice, Andrew, 2014. *Sovereignty, Property and Empire, 1500-2000*. Cambridge: Cambridge University Press.

Fleisher, Michael, 2000. 'Kuria Cattle Raiding: Capitalist Transformation, Commoditization, and Crime Formation among an East African Agro-Pastoral People', *Comparative Studies in Society and History*, **42**/4: 745–69.

Fleming, Robin, 2010. *Britain After Rome: The Fall and Rise*. London: Penguin.

Fortescue, John, [ca. 1460] 1869. *De Natura Legis Naturae*, ed. by T. Fortescue, Lord Clermont. London: privately printed.

Frank, Tenney, 1927. '*Dominium in solo provinciali and ager publicus*', *Journal of Roman Studies*, **17**: 141–61.

Frankopan, Peter, 2015. *Silk Roads: A New History of the World*. London: Bloomsbury.

Frier, Bruce W., 1980. *Landlords and Tenants in Imperial Rome*. Princeton, NJ: Princeton University Press.

Frier, Bruce W., 1982–3. 'Bees and Lawyers', *Classical Journal*, **78**: 105–14.

Frier, Bruce W., 1985. *The Rise of Roman Jurists: Studies in Cicero's Pro Caecina*. Princeton, NJ: Princeton University Press.

Frier, Bruce W., 1994. 'Why Did the Jurists Change Roman Law? Bees and Lawyers Revisited', *Index*, **22**: 135–49.

Frier, Bruce W., and Dennis P. Kehoe, 2007. 'Law and Economic Institutions', in W. Scheidel, I. Morris, and R. P. Saller (eds.), *The Cambridge Economic History of the Graeco-Roman World*. Cambridge: Cambridge University Press, 113–43.

Fynn-Paul, J., 2009. 'Empire, Monotheism and Slavery in the Greater Mediterranean Region from Antiquity to the Early Modern Era', *Past and Present*, 205: 3–40.

Gagliardi, Lorenzo, 2015. 'Fondazione di colonie romane ed espropriazioni di terre a danno degli indigeni', *Mélanges de l'Ecole française de Rome. Antiquité*, **127**/2: 353–70.

Gallagher, Mary E., 2006. 'Mobilizing the Law in China: "Informed Disenchantment" and the Development of Legal Consciousness', *Law & Society Review*, **40**/4: 783–816.

Galsterer, Hartmut, 1987. 'La loi municipale des romains: chimère ou réalité', *Revue historique de droit français et étranger*, **65**: 181–203.

Gardinier, David E., 1989. 'Muhammad Awuda Oulech at Abéché: A Reformist Islamic Challenge to French and Traditionalist Interests in Ouaddaï, Chad, 1947–1956', *Islam et sociétés au sud du Sahara*, **3**: 159–85.

Garnsey, Peter, 1996. *Ideas of Slavery from Aristotle to Augustine*. Cambridge: Cambridge University Press.

Garnsey, Peter, 2007. *Thinking about Property: From Antiquity to the Age of Revolution.* Cambridge: Cambridge University Press.

Gell, Alfred, 1992. *The Anthropology of Time: Cultural Constructions of Temporal Maps and Images.* Oxford: Berg.

Gerriets, Marilyn, 1983. 'Economy and Society: Clientship according to the Irish Laws', *Cambridge Medieval Celtic Studies*, **6**: 43–61.

Gervais, Raymond, 1982. 'La plus riche des colonies pauvres: la politique monétaire et fiscale de la France au Tchad', *Canadian Journal of African Studies*, **16**/1: 93–112.

Geschiere, Peter, 1993. 'Chiefs and Colonial Rule in Cameroon: Inventing Chieftaincy, French and British Style', *Africa*, **63**/2: 151–75.

Giachi, Cristina, and Valerio Marotta, 2014. *Diritto e giurisprudenza in Roma antica*, 2nd edn. Rome: Carocci.

Gilchrist, John, 1976. 'The Medieval Canon Law on Unfree Persons', *Studia Gratiana*, **19**: 271–301.

Gillespie, John, and Hualing Fu, 2014. 'Resolving Land Disputes in East Asia: Exploring the Limits of the Law', in H. Fu and J. Gillespie (eds.), *Resolving Land Disputes in East Asia.* Cambridge: Cambridge University Press, 3–36.

Gladney, Dru C., 1987. 'Muslim Tombs and Ethnic Folklore: Charters for Hui Identity', *Journal of Asian Studies*, **46**/3: 495–532.

Gladney, Dru C., [1991] 1996. *Muslim Chinese: Ethnic Nationalism in the People's Republic*, 2nd edn. Cambridge, MA: Council on East Asian Studies, Harvard University.

Gladney, Dru C., 1999. 'The Salafiyya Movement in Northwest China: Islamic Fundamentalism among the Muslim Chinese?', in L. Manger (ed.), *Muslim Diversity: Local Islam in Global Contexts.* Surrey: Curzon Press, 102–49.

Glickman, M., 1971. 'Kinship and credit among the Nuer', *Africa*, **41**/4: 306–19.

Goebel, Julius Jr., 1937. *Felony and Misdemeanor: A Study in the History of English Criminal Procedure.* New York: Commonwealth Fund.

Gordon, H. Scott, 1954. 'The Economic Theory of a Common-Property Resource: The Fishery', *Journal of Political Economy*, **62**/2: 124–42.

Goswami, Manu, 2004. *Producing India: From Colonial Economy to National Space.* Chicago and London: University of Chicago Press.

Graeber, David, 2001. *Toward an Anthropological Theory of Value: The False Coin of Our Own Dreams.* New York: Palgrave.

Graeber, David, 2011. *Debt, the First 5000 years.* New York: Melville House.

Grant, Bruce, 2009. *The Captive and the Gift: Cultural Histories of Sovereignty in Russia and the Caucasus.* Ithaca, NY: Cornell University Press.

Gray, Kevin, 1991. 'Property in Thin Air', *Cambridge Law Journal*, **50**/2: 252–307.

Green, Thomas Hill, [1895] 1941. *Lectures on the Principles of Political Obligation.* London: Longmans, Green & Co.

Greene, David (ed.), 1955. *Fingal Rónáin and Other Tales.* Dublin: Dublin Institute for Advanced Studies.

Greenhouse, Carol J., 1996. *A Moment's Notice: Time Politics Across Cultures.* Ithaca, NY: Cornell University Press.

Grelle, Francesco, 1966. 'La signoria sul suolo provinciale nella Parafrasi di Teofilo', *Labeo*, **12**: 209–18.

Grelle, Francesco, 1990. 'L'appartenenza del suolo provinciale nell'analisi di Gaio 2.7 e 2.21', *Index*, **18**: 167–83.

Grosso, Giuseppe, 1974. 'La condizione del suolo provinciale negli schemi giuridici della giurisprudenza del principato', in G. I. Luzzato et al. (eds.), *I diritti locali nelle province romane con particolare riguardo alle condizioni giuridiche del suolo*. Rome: Accademia Nazionale dei Lincei, 65–76.

Grotius, Hugo, [1625] 2005. *The Rights of War and Peace*, ed. and with an intro. by Richard Tuck, 3 vols. Indianapolis: Liberty Fund. [First published as *De jure belli ac pacis*.]

Guarino, Antonio, 2001. *Diritto privato romano*, 12th edn. Naples: Editore Jovene.

Habachy, Saba, 1962. 'Property, Right, and Contract in Muslim Law', *Columbia Law Review*, **62**/3: 450–73.

Hallaq, Wael, 2003–4. 'Juristic Authority versus State Power: The Legal Crises of Modern Islam', *Journal of Law and Religion*, **19**/2: 243–58.

Hallaq, Wael, 2009. *Sharīʿa. Theory, Practice, Transformations*. Cambridge: Cambridge University Press.

Halverson, Jeffrey E., 2010. *Theology and Creed in Sunni Islam: The Muslim Brotherhood, Ash'arism, and Political Sunnism*. Basingstoke: Palgrave Macmillan.

Hann, Chris M., 1998. 'Introduction: The Embeddedness of Property', in C. M. Hahn (ed.), *Property Relations: Renewing the Anthropological Tradition*. Cambridge: Cambridge University Press, 1–47.

Hann, Chris M., 2007. 'A New Double Movement? Anthropological Perspectives on Property in the Age of Neoliberalism', *Socio-Economic Review*, **5**: 287–318.

Hann, Chris M., 2014. 'The Economistic Fallacy and Forms of Integration under and after Socialism', *Economy and Society*, **43**: 626–49.

Hann, Chris M., and Keith Hart, 2011. *Economic Anthropology: History, Ethnography, Critique*. Cambridge: Polity.

Hansen, Stig Jarle, 2009. *Piracy in the Greater Gulf of Aden: Myths, Misconceptions and Remedies*. (Norwegian Institute for Urban and Regional Research; Report 2009: 29.) Oslo.

Hardin, Garret, 1968. 'The Tragedy of the Commons', *Science*, **162**: 1243–48.

Harmer, Florence E. (ed.), 1952. *Anglo-Saxon Writs*. Manchester: Manchester University Press.

Harper, Kyle, 2011. *Slavery in the Late Roman World, AD 275–425*. Cambridge: Cambridge University Press.

Harris, Edward M., 2008. 'Response to Gerhard Thür', in E. Harris and G. Thür (eds.), *Symposion 2007: Vorträge zur griechischen und hellenistischen Rechtsgeschichte*. Vienna: Verlag der Österreichischen Akademie der Wissenschaften, 189–200.

Harrison, Alick Robin Walsham, 1968. *The Law of Athens: The Family and Property*. Oxford: Clarendon Press.

Harvey, David, 1990. 'Between Space and Time: Reflections on the Geographical Imagination', *Annals of the Association of American Geographers*, **80**/3: 418–34.

Harvey, Sally, 2014. *Domesday: Book of Judgement*. Oxford: Oxford University Press.

Hatcher, John, and Mark Bailey 2001. *Modelling the Middle Ages: The History and Theory of England's Economic Development*. Oxford: Oxford University Press.

Hatzopoulos, Miltiade B., 2015. 'Roi et cité en Macédoine', *Studi ellenistici*, **29**: 77–87.

Haykel, Bernard, 2002. 'Dissembling Descent, or How the Barber Lost His Turban: Identity and Evidence in Eighteenth-Century Zaydî Yemen', *Islamic Law and Society*, **9**/2: 194–230.

Heers, Jacques, 1981. *Esclaves et domestiques au Moyen-Âge dans le monde méditérannéen*. Paris: Fayard.

Hegel, Georg Wilhelm Friedrich, [1821] 1967. *The Philosophy of Right*, trans. T. M. Knox. Oxford: Oxford University Press. [First published as *Grundlinien der Philosophie des Rechts*.]

Heller, Michael A., 1998. 'The Tragedy of the Anticommons: Property in the Transition for Marx to Markets', *Harvard Law Review*, **111**/3: 621–88.

Helmholz, Richard, 2012. 'The Law of Slavery and the Ius Commune', in Jean Allain (ed.), *The Legal Understanding of Slavery: From the Historical to the Contemporary*. Oxford: Oxford University Press, 17–39.

Helmreich, Stefan, 2009. *Alien Ocean: Anthropological Voyages in Microbial Seas*. Berkeley, CA: University of California Press.

Herskovits, Melville J., 1926. 'The Cattle Complex in East Africa', *American Anthropologist*, **28**/1: 230–72.

Heuss, Alfred, 1933. *Die völkerrechtlichen Grundlagen der römischen Aussenpolitik in republikanischer Zeit*. Leipzig: Dieterich.

Hickey, Robin, 2012. 'Seeking to Understand the Definition of Slavery', in Jean Allain (ed.), *The Legal Understanding of Slavery: From the Historical to the Contemporary*. Oxford: Oxford University Press, 220–42.

Hicks, Zehra, 2015. *All Mine!* London: Macmillan.

Hivon, Myriam, 1998. 'The Bullied Farmer: Social Pressure as Survival Strategy?', in Frances Pine and Sue Bridger (eds.), *Surviving Post-Socialism: Local Strategies and Regional Responses in Eastern Europe and the Former Soviet Union*. London: Routledge, 33–51.

Ho, Peter, 2013. 'In Defense of Endogenous, Spontaneously Ordered Development: The Institutional Structure of China's Rural Urban Property Rights', *Journal of Peasant Studies*, **40**/6: 1–32.

Hobbes, Thomas, [1647] 1983. *De Cive: The English Version*, ed. by H. Warrender. Oxford: Clarendon Press.

Hobsbawm, Eric J., 1959. *Primitive Rebels: Studies in Archaic Forms of Social Movements in the 19th and 20th Centuries*. Manchester: Manchester University Press.

Hoebel, E. Adamson, 1966. *Anthropology: The Study of Man*, 3rd edn. New York: McGraw Hill.

Hohfeld, Wesley Newcomb, 1913. 'Some Fundamental Legal Conceptions as Applied in Judicial Reasoning', *Yale Law Journal*, **23**/1: 16–59.

Hohfeld, Wesley Newcomb, 1917. 'Fundamental Legal Conceptions as Applied in Judicial Reasoning', *Yale Law Journal*, **26**/8: 710–70.

Holling, Crawford S., 1973. 'Resilience and Stability of Ecological Systems', *Annual Review of Ecology and Systematics*, **4**: 1–23.

Holt, Richard, 2010. 'The Urban Transformation in England, 900–1100', *Anglo-Norman Studies*, **32**: 57–78.

Honoré, A. M. (Tony), 1961. 'Ownership', in A. G. Guest (ed.), *Oxford Essays in Jurisprudence*, Oxford: Oxford University Press, 107–47.

Honoré, A. M. (Tony), 1962. *Gaius: A Biography*. Oxford: Clarendon Press.

Honoré, A. M. (Tony), 2012. 'The Nature of Slavery', in Jean Allain (ed.), *The Legal Understanding of Slavery: From the Historical to the Contemporary*. Oxford: Oxford University Press, 9–16.

Hough, Carole, 1997. 'Alfred's *Domboc* and the Language of Rape: A Reconsideration of Alfred, ch. 11', *Medium Ævum*, **66**: 1–27.

Hourani, Albert, 1991. *A History of the Arab Peoples*. Cambridge, MA: Belknap Press of Harvard University Press.

Hozier, H. M., July 1906. 'Wireless Telegraphy', *The Nineteenth-Century and After: A Monthly Review*, **60**/353: 49–56.

Hua, Xinmin [华新民], 2011. 'Weishenme huaqian qumai chaobubaoxi de fangzi? [Why spend money to buy a house that's in a precarious state?]', *Sina*, 24 February. Online at <http://blog.sina.com.cn/s/blog_4ab3874b0100one9.html>.

Hua, Xinmin [华新民], 2014. 'Beijing de zuchuan siyou siheyuan he zuzhai zhuren [Beijing's privately owned handed-down four-walled courtyards and the ancestral house master]', blog.163.com, 21 September. Online at <http://huaxinmin.blog.163.com/blog/static/118909964201482185340687/>.

Hudson, John, 2012. *The Oxford History of the Laws of England. Volume II: 871–1216*. Oxford: Oxford University Press.

Hull, Vernam (ed.), 1968. '*Noínden Ulad*: The Debility of the Ulidians', *Celtica*, **8**: 1–42.

Hume, David, [1739] 1978. *A Treatise of Human Nature*, eds. L. A. Selby-Bigge and P. H. Nidditch. Oxford: Clarendon Press.

Humfress, Caroline, 2007. 'Law and Justice in the Later Roman Empire', in D. M. Gwynn (ed.), *A. H. M. Jones and the Later Roman Empire*. Leiden: Brill, 121–42.

Humfress, Caroline, 2013. 'Thinking through Legal Pluralism: "Forum Shopping" in the Later Roman Empire', in J. Duindam, J. Harries, C. Humfress, and N. Hurvitz (eds.), *Law and Empire: Ideas, Practices, Actors*. Leiden and Boston, MA: Brill, 225–50.

Humfress, Caroline, 2015. 'Telling Stories about (Roman) Law: Rules and Concepts in Legal Discourse', in P. Dresch and J. Scheele (eds.), *Legalism: Rules and Categories*. Oxford: Oxford University Press, 79–104.

Humphrey, Caroline, 1998. *Marx Went Away—But Karl Stayed Behind*. Ann Arbor, MI: University of Michigan Press.

Hutchinson, Sharon, 1992. 'The Cattle of Money and the Cattle of Girls among the Nuer, 1930–83', *American Ethnologist*, **19**/2: 294–316.

Hyams, Paul, 2016. 'Property Talk in Old English: Did Anglo-Saxon England Know the Concept of Seisin?', in John Witte, Jr., Sara McDougall, and Anna di Robilant (eds.), *Texts and Contexts in Legal History: Essays in Honor of Charles Donahue*. Berkeley, CA: Robbins Collection, 37–59.

Ingold, Tim, 1986. *The Appropriation of Nature: Essays on Human Ecology and Social Relations*. (Themes in Social Anthropology.) Manchester: Manchester University Press.

International Crisis Group (ICG), 2009. 'Somalia: The Trouble with Puntland', *Crisis Group Africa Briefing*, **64**. Online at <https://www.crisisgroup.org/africa/horn-africa/somalia/somalia-trouble-puntland>.

Iqbal, Zamir, and Abbas Mirakhor, 2011. *An Introduction to Islamic Finance: Theory and Practice*, 2nd edn. Singapore: Wiley.

Isaac, Barry L., 2012. 'Karl Polanyi', in J. G. Carrier (ed.), *A Handbook of Economic Anthropology*, 2nd edn. Cheltenham and Northampton, MA: Edward Elgar, 1–25.

Islam, Muhammad Wohidul, 1999. 'Al-Mal: The Concept of Property in Islamic Legal Thought', *Arab Law Quarterly*, **14**: 361–68.

Issawi, Charles, 1954. *Egypt at Mid-century: An Economic Survey*. London: Oxford University Press.

Jakab, Éva, 2014. 'Auctions and Ownership in Ptolemaic Egypt: A Social and Economic Approach', in M. Gagarin and A. Lanni (eds.), *Symposion 2013: Papers on Greek and Hellenistic Legal History*. Vienna: Verlag der Österreichischen Akademie der Wissenschaften, 313–37.

Jakab, Éva, 2015. 'Property Rights in Ancient Rome', in P. Erdkamp, K. Verboven, and A. Zuiderhoek (eds.), *Ownership and Exploitation of Land and Natural Resources in the Roman World*. Oxford: Oxford University Press, 106–31.

James, William, 1890. *The Principles of Psychology*, 2 vols. London: Macmillan.

Jeffers, Oliver, 2012. *This Moose Belongs to Me*. London: HarperCollins.

Jenkins, Dafydd (trans.), 1986. *The Law of Hywel Dda: Law Texts from Medieval Wales*. Llandysul: Gomer Press.

Jing, Jun, 1996. *The Temple of Memories*. Stanford: Stanford University Press.

Johansen, Baber, 1990. 'Le jugement comme preuve. Preuve juridique et vérité religieuse dans le droit islamique hanéfite', *Studia Islamica*, **72**: 5–17.

Johansen, Julian, 1996. *Sufism and Islamic Reform in Egypt: The Battle for Islamic Tradition*. Oxford: Oxford University Press.

Johannes, Robert E., Milton M. R. Freeman, and Richard J. Hamilton, 2000. 'Ignore Fishers' Knowledge and Miss the Boat', *Fish and Fisheries*, **1**/3: 257–71.

Johnson, Ian, 2013. 'China's Great Uprooting: Moving 250 Million into Cities', *New York Times*, June 15. Online at <http://www.nytimes.com/2013/06/16/world/asia/chinas-great-uprooting-moving-250-million-into-cities.html>.

Johnson, Tom, 2015. 'Medieval Law and Materiality: Shipwrecks, Finders, and Property on the Suffolk Coast, ca. 1380–1410', *American Historical Review*, **120**/2: 407–32.

Johnson, Tom, forthcoming 2017. 'The Tree and the Rod: Jurisdiction in Late Medieval England', *Past and Present*, **237**: 1–39.

Johnston, David, 1999. *Roman Law in Context*. Cambridge: Cambridge University Press.

Jomard, Edme-François, 1851. 'Préface', in M. El Tounsy (ed.), *Voyage au Soudan oriental. Le Ouadây*. Paris: B. Duprat, i–lxxi.

Jones, Arnold Hugh Martin, 1941. 'In eo solo dominium populi Romani est vel Caesaris', *Journal of Roman Studies*, **31**: 26–31. [Reprinted in his *Studies in Roman Government and Law* (Oxford: Blackwell, 1960), ch. 9.]

Jones, Jeffrey Douglas, 2011. 'Property and Personhood Revisited', *Wake Forest Journal of Law & Policy*, **1**/1: 93–136.

Jones, John D. (trans.), 1999. *Hervaeus Natalis: The Poverty of Christ and the Apostles*. (Mediaeval Sources in Translation 37. Studies in Medieval Moral Teaching 2.) Toronto: Pontifical Institute of Medieval Studies.

Jördens, Andrea, 2016. 'Possession and Provincial Practice', in P. J. du Plessis, C. Ando, and K. Tuori (eds.), *The Oxford Handbook of Roman Law and Society*. Oxford: Oxford University Press, 553–65.

Jullien de Pommerol, P., 1994. *L'arabe tchadien. Emergence d'une langue véhiculaire*. Paris: Karthala.

Kamali, Mohammad Hashim, 2003. *Principles of Islamic Jurisprudence*, 3rd edn. Cambridge: Islamic Texts Society.

Kammel, Frank Matthias, 2001. 'Gefährliche Heiden und gezähmte Exoten: Bemerkungen zum europäischen Türkenbild im 17. und frühen 18. Jahrhundert' in Ronald Asch, Wulf Eckart Voß, and Martin Wrede (eds.), *Frieden und Krieg in der Frühen Neuzeit*. Munich: Wilhelm Fink, 503–25.

Kant, Immanuel, [1797] 1996. *The Metaphysics of Morals*, transl. and ed. by Mary Gregor and Roger J. Sullivan. Cambridge: Cambridge University Press.

Kantor, Georgy, 2012. 'Ideas of Law in Hellenistic and Roman Legal Practice', in P. Dresch and H. Skoda (eds.), *Legalism: Anthropology and History*. Oxford: Oxford University Press, 55–83.

Kantor, Georgy, 2014. 'Roman Legal Administration in the Province of Asia: Hellenistic Heritage vs. Innovation', in J. Dubouloz, S. Pittia, and G. Sabatini (eds.), L'imperium Romanum *en perspective. Les savoirs d'empire dans la République romaine et leur héritage dans l'Europe médiévale et moderne*. Besançon: Presses universitaires de Franche-Comté, 243–68.

Kaplan, Robert D., 2010. *Monsoon: The Indian Ocean and the Future of American Power*. New York: Random House.

Kapteijns, Lidwien, 1995. 'Gender Relations and the Transformation of the Northern Somali Pastoral Tradition', *International Journal of African Historical Studies*, **28**/2: 241–59.

Kapteijns, Lidwien, 2008. 'The Disintegration of Somalia: A Historiographical Essay', *Bildhaan: An International Journal of Somali Studies*, **1**/1: 6–17.

Kaser, Max, 1942. 'Die Typen des römischen Bodenrechts in der späten Republik', *Zeitschrift der Savigny-Stiftung für Rechtsgeschicte. Romanistische Abteilung*, **62**: 1–81.

Kaser, Max, 1964. 'The Concept of Roman Ownership', *Tydskrif vir Hedendaagse Romeins-Hollandse Reg*, **27**: 5–19.

Kaser, Max, 1971–5. *Das römische Privatrecht*, 2nd edn, 2 vols. Munich: C. H. Beck.

Kassab, Elizabeth Suzanne, 2010. *Contemporary Arab Thought: Cultural Critique in Contemporary Perspective*. New York: Columbia University Press.

Kehoe, Dennis P., 2007. *Law and the Rural Economy in the Roman Empire*. Ann Arbor, MI: University of Michigan Press.

Kehoe, Dennis P., 2015. 'Property Rights over Land and Economic Growth in the Roman Empire', in P. Erdkamp, K. Verboven, and A. Zuiderhoek (eds.), *Ownership and Exploitation of Land and Natural Resources in the Roman World*. Oxford: Oxford University Press, 88–106.

Kehoe, Dennis P., Ratzan, David M., and Uri Yiftach, 2015. 'Transaction Costs, Ancient History, and the Law', in D. P. Kehoe, D. M. Ratzan, and U. Yiftach (eds.), *Law and Transaction Costs in the Ancient Economy*. Ann Arbor, MI: University of Michigan Press, 1–35.

Kelinguen, Yves, 1957. 'Renaissance d'un sultanat dans l'Afrique centrale française. Le Ouaddaï', *L'Afrique et l'Asie modernes*, **13**: 36–40.

Kelly, Fergus, 1988. *A Guide to Early Irish Law*. Dublin: Dublin Institute for Advanced Studies.

Kelly, Fergus, 1997. *Early Irish Farming: A Study Based Mainly on the Law-Texts of the 7th and 8th Centuries AD*. Dublin: Dublin Institute for Advanced Studies.

Kennedy, Duncan, 2006. 'Three Globalizations of Law and Legal Thought: 1850–2000', in David M. Trubek and Alvaro Santon (eds.), *The New Law and Economic Development: A Critical Appraisal*. Cambridge: Cambridge University Press, 19–73.

Keynes, Simon, 1980. *The Diplomas of Æthelred 'the Unready', 978–1016: A Study in Their Use as Historical Evidence.* Cambridge: Cambridge University Press.

Keynes, Simon, and Michael Lapidge, 1983. *Alfred the Great: Asser's Life of King Alfred and Other Contemporary Sources*. London: Penguin.

Khan, Naveed, 2012. *Muslim Becoming: Aspiration and Skepticism in Pakistan*. Durham, NC: Duke University Press.

Khatab, Sayed, 2006. *The Power of Sovereignty: The Political and Ideological Philosophy of Sayyid Qutb*. London and New York: Routledge.

Khayar, I. H., 1994. *Tchad. Regard sur les elites ouadaïennes*. Paris: Éditions du CNRS.

Khazanov, Anatoly M. 2012. 'Pastoralism and Property Relations in Contemporary Kazakhstan', in Anatoly M. Khazanov and Günther Schlee (eds.), *Who Owns the Stock?: Collective and Multiple Property Rights in Animals*. New York and Oxford: Berghahn, 141–57.

Kinsey, Christopher Paul, Hansen, Stig Jarle, and George Franklin, 2009. 'The Impact of Private Security Companies on Somalia's Governance Networks', *Cambridge Review of International Affairs*, **22**/1: 147–61.

Klassen, Jon, 2012. *This Is Not My Hat*. London: Walker.

Klingmüller, Fritz, 1910. 'Die Idee des Staatseigentums am römischen Provinzialboden', *Philologus*, **69**: 71–113.

Kniep, Ferdinand, 1912. *Gai Institutionum Commentarius Secundus (§§1–96)*. Jena: Fischer.

Knudsen, Ståle, 2008. *Fishers and Scientists in Modern Turkey: The Management of Natural Resources, Knowledge and Identity on the Eastern Black Sea Coast*. New York and Oxford: Berghahn.

Knudsen, Ståle, and Hege Toje, 2008. 'Post-Soviet Transformations in Russian and Ukrainian Black Sea Fisheries: Socio-Economic Dynamics and Property Relations', *Southeast European and Black Sea Studies*, **8**/1: 17–32.

Koch, John T., and John Carey (eds.), 2003. *The Celtic Heroic Age: Literary Sources for Ancient Celtic Europe and Early Ireland and Wales*, 4th edn. Aberystwyth: Celtic Studies Publications.

Kopytoff, Igor, 1982. 'Slavery', *Annual Review of Anthropology*, **11**: 207–30.

Kornai, János. 1980. *Economics of Shortage*. Amsterdam; London: North-Holland.

Kränzlein, Arnold, 1963. *Eigentum und Besitz im griechischen Recht des fünften und vierten Jahrhunderts v. Chr.* Berlin: Duncker & Humblot.

Krekić, B., 1997. *Dubrovnik: A Mediterranean Urban Society*. Aldershot, Hampshire: Ashgate.

Kuehn, Thomas, 1998. 'Adoption à Florence à la fin du Moyen Age', *Médiévales*, **35**: 69–81.

Kuper, Adam, 1982. *Wives for Cattle: Bridewealth and Marriage in Southern Africa*. London: Routledge & Kegan Paul.

Kuran, Timur, 2001. 'The Provision of Public Goods under Islamic Law: Origins, Impact, and Limitations of the Waqf System', *Law and Society Review*, **35**/4: 841–98.

Kuran, Timur, 2004. *Islam and Mammon: The Economic Predicaments of Islamism*. Princeton, NJ: Princeton University Press.

Laffi, Umberto, 1967. 'Le iscrizioni relative all'introduzione nel 9 a.C. del nuovo calendario della provincia d'Asia', *Studi classici e orientali*, **16**: 5–98.

Laidlaw, James, 2014. *The Subject of Virtue: An Anthropology of Ethics and Freedom*. Cambridge: Cambridge University Press.

Laitin, David, and Said Samatar, 1984. 'Somalia and the World Economy', *Review of African Political Economy*, **30**/1: 58–72.

Laitin, David, and Said Samatar, 1987. *Somalia: Nation in Search of a State*. Boulder, CO: Westview Press.

Lambek, Michael, 2008. 'Value and Virtue', *Anthropological Theory*, **8**/2: 133–57.

Lambert, Malcolm, 1977. *Medieval Heresy: Popular Movements from the Gregorian Reform to the Reformation*. Oxford: Blackwell.

Lambert, Malcolm, 1998. *Franciscan Poverty: The Doctrine of Absolute Poverty of Christ and the Apostles in the Franciscan Order, 1210–1323*, rev. and expanded edn. St Bonaventure, NY: Franciscan Institute, St Bonaventure University.

Lambert, Tom, 2017. *Law and Order in Anglo-Saxon England*. Oxford: Oxford University Press.

Lampland, Martha, 1995. *The Object of Labor: Commodification in Socialist Hungary*. Chicago: University of Chicago Press.

Lane, Anthony, 2013. 'Dangerous Waters', *New Yorker*, 24 October. Online at <http://www.newyorker.com/magazine/2013/10/14/dangerous-waters>.

Largeau, Victor-Emmanuel, [1913] 2001. *A la naissance du Tchad (1903–1913)*, ed. L. Caron. Saint-Maur-des-Fossés: Editions Sépia.

Larkin, Peter A., 1977. 'An Epitaph for the Concept of Maximum Sustained Yield', *Transactions of the American Fisheries Society*, **106**/1: 1–11.

Latour, Bruno, 2010. *The Making of Law: An Ethnography of the Conseil d'État*, trans. Marina Brilman and Alain Pottage. Cambridge: Polity.

Lawson, M. K., 1984. 'The Collection of Danegeld and Heregeld in the Reigns of Æthelred II and Cnut', *English Historical Review* 99: 721–738.

Layish, Aharon, 2006. 'Interplay between Tribal and *shar'î* Law: A Case of tibbawî Blood Money in the sharî'a Court of Kufra', *Islamic Law and Society*, **13**/1: 63–75.

Le Cornec, J., 1963. *Histoire politique du Tchad de 1900 à 1962*. Paris: Librairie générale de droit et de jurisprudence.

Le Goff, Jacques, 2012. *Money and the Middle Ages: An Essay in Historical Anthropology*, transl. from French by J. Birrell. London: Polity Press.

Le Teuff, Béatrice, 2016. 'Enregistrer les propriétés dans les cités de l'Orient romain: archives civiques et documents cadastraux sous le Haut-Empire', in F. Lerouxel and A.-V. Pont (eds.), *Propriétaires et citoyens dans l'Orient romain*. Bordeaux: Ausonius, 157–73.

Lee, Robert Warden, 1925. *An Introduction to Roman-Dutch Law*, 2nd edn. Oxford: Clarendon Press.

Leeson, Peter T., 2012. *The Invisible Hook: The Hidden Economics of Pirates*. Princeton, NJ: Princeton University Press.

Leff, Gordon, 1967. *Heresy in the Later Middle Ages: The Relation of Heterodoxy to Dissent, c.1250–1450*. Manchester: Manchester University Press.

Lenel, Otto, 1927. *Das Edictum perpetuum: ein Versuch zu seiner Wiederherstellung*, 3rd edn. Leipzig: Tauschnitz.

Lenin, Vladimir Il'ich, [1917] 1964. 'Decree on Land', in V. I. Lenin, *Collective Works*, vol. 26, transl. Y. Sdobnikov and G. Hanna. Moscow: Progress Publishers, 258.

Lenski, Noel, 2016. *Constantine and the Cities: Imperial Authority and Civic Politics*. Philadelphia: University of Pennsylvania Press.

Lepselter, Susan, 2012. 'The Resonance of Captivity: Aliens and Conquest', *HAU: Journal of Ethnographic Theory*, **2**/2: 84–104.

Lerouxel, François, and Anne-Valerie Pont (eds.), 2016. *Propriétaires et citoyens dans l'Orient romain*. Bordeaux: Ausonius.

Leroy, E., 1987. *La réforme du droit de la terre dans certains pays d'Afrique francophone*. Rome: FAO.

Leuchtenburg, William E., 1996. *The Supreme Court Reborn: The Constitutional Revolution in the Age of Roosevelt*. New York: Oxford University Press.

Levick, Barbara, 1967. *Roman Colonies in Southern Asia Minor*. Oxford: Clarendon Press.

Levick, Barbara, 2000. *The Government of the Roman Empire: A Sourcebook*, 2nd edn. London and New York: Routledge.

Levy, Ernst, 1951. *West Roman Vulgar Law: The Law of Property*. Philadelphia: American Philosophical Society.

Lewis, Ioan M., 1994. *Blood and Bone: The Call of Kinship in Somali Society*. Lawrenceville: Red Sea Press.

Lewis, Ioan M., 1999. *A Pastoral Democracy: A Study of Pastoralism & Politics Among the Northern Somali of the Horn of Africa*. Oxford: James Currey Publishers.

Lewis, Ioan M., 2003. *A Modern History of the Somali: Nation and State in the Horn of Africa*, 4th edn. Athens, OH: Ohio University Press, 2003.

Li, Tania Murray, 1996. 'Images of Community: Discourse and Strategy in Property Relations', *Development and Change*, **27**/3: 501–27.

Li, Tania Murray, 2002. 'Engaging Simplifications: Community-Based Resource Management, Market Processes, and State Agendas in Upland Southeast Asia', *World Development*, **30**/2: 264–83.

Lia, Brynjar, 1998. *The Society of the Muslim Brothers in Egypt: The Rise of an Islamic Mass Movement 1928-1942*. Reading: Ithaca Press.

Lightman, Alan, 2004. *Einstein's Dreams*. New York: Vintage Books.

Lim, Louisa, 2014. *The People's Republic of Amnesia: Tiananmen Revisited*. Oxford: Oxford University Press.

Linklater, Andro, 2013. *Owning the Earth: The Transforming History of Land Ownership*. New York and London: Bloomsbury.

Lipman, Jonathan N., 1999. 'Sufism in the Chinese Courts: Islam and Qing Law in the Eighteenth and Nineteenth Centuries', in F. D. Jong and B. Radtke (eds.), *Islamic Mysticism Contested: Thirteen Centuries of Controversies and Polemics*. Leiden: Brill, 553–74.

Lipman, Jonathan N., 2005. '"A Fierce and Brutal People": On Islam and Muslims in Qing Law', in P. Crossley (ed.), *Empire at the Margins: Culture, Ethnicity, and Frontier in Early Modern China*. Berkeley, CA: University of California Press, 83–112.

Little, Peter D., 1992. 'Traders, Brokers and Market "Crisis" in Southern Somalia', *Africa*, **62**/1: 94–124.

Locke, John, [1689] 1988. *Two Treatises of Government*, ed. Peter Laslett. Cambridge: Cambridge University Press.

Lonza, Nella, 2012. 'The Statute of Dubrovnik of 1272: Between Legal Code and Political Symbol', in Vesna Rimać (trans.) and Nella Lonza (ed.), *The Statute of Dubrovnik of 1272 = Liber statutorum Civitatis Ragusii compositus anno MCCLXXII*. Dubrovnik: Drzavni arhiv u Dubrovnik, 7–26.

Lucić, Hanibal, [1556] 1988. *Robinja*, ed. and trans. into modern Croatian by M. Grčić, with T. Maroević and M. Tomasović. Zagreb: Grafički Zavod Hrvatske.

Lucić, Josip, 1979. *Obrti i usluge u Dubrovniku do početka XIV. stoljeća*. Zagreb: Sveučilište u Zagrebu, Institut za hrvatsku povijest.

Ludwig, Donald, Ray Hilborn, and Carl Walters, 1993, 'Uncertainty, Resource Exploitation, and Conservation: Lessons from History', *Science*, **260** (5104): 17–36.

Lund, C., 2006. 'Twilight Institutions: Public Authority and Local Politics in Africa', *Development and Change*, **37**/4: 685–706.

Luzzato, Giuseppe Ignazio, et al., 1974. *I diritti locali nelle province romane con particolare riguardo alle condizioni giuridiche del suolo*. Rome: Accademia Nazionale dei Lincei.

Ma, John, 2002. *Antiochos III and the Cities of Western Asia Minor*, 2nd edn. Oxford: Oxford University Press.

McCay, Bonnie J., and James M. Acheson (eds.), 1987. *The Question of the Commons: The Culture and Ecology of Communal Resources*. Tucson: University of Arizona Press.

MacDowell, Douglas M., 1986. *Spartan Law*. Edinburgh: Scottish Academic Press.

McEvoy, Arthur F., 1990. *The Fisherman's Problem: Ecology and Law in the California Fisheries, 1850–1980*. Cambridge: Cambridge University Press.

McGranahan, Carole, and Ralph Litzinger, 2012. 'Self-Immolation as Protest in Tibet', Hot Spots, *Cultural Anthropology* website, published 9 April 2012. Online at <https://culanth.org/fieldsights/93-self-immolation-as-protest-in-tibet>.

McGuire, Gabriel, 2014. 'By Coin or by Kine? Barter and Pastoral Production in Kazakhstan', *Ethnos*, **81**/1: 53–74.

McKee, S., 2008. 'Domestic Slavery in Renaissance Italy', *Slavery and Abolition*, **29**/3: 1–21.

McKinley, Michelle, 2010. 'Fractional Freedoms: Slavery, Legal Activism and Ecclesiastical Courts in Colonial Lima, 1593–1689', *Law and History Review*, **28**/3: 749–90.

McKinnell, John S., 2009. 'The Ideology of Vengeance in Old Norse Mythology', in T. B. Lambert and D. Rollason (eds.), *Peace and Protection in the Middle Ages*. Durham: Centre for Medieval and Renaissance Studies, 181–94.

Macray, W. Dunn (ed.), 1886. *Chronicon Abbatiae Rameseiensis*. London: Longman.

Maddock, Kenneth, 1983. *Your Land is Our Land: Aboriginal Land Rights*. Harmondsworth: Penguin.

Mahmood, Hussain Abdullahi, 2008. 'Risky Trade, Resilient Traders: Trust and Livestock Marketing in Northern Kenya', *Africa*, **78**/4: 561–81.

Maine, Henry Sumner, 1861. *Ancient Law: Its Connection with the Early History of Society, and Its Relation to Modern Ideas*. London: John Murray.

Maitland, Frederic William, 1897. *Domesday Book and Beyond: Three Essays in the Early History of England*. Cambridge: Cambridge University Press.

Maiuro, Marco, 2012. *Res Caesaris: Ricerche sulla proprietà imperiale nel Principato*. Bari: Epiduglia.

Mäkinen, Virpi, 2001. *Property Rights in the Late Medieval Franciscan Discussion on Property*. Leuven: Peeters.

Malavolta, Mariano, 1985. 'Ius Italicum', in *Dizionario epigrafico* IV: 2333–9.

Mann, Gregory, 2015. *From Empires to NGOs in the West African Sahel. The Road to Nongovernmentality*. Cambridge: Cambridge University Press.

Mantovani, Dario, 1999. *Le formule del processo privato romano. Per la didattica delle Istituzioni di diritto romano*, 2nd edn. Padova: CEDAM.

Marchal, Roland, 1996. *The Post Civil War Somali Business Class*. Brussels: European Commission, Somalia Unit.

Marchal, Roland, 2006. 'Tchad/Soudan: vers un système de conflits', *Politique Africaine*, **102**: 135–54.

Marshall, Anthony J., 1969. 'Romans under Chian Law', *Greek, Roman, and Byzantine Studies*, **10**: 255–71.

Marston, Thomas E., 1961. *Britain's Imperial Role in the Red Sea Area, 1800–1878*. Hamden, CT: Shoe String Press.

Marty, André, Antoine Eberschweiler, and Zakinet Dangbet, 2009. *Au cœur de la transhumance: un campement chamelier au Tchad central, septembre 2006—avril 2007*. Paris: Karthala.

Marx, Karl, 1963. *Early Writings*, trans. and ed. T. B. Bottomore. London: Watts.

Marx, Karl, 1973. *Grundrisse: Foundations of the Critique of Political Economy*, trans. with a foreword by M. Nicolaus. Harmondsworth: Penguin.

Mauss, Marcel, [1950] 1990. *The Gift: The Form and Reason for Exchange in Archaic Societies*, trans. W. D. Halls. New York: Norton.

Mawdudi, Sayyid Abu A'la, 1947. *The Economic Problem of Man and Its Islamic Solution*. Lahore: Islamic Publications.

Mbembe, Achille, 2000. *De la postcolonie: essai sur l'imagination politique dans l'Afrique contemporaine*. Paris: Karthala.

Mbembe, Achille, and Janet Roitman, 1995. 'Figures of the Subject in Times of Crisis', *Public Culture*, **7**/2: 323–52.

Meillassoux, Claude, 1996. *The Anthropology of Slavery: The Womb of Iron and Gold*. London: Athlone Press.

Melissaris, Emmanuel, 2007. 'The Concept of Appropriation and the Law of Theft', *Modern Law Review*, **70**/4: 581–97.

Menkhaus, Kenneth, 2006. 'Governance without Government in Somalia: Spoilers, State Building, and the Politics of Coping', *International Security*, **31**/3: 74–106.

Merrill, Thomas W., 2011. 'The Property Prism', *Econ Journal Watch*, **8**/3: 247–54.

Merry, Sally Engle, 1990. *Getting Justice and Getting Even: Legal Consciousness among Working-Class Americans*. Chicago: University of Chicago Press.

Meyer, Elizabeth A., 2004. *Legitimacy and Law in the Roman World:* Tabulae *in Roman Belief and Practice*. Cambridge: Cambridge University Press.

Micklin, Philip P., 2007. 'The Aral Sea Disaster', *Annual Review of Earth and Planetary Sciences*, **35**: 47–72.

Micklin, Philip P., and Nikolay V. Aladin, 2008. 'Reclaiming the Aral Sea', *Scientific American*, **298**/4: 64–71.

Migeotte, Léopold, 2014. *Les finances des cités grecques aux périods classique et hellénistique*. Paris: Les Belles Lettres.

Mileta, Christian, 2008. *Der König und sein Land: Untersuchungen zur Herrschaft der hellenistischen Monarchen über das königliche Gebiet Kleinasiens und seine Bevölkerung*. Berlin: Akademie Verlag.

Millar, Fergus, 2002. *The Roman Republic and the Augustan Revolution*. Chapel Hill: University of North Carolina Press.

Miller, William Ian, 1990. *Bloodtaking and Peacemaking: Feud, Law, and Society in Saga Iceland*. Chicago: University of Chicago Press.

Miller, William Ian, 2006. *Eye for an Eye*. Cambridge: Cambridge University Press.

Milsom, Stroud Francis Charles, 1981. *Historical Foundations of the Common Law*, 2nd edn. London: Butterworths.

Minnegal, Monica, and Peter Dwyer, 2011. 'Appropriating Fish, Appropriating Fishermen: Tradable Permits, Natural Resources, and Uncertainty', in Veronica Strang and Mark Busse (eds.), *Ownership and Appropriation*. Oxford: Berg, 197–215.

Minzner, Carl F., 2006. 'Xinfang: An Alternative to Formal Chinese Legal Institutions', *Stanford Journal of International Law*, **42**: 103–80.

Mitchell, Richard P., [1969] 1993. *The Society of the Muslim Brothers*, with a foreword by John O. Voll. New York: Oxford University Press.

Mitchell, Stephen, 1980. 'Population and the Land in Roman Galatia', in *Aufstieg und Niedergang der römischen Welt*, vol. II.7.2. Tübingen, 1053–81.

Mitteis, Ludwig, 1891. *Reichsrecht und Volksrecht in den östlichen Provinzen des römischen Kaiserreichs*. Leipzig: Teubner.

Moatti, Claude, 1993. *Archives et partage de la terre dans le monde romain (IIe s. av.—Ier s. apr. J.-C.)*. Rome: École française de Rome.

Mommsen, Theodor, 1887. *Römisches Staatsrecht*, vol. III.1. Leipzig: S. Hirzel.

Monson, Andrew, 2005. 'Sacred Land in Ptolemaic and Roman Tebtunis', in S. L. Lippert and M. Schentuleit (eds.), *Tebtynis und Soknopaiu Nesos: Leben im römerzeitlichen Fajum*. Wiesbaden: Harrassowitz, 84–91.

Monson, Andrew, 2012. *From the Ptolemies to the Romans: Political and Economic Change in Egypt*. Cambridge: Cambridge University Press.

Montesquieu, Charles de, [1748] 1989. *The Spirit of the Laws*, ed. and trans. A. Cohler, B. Miller and H. Stone. Cambridge: Cambridge University Press.

Morgan, Lewis Henry, 1877. *Ancient Society; Or, Researches in the Lines of Human Progress from Savagery, Through Barbarism to Civilization*. Chicago: Charles H. Kerr.

Morris, William Alfred, 1910. *The Frankpledge System*. London: Longmans, Green and Co.

Morris, William Alfred, 1927. *The Medieval English Sheriff to 1300*. Manchester: Manchester University Press.

Mosher Stuard, Susan, 1983. 'Urban Domestic Slavery in Medieval Ragusa', *Journal of Medieval History*, **9**/3: 155–71.

Mosher Stuard, Susan, 1992. *A State of Deference: Ragusa/Dubrovnik in the Medieval Centuries*. Philadelphia: University of Pennsylvania Press.

Moukhtar, B. M., 1982. *De 1909 à 1960. Aux confins des états: les peuples du Tchad oriental et leur évolution dans un Ouadaï statique*. Thèse de troisième cycle, Paris VII.

Mouritsen, Henrik, 2011. *The Freedman in the Roman World*. Cambridge: Cambridge University Press.

Mousourakis, George, 2012. *Fundamentals of Roman Private Law*. Berlin: Springer.

Moussalli, Ahmad, S., 1992. *Radical Islamic Fundamentalism: The Ideological and Political Discourse of Sayyid Qutb*. Beirut: American University of Beirut.

Mueggler, Erik, 2001. *The Age of Wild Ghosts: Memory, Violence, and Place in Southwest China*. Berkeley, CA: University of California Press.

Mundy, Martha, 2007. *Governing Property, Making the Modern State: Law, Administration and Production in Ottoman Syria*. London: I.B. Tauris.

Munn, Nancy D., 1992. 'The Cultural Anthropology of Time: A Critical Essay', *Annual Review of Anthropology*, **21**: 93–123.

Murphy, Martin N., 2011. *Somalia, the New Barbary?: Piracy and Islam in the Horn of Africa*. New York: Columbia University Press.

Murray, Alexander Callander, 2010. 'Merovingian Immunity Revisited', *History Compass*, **8**: 913–28.

Musallam, Adnan A., 2005. *From Secularism to Jihad: Sayyid Qutb and the Foundations of Radical Islamism*. Westport, CT and London: Praeger.

Nachtigal, Gustav, 1889. *Sahârâ und Sûdân: Ergebnisse sechsjähriger Reisen in Afrika. Dritter Band: Wadâï und Dâr-Fôr*. Berlin: Weidmannsche Buchhandlung.

Nakhshina, Maria, 2012. 'Community Interpretations of Fishing Outside Legal Regulations: A Case Study from Northwest Russia', in Courtney Carothers, Catherine P. Chambers, and Keith R. Criddle (eds.), *Fishing People of the North: Cultures, Economies, and Management Responding to Change*. Fairbanks: University of Alaska, 229–41.

Neesen, Lutz, 1980. *Untersuchungen zu den direkten Staatsabgaben der römischen Kaiserzeit (27 v. Chr.–284 n. Chr.)*. Bonn: Rufolf Habelt.

Néné Tassi, I., 2000. *La place des coutumes dans la pratique judiciaire au Tchad*. Mémoire de fin d'étude du premier cycle de l'ENAM, N'Djamena.

Ní Dhonnchadha, Máirín (trans.), 2003. 'The Kin-slaying of Rónán', in J. T. Koch and J. Carey (eds.), *The Celtic Heroic Age: Literary Sources for Ancient Celtic Europe and Early Ireland and Wales*. Aberystwyth: Celtic Studies Publications, 274–82.

Nicholson, William, 1922. *The Velveteen Rabbit: Or How Toys Become Real*. London: Heinemann.

Nicolet, Claude, 1976. *Le métier de citoyen dans la Rome républicaine*, 2nd edn. Paris: Gallimard.

Nicolet, Claude, 1991. *Space, Geography, and Politics in the Early Roman Empire*. Ann Arbor, MI: University of Michigan Press.

Nieboer, H. J., 1910. *Slavery as an Industrial System: Ethnological Researches*. The Hague: Martinus Nijhoff.

Nörr, Dieter, 2012. 'Der Kaiser und sein Interpret. MAMA IX p. xxxvi sq. Dossier über den *ager Aezanensis Iovi dicatus*', *Zeitschrift der Savigny-Stiftung für Rechtsgeschichte. Romanistische Abteilung*, **129**: 315–63.

Ober, Josiah, 2015. *The Rise and Fall of Classical Greece*. Princeton, NJ: Princeton University Press.

O'Brien, Bruce R., 1999. *God's Peace and King's Peace: The Laws of Edward the Confessor*. Philadelphia: University of Pennsylvania Press.

O'Fahey, R. S., 1977. 'The Office of qadi in Dar Fur: A Preliminary Inquiry', *Bulletin of the School of Oriental and African Studies*, **50**/1: 110–24.

O'Fahey, R. S., 1997. 'Endowment, Privilege and Estate in the Central and Eastern Sudan', *Islamic Law and Society*, **4**/3: 333–51.

Opwis, Felicitas, 2005. '*Maslaha* in Contemporary Islamic Legal Theory', *Islamic Law and Society*, **12**/2: 182–223.

O'Rahilly, Cecile (ed. and trans.), 1976. *Táin Bó Cúailnge: Recension I*. Dublin: Dublin Institute for Advanced Studies.

Origo, Iris, 1955. 'The Domestic Enemy: The Eastern Slaves in Tuscany in the Fourteenth and Fifteenth Centuries', *Speculum*, **30**/3: 321–66.

Ostrom, Elinor, 1990. *Governing the Commons: The Evolution of Institutions for Collective Action*. (Political Economy of Institutions and Decisions.) Cambridge: Cambridge University Press.

Otto, Ton, and Rane Willerslev, 2013. 'Introduction: Value as Theory: Comparison, Cultural Critique, and Guerrilla Ethnographic Theory', *HAU: Journal of Ethnographic Theory*, **3**/1: 1–20.

Oxé, August, 1923. 'Die römische Vermessung steuerpflichtigen Bodens', *Bonner Jahrbücher*, **128**: 20–27.

Pahuja, Sundhya, 2011. *Decolonising International Law: Development, Economic Growth and the Politics of Universality*. Cambridge: Cambridge University Press.

Palmer, Robert C., 1985. 'The Origins of Property in England', *Law and History Review*, **3**/1: 1–50.

Pálsson, Gísli, 1994. 'Enskilment at Sea', *Man*, **29**/4: 901–27.

Pálsson, Gísli, 2006. 'Nature and Society in the Age of Postmodernity', in Aletta Biersack and James B. Greenberg (eds.), *Reimagining Political Ecology*. (New Ecologies for the Twenty-First Century.) Durham, NC: Duke University Press, 70–93.

Parry, Jonathan P., and Maurice Bloch (eds.), 1989. *Money and the Morality of Exchange*. Cambridge: Cambridge University Press.

Patterson, Orlando, 1982. *Slavery and Social Death: A Comparative Study*. Cambridge: Harvard University Press.

Patterson, Orlando, 2012. 'Trafficking, Gender and Slavery: Past and Present', in J. Allain (ed.), *The Legal Understanding of Slavery: From the Historical to the Contemporary*. Oxford: Oxford University Press, 322–34.

Payne, Matthew J., 2011. 'Seeing like a Soviet State: Settlement of Nomadic Kazakhs, 1928–1934', in Golfo Alexopoulos, Julie Hessler, and Kiril Tomoff (eds.), *Writing the Stalin Era: Sheila Fitzpatrick and Soviet Historiography*. New York and Basingstoke: Palgrave Macmillan, 59–86.

Peirce, Leslie, 1998. 'Le dilemme de Fatma. Crime sexuel et culture juridique dans une cour ottomane au début des temps modernes', *Annales. Histoire, Sciences sociales*, **53**/2: 291–319.

Peñalver, Eduardo Moisés, and Sonia K. Katyal, 2007. 'Property Outlaws', *University of Pennsylvania Law Review*, **155**: 1097–186.

Penner, J. E., 2012. 'The Concept of Property and the Concept of Slavery', in Jean Allain (ed.), *The Legal Understanding of Slavery: From the Historical to the Contemporary*. Oxford: Oxford University Press, 242–52.

Percy, Sarah, and Anja Shortland, 2010. *The Business of Piracy in Somalia*. (Deutsches Institut für Wirtschaftsforschung Discussion Paper no. 1033.) Berlin.

Perović, Z., 1992. 'Trgovina Robljem u Dubrovniku', unpublished master's dissertation, University of Zagreb.

Perrot, C.-H. and F.-X. Aymar (eds.), 2003. *Le retour des rois: les autorités traditionnelles et l'État en Afrique contemporaine*. Paris: Karthala.

Perrotta, Louise, 2002. 'Rural Identities in Transition: Partible Persons and Partial Peasants in Post-Soviet Russia', in Pamela Leonard and Deema Kaneff (eds.), *Post-Socialist Peasant? Rural and Urban Constructions of Identity in Eastern Europe, East Asia and the Former Soviet Union*. Basingstoke: Palgrave Macmillan, 117–35.

Peters, Rudolph, 2005. *Crime and Punishment in Islamic Law: Theory and Practice from the Sixteenth to the Twenty-first Century*. Cambridge: Cambridge University Press.

Pianciola, Niccolò, 2001. 'The Collectivization Famine in Kazakhstan, 1931–1933', *Harvard Ukrainian Studies*, **25**/3–4: 237–51.

Pianciola, Niccolò, forthcoming. 'Fish, Livestock, Railroads and People: Imperial Infrastructures and the Great Famine around the Aral Sea, 1906–1934'.

Piganiol, André, 1962. *Les documents cadastraux de la colonie romaine d'Orange*. Paris: CNRS.

Pils, Eva, 2005. 'Land Disputes, Rights Assertion, and Social Unrest in China: A Case from Sichuan', *Columbia Journal of Asian Law*, **19**/1: 235–92.

Pils, Eva, 2009. 'Chinese Property Law as an Image of PRC History', *Hong Kong Law Journal*, **39**/3: 595–611.

Pinelli, P., 2008. 'From Dubrovnik (Ragusa) to Florence: Observations on the Recruiting of Domestic Servants in the Fifteenth Century', *Dubrovnik Annals*, **12:** 57–71.

Ping, Li, 2007. *The Impact of Regulatory Takings by the Chinese State on Rural Land Tenure and Property Rights*. Washington, DC: Rural Development Institute.

Pirie, Fernanda, 2014. 'Community, Justice, and Legalism', in F. Pirie and J. Scheele (eds.), *Legalism: Community and Justice*. Oxford: Oxford University Press, 227–52.

Pirie, Fernanda, 2015. *The Anthropology of Law*. Oxford: Oxford University Press.

Plotnikov, Igor S., Nikolay V. Aladin, Zaualkhan K. Ermakhanov, and Lyubov V. Zhakova. 2014. 'Biological Dynamics of the Aral Sea Before Its Modern Decline (1900–1960)', in P. Micklin, N. V. Aladin, and I. Plotnikov (eds.), *The Aral Sea: The Devastation and Partial Rehabilitation of a Great Lake*, Springer Earth System Sciences 10178. Berlin: Springer, 41–76.

Polanyi, Karl, [1944] 2001. *The Great Transformation: The Political and Economic Origins of Our Time*, 2nd edn., foreword by J. E. Stiglitz, with a new intro. by F. Block. Boston, MA: Beacon Press.

Polanyi, Karl, 1957. 'The Economy as Instituted Process', in K. Polanyi, C. M. Arensberg, and H. W. Pearson (eds.), *Trade and Market in the Early Empires: Economies in History and Theory*. Glencoe: Free Press & Falcon's Wing Press, 243–70.

Polanyi, Karl, Arensberg, Conrad M., and Harry W. Pearson (eds.), 1957. *Trade and Market in the Early Empires: Economies in History and Theory*. Glencoe: Free Press & Falcon's Wing Press.

Policy and Law Department of the Bureau of Religious Affairs [Zongjiao shiwuju zhengce faguisi], 1995. *Xin shiqi zongjiao gonguo wengong xuanbian* [Anthology of New Period Religious Work Documents]. Beijing: Zongjiao wenhua chubanshe [Religion Culture Publishers].

Pollock, Frederick, and Frederic William Maitland, 1898. *The History of English Law before the Time of Edward I*, 2nd edn., 2 vols. Cambridge: Cambridge University Press.

Post, Gaines, Giocarinis, Kimon, and Richard Kay, 1955. 'The Medieval Heritage of a Humanistic Ideal: *Scientia donum Dei est, unde vendi non potest*', *Traditio*, **11**: 195–234.

Potter, Beatrix, 1902. *The Tale of Peter Rabbit*. London: Frederick Warne.

Pouillon, François, 1988. 'Cens et puissance, ou pourquoi les pasteurs nomades ne peuvent pas compter leur bétail', *Cahiers d'études africaines*, **28**/110: 177–205.

Premerstein, Anton von, 1919. 'Ius Italicum', in *Paulys Real-Encyclopädie der klassischen Altertumswissenschaft* **X**: cols. 1238–53.

Purdy, Jededia, 2010. *The Meaning of Property: Freedom, Community, and the Legal Imagination*. New Haven, CT: Yale University Press.

Qiao, Shitong, 2013. 'Planting Houses in Shenzhen: A Real Estate Market without Legal Titles', *Canadian Journal of Law and Society/Revue Canadienne Droit et Société*. Online at <http://dx.doi.org/10.2139/ssrn.2391012>.

Qiao, Shitong, 2015. 'Small Property, Adverse Possession, and Optional Law', in Yun-chien Chang (ed.), *Law and Economics of Possession*. Cambridge: Cambridge University Press, 290–319.

Qiao, Shitong, and Frank K. Upham, 2015. 'The Evolution of Relational Property Rights: A Case of Chinese Rural Land Reform', *Iowa Law Review*, **100**/6: 2479–2506.

Qutb, Sayyid, [1949] 1996. *Social Justice in Islam*, trans. William E. Shepard, *Sayyid Qutb and Islamic Activism: A Translation and Critical Analysis of Social Justice in Islam*. Leiden: Brill. [First published as *Al-'Adala al-Ijtima'iyya fi al-Islam*.]

Qutb, Sayyid, [1962] 1991. *The Islamic Concept and Its Characteristics*, trans. Mohammed Moinuddin Siddiqui. Indianapolis: American Trust Publications. [First published as *Khasa'is al-Tasawwur al-Islami wa Muqawwimatuhu*.]

Qutb, Sayyid, [1964] 2005. *Milestones*. USA: SIME E-Publishing. [First published as *Ma'alim fi al-Tariq*.]

Qutb, Sayyid, [1952–9] 2008. *In the Shade of the Qur'an*, trans. and ed. Adil Salahi and Ashur Shamis. Leicester: Islamic Foundation. [First published as *Fi Zilal al-Qur'an*.]

Radin, Margaret Jane, 1982. 'Property and Personhood', *Stanford Law Review*, **34**/5: 957–1015.

Radin, Margaret Jane, 1987. 'Market-Inalienability', *Harvard Law Review*, **100**: 1903–8.

Radin, Margaret Jane, 1993. *Reinterpreting Property*. Chicago: University of Chicago Press.

Raffles, Hugh, 2010. *Insectopedia*. New York: Random House.

Ramsay, William Mitchell, 1890. *The Historical Geography of Asia Minor*. London: John Murray.

Ramsay, William Mitchell, 1895–97. *The Cities and Bishoprics of Phrygia*, vol. 1. Oxford: Clarendon Press.

Ramsay, William Mitchell, 1906. *Studies in the History and Art of the Eastern Provinces of the Roman Empire*. Aberdeen: Aberdeen University Press.

Randolph, Patrick A., and Jianbou Lou, 2000. *Chinese Real Estate Law [Zhongguo fangdichan falü]*. The Hague: Kluwer Law International.

Rathbone, Dominic, 2013. 'The Romanity of Roman Egypt: A Faltering Consensus?', *Journal of Juristic Papyrology*, **43**: 73–95.

Rathje, William, and Cullen Murphy, 2001. *Rubbish!: The Archaeology of Garbage*. Tucson: University of Arizona Press.

Rautmann, Marcus Louis, 2006. *Daily Life in the Byzantine Empire*. London: Greenwood.

Rediker, Marcus, 2004. *Villains of all Nations: Atlantic Pirates in the Golden Age*. London: Verso.

Reese, Scott Steven, 1999. 'Urban Woes and Pious Remedies: Sufism In Nineteenth-Century Benaadir (Somalia)', *Africa Today*, **46**/3: 169–92.

Reeves, Madeleine, 2012. 'Black Work, Green Money: Remittances, Ritual, and Domestic Economies in Southern Kyrgyzstan', *Slavic Review*, **71**/1: 108–34.

Reynolds, Susan, 1994. *Fiefs and Vassals: The Medieval Evidence Reinterpreted*. Oxford: Oxford University Press.

Richardson, John, 2008. *The Language of Empire: Rome and the Idea of Empire from the Third Century BC to the Second Century AD*. Cambridge: Cambridge University Press.

Richardson, Tanya, and Gisa Weszkalnys, 2014. 'Introduction: Resource Materialities'. *Anthropological Quarterly*, **87**/1: 5–30.

Rimać, Vesna (trans.) and Lonza, Nella (ed.) 2012. *The Statute of Dubrovnik of 1272 = Liber statutorum Civitatis Ragusii compositus anno MCCLXXII*. Dubrovnik: Drzavni arhiv u Dubrovnik.

Rives, James, 2012. 'Control of the Sacred in Roman Law', in O. Tellegen-Couperus (ed.), *Law and Religion in the Roman Republic*. Leiden: Brill, 165–80.

Robertson, A. J., 1925. *The Laws of the Kings of England from Edmund to Henry I.* Cambridge: Cambridge University Press.

Robinson, Glenn E., 2004. 'Hamas as a Social Movement', in Quintan Wiktoriwicz (ed.), *Islamic Activism*. Bloomington and Indianapolis: Indiana University Press, 112–39.

Römer, Zdenka Janeković, 2011. 'O napuštanju, udomljivanju i posvojenju djece u srednjovjekovnom Dubrovniku i Dalmaciji', *Zbornik radova*, **4:** 14–32.

Rose, Carol M., 1985. 'Possession as the Origin of Property', *University of Chicago Law Review*, **52**/1: 73–88.

Rose, Carol M., 1994. *Property and Persuasion: Essays on the History, Theory, and Rhetoric of Ownership*. Boulder, CO: Westview Press.

Rose, George A., 2007. *Cod: The Ecological History of the North Atlantic Fisheries*. St Johns, NL: Breakwater Books.

Roselaar, Saskia T., 2010. *Public Land in the Roman Republic: A Social and Economic History of Ager Publicus in Italy, 396–89 BC*. Oxford: Oxford University Press.

Rosenwein, Barbara, 1999. *Negotiating Space: Power, Restraint and Privileges of Immunity in Early Medieval Europe*. Manchester: Manchester University Press.

Rostowzew, Michael, 1910. *Studien zur Geschichte des römischen Kolonates*. Leipzig: Teubner.

Rousseau, Jean-Jacques, [1755] 1994. *Discourse on the Origin of Inequality*, trans. F. Philip. Oxford: Oxford University Press. [First published as *Discours sur l'origine et les fondements de l'inégalité parmi les hommes*.]

Rüfner, Thomas, 2010. 'The Roman Concept of Ownership and the Medieval Doctrine of *dominium utile*', in J. W. Cairns and P. J. du Plessis (eds.), *The Creation of the Ius Commune. From Casus to Regula*. Edinburgh: Edinburgh University Press, 127–42.

Sacchi, Osvaldo, 2006. *Regime della terra e imposizione fondiaria nell'età dei Gracchi*. Naples: Jovene.

Sahlins, Marshall, 1972. *Stone Age Economics*. Chicago: Aldine-Atherton.

St German, Christopher, [1532] 1874. *Doctor and Student: Or Dialogues Between a Doctor of Divinity and a Student in the Laws of England Containing the Grounds of Those Laws Together with Questions and Cases Concerning the Equity Thereof*, ed. T. Muchall. Cincinnati: Robert Clarke.

Samatar, Abdi Ismail, 1989. *The State and Rural Transformation in Northern Somalia, 1884–1986*. Madison, WI: University of Wisconsin Press.

Samatar, Abdi Ismail, Mark Lindberg, and Basil Mahayni, 2010. 'The Dialectics of Piracy in Somalia: The Rich versus the Poor', *Third World Quarterly*, **31**/8: 1377–94.

Samatar, Abdi Ismail, Lance Salisbury, and Jonathan Bascom, 1988. 'The Political Economy of Livestock Marketing in Northern Somalia', *African Economic History*, **17**: 81–97.

Sandars, Thomas Collett (ed. and trans.), 1876. *The Institutes of Justinian*. Chicago: Callaghan and Company.

Sawyer, Peter, 2013. *The Wealth of Anglo-Saxon England*. Oxford: Oxford University Press.

Sayers, Sean, 2011. *Marx and Alienation: Essays on Hegelian Themes*. Basingstoke: Palgrave Macmillan.

Schacht, Joseph, 1964. *An Introduction to Islamic Law*. Oxford: Clarendon Press.

Scheele, Judith, 2012. 'Rightful Measures: Irrigation, Land, and the Shari'ah in the Algerian Touat', in P. Dresch and H. Skoda (eds.), *Legalism: Anthropology and History*. Oxford: Oxford University Press, 197–227.

Scheele, Judith, 2015. 'In Praise of Disorder: Breaking the Rules in Northern Chad', in P. Dresch and J. Scheele (eds.), *Legalism: Rules and Categories*. Oxford: Oxford University Press, 153–76.

Schiel, Juliane, 2015. 'Slaves' Religious Choice in Renaissance Venice', *Archivio Veneto*, **146**: 23–45.

Schielke, Samuli, 2009. 'Ambivalent Commitments: Troubles of Morality, Religiosity and Aspiration among Young Egyptians', *Journal of Religion in Africa*, **39**: 158–85.

Schielke, Samuli, 2015. *Egypt in the Future Tense: Hope, Frustration, and Ambivalence Before and After 2011*. Bloomington: Indiana University Press.

Schiffer, Michael B., 1987. *Formation Processes of the Archaeological Record*. Albuquerque: University of New Mexico Press.

Schmitt, Carl, 1985, *Political Theology: Four Chapters on the Concept of Sovereignty*, trans. Georg Schwab. Cambridge, MA: MIT Press. [First published as *Politische Theologie. Vier Kapitel zur Lehre von der Souveranität*, 1922.]

Schnably, Stephen J., 1993. 'Property and Pragmatism: A Critique of Radin's Theory of Property and Personhood', *Stanford Law Review*, **45**/2: 347–407.

Schulz, Fritz, 1951. *Classical Roman Law*. Oxford: Clarendon Press.

Schwarzwalder, Brian, Roy Prosterman, and Li Ping, 2003. *Land Takings in China: Policy Recommendations*. Seattle, WA: Rural Development Institute.

Seed, Patricia, 1995. *Ceremonies of Possession in Europe's Conquest of the New World, 1492–1640*. Cambridge: Cambridge University Press.

Seipp, David J., 1994. 'The Concept of Property in the Early Common Law', *Law and History Review*, **12**/1: 29–91.

Sen, Amartya, 1988. 'Property and Hunger', *Economics and Philosophy*, **4**/1: 57–68.

Shabi, Rachel, 2012. 'Egyptians are Being Held Back by Neoliberalism, Not Religion', *Guardian*, 21 December. Online at <http://www.theguardian.com/commentisfree/2012/dec/21/egyptians-held-back-neoliberalism-not-religion>.

Shalakany, Amr, 2001. 'Between Identity and Redistribution: Sanhuri, Genealogy and the Will to Islamise', *Islamic Law and Society*, **8**/2: 201–44.

Sharpe, Richard, 2003. 'The Use of Writs in the Eleventh-Century', *Anglo-Saxon England*, **32**: 247–91.

Shepard, William E., 1996. *Sayyid Qutb and Islamic Activism: A Translation and Critical Analysis of 'Social Justice in Islam'*. Leiden: Brill.

Sherwin-White, Adrian Nicholas, 1973. *The Roman Citizenship*, 2nd edn. Oxford: Clarendon Press.

Shreeves, Rosamund, 2002. 'Broadening the Concept of Privatization: Gender and Development in Rural Kazakhstan', in Ruth Mandel and Caroline Humphrey (eds.), *Markets and Moralities: Ethnographies of Postsocialism*. Oxford: Berg, 211–35.

Shryock, Andrew, and Daniel L. Smail, 2011. *Deep History: The Architecture of Past and Present*. Berkeley, CA: University of California Press.

Siegrist, Hannes, 2003. 'Geschichte und aktuelle Probleme des geistigen Eigentums (1600–2000)', in A. Zerdick et al. (eds.), *E-Merging Media: Kommunikation und Medienwirtschaft der Zukunft*. Berlin: Springer, 313–32.

Sikor, Thomas, 2006. 'Land as Asset, Land as Liability: Property Politics in Rural Central and Eastern Europe', in F. von Benda-Beckmann, K. von Benda-Beckmann, and M. Wiber (eds.), *Changing Properties of Property*. New York and Oxford: Berghahn, 106–25.

Silver, Morris, 2011. 'Contractual Slavery in the Roman Economy', *Ancient History Bulletin*, **25**: 73–132.
Simons, Anna, 1995. *Networks of Dissolution: Somalia Undone*. Boulder, CO: Westview Press.
Sirks, Boudewijn, 1983. 'The *lex Junia* and the Effect of Informal Manumission and Iteration', *Revue Internationale des Droits de l'Antiquité*, **30**: 211–92.
Smith, Adam, [1776] 2014. *An Enquiry into the Nature and Causes of the Wealth of Nations*, ed. William B. Todd, 2 vols. Oxford: Oxford University Press; Glasgow Edition of the Works and Correspondence of Adam Smith.
Smith, Henry E., 2012. 'Property as the Law of Things', *Harvard Law Review*, **125**/7: 1691–726.
Stafford, Pauline, 2014. 'Reeve', in Michael Lapidge et al. (eds.), *The Wiley-Blackwell Encyclopedia of Anglo-Saxon England*, 2nd edn. Chichester: Wiley-Blackwell, 397–8.
Stein, Peter, 1999. *Roman Law in European History*. Cambridge: Cambridge University Press.
Steins, Nathalie A. 2001. 'New Directions in Natural Resource Management: The Offer of Actor-Network Theory', *IDS Bulletin*, **32**/4: 18–25.
Stenton, Doris M. (ed.), 1952–67. *Pleas before the King or His Justices, 1189–1212*, 4 vols. London: Quaritch.
Stevenson, W. H. (ed.), 1904. *Asser's Life of King Alfred Together with the Annals of St Neot's Erroneously Ascribed to Asser*. Oxford: Clarendon Press.
Stewart, Frank H., 2003. 'The Contract with Surety in Bedouin Customary Law', *UCLA Journal of Islamic and Near Eastern Law*, **2**/2: 163–280.
Stójkovski, Boris, 2011. 'Facts and Fates: Slave Women and Prostitutes as Socially Excluded Groups in Medieval Dubrovnik', in Dubravka Valić Nedeljković (ed.), *Media Discourse of Poverty and Exclusion*. Novi Sad: Faculty of Philosophy, 247–56.
Stout, Matthew, 1997. *The Irish Ringfort*. Dublin: Four Courts Press.
Strang, Veronica, and Mark Busse (eds.), 2011. *Ownership and Appropriation*. Oxford: Berg.
Strathern, Marilyn, 1990. *The Gender of the Gift: Problems with Women and Problems with Society in Melanesia*. Berkeley, CA: University of California Press.
Strathern, Marilyn, 1996. 'Potential Property: Intellectual Rights and Property in Persons', *Social Anthropology*, **4**/1: 17–32.
Strathern, Marilyn, 1999. *Property, Substance, and Effect: Anthropological Essays on Persons and Things*. London and New Brunswick, NJ: Athlone Press.
Straumann, Benjamin, 2016. *Crisis and Constitutionalism: Roman Political Thought from the Fall of the Republic to the Age of Revolution*. Oxford: Oxford University Press.
Sturgeon, Janet C., 2004. 'Post-Socialist Property Rights for Akha in China: What is at Stake?', *Conservation & Society*, **2**/1: 137–61.
Sturgeon, Janet C., and Thomas Sikor, 2004. 'Post-Socialist Property in Asia and Europe: Variations on "Fuzziness"', *Conservation & Society*, **2**/1: 1–17.
Sutherland, Donald W, 1963. *Quo Warranto Proceedings in the Reign of Edward I, 1278–1294*. Oxford: Oxford Clarendon Press.
Swain, Simon, 2013. *Economy, Family, and Society from Rome to Islam: A Critical Edition, English Translation and Study of Bryson's Management of the Estate*. Cambridge: Cambridge University Press.

Swanson, Scott Gordon, 1997. 'The Medieval Foundations of John Locke's Theory of Natural Rights: Rights of Subsistence and the Principle of Extreme Necessity', *History of Political Thought*, **18**: 399–456.

Tabiu, M., 1989. 'Shari'ah in an Era of Transition: Some Judicial Practices in the Early Days of the Sokoto Caliphate', *Islamic Studies*, **28**/4: 382.

Tate, Joshua C., 2006. 'Ownership and Possession in the Early Common Law', *American Journal of Legal History*, **48**/3: 280–313.

Taylor, Alice, 2013. 'Crime without Punishment: Medieval Scottish Law in Comparative Perspective', *Anglo-Norman Studies*, **35**: 287–304.

Taylor, Alice, 2014. 'Lex Scripta and the Problem of Enforcement: Anglo-Saxon, Scottish and Welsh Law Compared', in F. Pirie and J. Scheele (eds.), *Legalism: Community and Justice*. Oxford: Oxford University Press, 47–75.

Teja, A., 1942. 'Aspetti della vita economimica di Zara dal 1289 al 1409, parte II: La schiavitù domestica ed il traffico degli schiavi', *La Rivista Dalmatica*, **4**: 35–40.

Thompson, Elizabeth F., 2014. 'Social Justice in the Middle East', in Michael Reisch (ed.), *Routledge International Handbook of Social Justice*. London and New York: Routledge, 61–73.

Thonemann, Peter, 2007. 'Estates and the Land in Late Roman Asia Minor', *Chiron*, **37**: 435–78.

Thonemann, Peter, 2011. *The Maeander Valley: A Historical Geography from Antiquity to Byzantium*. Cambridge: Cambridge University Press.

Thür, Gerhard, 2008. 'Ownership and Security in Macedonian Sale Documents', in E. Harris and G. Thür (eds.), *Symposion 2007: Vorträge zur griechischen und hellenistischen Rechtsgeschichte*. Vienna: Verlag der Österreichischen Akademie der Wissenschaften, 173–87.

Thurneysen, Rudolf, 1923–5. 'Aus dem irischen Recht I. Das Unfrei-Lehen', *Zeitschrift für celtische Philologie*, 14: 335–94, with corrections and additions *Zeitschrift für celtische Philologie*, 14: 393, *Zeitschrift für celtische Philologie*, 15: 238–39.

Tierney, Brian, 1997. *The Idea of Natural Rights: Studies on Natural Rights, Natural Law and Church Law 1150-1625*. Atlanta, GA: Scholars Press.

Toleubayev, Kazbek, Kees Jansen, and Arnold van Huis, 2010. 'Knowledge and Agrarian De-Collectivisation in Kazakhstan', *Journal of Peasant Studies*, **37**/2: 353–77

Tolybekov, Sergali Esbembetovich, 1959. *Obshchestvenno-ėkonomicheskiĭ stroĭ kazakhov v XVII–XIX vekakh*. Alma-Ata: Kazakhskoe gosizd-vo.

Travis, William, 1967. *The Voice of the Turtle*. London: Allen & Unwin.

Trevisani, Tommaso. 2016. 'Modern Weddings in Uzbekistan: Ritual Change from "above" and from "below"', *Central Asian Survey*, **35**/1: 61–75.

Triantaphyllopoulos, Jean, 1974. '*Ius Italicum* personale (Inschr. Didyma 331)', in G. I. Luzzato et al. (eds.), *I diritti locali nelle province romane con particulare riguardo alle condizione giuridiche del suolo*. Rome: Accademia Nazionale dei Lincei, 135–70.

Tripp, Charles, 2006. *Islam and the Moral Economy: The Challenge of Capitalism*. Cambridge: Cambridge University Press.

Tsing, Anna Lowenhaupt, 2005. *Friction: An Ethnography of Global Connection*. Princeton, NJ: Princeton University Press.

Tubiana, M.-J., 1960. 'Un document inédit sur les sultans du Waday', *Cahiers d'études africaines*, **1**/2: 29–112.

Tuck, Richard, 1979. *Natural Rights Theories: Their Origin and Development.* Cambridge: Cambridge University Press.

Tuck, Richard, 1999. *The Rights of War and Peace: Political Thought and the International Order from Grotius to Kant.* Oxford: Oxford University Press.

Upham, Frank K., 2014. 'Property Rights, Commodification, and Land Disputes in Contemporary Socialist Asia', in H. Fu and J. Gillespie (eds.), *Resolving Land Disputes in East Asia: Exploring the Limits of Law.* Cambridge: Cambridge University Press, 37–56.

Vacca, Letizia, 2015. *Possesso e acquisto della proprietà: Saggi romanistici.* Torino: G. Giappichelli.

Van Ittersum, Martine Julia, 2006. *Profit and Principle: Hugo Grotius, Natural Rights Theories and the Rise of Dutch Power in the East Indies 1595–1615.* Leiden and Boston, MA: Brill.

Velissaropoulos-Karakostas, Julie, 2011. *Droit grec d'Alexandre à Auguste (323 av. J.-C.—14 ap. J.-C.)*, 2 vols. Athens.

Verdery, Katherine, 1996. *What Was Socialism, and What Comes Next?* Princeton, NJ: Princeton University Press.

Verdery, Katherine, 1998. 'Property and Power in Transylvania's Decollectivization', in C. M. Hann (ed.), *Property Relations: Renewing the Anthropological Tradition.* Cambridge: Cambridge University Press, 160–80.

Verdery, Katherine, 1999. 'Fuzzy Property: Rights, Power, and Identity in Transylvania's Decollectivization', in M. Burawoy and K. Verdery (eds.), *Uncertain Transition: Ethnographies of Change in the Postsocialist World.* Lanham, MD: Rowman & Littlefield, 53–82.

Verdery, Katherine, 2003. *The Vanishing Hectare: Property and Value in Postsocialist Transylvania.* Ithaca, NY: Cornell University Press.

Verdery, Katherine, 2004. 'The Obligations of Ownership: Restoring Rights to Land in Postsocialist Transylvania', in K. Verdery and C. Humphrey (eds.), *Property in Question: Value Transformation in the Global Economy.* Oxford: Berg, 139–59.

Verdery, Katherine, and Caroline Humphrey (eds.), 2004. *Property in Question: Value Transformation in the Global Economy.* Oxford: Berg.

Verlinden, Charles, 1955–77. *L'esclavage dans l'Europe médiévale*, 2 vols. Bruges: De Tempel.

Vinaver, Vuk, 1953. 'Trgovina Bosanskim robljem tokom XIV veka u Dubrovniku', *Dubrovnik Anali*, **2**: 125–47.

Visscher, Fernand de, 1966. 'Auctoritas, res mancipi et usucapio', in *Études de droit romain public et privé. Troisième série.* Milan: A. Giuffrè, 233–61.

Visser, Oane, 2006. 'Property, Labour Relations and Social Obligations in Russia's Privatised Farm Enterprises', in F. von Benda-Beckmann, K. von Benda-Beckmann, and M. Wiber (eds.), *Changing Properties of Property.* New York and Oxford: Berghahn, 126–46.

Vlassopoulos, Kostas, 2011. 'Greek Slavery: From Domination to Property and Back Again', *Journal of Hellenic Studies*, **131**: 115–30.

Waelkens, Laurent, 2015. *Amne adverso: Roman Legal Heritage in European Culture.* Leuven: Leuven University Press.

Wakelin, Daniel, 2005. 'Scholarly Scribes and the Creation of Knyghthode and Bataile', in P. Beal and A. Edwards (eds.), *Scribes and Transmission in English Manuscripts 1400–1700*, English Manuscript Studies vol. 12. London: British Library, 26–46.

Waldron, Jeremy, 1990. *The Right to Private Property*. Oxford: Oxford University Press.

Waldron, Jeremy, 2004. 'Property and Ownership', in Stanford Encyclopedia of Philosophy. Online at <https://plato.stanford.edu/entries/property/>.

Wallace, Jeremy L., 2014. *Cities and Stability: Urbanization, Redistribution, & Regime Survival in China*. Oxford: Oxford University Press.

Walters, D. B., 1986. 'The General Features of Archaic European Suretyship', in T. M. Charles-Edwards, Morfydd E. Owen, and D. B. Walters (eds.), *Lawyers and Laymen*. Cardiff: University of Wales Press, 92–116.

Wasserschleben, Hermann, 1885. *Die irische Kanonensammlung*, 2nd edn. Leipzig: Bernhard Tauchnitz. [Reprinted 1966, Aalen: Scientia Verlag.]

Watkins, Calvert, 1963. 'Indo-European Metrics and Archaic Irish Verse', *Celtica*, **6**: 194–249.

Watson, Alan, 1968. *The Law of Property in the Later Roman Republic*. Oxford: Clarendon Press.

Watson, Alan, 1971. *Roman Private Law around 200 BC*. Edinburgh: Edinburgh University Press.

Watson, Alan, 1975. *Rome of the XII Tables: Persons and Property*. Princeton, NJ: Princeton University Press.

Watson, Alan, 1987. *Roman Slave Law*. Baltimore: Johns Hopkins University Press.

Weiner, Annette B., 1992. *Inalienable Possessions: The Paradox of Keeping-While-Giving*. Berkeley, CA: University of California Press.

Weldemichael, Awet T., 2012. 'Maritime Corporate Terrorism and Its Consequences in the Western Indian Ocean: Illegal Fishing, Waste Dumping and Piracy in Twenty-First-Century Somalia', *Journal of the Indian Ocean Region*, **8**/2: 110–26.

Wheeler, William, 2016. 'Aral-88: Catastrophe, Critique and Hope', *Slavonic and East European Review*, **94**/2: 295–324.

Whitelock, Dorothy (ed.), 1979. *English Historical Documents. Volume 1: c. 500–1042*, 2nd edn. London: Eyre Methuen.

Wickham, Chris, 2005. *Framing the Early Middle Ages*. Oxford: Oxford University Press.

Widlok, Thomas, and Wolde Gossa Tadesse (eds.), 2004. *Property and Equality*. New York and Oxford: Berghahn.

Willford, Andrew, 2014. *Tamils and the Haunting of Justice: History and Recognition in Malaysia's Plantations*. Honolulu: Hawaii University Press.

Williams, Margery, 1922. *The Velveteen Rabbit or How Toys Become Real*. London: Heinemann.

Wilson, Emma. 2002. 'Est' Zakon, Est' I Svoi Zakoni: Legal and Moral Entitlements to the Fish Resources of Nyski Bay, North-East Sakhalin', in E. Kasten (ed.), *People and the Land: Pathways to Reform in Post-Soviet Siberia*. Berlin: Dietrich Riemer, 149–68.

Wilson, James. 2002. 'Scientific Uncertainty, Complex Ecosystems and the Design of Common-Pool Institutions', in Elinor Ostrom, Thomas Dietz, Nives Dolsak, Paul C. Stern, and Susan Stonich (eds.), *The Drama of the Commons*. Washington, DC: National Academies Press, 327–59.

Wilson, James A., James M. Acheson, Mark Metcalfe, and Peter Kleban. 1994. 'Chaos, Complexity and Community Management of Fisheries', *Marine Policy*, **18**/4: 291–305.

Winkler, Andreas, 2015. 'A Contribution to the Revenues of the Crocodile in the Imperial Fayum: The Temple Tax on Property Transfer Revisited', *Bulletin of the American Society of Papyrologists*, **52**: 239–63.

Woodburn, James, 1982. 'Egalitarian Societies', *Man*, **17**/3: 431–51.

World Bank, 2004. Innovations in Fisheries Management for Kazakhstan. Washington, DC: World Bank. Online at <http://siteresources.worldbank.org/INTKAZAKHSTAN/Data%20and%20Reference/20292610/KZ%20Fish-Draft%20Report-V4-pdf>.

World Bank, and Development Research Center of the State Council of the People's Republic of China, 2014. *Urban China: Toward Efficient, Inclusive, and Sustainable Urbanization*. Washington, DC: World Bank Group.

Wormald, Patrick, [1986] 1999. 'Charters, Law and the Settlement of Disputes in Anglo-Saxon England' in his *Legal Culture in the Early Medieval West: Law as Text, Image and Experience*. London: Hambledon Press, 289–311. [Reprinted from Davies and Fouracre (eds.) 1986: 149–68.]

Wormald, Patrick, [1995] 1999. 'Lordship and Justice in the Early English Kingdom: Oswaldslow Revisited' in his *Legal Culture in the Early Medieval West: Law as Text, Image and Experience*. London: Hambledon Press, 313–32. [Reprinted from Davies and Fouracre (eds.) 1995: 114–36.]

Xu, Ting, 2014. *The Revival of Private Property and its Limits in Post-Mao China*. London: Wildy, Simmonds and Hill.

Yanagihashi, Hiroyuki, 2004. *A History of the Early Islamic Law of Property: Reconstructing the Legal Development, 7th–9th Centuries*. Leiden and Boston, MA: Brill.

Yeh, Emily T., 2004. 'Property Relations in Tibet Since Decollectivisation and the Question of "Fuzziness"', *Conservation & Society*, **2**/1: 164–187.

Zanca, Russell G., 2007. 'Fat and All That: Good Eating the Uzbek Way', in J. Sahadeo and R. G. Zanca (eds.), *Everyday Life in Central Asia: Past and Present*. Bloomington and Indianapolis: Indiana University Press, 178–97.

Zemon Davis, Natalie, 2011. 'Judges, Masters, Diviners: Slaves' Experience of Criminal Justice in Colonial Suriname', *Law and History Review*, **29**/4: 925–84.

Zhang, Everett Y., 2013. 'Grieving at Chongqing's Red Guard Graveyard: In the Name of Life Itself', *China Journal*, **70**: 24–47.

Zhao, Xudong, and Duran Bell, 2005. 'Destroying the Remembered and Recovering the Forgotten in Chai', *China Information*, **19**/3: 489–503.

Zhu, Jiangang, and Chao Wang, 2008. 'Seniors Defending their Rights: Strategies and Culture in Collective Action', *Chinese Sociology and Anthropology*, **40**/2: 5–34.

Zurbach, Julien, 2013. 'La formation des cités grecques. Statuts, classes et systèmes fonciers', *Annales. Histoire, sciences sociales*, **68**: 957–98.

Index

The manufacturer's authorised representative in the EU for product safety is Oxford University Press España S.A. of el Parque Empresarial San Fernando de Henares, Avenida de Castilla, 2 – 28830 Madrid (www.oup.es/en or product.safety@oup.com). OUP España S.A. also acts as importer into Spain of products made by the manufacturer.

www.ingramcontent.com/pod-product-compliance
Lightning Source LLC
LaVergne TN
LVHW011915200926
848484LV00002B/630
* 9 7 8 0 1 9 8 8 1 3 4 1 5 *